Humanitarianism, empire and transnationalism, 1760–1995

Manchester University Press

STUDIES IN IMPERIALISM

General editors: Andrew S. Thompson and Alan Lester
Founding editor: John M. MacKenzie

When the 'Studies in Imperialism' series was founded by Professor John M. MacKenzie more than thirty years ago, emphasis was laid upon the conviction that 'imperialism as a cultural phenomenon had as significant an effect on the dominant as on the subordinate societies'. With well over a hundred titles now published, this remains the prime concern of the series. Cross-disciplinary work has indeed appeared covering the full spectrum of cultural phenomena, as well as examining aspects of gender and sex, frontiers and law, science and the environment, language and literature, migration and patriotic societies, and much else. Moreover, the series has always wished to present comparative work on European and American imperialism, and particularly welcomes the submission of books in these areas. The fascination with imperialism, in all its aspects, shows no sign of abating, and this series will continue to lead the way in encouraging the widest possible range of studies in the field. 'Studies in Imperialism' is fully organic in its development, always seeking to be at the cutting edge, responding to the latest interests of scholars and the needs of this ever-expanding area of scholarship.

To buy or to find out more about the books currently available in this series, please go to: https://manchesteruniversitypress.co.uk/series/studies-in-imperialism/

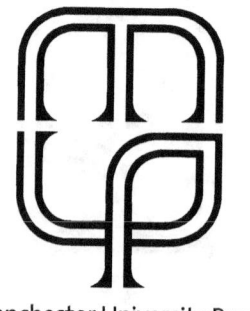

Manchester University Press

Humanitarianism, empire and transnationalism, 1760–1995

Selective humanity in the Anglophone world

Edited by
Joy Damousi, Trevor Burnard and
Alan Lester

MANCHESTER UNIVERSITY PRESS

Copyright © Manchester University Press 2022

While copyright in the volume as a whole is vested in Manchester University Press, copyright in individual chapters belongs to their respective authors, and no chapter may be reproduced wholly or in part without the express permission in writing of both author and publisher.

Published by Manchester University Press
Oxford Road, MANCHESTER M13 9PL

www.manchesteruniversitypress.co.uk

British Library Cataloguing-in-Publication Data

A catalogue record for this book is available from the British Library

ISBN 978 1 5261 5955 7 hardback
ISBN 978 1 5261 8241 8 paperback

First published 2022

The publisher has no responsibility for the persistence or accuracy of URLs for any external or third-party internet websites referred to in this book, and does not guarantee that any content on such websites is, or will remain, accurate or appropriate.

Typeset
by Deanta Global Publishing Services, Chennai, India

Contents

Notes on contributors — page vii
Acknowledgements — x

Introduction: Selective humanity: Three centuries of Anglophone humanitarianism, empire and transnationalism – Trevor Burnard, Joy Damousi and Alan Lester — 1

I Transatlantic humanitarianism, 1760–1838

1. Anthony Benezet: *A Short History of Guinea* and its impact on early British abolitionism – Trevor Burnard — 37
2. An incident at the Sun Tavern: Changing the discourse on Indigenous visitors to Georgian Britain – Kate Fullagar — 60
3. Humanity amidst calamity: Humanitarian discourse in New South Wales, 1788–1830 – Jillian Beard — 82
4. 'Nor do they harbour vermin': Material culture approaches to exploring humanitarian exchanges – Amanda B. Moniz — 99
5. The realpolitik of emancipation in the British Empire, 1833–38 – Alan Lester — 119

II Humanitarianism and Indigenous peoples, 1838–c. 1950

6. Humanitarianism in a genocidal age: The tragic story of the Aboriginal prison on Rottnest Island, Western Australia, 1838–1903 – Ann Curthoys — 147
7. From humanitarianism to humane governance: Aboriginal slavery and white Australia – Amanda Nettelbeck — 179
8. Humanitarian priorities and West African agency in the British Empire – Bronwen Everill — 199
9. The origins of exemption: The individual exception in the discourse of humanitarianism – Katherine Ellinghaus — 217

III A new international order, 1918–95

10 Gender, personalities and the politics of humanitarianism: Nursing leaders of the League of Red Cross Societies between the wars – Melanie Oppenheimer ... 241
11 'Springs of love': Sentiment and affect in mid-twentieth-century development volunteering – Agnieszka Sobocinska ... 264
12 Humanitarian activism during the Vietnam War: The case of Rosemary Taylor, Elaine Moir and Margaret Moses – Joy Damousi ... 283
13 Humanitarianism in the age of human rights: Amnesty International in Australia – Jon Piccini ... 305
14 Palliation, poverty and child welfare: Human rights and humanitarianism in the 1980s – Roland Burke ... 327

Index ... 347

Notes on contributors

Dr Jillian Beard, Griffith University. Recent publications include: 'Conciliation in New South Wales, 1788–1815: A Colonial Governance Policy', in Joelle Bonnevin, David Waterman and Sue Ryan-Fazilleau (eds), *Aboriginal Australians and Other 'Others'* (Paris, France: Les Indes Savantes, 2014), pp. 169–85.

Dr Roland Burke, LaTrobe University. Recent publications include: 'The Rites of Human Rights at the United Nations', *Humanity: An International Journal of Human Rights, Humanitarianism, and Development* (2018), 9, pp. 127–42; 'Disseminating Discord and Discovering the World: UN Advisory Services on Human Rights and the Illusory Faith in Specialist Knowledge', *The International Journal of Human Rights* (2017), 21, pp. 589–610.

Professor Trevor Burnard, Director of the Wilberforce Institute, University of Hull; Editor in Chief, Oxford Online Bibliography in Atlantic History. Recent publications include: 'Plantations and the Great Divergence' in Tirthankar Roy and Giorgio Riello (eds), *Global Economic History* (London, UK: Bloomsbury, 2019); 'Living Costs, Real Incomes and Inequality in Colonial Jamaica', *Explorations in Economic History* (2018), 71, pp. 55–71; *Jamaica in the Age of Revolution* (Philadelphia, PA: University of Pennsylvania Press, 2020); and *The Atlantic in World History* (London, UK: Bloomsbury, 2020).

Professor Ann Curthoys, University of Western Australia. Recent publications include: *Taking Liberty: Indigenous Rights and Settler Self-Government in Colonial Australia, 1830–1890* with Jessie Mitchell (Cambridge, UK: Cambridge University Press, 2018); 'The Impossibility of Section 70: Aboriginal Protection, Amelioration, and the Contradictions of Humanitarian Governance', *Studies in Western Australian History* (2016), 30, pp. 13–28.

Professor Joy Damousi, Director of the Institute of Humanities and Social Sciences, Australian Catholic University. Author of *Memory and Migration* *in the Shadow of War* (Cambridge, UK: Cambridge University Press, 2015). Recent publications include: 'Humanitarianism and Children Refugee Sponsorship: The Spanish Civil War and the Global Campaign of Esme Odgers', *Journal of Women's History* (Spring 2020), 32 (1), pp. 111–34; *The Cambridge World History of Violence*, four volumes, general editor with Phillip Dwyer (Cambridge, UK: Cambridge University Press, 2020).

Associate Professor Katherine Ellinghaus, LaTrobe University. Recent publications include: *Blood Will Tell: Native Americans and Assimilation Policy* (Lincoln, NE: University of Nebraska Press, 2017); and with Judi Wickes, 'A Moving Female Frontier: Aboriginal Exemption and Domestic Service in Queensland, 1897–1914', *Australian Historical Studies* (2020), 51 (1), pp. 19–37.

Dr Bronwen Everill, Class of 1973 Lecturer in History, Gonville & Caius College, University of Cambridge. Author of *Not Made By Slaves: Ethical Capitalism in the Age of Abolition* (Cambridge, MA: Harvard, 2020); *Abolition and Empire in Sierra Leone and Liberia* (London, UK: Palgrave, 2013); and editor of *The History and Practice of Humanitarian Intervention and Aid in Africa* (London, UK: Palgrave, 2013).

Professor Kate Fullagar, Australian Catholic University. Recent publications include: *Facing Empire*, edited with M. A. McDonnell (Baltimore, MD: Johns Hopkins University Press, 2018); *The Warrior, the Voyager, and the Artist: Three Lives in an Age of Empire* (New Haven, CT: Yale University Press, 2020); 'Voyagers from the Havai'i Diaspora: Polynesian Mobility, 1760s–1860s' in L. Russell and A. McGrath (eds), *The Routledge Companion to Indigenous Global History* (London, UK: Routledge, 2021).

Professor Alan Lester, La Trobe University/University of Sussex. Author of *Ruling the World: Freedom, Civilisation and Liberalism in the Nineteenth Century British Empire* (Cambridge, UK: Cambridge University Press, 2021) with Kate Boehme and Peter Mitchell; *Imperial Networks: Creating Identities in Nineteenth Century South Africa and Britain* (London, UK: Routledge, 2001); *Colonial Lives Across the British Empire: Imperial Careering in the Long Nineteenth Century* (Cambridge, UK: Cambridge University Press, 2006) with David Lambert; and *Colonization and the Origins of Humanitarian Governance* (Cambridge, UK: Cambridge University Press, 2014) with Fae Dussart. Recent publications include 'Reforming Everywhere and All at Once: Transitioning to Free Labor across the British Empire, 1837–1838', *Comparative Studies in Society and History* (2018), 60 (3), pp. 688–718, with Peter Mitchell and Kate Boehme.

Dr Amanda B. Moniz, David M. Rubsenstein Curator of Philanthropy, Smithsonian Institution, National Museum of American History. Recent publications include: *From Empire to Humanity: The American Revolution and the Origins of Humanitarianism* (Oxford, UK: Oxford University Press, 2016).

Professor Amanda Nettelbeck, Australian Catholic University. Recent publications include: *Indigenous Rights and Colonial Subjecthood: Protection and Reform in the Nineteenth-Century British Empire* (Cambridge, UK: Cambridge University Press, 2019); *Aboriginal Protection and Its Intermediaries in Britain's Antipodean Colonies* (edited with S. Furphy) (London, UK: Routledge, 2020); 'Frontier Violence in the Nineteenth-Century British Empire' (with L. Ryan) in *The Cambridge World History of Violence*, vol. IV (Cambridge, UK: Cambridge University Press, 2020), pp. 227–45.

Professor Melanie Oppenheimer, Australian National University. Recent publications include a short biography of the founder of the IFRC, *Henry Pomeroy Davison, 1867–1922* (Geneva, Switzerland: IFRC, 2019), and *The Red Cross Movement: Myths, Practices and Turning Points* (Manchester, UK: Manchester University Press, 2020) with Neville Wylie and James Crossland.

Dr Jon Piccini, Australian Catholic University. Recent publications include: *Human Rights in Twentieth Century Australia* (Cambridge, UK: Cambridge University Press, 2019); '"That Brotherhood May Prevail": International House Brisbane, Race and the Humanitarian Ethic in Cold War Australia', *History Australia* (2020), 17 (4), pp. 695–710; and '"Women Are a Colonised Sex": Elizabeth Reid, Human Rights and International Women's Year 1975', *Australian Historical Studies* (2018), 49 (3), pp. 307–23.

Dr Agnieszka Sobocinska, Monash University. Recent publications include: *Saving the World? Western Volunteers and the Rise of the Humanitarian-Development Complex* (Cambridge, UK: Cambridge University Press, 2021); 'How to win friends and influence nations: The international history of Development Volunteering', *Journal of Global History* (2017), 12 (1), pp. 49–73.

Acknowledgements

This collection arose initially from a workshop hosted by Joy Damousi at the University of Melbourne in 2019 on 'Three Centuries of Humanitarianisms' which was generously funded under the auspices of her Australian Research Council Laureate Fellowship. She would like to dedicate this book to members of the Laureate research team on the history of child refugees: Sarah Green, Niro Kandasamy, Anh Nguyen Austen, Rachel Stevens, Jordy Silverstein and Mary Tomsic.

Trevor Burnard would like to thank Bertrand Van Ruymbeke and Marie-Jeanne Rossignol for assistance in understanding the context of French humanitarianism and for a stimulating session on French humanitarianism at the Sorbonne, Paris, and wishes to dedicate this book to them. His work was funded under an Australian Research Council Discovery Project Grant, 1510104051.

Alan Lester would like to acknowledge the funding from the Leverhulme Trust that has enabled his research of the last few years. He would like to dedicate this book to Jo, Daisy, Evan and Alfred.

This paperback edition is dedicated to our co-editor Trevor Burnard, a friend, colleague, and incredibly gifted and generous historian, who tragically passed away before it could be issued.

Introduction: Selective humanity: Three centuries of Anglophone humanitarianism, empire and transnationalism

Trevor Burnard, Joy Damousi and Alan Lester

David Cameron, Prime Minister of the United Kingdom between 2010 and 2016, when challenged to explain why Britain expected its voice to have particular resonance in discussions about global governance, rooted his response in his nation's exceptional history. That exceptionalism was based on what Cameron believed was Britain's particular devotion to the concept of freedom and to humanitarian efforts to enhance the welfare of people in other parts of the world. Ignoring the several centuries through which Cameron's own ancestors and other Britons refined, scaled up and profited from the institution of slavery, he spelt out that Britain deserved to be thought of as a nation devoted to these virtues primarily due to its role in pioneering slavery's abolition.[1] Patriotic British politicians and historians who, in the wake of the 2020 Black Lives Matter protests, see their cherished version of Britain's past threatened by imagined hordes of 'woke protesters' tearing down statues across the nation, pay special attention to Britain's abolition of the slave trade in 1807 and of slavery in the British Empire in 1834.[2]

Historians have also drawn attention to the British campaigns mobilising public support for these measures as a foundational example of the long-distance projection of empathy and concern for the welfare of others that has come to be known as humanitarianism.[3] In particular, they point to the earliest manifestation of humanitarian intervention, when one state acts, sometimes employing the military, against others in the interests of foreign subjects' welfare. The instance they have in mind was the operation of the Royal Navy's West Africa squadron antislavery patrols against other nations' slave ships. While the Conservative Education Secretary, Michael Gove, insisted that the national curriculum in British schools 'celebrate the distinguished role of these islands in the history of the world' by highlighting the Royal Navy's rescue of some 160,000 captives destined for the Americas between 1808 and 1867, certain contextual features of the enterprise, including the fate of the Africans thus 'liberated' – most of whom were allocated as unpaid apprentices to free settlers in Sierra Leone or impressed into the British military – were less imperative for young Britons to appreciate.[4] It is not coincidental that one of Cameron's predecessors as leader of the Conservative Party, William Hague, wrote a biography of the leading (and Tory-leaning) abolitionist, William Wilberforce. The legacy of humanitarianism remains one that many people want to claim.[5]

Of course, that politicians claim that the nations they represent have particular virtues and are especially good is a commonplace of political discourse. We should not pay too much attention to such statements. We should perhaps pay even less attention to statements from British prime ministers that glory in Britain's imperial past, knowing that disavowal of the racial discrimination and violence of colonialism overseas was intrinsic both to governance and public understanding of the Empire within Britain.[6] If the popular memory of British antislavery activities can be selective, so too is its focus on British agency. As J. R. Oldfield highlights, late eighteenth-century antislavery was far more than a British national project. Rather, 'the early abolitionist movement is best understood as an international movement that rested on dense networks that linked activists in large metropolitan centres such as Paris and London with those in more remote outposts such as Washington and Pennsylvania', all of them interacting with those who had first-hand knowledge of slavery in the Caribbean and Americas.[7]

As with most nationalist mythologies, there is a seed of truth from which these exceptionalist narratives are constructed. From the eighteenth century to the mid-twentieth century, as the essays collected in this volume demonstrate, the British Empire acted as a vast engine for the generation of new, long-distance relationships of all kinds. As a result of connections forged by imperial sail, steam ship, rail, telegraphic and airborne communications, and as a result of the circulation of newspapers, illustrations, photographs and film through these networks, humanitarian relationships, along with those of trade, governance, settlement and science, were stretched across the globe by the British Empire in unprecedented ways. Furthermore, there is a reasonable claim that late eighteenth- and early nineteenth-century antislavery was specifically Anglophone, if not exclusively British. French humanitarianism started more slowly than in Britain and had a different focus. The northern colonies of British America and England were in the vanguard of the development of humanitarianism while France, Britain's greatest imperial rival of the early nineteenth century, despite its centrality to Enlightenment thought and culture, lagged behind. French *philosophes* did not concentrate on humanitarian matters, notably antislavery, until relatively late in the eighteenth century. The most important antislavery initiative was La Sociétè des Amis des Noirs, founded in Paris in February 1788, led by France's most important antislavery activist, Jacques-Pierre Brissot de Warville, an intimate of Anthony

Brissot. Nevertheless, as Marie-Jeanne Rossignol insists, even though the Amis des Noirs organised some of Anthony Benezet's work, addressed by Trevor Burnard in this volume, to be translated into French, 'his humanitarian and religious rationale could do little to shape the French antislavery argument, which was characterized by the prevalence of philosophical, administrative and economic arguments, together with moral indignation targeted at colonial planters'.[8]

In contrast with the other European empires, Anglophone humanitarian networks connected those in Britain concerned about slavery, heathenism, dispossession, a perceived lack of civilisation and poverty to the British emigrant diaspora of some two million people and even larger Anglophone settler populations by the beginning of the twentieth century, and to further millions of subjects of humanitarian concern who were largely (but not exclusively) colonised people of colour. Anglophone humanitarianism was dispensed via intermediaries including missionaries and colonial activists (many of them also people of colour), official protectors of slaves and Aborigines, and concerned travellers, writers, colonists and government officials; an array of actors which morphed into newly entangled relationships between nation states, international and local NGOs as the largest and most dispersed of the modern empires fragmented from the mid-twentieth century.

As Britain's temperate colonies were consolidated through emigration and colonial population growth (and corresponding relative Indigenous demographic decline) and as British settlers there developed self-governing institutions, they became centres of humanitarian gravity in their own right, often eclipsing the efforts of the United Kingdom itself. Beginning with the USA, British settler colonial offshoots in North America, southern Africa and Australasia contended for global influence as donor nations, creating a modern global Anglophone humanitarian sphere.

This extended Anglophone humanitarianism had a long afterlife beyond empire. C. P. Cullen, S. McCorriston and A. S. Thompson's analysis of the International Council of Voluntary Agencies (ICVA) 'Repertory of Africa's NGOs' (1968), for instance, indicates that former colonies of Britain dominated in the proliferation of humanitarian NGOs in post-colonial Africa. The top five host countries were 'all former British colonies, together accounting for 553 NGOs and representing 30 per cent of the total number of NGOs'.[9] The existence of these Anglophone humanitarian networks across, beyond and after the British Empire, with especially dense nodal points in the USA and settler colonies, is what encourages contemporary British apologists for empire to claim that the nation had a strongly benevolent nature and beneficial effect in shaping the modern world. As this book shows, recognising the lasting link between Anglophone humanitarian movements over time is important but what humanitarianism meant at various points in time is too complicated to be placed within a single framework of national benevolence.[10]

One of the purposes of this book is to sample repeatedly the *longue durée* of Anglophone humanitarianism over 300 years that national myth makers so neatly step across to dwell on particular moments. We examine how the discourses and practices of Anglophone humanitarianism emerged as particular projects which waxed and waned over the period. Our focus shifts to follow the changing contours of the British Empire, beginning with a primarily transatlantic axis in the late eighteenth century and extending to encompass the settler colonies including the United States, which brought new Indigenous and foreign subjects within Anglophone humanitarians' view in the early nineteenth century. Our contributors pay special attention to Australia as a focal point, initially of British metropolitan humanitarian concern, and then as a settler colonial hub of international humanitarianism in its own right. In the later nineteenth century, Anglophone humanitarians alighted upon East, West and then Central Africa, before their enterprise contributed to an NGO-based international industry, fostered by other European states too, in the late nineteenth and twentieth centuries.

Throughout the 300 years of its dynamic historical geography, episodic crises called forth Anglophone humanitarian interventions within Europe too. Dipping in and out of this extended trajectory, our contributors range across many regions as well as multiple time periods, from the major cities of the Atlantic world – Philadelphia, London and New York – in the late eighteenth century, through the Caribbean, West Africa and the Australian colonies in the early-mid nineteenth century, to Geneva, the centre of post-imperial non-governmental and transnational organisations devoted to human rights, in the late twentieth century.

In this introduction, we sketch out some of the main features of this *longue durée* of Anglophone humanitarianism. We draw attention to three insights in particular that have emerged from our contributors' collective temporal and spatial breadth. The first concerns humanitarian *governance*, the second the relationship between humanitarianism and *human rights*, and the third humanitarian *intervention*. After introducing the genesis of Anglophone humanitarianism in the post-1760 convergence of evangelical Christianity, ideas of freedom and Enlightenment understandings of civilisation, we suggest first that the fervour of antislavery was soon incorporated into governmental forms of humanitarianism intended to ameliorate imperial subjects' conditions. This project of humanitarian *governance* served two purposes. The first was to anglicise an expanded empire including polyglot territories newly captured from European rivals.[11] The second, which we emphasise here, was to dilute the potency of a revolutionary discourse of the Rights of Man, which threatened British security first in the American colonies and then from France and Haiti.[12]

Our second insight is related to this relationship between the ameliorative function of humanitarian governance and the revolutionary potential of the Rights of Man. Samuel Moyn has argued that humanitarianism and human rights, often thought of as sharing a common point of origin in late eighteenth-century Enlightenment ideas of humanity, are more accurately thought of as distinct.[13] Both may have had origins related to aspects of Enlightenment thought, but drew very different conclusions from it. The internationalist human rights discourse of the 1970s identified by Moyn was quite different from the idea of the Rights of Man that underpinned the late eighteenth-century Age of Revolution. Nevertheless, Moyn argues, it was rapidly absorbed within more moderate forms of twentieth-century humanitarianism. While our overview of Anglophone humanitarianism broadly supports the contention that human rights' destabilising radical potential tends to be mitigated by a humanitarianism that alleviates suffering while sustaining unequal power relations, we advise as much caution about defining the two discourses in consistently binary terms as we would about seeing them as co-constituted products of Enlightenment.

As Moyn and others have argued, the relationship between these ameliorative and radical discourses has been especially entangled since the end of empire, but not in any neat and predictable way.[14] Individuals acting in the interests of a broader humanity are complex assemblages in their own right. They have internal tensions that are magnified when they operate collectively, such that humanitarianism and human rights can be variously antithetical, separate and subordinated or can be mutually reinforcing at the scale of both the individual and the social. The complexity of this relationship is further revealed when the practices of NGOs during the 1960s and 1970s are considered. As Andrew Thompson has argued in relation to apartheid South Africa and protecting detainees, Amnesty International – a human rights organisation – and the International Committee of the Red Cross – a humanitarian group – came together in activities such as the documentation of abuses and collection of personal testimonies. This coming together demonstrated that there was a greater intersection within and between organisations than has often been discussed. Through their interventions, practices and discourses, humanitarian and human rights activists converged for a common cause.[15] The intersecting narratives between humanitarian and human rights groups and evidence of their co-operation suggest organisations were in close dialogue with each other over certain campaigns. Kevin O'Sullivan demonstrates that this was pronounced in the global campaigns against poverty during the 1970s when the NGO community drew inspiration from a diverse range of discourses, including Christian theology, the New Left and the United Nations coalition of developing nations, the Group of 77.[16] Both these examples suggest the sharp distinctions which have been drawn in recent accounts between humanitarian and human rights organisations requires reconsideration. A more nuanced examination of the intersection and convergence between humanitarianism and human rights would challenge current periodisation and explanations of when and how the two co-existed and when they did not. At present, emphasis is placed upon the period immediately after the end of World War II as a crucial point of transition but the essays in this collection point to other periods, such as the aftermath of World War I and various points in the 1960s and 1970s as being just as significant as times of change in the conceptualisation of modern humanitarian practice.

Our third insight concerns the rather more peripatetic phenomenon of humanitarian *intervention*. Episodic waves of humanitarian lobbying have carried politicians and governments before them, resulting in sometimes surprising interventions against other states in the interests of suffering foreign subjects. While the crises of the 1990s–2000s led many commentators to believe that such interventions, articulated especially by British Prime Minister Tony Blair as a new doctrine of humanitarian protection in respect of the Balkans, were a new phenomenon, this is very far from the case.[17] From the campaign against the slave trade in the 1780s, through mobilisation on behalf of Greek independence in the 1820s and the renewed antislavery petitioning spurred by David Livingstone in the 1860s, to Gladstone's Midlothian campaign in the late 1870s and outrage at Belgian atrocities in the Congo in the 1880s–90s, surges of Anglophone humanitarian intervention have been fickle companions to more continuous currents of humanitarian organisation, subject to the whims of an electorate swayed by selective reporting and celebrity culture.[18]

Colonisation, humanity and antislavery, c. 1760–c. 1800

The idea that humans owe a duty to other humans is rooted in all of the major religions, not least Christianity. Jesus might be considered the original Western humanitarian, with his formulation of the golden rule that 'one should do to others what one would want to have done to yourself'. Nevertheless, modern humanitarianism took on a distinctive form in the years of imperial transformation in Britain and its empire following the Seven Years War, from 1756 to 1763, with an important expansion and acceleration in Anglophone humanitarian sentiment after the end of the American Revolution in what Maya Jasanoff has called the 'spirit of 1783'.[19] This transatlantic Anglophone humanitarianism connected to earlier theological concepts which focused around the view that Jesus's nature is only human, not divine. Humanitarianism from around the early 1760s moved to being benevolent activism, informed by largely Christian doctrine about Jesus's human nature that was designed to improve the lot of humanity.

Kate Fullagar's chapter in this volume marks a distinctive shift at this crucial moment in imperial and humanitarian affairs, when a British court decreed that two Mohawk men should no longer be put on display in London. Previously, the reasoning for such a prohibition would have focused on the men's utility as allies of the British in North America and the need to maintain diplomatic relations with them, but in the 1760s a further rationale was added, consisting of 'an early instance of modern humanitarian thinking'. These men should not be displayed because they were human subjects whose welfare was of intrinsic value in its own right. As with so many of the contributors to this volume, however, Fullagar notes the Janus-faced nature of this early humanitarian act. The men's transition from independent allies to subjects of Britons' humane concern marked at the same time a 'growing British certainty in the inevitability of Empire' and the start of a discussion of what kind of empire Britons should maintain, rather than whether they should have one. Jillian Beard's contribution indicates a similar point of transition, very shortly afterwards in Australia, as an early penal colony's need to conciliate with Aboriginal people for its very survival was succeeded by the need to position Aboriginal groups as beneficiaries of British benevolence in return for their colonisation.

As Thomas Haskell has famously argued, the rise of humanitarianism in this period had less to do with new ideological or theological formulations – anyone who was Christian accepted that the golden rule ought to be a fundamental tenet by which humans governed themselves – than an expansion in the possibilities of extending help to others, including, for almost the first time in history, people suffering misfortune who did not belong to the same ethnic or religious group as oneself.[20] Haskell argued that the key impulse causing changes in conventions of moral responsibility was the rise of capitalism understood as a contractually based economy of exchange. Recent scholarship, notably that of Amanda Moniz, whose chapter in this collection examines the role of material culture in transatlantic humanitarian discourse, has modified Haskell by suggesting that his interpretation is too narrowly focused – capitalism was important but not overwhelmingly so in creating a humanitarian sensibility in the aftermath of the Seven Years War. Moniz among others insists that change was not revolutionary but gradual and was influenced by the development of a booming print media from the second quarter of the eighteenth century, by increasing patterns of transatlantic consumption and especially by ideological changes around mid-century in how race and 'otherness' was understood, notably in a changing medical environment. She notes, moreover, that a burgeoning culture of sensibility, encouraged by the emergence of novels and a republic of letters, led to a growth and extension of humanitarianism.[21]

Crucially, this humanitarianism was routed and channelled by specific sets of connections and embedded in broader strategic and governmental issues. The Christian religion remained central to its emerging and targeted sensibility. For contemporaries in the eighteenth century and for historians in the nineteenth and twentieth centuries, the growth of humanitarianism was a direct consequence of God's involvement in the world and a successful way of assuaging a deity angry at man's inhumanity and violations of His moral commands.[22] The rise of humanitarianism mapped on closely to the realisation among Britons, noted by Fullagar, that after the acquisition of a worldwide empire in the Americas, Asia and, through the Atlantic slave trade, Africa, control of a polyglot, multi-ethnic and multicultural imperial melange forced Christian reflection on the relations they had with the particular distant peoples they ruled. Many Britons came to argue that imperial rule brought unique responsibilities as much as it bestowed rights and privileges.

Edmund Burke summarised in eloquent prose in a speech in Parliament on the East India Bill in 1783 what were Britain's obligations, as the possessor of power, over seemingly less fortunate people. He noted that 'all political power which is set over men ... ought to be in some way or other exercised for their benefit ... Such rights or privileges ... are all in the strictest sense *a trust*; and it is of the very essence of every trust to be rendered *accountable* and even totally to *cease*, when it substantially varies from the purpose to which alone it could have a lawful existence'.[23] The idea that the British Empire was a form of trust strongly influenced humanitarian discourse during the nineteenth century. As Andrew Porter notes, 'territorial conquest, white settlement, commercial growth, economic development, and above all issues of slavery and the slave trade, raised questions about the ethics of economic exchange, the politics of equal rights or racial differences, and the purpose of Imperial power'.[24]

Without discounting the religious sensibilities of early humanitarianism, the movement arose within a larger and seemingly equally universal context, that eighteenth-century moment of inquiry, experiment and speculation that historians term the Enlightenment. It was a period in which Europeans thought hard about what features of political and cultural life distinguished the 'civilised' world from what they perceived as the 'uncivilised'. That world was related to, but was not necessarily quite the same as, the distinction between Christian and heathen. They wondered about what responsibility the 'civilised' owed to the 'uncivilised'. No one thought harder about this problem than Adam Smith, the Scottish philosopher.

He applied the newly developed culture of sensibility and the values and instincts of the 'man of feeling' as outlined in the new literary form of the novel to such seemingly abstract matters as the economy. In *The Theory of Moral Sentiments* (1759), he tried to explain why people routinely do well by each other without a judge, secular or divine, making them do things. He suggested that morality was a matter of feeling, about not doing things that were wrong, an extension of the Biblical assertion of the golden rule, of not doing to others what you would not want to be done to you, from the immediate neighbourhood to larger environs, even to people who were strangers, not neighbours.[25]

By raising the problem of humans' tendency to ignore the fate of anyone outside their immediate circle, Smith gave voice to essential concerns that animated Anglophone humanitarianism from its start in the mid-eighteenth-century – what is the duty of humans to each other, how far should humans go to end suffering, anywhere it was found, and what did adopting humanitarian approaches say about the society that took such approaches? Such questions could be answered, Smith posited, by responding to the dictates of conscience: 'reason, principle ... the inhabitant of the breast, the man within, the great judge and arbiter or our conduct'.[26] Early humanitarians, similar to Smith, believed that humans had instinctive regard for other human beings. The trick was harnessing it, and directing it, since while humanitarian concern might be universally projected, the assistance that it called forth could never be universally applied.

As Trevor Burnard shows in this volume, one of the early antislavery activists who sought to harness that early humanitarian regard was Anthony Benezet. Abolitionism, as a foundational long-distance humanitarian project started in earnest during the Seven Years War, when a tiny number of religiously minded Quakers began to consider slavery and the slave trade as not just morally indefensible and economically less desirable than wage labour, but also a sin, one that violated religious norms and stained the good name of Britain. Benezet, an American Quaker, helped initiate this historically significant process with his *Some Historical Account of Guinea ...*, first published in 1762 and influencing the more famous British abolitionists Granville Sharp, Thomas Clarkson and William Wilberforce in their work of educating the British public on the horrors of the slave trade and their own culpability in the 1780s.[27]

During the 1790s antislavery activism in Britain became cautious and somewhat muted given its potential to become conflated politically with the incendiarism of Revolutionary Terror across the Channel in France. As antislavery activists articulated the differences between their project of national preservation through atonement and the overthrow of the aristocratic order, Rights of Man fervour and the rule of the mob across the English Channel, so they introduced an explicit rupture between the discourses of humanitarianism and human rights.[28] Marcel Dorigny argues that contemporaneous French antislavery was less a humanitarian than a political creed. Because of the strong and often resented weight of the Catholic Church in France, humanitarianism was never as powerful a force in France as it was in Britain or the USA.[29] And humanitarianism was less connected to liberalism in France than in the English-speaking world. Naomi Andrews sees humanitarianism as rooted in ideas of a collective humanity and privileged solidarity with others rather than liberal individualism, narrowing and making more overtly political humanitarianism's reach.[30]

What was true of Benezet was true for other topics that provoked humanitarian discourse in Britain and America. There were astonishingly few French literary texts, for example, on the topic of slave revolts, except for Jean-François de Saint-Lambert's *Ziméo* of 1769, a wildly popular play on an imagined slave rebellion in Jamaica. Indeed, Michel-Rolph Trouillot has argued that the remarkable silence of French intellectuals to what occurred in Haiti between 1791 and 1804 came about due to the lack of appropriate categories in French Enlightenment discourse to think about and represent slave rebellion.[31] Sentimentality – so important in developing humanitarian writing in Britain – was less pronounced in France, in part showing more limited interaction by *philosophes* in the colonial venture.[32] As Matthias Middell argues, 'the intellectual pathway was a different one in Catholic France compared to Protestant Britain, with its many religions. In French public opinion, the discussion of Roman slavery and its critique by Montesquieu, played a much bigger role than the contemporary reality of plantations in the Americas. As a result, the debate remained abstract for a long time'.[33] When abolitionism and thus humanitarianism did emerge, it was created very much in the British image. It diverged over time, in part due to greater involvement of free men of colour in the Société, its lack of infrastructure and limited penetration into the provinces and outside Paris, and its inability to influence the French government, especially in the complicated context of the dual French and Haitian Revolutions.[34]

By the time William Wilberforce had led the British parliamentary antislavery lobby through the abolition of the slave trade in 1807, a new terrain for the exercise of a conservative British humanitarian sensibility, identified by Jillian Beard in this collection, was opening, as the convict colony of New South Wales became better established. Early encounters between Britons and Australian Aboriginal peoples had not yet taken the form of a settled humanitarian narrative. There was a key distinction between the discourse of conciliation pursued by Governor Phillip and that which the humanitarian lobby would apply to Aboriginal people in the coming decades. In a process mirroring Fullager's conversion of Mohawk from independent allies to objects of humane concern, it was only as the institutions of an established settler colony, including the newspaper press, emerged that, as Beard writes, 'conciliation and acculturation gave way to education and Christianisation at the hands those who would come to be labelled as humanitarians'.

The foundational Anglophone humanitarian campaign, antislavery, then, had its origins in both religious and secular regimes intended to rest upon universalism – Christianity and Enlightenment. However, the empathy with others that the campaign manifested was generated and channelled in specific ways. While writers like Benezet encouraged Britons to think of fellowship with enslaved Africans as a function of being human, it was not until the loss of the American colonies that many Britons saw participation in the slave trade as a national sin requiring moral action.[35] Exactly concurrent with that action was a shift in the perception of certain Indigenous peoples with whom British colonists had interacted for some time. As settlement proceeded and the demographic and military balance shifted towards those colonists, Indigenous subjects like the Mohawk and Aboriginal people of New South Wales morphed from independent peoples to people who needed to be conciliated into objects of British responsibility and humanitarian concern. Anglophone humanitarianism was emerging as a moral investment in specific peoples for whom Britons were assuming responsibility without jeopardising the conservative foundations of their state in church and crown by succumbing to a more revolutionary discourse of natural civic rights evident in France. Antislavery, with the unprecedented scale of public mobilisation that it entailed, needs to be set in this broader context rather than seen as a singular foundation stone for subsequent histories of both humanitarianism and human rights.

The uneven spread of philanthropy, c. 1800–c. 1880

After the abolition of the slave trade in 1807, the work of abolishing slavery continued among enslaved people themselves and in Britain. But a new generation of Anglophone philanthropic campaigners was emerging with a more diffuse set of targets for welfare in mind, scattered across a far broader terrain. With the primary object of mass campaigning on the grounds of humanity – abolition of the slave trade – accomplished, the objects and locations of Anglo-American philanthropists' concerns proliferated.[36]

Amanda Moniz's chapter in this volume charts the institutionalisation of such philanthropy in the New York Hospital, highlighting how control of the flow of material resources necessary to its dispensation consolidated the position of white male merchants and doctors while relegating female nurses and African-Americans to a subordinated role. This chapter in particular reveals the critical importance of humanitarianism's materialities. Who gets to obtain and utilise which resources is just as significant in conditioning philanthropic selectivity as is the identification of particular recipients. It is no coincidence that, at the same time as philanthropy was being dispensed in ways which shored up privilege in New York, and which consolidated middle-class British reformers' status in Britain, former slave owners in receipt of compensation funds for the loss of their enslaved 'property' were often in the forefront of charitable enterprises.[37]

The reach of British humanitarianism was extended, with uneven effects around the world, as the empire's centre of gravity shifted from the former slave societies of the Atlantic world to the eastern and southern hemispheres, aided in part by the reinvestment of slave owners and East India Company shareholders in a surge of Australian colonisation.[38] This diffusion of philanthropy was embodied in Britain by the passing of the mantle of antislavery activism from William Wilberforce to Thomas Fowell Buxton, whose reformist interests extended well beyond slavery to include the conduct of rapidly increasing numbers of British settlers towards Indigenous peoples in North America, Australasia and southern Africa, and the need for Christian reformist intervention in India.[39]

This geographical expansion of British concern was, as always, balanced by a greater selectivity as certain potential recipients were valorised at the expense of others. Bronwen Everill's chapter in this collection shows how, building on its antislavery credentials, 'British imperial humanitarian policy often responded to British West African subjects' appeals to intervene in the slave trade', while their 'other humanitarian concerns, including famine and disease, were regularly not prioritised by the colonial government, despite lobbying from the same groups'. Antislavery, as we will see, was a perennial, indeed dominant, part of British humanitarianism's repertoire during the nineteenth century, but it was swiftly accompanied by episodic attention to European objects of pity and remedial action.

In the 1820s, as philanthropic campaigners remained focused on the amelioration of slavery in the Caribbean prior to its abolition in 1833, Lord Byron mobilised a philhellene movement that took the government by surprise. Byron's poetry, combined with the appeals of classically educated men of letters, saw British public opinion brought to bear in defence of the Christian descendants of the 'noble' ancient Greeks, railing against oppressive Muslim Ottoman occupation.[40] Byron's romantic death in the struggle for Greek freedom inspired revolutionaries elsewhere but was also fuel for the reluctant British naval action against the Ottomans at the Battle of Navarino in 1827.[41] This early 'humanitarian intervention' was one of a number of the proliferating forms that a somewhat fickle Anglophone humanitarianism was taking in the aftermath of the initial campaign against the Atlantic slave trade.

The period of the philanthropically induced amelioration of slavery between 1807 and 1833 saw humanitarianism increasingly incorporated into the government of an empire seeking to fend off the radical implications of a new and revolutionary Rights of Man discourse, manifested in the American, French and Haitian Revolutions. As Alan Lester and Fae Dussart argue, the philanthropic sentiments expressed and enacted by governing men like George Arthur, Governor of Tasmania, Honduras, Upper Canada and Bombay were intended to ameliorate the conditions of first enslaved and then Indigenous subjects in order to preserve a hierarchical order founded on church and crown.[42] Arthur's conservative humanitarian trajectory saw him release illegally enslaved Mosquito Coast Indians in British Honduras in the 1820s, and insist upon the establishment of protectorates of Aborigines in the Port Phillip District of the colony of New South Wales so as to avoid a repeat of the Tasmanian Aboriginal genocide that he had overseen in the mid-1830s, while ruthlessly executing the American patriots who raided the Canadian colonies in support of rebels espousing the Rights of Man in 1838.[43]

By the time the philanthropists led by Buxton in Britain had articulated their most coherent vision of a more benevolent empire in the Select Committee report on Aborigines in British Settlements (1837), humanitarianism was already being encompassed within the discourse of the empire's governing men – indeed it can be seen as performing both a moral justification for, and technique of, imperial governance.[44] We see the conservative selectivity of British governmental humanitarianism even more explicitly in Alan Lester's chapter in this collection on how British officials interpreted and acted upon the implementation of the law abolishing slavery passed in 1833. He notes that humanitarians' mobilisation of empathy was directed towards certain kinds of precarious people rather than others. Attacks on slavery in the West Indies, leading to its abolition in the 1830s, were accompanied by the indifference of British activists towards slavery elsewhere, notably in India, where it was allowed to continue as before. As Andrea Major points out, the abolitionist Zachary Macaulay spoke for many when distinguishing between West and East Indian slaves' entitlement to freedom. 'There is a difference', Macaulay maintained, 'between the slavery of the East and West, that of the latter we ourselves are the sole authors, and are chargeable, therefore, with its whole guilt and turpitude. In the East whatever slavery exists we found there; we did not create it ourselves', although it certainly proved useful to the production of the rent paid to Company shareholders after the abolition of the East India Company's commercial functions in 1833.[45]

A second, and as far as the government was concerned, somewhat unanticipated, British antislavery campaign emerged in the 1860s–70s. Just as Byron had rendered the Greeks proper subjects for humanitarian intervention in the 1820s, so David Livingstone's muscular Christian exploration of southern and central Africa brought different forms of slavery to the attention of the British public. The celebrity Livingstone's highlighting of East African slavery, perpetuated by Portuguese and Arabs, generated mass interest and mobilisation in Britain, leaving imperial administrators somewhat bewildered. A popular call to action mobilised by Livingstone's writings and lecture tours across the country led first to Henry Bartle Frere's gunboat diplomacy to close down the Zanzibar slave trade and then the awkward extension of Protectorates intended to stamp out slavery beyond the crown colonies of West Africa (covered by Bronwen Everill in this volume) and in the Pacific.[46] As Richard Huzzey notes, 'After 1874, anti-slavery rhetoric infused the expansionist campaigns that annexed British Central Africa, the Ugandan protectorate and northern and southern Nigeria ... If Victorian commentators could agree that slavery was evil, they could not always agree on how, when and where to combat it [although] foreign, external slave trades loomed large in differing recipes for British agency and intervention'.[47] This resurgence of antislavery campaigning and governance at the height of Victoria's empire, unrivalled by any other European imperial power, revitalised Britons' understandings of their special place in the history of human benevolence and provided further grist for later generations of imperial apologists.[48] By 1879, however, Bartle Frere, the celebrated antislavery crusader, was waging bloody wars of confederation against independent African polities in southern Africa while 5.5 million British Indian subjects were starving to death, with barely a ripple of concern among the British public.[49]

In the early nineteenth century the British Empire was in transition, from a geographical axis linking Britain to the Americas and Caribbean, to one focused on emigration and settlement in the southern hemisphere. Humanitarian concern and governance followed, as Indigenous peoples joined the ranks of the enslaved as intended recipients of a discourse of British benevolence, even if their experiences of colonialism differed vastly from those imagined by the majority of Britons. Accompanying this proliferation, expansion and redirection of Anglophone humanitarianism was a periodic resurgence of campaigning for particular humanitarian interventions. With an increasingly enfranchised male population and an electorate to which British ministers needed to be ever more attentive, such campaigns could result in unexpected and not necessarily strategically advantageous ventures overseas. As Richard Huzzey puts it, the revitalisation of British antislavery in the later nineteenth century provided Anglophone humanitarianism with a 'dual identity – of philanthropic restraint and imperial chauvinism'.[50] In the meantime, as emancipation was accompanied by settler colonial expansion and self-government, middle-class metropolitan reformers like Thomas Hodgkin and Buxton organised new networks of concern and new forms of lobbying through correspondents in the settler colonies, particularly in Australasia.[51]

Settler colonial humanitarianism and protection, c. 1850–c. 1900

Although humanitarian concern had been brought to bear unevenly in the abolition of slavery, the fact of legal abolition settled the issue of imperial freedoms as far as many Britons were concerned. As we have seen from the ruminations of Burke, Smith and others, however, humanitarianism was driven too by the notion of attending to the welfare of others by propagating their 'civilisation'. Anglophone humanitarians' sense of obligation to bring civilisation, as well as freedom and Christianity, became especially urgent as the British Empire was rocked by a variety of crises in the 1850s and 1860s, notably the Uprising in India in 1857, but was also manifested in conflict between settlers and Indigenous peoples in Canada, New Zealand, South Africa and the Caribbean.[52] At the heart of these conflicts were vexed questions for imperial humanitarians: To what extent should Britons impose their own civilisation on others whom they now ruled? When colonial subjects resisted, was it right to use violence against them, assuming that it was for their own long-term benefit? What kinds of violence used and against whom could be reconciled with a progressive and beneficial empire?[53]

Humanitarian governance in the middle of the nineteenth century was marked by the dissemination of British civilisational norms alongside the denial of another people's self-determination. George Grey, the ethnographer who governed South Australia, New Zealand (twice) and the Cape Colony in southern Africa, epitomised the way in which Britons justified forced assimilation of Indigenous peoples into settler societies (a form of cultural genocide, as Curthoys argues in this volume) as a humanitarian act, which would save at least some individuals among them from their otherwise inevitable fate of extinction as a race.[54] While Lt Governor George Arthur had envisaged Protection as the project of safeguarding Indigenous communities on certain of their own lands until such time as they had survived the first onslaught of settler colonialism and could begin the task of adaptation, 'protection' came to mean something quite different in mid-century Australia. It is a word that Curthoys, Nettelbeck and Ellinghaus all interrogate in their chapters on settler policies towards Aboriginal Australians as the intended recipients of civilisational 'welfare'.[55]

The settler colonies provided Britain with an arena for the exercise of colonial humanitarianism that was quite distinctive among the nineteenth-century European empires, the others of which lacked colonies of mass emigration and settlement on such a scale. Nineteenth-century Australia is an ideal place to test the changing notions of humanitarian governance and of humanitarianism more generally within the Anglophone world. Once federated it was the settler colony par excellence – with wealthy, confident and humanitarian-inclined white residents in a country in which the Aboriginal inhabitants had been dispossessed, incarcerated and subjected to forcible policies of assimilation. The chapters by Curthoys, Nettelbeck and Ellinghaus examine, in different ways, the complicated relationship between Australian settlers and Aboriginal people as they tease out the complexities of humanitarian feeling in an Anglophone society committed to white supremacy. More importantly, it was a society that believed in the assertion of British civilisation and British values as the only ideals worth living up to while being a full participant in what Ann Curthoys calls a genocidal age.

Curthoys powerfully analyses the genocidal implications of this humanitarianism in the tragic story of the Aboriginal prison, Rottnest Island or Wadgemup as known by the Whadjuk Nganger people living near Perth, West Australia. As Nettelbeck and Ellinghaus also argue, the relationship between the general concept of 'protection' and the ways in which Aboriginal people were treated by Protection as a governmental regime was tenuous to say the least. This treatment was frequently brutal, as Curthoys shows in the horrific punishment data about Aboriginal prisoners at Rottnest; as Nettelbeck illustrates in her examination of the malign sexual environment that existed on the large Minderoo station on Australia's north-west frontier; and as Ellinghaus discusses in respect of the process by which certain Aboriginal people were granted 'exemption' certificates, to be allowed to drink in public houses. By showing that they could qualify as civilised by the standards of the state, they were also demonstrating their exemption from their own, Aboriginal, humanity. Exemption was deeply humanitarian – paternalistic, ameliorative and based on the conscience-salving idea that some special individuals could escape the controls imposed on the majority of the rest of the community – and deeply problematic – requiring individuals to surpass the barrier of 'civilisation' or 'progress' or else to be excluded from the benefits of civilisation, some of which, like drinking in public houses, were dubious benefits in any case. Ellinghaus argues that exemption reflected the humanitarian fantasy of the civilised, Christianised, acculturated Indigenous person. Nettelbeck's focus is on the ways that a revived antislavery discourse within Australia brought forth yet greater intervention into the lives of Aboriginal people by a settler state intent on civilising them out of existence, while shoring up its credentials as a federated white nation.

As Nettelbeck's previous work demonstrates, these intra-Australian discussions fed directly into trans-imperial arguments about the proper targets of Anglophone empathy in both colony and metropole.[56] Harriet Beecher Stowe's call for sympathy with enslaved black people in *Uncle Tom's Cabin*, a massively popular book across the Anglophone world, was directly challenged by Charles Dickens's scathing critique of 'telescopic philanthropy' in *Bleak House*. Dickens expressed his distaste for Stowe's romantic sympathy with black people both in personal correspondence with Stowe, and in his character Mrs Jellyby, who was intended to highlight the pernicious effect of such selective humanitarian concern. In dedicating herself to the missionary cause in Africa, Mrs Jellyby ignores her own impoverished children. The contest between these two authors' visions of where Anglophone empathy should be directed during the 1840s–60s was itself constitutive of a turn in imperial humanitarianism away from empathy with Indigenous and formerly enslaved people, and towards fellow feeling with racial kin. This was manifest especially in the outpouring of emotional plays and readings in Australia, the USA and Britain about the death of another of Dickens's characters, the poor London road sweep, Jo. Dickens, alongside other prominent commentators like Thomas Carlyle, helped to generate a new sense of the very word 'humanitarian'. It came into popular use for the first time to refer to those who had previously been designated 'philanthropists', as a scathing condemnation of their partiality for black people at the expense of more proximate racial kin.

At the same time as a growing critique of humanitarianism's focus on 'undeserving' black subjects was mounting in the aftermath of British humanitarians' disappointment at the progress made by emancipated slaves in the Caribbean, however, settler colonies like the Australian ones were striving to become recognised as upstanding centres of international humanitarian concern in their own right.[57] Even before Federation at the end of the century, this was demonstrated especially by Australian critiques of the British imperial government's management of Indian famines and offers of alternative forms of assistance from the seemingly more progressive parts of the Anglophone world.[58] As settler colonies federated and gained self-government and the British Empire transitioned and expanded again during the late nineteenth and early twentieth centuries, a new international context for Anglophone humanitarianism was developing. Settler nations like Australia, as well as the United States, emerged as alternative focal points for the projection of Anglophone humanitarian intervention overseas. This diffusion of humanitarian responsibility from the 'centre' of the British Empire to its former 'peripheries' was a transition foreshadowing the internationalisation of humanitarianism involving other European powers in the twentieth century, and, we suggest, is deserving of far greater attention as an episode in its own right.

Late imperial transitions, c. 1880–1919

The rhetorical and political power of episodic British mobilisation for humanitarian intervention was demonstrated once again when the Liberal leader William Ewart Gladstone came out of retirement to appeal to British voters for empathy with the victims of the Turkish atrocities in Bulgaria in the late 1870s. Gladstone waded in after the massacre of some 30,000 Bulgarians by Turks and their supporters was reported in the British press, publishing his sensational *Bulgarian Horrors and the Question of the East* in 1879. The book was primarily an attack on the Conservative Disraeli not only for supporting the Ottoman Empire as a bulwark against Russian expansion, but also for withholding information on the scale of the atrocities from the British public and preventing parliamentary debate of them. 'We learn with astonishment and horror', Gladstone lamented, that 'we have been involved, in ... moral complicity with the basest and blackest outrages upon record within the present century ... crimes and outrages, so vast in scale as to exceed all modern example, and so unutterably vile as well as fierce in character, that it passes the power of heart to conceive, and of tongue and pen adequately to describe them'. A byproduct of Gladstone's newfound humanitarianism was the sponsoring of a new racism against Turks. The 'Turkish race was and what it is', he wrote, 'are not the mild Mahometans of India, nor the chivalrous Saladins of Syria, nor the cultured Moors of Spain. They were, upon the whole, from the black day when they first entered Europe, the one great anti-human specimen of humanity. Wherever they went, a broad line of blood marked the track behind them; and, as far as their dominion reached, civilisation disappeared from view'.[59]

The effect of potent humanitarian lobbying on the politics of empire emerged again in criticisms of the methods employed by the British army in the latter stages of the South African War, with Emily Hobhouse's exposé of the conditions in the concentration camps set up as part of its 'scorched earth' tactics.[60] In the wake of this critique, Edmund Morel, the Irish nationalist Roger Casement and the Congo Reform Association mobilised public campaigns against the conduct of Belgian colonialism in the Congo, reinvigorating humanitarian networks once again with the spirit of the abolitionist movement.[61] Both campaigns fused a sense of imperial responsibility with standards of international behaviour that were now being increasingly articulated in treaties and agreements between the major European imperial powers, as they outlined particular spheres of interest, legitimising their intervention on the grounds of a pan-European mission to spread Christianity, commerce and civilisation.[62]

The revived late nineteenth-century imperial competition and co-operation that lay behind the Scramble for Africa prompted Britain's European state rivals to forge their own humanitarianisms as counterpart legitimations to those which British elites had long wielded. Perhaps the most famously cynical use of humanitarianism as a cover for economic exploitation was King Leopold's protestation that he was acting against the slave trade in his colonisation of Congo, at the same time that Britain was conquering southern African kingdoms in pursuit of confederation.[63] But the 1880s also saw an increasing pan-European Catholic intervention, as the French Société Antiesclavagiste de France (1888) and the Italian Società Antischiavista d'Italia (1888) joined efforts with the British Antislavery Society and with humanitarians in Switzerland to raise Europeans' awareness of the persistence of domestic slavery and slave trading in Africa.[64] Such newly internationalised antislavery discourse fed into notions of a 'civilising mission' which seemed to legitimise imperial expansion. Portrayals that contrasted the actions of Western powers with those of so-called 'Arab' slave traders (a term which Europeans also applied to African Muslims) were one element of this discourse from the 1880s.[65]

As Richard Drayton points out, however, and as was borne out by the Scramble for Africa, 'The problem in all humanitarian interventions is that those powers with the capacity to apply force at a distance for humanitarian or other ends are generally also those with economic and strategic interests overseas and are often also states which refuse any cosmopolitan restraint on their own military action'. Such was particularly true of the period of unbridled European rivalry to gain territory in Africa.[66] Roger Casement's own radical critique of British imperial governance, articulated initially from within the Foreign Office itself, would ultimately reveal starkly the rift between a more revolutionary human rights discourse and this conflicted discourse of late imperial humanitarian intervention. It would end in his execution for participation in the 1916 Easter Rising in Dublin.[67]

Even before the outbreak of World War I, itself associated with these European imperial rivalries, Anglophone humanitarian rhetoric was tending increasingly towards an apolitical neutralism designed to enable the transfer of aid and expertise in contested regions. The global conditions at the end of World War I, including the mass displacement of refugees on an unprecedented scale, the Armenian genocide and ethnic cleansing, food shortages and famines, and health crises including the influenza pandemic of 1918–19, increasingly gave rise to international, state-directed, secular and institutionalised humanitarian aid efforts.[68] The scale and gravity of post-war conditions demanded that humanitarian interventions could not rely on aid from the philanthropic and charity sector but required interventions and support by states and governments. These endeavours were increasingly influenced not so much by imperial Britain as by a newly assertive USA, intent on promoting a post-imperial world.[69]

The British Empire, however, remained a powerful reference point and model for Anglophone humanitarianism well into the twentieth century. Despite American endeavours, many of the architects of international organisations following World War I saw bodies such as the League of Nations as a means to secure imperial interests, rather than undermine them.[70] British inter-war humanitarians sought to extend compassion 'without undermining the imperialist attitudes and projects with which [humanitarianism] was normally entangled'.[71] While humanitarianism had begun to operate within an international arena in the 1880s, the ideological foundations of liberal internationalism were themselves shaped by the moral and political frameworks of empire.[72] The vocabulary of a benign empire in particular still enhanced the appeal of post-war humanitarian efforts, particularly with the more conservative faction of the British public.[73]

Anglophone humanitarianism moved between the imperial and the new 'international' frames of reference, through a long, complicated and often fraught process until the onset of World War II. The rise of an innovative and professional charity fundraising sector within Edwardian Britain was a key, but often overlooked part of this process.[74] So too was the tendency, noted above, for Anglophone societies outside of Britain, especially but not exclusively those in the settler colonies, to become donor and organisational hubs in their own right.[75] During and immediately after World War I, the new medium of film assisted in this diffusive process.[76]

Within this context, 1919 was an auspicious year for the establishment of a number of Anglophone humanitarian organisations presaging the new world order of humanitarian intervention.[77] These organisations both reflected and contributed to the waning of the British Empire as a dominant form of global governance. The League of Nations, formed out of the 1919 Treaty of Versailles, aspired to build peace and global co-operation through the League's Covenants and treaties which dealt with questions of the conditions of displaced refugees, the treatment of Indigenous peoples and the slavery of women and children.[78] Dame Rachel Crowdy, Chief of the Opium and Social Questions Section of the League of Nations, claimed that within its first six years the League completed 'the work of a temporary nature resulting from post-War conditions' including the repatriation of 400,000 prisoners from Siberia, the suppression of typhus in Poland, and the resettlement of Russian and Armenian refugees. 'Then, as a result of the Committees on Slavery, we have a Convention [1926] ... the best thing of its kind which we could get at the time, for the abolition of slavery'.[79]

Despite the ensuing pusillanimity of this convention, the creation of the League opened up a new space in Geneva where different national and international humanitarian organisations could compete for resourcing and political support. As Amalia Ribi Forclaz shows, the internationalisation of antislavery was especially marked there in the inter-war years with Fascist Italy proclaiming its own imperial virtue through the discourse and thereby asserting its right to be seen as a trustee for mandated colonies in the same way as were Britain and France. Ethiopian 'slavery not only played a tangible role in the build up to the Italo/Ethiopian War in 1835/6; humanitarian propaganda became one of the main vehicles through which Italy attempted to sell the conflict to public opinion in Italy and abroad'.[80]

The establishment of the Save the Children Fund in the same year as the League of Nations marked the emergence of a distinctive Anglophone humanitarian organisation within this proliferating international humanitarian landscape, which was secular and transnational.[81] The rise of international organisations was especially pronounced in the field of health with the establishment of the League of Red Cross Societies (LRCS) which aimed to co-ordinate the existing Red Cross societies globally in an international response to health management. These new international organisations shared targets and techniques through international congresses and the exchange of information but remained in an 'interdependent and mutually formative relationship with government authorities', their activities still manifesting, ultimately, through national channels.[82] Focusing on the LRCS and the international development of public health programmes, Melanie Oppenheimer's chapter demonstrates how Anglophone humanitarianism began to manifest in distinctive ways during the inter-war years. By drawing in a biographical approach to the study of interwar humanitarianism, Oppenheimer directs our attention to the gendered aspects of humanitarian work. Oppenheimer weaves the narratives of the lives of these women to illustrate the conservatism of the LRCS and its impact on the role of women, their agency and the nature of humanitarianism at this time.

As Oppenheimer's chapter indicates, much of the internationally collaborative Anglophone humanitarianism of the inter-war years served the same palliative function that earlier iterations of imperial humanitarianism had served, only with a more acute focus on the role of women as both practitioners and targets. As Jean Allman observes, 'In seeking to address the welfare of African women and children almost exclusively through social and educative solutions aimed at women and children (particularly at their hygiene and nutrition)', a conference comprising 'government, church and business representatives from eight European countries and from several colonial territories in Africa' in Geneva in June 1931, 'avoided the obvious issues of economic exploitation and political expediency. In this sense, its proceedings both reflected and inspired an international discourse aimed at constructing proper, nurturing motherhood (according to European middle-class criteria) out of biological maternity, irrespective of economic, cultural or social context'.[83]

Decolonisation and the new empire of humanity, c. 1945–90

As Andrew Thompson has noted, 'The speed with which the world's largest empire was liquidated – more than forty new States emerged from the late 1950s to the early 1960s – caught humanitarians by surprise as much as it did colonial administrators'.[84] While British officials sought to control a narrative of largely peaceful and voluntary decolonisation, the counter-revolutionary violence of the British Empire's transition is coming increasingly to light as the Colonial and Foreign Offices' concealed, or 'migrated archive' is explored.[85] While the ICRC called for new international rules to manage the wars of decolonisation, 'Britain did not even ratify the four Geneva Conventions until 1957, out of concern that they would restrict the operations of its security forces when fighting insurgents in anti-colonial struggles'.[86]

Nevertheless, the British Red Cross played an ameliorative role within each of Britain's wars of decolonisation. They worked among the half a million 'Chinese squatters' relocated during the Malaya conflict into 'new villages' in an attempt to cut them off from Communist insurgents. In Kenya, their workers were present among captured Mau Mau insurgents and in the African reserves, distributing food, promoting health services and managing a home for abandoned and orphaned Kikuyu children. In Cyprus, they launched an island-wide rural health scheme and in Aden they 'prioritized maternity care, child welfare and the training of local women as health visitors'. As Thompson concludes, 'Nowhere are the moral hazards of humanitarianism during decolonisation more apparent than in relation to the forced resettlement of civilians – a recurrent feature of military operations in counter-insurgencies that remains poorly regulated by international law to this day'.[87]

Decolonisation was a time of considerable flux for international humanitarian organisations seeking to gain access and promote welfare in the midst of numerous conflicts of independence and rivalry between USA- and Soviet-dominated blocs for the allegiance of new states. The humanitarian paradox of the end of empire noted by Thompson was that on the one hand 'the security measures undertaken by late-colonial States were responsible for much of the suffering that humanitarians brought to the public eye'. On the other hand, 'by extending bureaucratic power into new spheres of social and economic life, cash-strapped late-colonial States were compelled to draw more and more on the resources of the voluntary, charitable and humanitarian sectors' to ameliorate that suffering.[88]

From the 1960s, NGO appeals to donor publics, Matthew Hilton argues, 'were a formative factor in how European electorates engaged with decolonization … these organizations gained the capacity to direct the sympathies of their supporters in one direction or another, even to the point of determining whether different categories of victim were felt to be genuinely deserving or, conversely, to deserve their own plight'.[89] As Hilton points out, British 'NGOs and charities were popular because they represented many things for many people. For the late colonial state, they were the agents that would step in where government retreated, providing vital lessons in self-help for the future leaders of the country. For newly independent governments, they were both suppliers of Western funds and props to impoverished social service departments. For donors and international aid agencies, they were a route through which liberal internationalist sympathies could be directed. That no one in these early decades of development was certain which aid initiatives actually worked on the ground was therefore of less importance than the optimistic hopes placed upon charity to tackle global poverty'.[90]

The ways in which Anglophone humanitarianism was transformed with the end of formal empire can be seen in the changing nature of Australia's international involvement in humanitarian work during the Cold War. Civil wars in Korea (1950–53) and Vietnam (1955–75) and Australia's involvement in these wars pivoted Australia away from one empire – the British – towards another – through its alliance with the United States. The proliferation of humanitarian organisations resulted in a boom in aid agencies in the era of development. With the collapse of the League of Nations on the brink of World War II and with the emergence of the United Nations in 1945, the post-war era created a new, internationally sanctioned human rights framework, different from the revolutionary Rights of Man against which ameliorative humanitarian governance had been pitched in the early nineteenth century. This framework included the 1948 Universal Declaration of Human Rights as well as the Convention on the Prevention and Punishment of the Crime of Genocide. Food aid became central to Western humanitarian efforts during this period especially to so-called Third World countries, culminating in the declaration in 1961 of the 'Decade of Development'.[91]

Anglophone humanitarian interventions from 1950 onwards took on various forms, ranging from the highly organised and structured humanitarian groups such as Oxfam and World Vision to the more individualised and independent form of humanitarian activity and intervention. In her chapter, Agnieska Sobocinska focuses on three major international volunteering schemes which were deeply embedded within Anglophone humanitarian interventions at this time: the Volunteer Graduate Scheme in Australia, Voluntary Service Overseas in Britain and the United States Peace Corps, developed in the 1950s and 1960s as a part of the movement of volunteers in the Global South. Sobocinska demonstrates, through her case study of emotion working within particular organisations devoted to furthering 'global friendship', how volunteerism blurred the distinction between international development and humanitarianism and drew on an emotional lexicon.[92]

By contrast, Joy Damousi examines a different form of humanitarian intervention which was based instead on individual rather than institutional, organisational or state-supported humanitarian activities. By examining the humanitarian activism of three women involved in Vietnam during the civil war – Rosemary Taylor, Elaine Moir and Margaret Moses – Damousi explores humanitarian practice and advocacy outside of organisational structures. Driven by attempts to promote inter-country adoption of war orphans, the independent nature of their humanitarian work informed their promotion of this cause – a practice not supported by the major humanitarian groups at the time. Such humanitarians have drawn less attention from scholars because they worked outside of organised groups and structures of humanitarian aid. This study also seeks to shed light on lesser-known humanitarian activists – invariably women – during this civil war.

Damousi develops three arguments. By working independently, the three women's very experience of their humanitarian work in wartime was distinctive and striking. Second, such a form of humanitarian practice allowed these women to take a distinctive advocacy role for inter-country adoption of refugee children. This role involved publicly lobbying government to shift public policy in ways which those in humanitarian organisations did not do at this time. Finally, Damousi intentionally moves her analysis outside of the debate on the relationship between humanitarianism and the reinvention of human rights which tends to dominate and define much of the scholarship of this period. Studies of humanitarian activists in practice, Damousi argues, point to a more fluid, evolving and dynamic form of humanitarian activism, which was shaped on the ground, in action, and was less shaped by human rights declarations and other decrees than by practical experience and the legacies of the past.

The final two essays in this volume take us back to organisational humanitarianism and recent debates by historians around human rights and humanitarianism throughout the 1970s and 1980s. It brings us full circle back to our point of origin in the late eighteenth century: the relationship between humanitarianism and human rights.[93] Broadly, our contributors reinforce Samuel Moyn's argument that humanitarianism and human rights have maintained distinct trajectories until relatively recently. Moyn suggests that when these discourses were conflated, from the late twentieth century on, the effect was that of a dominant humanitarian discourse of amelioration overawing and neutering the radical potential of human rights. As he puts it, 'Once comprising an anti-hierarchical language of egalitarian citizenship, human rights have frequently been humanitarianized, and their defenders are themselves victims of the repetitious confirmation of hierarchical relations which has been the central truth of humanitarian ethics for much longer'.[94]

While Damousi and Ellinghaus's chapters complicate any simplistic binary between humanitarianism and human rights, the essays by Jon Piccini and Roland Burke round off this volume by casting this fraught relationship within such a longer historical frame of reference. Jon Piccini focuses on Amnesty International in Australia to highlight the tension between practices and ideas of humanitarianism and human rights within the organisation. In particular, Piccini argues that the local expression of international non-government and humanitarian organisations raised challenges for the organisation when the platform of Amnesty International was translated and transplanted to a local and national context. Positioning this theme within the wider backdrop of Australia's human rights and humanitarian community after the war, Piccini focuses on two case studies. The first is the question of Indigenous rights and the second is conscientious objection to serving in the Vietnam War. On the question of Indigenous rights, Piccini documents that the Victorian branch of Amnesty in particular recognised the violations and dispossession of land of Indigenous populations with no adequate compensations. But what Amnesty should do about these injustices was unclear and received mixed responses.

Further, this case revealed the diversity of views within the organisation about what should have been the proper remit of the group. Similarly, differences of opinion on the issue of conscientious objection against military service in the Vietnam War divided Amnesty, often leading to bitter conflict between separate groups in the organisation. These cases, he suggests, reveal a divergence between humanitarian and human rights perspectives, co-existing in Amnesty and which were typical of humanitarian organising during the Cold War. One strength of Piccini's analysis is that it examines Amnesty in Australia over a long period, from the 1950s to the 1980s. He discusses the emergence during the 1970s of a parliamentary group of politicians who raised concerns about Amnesty's commitment to remain 'apolitical'. The emergence of this group of politicians provoked questions about the very nature of humanitarianism and human rights within nation states. Amnesty, Piccini argues, represented a continuation of existing humanitarianism rather than a sudden adoption of human rights, although as these examples demonstrate, both co-existed in tension.

Our final chapter develops the theme of human rights into the 1980s. Burke draws our attention to the need to explore the long-term effects of what Moyn has termed the 'breakthrough' of human rights during the mid-1970s.[95] He argues that it was during the 1980s that we should focus attention to examine the cumulative impact of the 1970s human rights movement. Burke argues that human rights in the 1980s was a struggle between anti-political groups of the human rights movement which focused on abuses by the states focused on human rights on the one hand, and on the other, Third World governments which framed human rights politically as a form of reparation of economic power. Burke argues that during this period, the utopianism of human rights ultimately 'retreated to humanitarian palliation'. Burke throws a spotlight on the 1980s as an especially distinctive decade when considering the impact of the human rights revolution. Beginning his discussion with the central role of torture to human rights discussions in the 1980s, Burke points to the Convention on Certain Conventional Weapons in October 1980 as emblematic and suggestive of a focus on and centrality of the human rights agenda at this time. Further, with the drafting of the United Nations' Convention Against Torture, Burke argues that 'the corporeal consolidated its place as a central priority in the first half of the 1980s'. Its adoption in 1984, he argues, was the 'breakthrough' moment. Shifting the analysis to a focus on the right to food, Burke draws on the activities of the Food and Agriculture Organization (FAO) and the UN's focus on the right to subsistence and food programmes introduced throughout the world. His final example is the Convention of the Rights of the Child in 1989 which he describes as the 'capstone' of the 1980s human rights movement, defusing its radical potential.

Conclusion

In examining the intersection between humanitarianism, human rights, governance and different methods and approaches of humanitarian intervention over the *longue durée*, this volume seeks to highlight the fluidity and contested meaning and practice of Anglophone humanitarianism and its relationship with the rise and fall of the British Empire. It spotlights the shifting forms of activity across periods, which were initially tied to colonialism and imperialism, and then, after World War II, to new realms of international political engagement. It contributes to the burgeoning literature on the histories both of humanitarianisms and of empire, aiming to further complicate methodologies, perspectives and approaches in each field.

Examining humanitarianism within an Anglophone context and within the context of settler societies that became nation states with British inheritances allows us to see the continuities in Anglophone humanitarianism over several centuries. These include the potential for humanitarian forms of governance to ameliorate the conditions of unequal subjects as a counter-revolutionary strategy, pitched against claims to universal rights of citizenship; the potency of antislavery as a humanitarian focal point, albeit with malleable definitions of what that institution is and who suffers from it, and the episodic power of humanitarian campaigns calling forth quite specific and delimited state interventions within both Anglophone and other imperial spheres.

Such continuities were sustained even into the different context of a twentieth century in which the British and other empires had been ended, and revised discourses of human rights competed with older yet still vibrant notions of humanitarianism and humane governance.

The dominance of humanitarians throughout this period has made it difficult for the voices of those acted upon by humanitarians to be heard or even recognised. Humanitarians' efforts, as Tehila Sasson and James Vernon note, 'generated a form of governmentality designed to produce a new type of colonial subject' rather than to include such subjects in governance.[96] But to see humanitarianism solely as a form of conservative governance which subsumed or assumed, rather than heeded, its recipients' demands, is too simplistic and stark. On occasion, this tendency to deny the agency of objects of humanitarianism could be subverted by humanitarians themselves. More importantly, while selective humanitarianism can tend to occlude the agency of its recipients, it can also be selectively utilised by those recipients to steer resources, and political capital, in certain directions rather than others – often in ways unintended by humanitarians themselves. A recent UK government Humanitarian Emergency Response Review noted a 'paradigm' in which 'the affected population' is still seen 'too much as ... "pawns" (passive individuals) and the international community as "knights" (extreme altruists)', meaning that 'local capacities are not utilised' and 'the beneficiary is not involved enough' in humanitarian projects.[97]

Yet the failure of humanitarians to *see* how recipients mobilise their aid does not mean that it is not mobilised. Humanitarians, as Jean Allman pointed out, 'were sowing seeds in ground they did not own, in a climate they could not predict and at intervals they did not determine'.[98] Three centuries of Anglophone humanitarianism may reveal broad tendencies for humanitarian governance to ameliorate precarious subjects' conditions and deflect the more radical agendas of human rights, and to respond unexpectedly to populist campaigns for intervention on behalf of certain subjects rather than others, but that does not mean that the redistribution of resources called forth by humane concern is without utility to its targets. 'Recipients' capacity to mobilise humanitarianism in unanticipated ways is the next stage in humanitarian historical research.

Notes

1 Claudia Rahout, 'The Link of a Former British Prime Minister's Ancestor to Caribbean Slavery Economy in the Current Call for Reparations in Jamaica',

in Olaf Kaltmeier, Mirko Petersen, Wilfried Raussert and Julia Roth (eds), *Cherishing the Past, Envisioning the Future: Entangled Practices of Heritage and Utopia in the Americas* (New Orleans, LA: University of New Orleans, 2021).
2. Robert Jenrick, 'We will save Britain's statues from the woke militants who want to censor our past', *The Telegraph*, 16 January 2021. In fact only one statue was spontaneously removed after decades of attempts to work through the local authorities – that of the prominent slave trader Edward Colston in Bristol.
3. See Michael Barnett, *Empire of Humanity: A History of Humanitarianism* (Ithaca, NY: Cornell University Press, 2011).
4. Richard Huzzey and John McAleer, 'History, Memory and the Commemoration of Atlantic Slave Trade Suppression', in R. Burroughs and R. Huzzey (eds), *The Suppression of the Atlantic Slave Trade: British Policies, Practices and Representations of Naval Coercion* (Manchester, UK: Manchester University Press, 2015), p. 182.
5. William Hague, *William Wilberforce: The Life of the Great Anti-Slave Trade Campaigner* (London, UK: Harper Perennial, 2008).
6. Alan Lester, Kate Boehme and Peter Mitchell, *Ruling the World: Freedom, Civilisation and Liberalism in the British Empire* (Cambridge, UK: Cambridge University Press, 2020).
7. J. R. Oldfield, *Transatlantic Abolitionism in the Age of Revolution: An International History of Antislavery, c. 1787–1820* (Cambridge, UK: Cambridge University Press, 2013), p. 2.
8. Marie-Jeanne Rossignol, 'Anthony Benezet's Antislavery Reputation in France: An Investigation', in Rossignol and Bertrand Van Ruymbeke (eds), *The Atlantic World of Anthony Benezet (1713–1784): From French Reformation to North American Quaker Antislavery Activism* (Leiden, Netherlands: Brill, 2017), p. 164.
9. Our thanks to Andrew Thompson for an early preview of the forthcoming C. P. Cullen, S. McCorriston and A. S. Thompson, 'The "Big Survey": Decolonisation, Development, and the First Wave of NGO Expansion in Africa after 1945', *International History Review*, Forthcoming.
10. For Britain see Jeremy Black, *Imperial Legacies: the British Empire Around the World* (New York, NY: Encounter Books, 2019); for the USA, Gary Jonathan Bass, *Freedom's Battle: The Origins of Humanitarian Intervention* (New York, NY: Knopf, 2008), pp. 11–24.
11. Lester, Boehme and Mitchell, *Ruling the World*.
12. Alan Lester, 'Humanitarian Governance and the Circumvention of Revolutionary Human Rights in the British Empire', in Michael Barnett (ed.), *Humanitarianism and Human Rights: A World of Differences?* (Cambridge, UK: Cambridge University Press, 2020), pp. 107–26.
13. Lynn Hunt, *Inventing Human Rights: A History* (New York, NY: Norton, 2007); Samuel Moyn, *Human Rights and the Uses of History* (London, UK: Verso, 2017); Samuel Moyn, *The Last Utopia: Human Rights in History* (Cambridge, MA: Harvard University Press, 2012).
14. Barnett, *Humanitarianism and Human Rights*.

15 Andrew Thompson, '"Restoring Hope Where All Hope Was Lost": Nelson Mandela, the ICRC and the Protection of Political Detainees in Apartheid South Africa', *International Review of the Red Cross* (2016), 98 (3), pp. 824–6.
16 Kevin O'Sullivan, 'The Search for Justice: NGOs in Britain and Ireland and the New International Economic Order, 1968–82', *Humanity: An International Journal of Human Rights, Humanitarianism, and Development* (Spring 2015), 6 (1), p. 183.
17 Bass, *Freedom's Battle*; Fabian Klose, *The Emergence of Humanitarian Intervention: Ideas and Practice from the Nineteenth Century to the Present* (Cambridge, UK: Cambridge University Press, 2015); Barnett, *Humanitarianism and Human Rights*; Barnett, *Empire of Humanity*; Brendan Simms and David J. B. Trim, *Humanitarian Intervention: A History* (Cambridge, UK: Cambridge University Press, 2011); Amanda B. Moniz, *From Empire to Humanity: The American Revolution and the Origins of Humanitarianism* (New York, NY: Oxford University Press, 2016); Alan Lester and Fae Dussart, *Colonization and the Origins of Humanitarian Governance: Protecting Aborigines across the Nineteenth-Century British Empire* (Cambridge, UK: Cambridge University Press, 2014); Amalia Ribi Forclaz, *Humanitarian Imperialism: The Politics of Anti-Slavery Activism, 1880–1940* (Oxford, UK: Oxford University Press, 2015).
18 This has not been a solely Anglophone phenomenon. For French examples see Bertrand Taithe, *The Killer Trail: A Colonial Scandal in the Heart of Africa* (Oxford, UK: Oxford University Press, 2009) and Max Jones, Berny Sèbe, Bertrand Taithe and Peter Yeandle, *Decolonising Imperial Heroes: Cultural Legacies of the British and French Empires* (London, UK: Routledge, 2018).
19 Maya Jasanoff, *Liberty's Exiles: American Loyalists in the Revolutionary World* (New York, NY: Random House, 2011); P. J. Marshall, *Remaking the British Atlantic: The United States and the British Empire after American Independence* (Oxford, UK: Oxford University Press, 2012), pp. 193–218.
20 Thomas L. Haskell, 'Capitalism and the Origins of the Humanitarian Sensibility, Parts 1 and 2', *American Historical Review* (1985), 90, pp. 339–61, 547–66.
21 Moniz, *From Empire to Humanity*, pp. 5–16; Thomas W. Laqueur, 'Bodies, Details, and the Humanitarian Narrative', in L. Hunt (ed.), *The New Cultural History* (Berkeley and Los Angeles, CA: University of California Press, 1989), pp. 176–204.
22 Thomas Clarkson, *The History of the Rise, Progress, and Accomplishment of the Abolition of the Slave Trade*, 2 vols. (London, UK: 1808); John Coffey, '"Tremble, Britannia!": Fear, Providence and the Abolition of the Slave Trade, 1758–1807', *English Historical Review* (2012), 127, pp. 848–81.
23 P. J. Marshall (ed.), *The Speeches of the Right Hon. Edmund Burke*, Vol. V, *India: Madras and Bengal, 1774–1785* (Oxford, UK: Oxford University Press, 1981), p. 385.
24 Andrew Porter, 'Trusteeship, Anti-Slavery, and Humanitarianism', in Porter (ed.), *The Oxford History of the British Empire: The Nineteenth Century* (Oxford, UK: Oxford University Press, 1999), p. 198.

25 Adam Smith, 'The Theory of Moral Sentiments', in Joseph Black and James Hutton (eds), *The Essays of Adam Smith*, 6th ed. (London, UK: Alexander Murray & Co., 1872), p. 118. See Jane Lydon, *Imperial Emotions: The Politics of Empathy Across the British Empire* (Cambridge, UK: Cambridge University Press, 2020), pp. 25–50.
26 Ibid., p. 120.
27 Dee E. Andrews and Emma Jones Lapsansky-Werner, 'Thomas Clarkson's Quaker Trilogy: Abolitionist Narrative as Transformative History', in Brycchan Carey and Geoffrey Plank (eds), *Quakers and Abolition* (Urbana, IL: University of Illinois Press, 2014), pp. 194–208; and Emma Gibson Wilson, *Thomas Clarkson: A Biography* (London, UK: Macmillan, 1989).
28 David Turley, *The Culture of English Antislavery, 1780–1860* (London, UK and New York, NY: Routledge, 1991).
29 Marcel Dorigny, *Les Abolitions de l'esclavage* (Paris, France: Que sais-je?, 2018).
30 Naomi J. Andrews, 'The Romantic Social Origins of Humanitarianism', *Modern Intellectual History* (2020), 17, pp. 737–68. See also Valentine Zuber, *Le Culte des droits de l'homme* (Paris, France: Gallimard, 2014).
31 Michel-Rolph Trouillot, *Silencing the Past: Power and the Production of History* (Boston, MA: Beacon Press, 1995), pp. 95–107. See also Jean Ehrard, *Lumières et Esclavage: L'Esclavage colonial et l'opinion publique en France au XVIII siècle* (Paris, France: Versaille, 2008); Madeleine Dobie, *Trading Places: Colonization and Slavery in Eighteenth-Century French Culture* (Ithaca, NY and London, UK: Cornell University Press, 2010); and Marie-Jeanne Rossignol, 'The Quaker Antislavery Commitment and How It Revolutionized French Antislavery through the Crèvecouer-Brissot Friendship, 1782–1789', in Brycchan Carey and Geoffrey Plank (eds), *Quakers and Abolition* (Urbana, IL: University of Illinois Press, 2014), pp. 180–94.
32 Anja Bandau, 'Jean-François de Saint-Lambert and His Moral *conte* "Ziméo" (1769) in the Context of Abolitionist and Imperial Activities', in Damien Tricoire (ed.), *Enlightened Colonialism; Civilization Narratives and Imperial Politics in the Age of Reason* (London, UK: Palgrave Macmillan, 2017), p. 206.
33 Matthias Middell, 'France, the Abolition of Slavery, and Abolitionisms in the Eighteenth Century', in Tricoire (ed.), *Enlightened Colonialism*, pp. 248–9.
34 Oldfield, *Transatlantic Abolitionism in the Age of Revolution*, pp. 83–7, 117–20.
35 Christopher Leslie Brown, *Moral Capital: Foundations of British Abolitionism* (Chapel Hill, NC: University of North Carolina Press, 2006).
36 See, for example, Zoë Laidlaw, *Protecting the Empire's Humanity: Thomas Hodgkin and British Colonial Activism 1830–1870* (Cambridge, UK: Cambridge University Press, 2021).
37 Catherine Hall et al., *Legacies of British Slaveholding: Colonial Slavery and the Formation of Victorian Britain* (Cambridge, UK: Cambridge University Press, 2014).
38 Alan Lester and Nikita Vanderbyl, 'The Restructuring of the British Empire and the Colonization of Australia, 1832–8', *History Workshop Journal* (Autumn 2020), 90, pp. 165–88.

39 Alan Lester, 'Thomas Fowell Buxton and the Networks of British Humanitarianism', in H. Gilbert and C. Tiffin (eds), *Burden or Benefit: Imperial Benevolence and its Legacies* (Bloomington, IN: Indiana University Press, 2008), pp. 31–48. See also Laidlaw, *Protecting the Empire's Humanity*.
40 Bass, *Freedom's Battle*.
41 In 1838, when American republican patriots were captured by Canadian militia as they raided in support of the 1837–38 rebellions in Upper and Lower Canada, they mentioned Byron's Greek struggle as inspiration for their endeavours to support the overthrow of British rule in the rest of North America: M. L. Harris, 'The Meaning of Patriot: The Canadian Rebellion and American Republicanism, 1837–1839', *Michigan Historical Review* (1997), 23 (1), pp. 33–69.
42 Lester, 'Humanitarian Governance and the Circumvention of Revolutionary Human Rights in the British Empire'; Lester and Dussart, *Colonization and the Origins of Humanitarian Governance*, p. 42.
43 Lester, Boehme and Mitchell, *Ruling the World*.
44 Rob Skinner and Alan Lester, 'Humanitarianism and Empire: New Research Agendas', *Journal of Imperial and Commonwealth History* (2012), 40 (5), pp. 729–47; Aoife O'Leary McNeice, 'Towards a History of Global Humanitarianism', *Historical Journal* (2020), 63, pp. 1378–89.
45 Andrea Major, '"The Slavery of East and West": Abolitionists and "Unfree" Labour in India, 1820–1833', *Slavery and Abolition* (2010), 31 (4), p. 503; Hazel Petrie, *Outcasts of the Gods?: The Struggle Over Slavery in Maori New Zealand* (Auckland, New Zealand: Auckland University Press, 2015).
46 R. J. Gavin, 'The Bartle Frere Mission to Zanzibar, 1873', *The Historical Journal* (1962), 5 (2), p. 129; R. E. Dumett, 'Pressure Groups, Bureaucracy, and the Decision-Making Process: The Case of Slavery Abolition and Colonial Expansion in the Gold Coast, 1874', *The Journal of Imperial and Commonwealth History* (1981), 9 (2), p. 198; Lester, Boehme and Mitchell, *Ruling the World*; Jane Samson, *Imperial Benevolence: Making British Authority in the Pacific Islands* (Honolulu, HA: University of Hawai'i Press, 1998).
47 Richard Huzzey, 'Minding Civilisation and Humanity in 1867: A Case Study in British Imperial Culture and Victorian Anti-Slavery', *The Journal of Imperial and Commonwealth History* (2012), 40 (5), pp. 807–25.
48 Jeremy Black, 'The Royal Navy in the Front Line against Slavery', *The Critic*, 18 October 2020, https://thecritic.co.uk/the-royal-navy-in-the-front-line-against-slavery/, accessed on 19 October 2020.
49 Lester, Boehme and Mitchell, *Ruling the World*.
50 Huzzey, 'Minding Civilisation and Humanity in 1867'.
51 Laidlaw, *Protecting the Empire's Humanity*.
52 For differing perspectives, see Catherine Hall, *Civilising Subjects: Metropole and Colony in the English Imagination, 1830–1867* (London, UK: Polity, 2002); John M. McKenzie, *Imperialism and Popular Culture* (Manchester, UK: Manchester University Press, 1989); and Andrew Porter, *The Oxford History of the British Empire*, vol III: *The Nineteenth Century* (Oxford, UK: Oxford University Press, 1999).

53 Lester, Boehme and Mitchell, *Ruling the World*.
54 Lester and Dussart, *Colonization and the Origins of Humanitarian Governance*.
55 See also Christina Twomey and Katherine Ellinghaus, 'Special Issue: Protection: Global Genealogies', *Pacific Historical Review* (2018), 87, pp. 1–149 and Amanda Nettelbeck, *Indigenous Rights and Colonial Subjecthood: Protection and Reform in the Nineteenth-Century British Empire* (Cambridge, UK: Cambridge University Press, 2019).
56 Nettelbeck, *Indigenous Rights and Colonial Subjecthood*.
57 For post-emancipation disillusionment, see Hall, *Civilising Subjects*.
58 C. Twomey, 'Framing Atrocity: Photography and Humanitarianism', *History of Photography* (2012), 36 (3), pp. 255–64; W. M. Kennedy, 'The Imperial Politics of Death: Australian Responses to India's Famines, 1874–1902', unpublished paper.
59 W. E. Gladstone, *Bulgarian Horrors and the Question of the East* (London, UK: J. Murray, 1876), pp. 9–10.
60 Rebecca Gill, 'Networks of Concern, Boundaries of Compassion: British Relief in the South African War', *The Journal of Imperial and Commonwealth History* (2012), 40 (5), pp. 827–44.
61 Kevin Grant, 'Christian Critics of Empire: Missionaries, Lantern Lectures, and the Congo Reform Campaign in Britain', *The Journal of Imperial and Commonwealth History* (2001), 29 (2), pp. 27–58.
62 Skinner and Lester, 'Humanitarianism and Empire'; Thomas Pakenham, *The Scramble for Africa*, 2nd ed. (London, UK: Abacus, 1992).
63 See Claude Kabemba, 'The History and Practice of Humanitarian Intervention and Aid in Africa', in Bronwen Everill and Josiah Kaplan (eds), *The Democratic Republic of Congo: The Land of Humanitarian Interventions* (London, UK and New York, NY: Palgrave Macmilllan, 2013), pp. 140–57.
64 Forclaz, *Humanitarian Imperialism*.
65 Daniel Laqua, 'The Tensions of Internationalism: Transnational Anti-Slavery in the 1880s and 1890s', *The International History Review* (2011), 33 (4), pp. 705–26.
66 Richard Drayton, 'Beyond Humanitarian Imperialism: The Dubious Origins of "Humanitarian Intervention" and Some Rules for Its Future', in Everill and Kaplan (eds), *The Democratic Republic of Congo*, pp. 140–57.
67 Gerry Kearns and David Nally, 'An Accumulated Wrong: Roger Casement and the Anticolonial Moments within Imperial Governance', *Journal of Historical Geography* (2019), 64, pp. 1–12.
68 Joy Damousi, 'An Appeal from Afar: The Challenges of Compassion and the Australian Humanitarian Campaigns for Armenia Relief, 1900–1930', in Joanne Laycock and Francesca Piana (eds), *Aid to Armenia: Humanitarianism and intervention from the 1890s to the present* (Manchester, UK: Manchester University Press, 2020), pp. 50–65.
69 Barnett, *Empire of Humanity*, pp. 82–94; Bruno Cabanes, *The Great War and the Origins of Humanitarianism, 1918–1924* (Cambridge, UK: Cambridge University Press, 2014); Adam Tooze: *The Deluge: The Great War, America*

and the Remaking of Global Order, 1916–1931 (London, UK: Allen Lane, 2014).
70 Branden Little, 'Humanitarianism in the Era of the First World War', special issue of *First World War Studies* (2014), 5 (1); Suzanne Miers, 'Slavery and the Slave Trade as International Issues, 1890–1939', in Suzanne Miers and Martin Klein (eds), *Slavery and Colonial Rule in Africa* (London, UK: Frank Cass, 1999), pp. 16–37; Suzanne Miers, *Slavery in the Twentieth Century: The Evolution of a Global Problem* (Walnut Creek, CA: AltaMira Press, 2013).
71 Moyn, *The Last Utopia*, p. 33.
72 See Mark Mazower, *No Enchanted Palace: The End of Empire and the Ideological Origins of the United Nations* (Princeton, NJ: Princeton University Press, 2009), pp. 28–9; Kevin Grant, *A Civilised Savagery: Britain and the New Slaveries in Africa, 1884–1926* (New York, NY and London, UK: Routledge, 2005).
73 Emily Baughan, 'The Imperial War Relief Fund and the All British Appeal: Commonwealth, Conflict and Conservatism within the British Humanitarian Movement, 1920–25', *The Journal of Imperial and Commonwealth History* (2012), 40 (5), pp. 845–61; Emily Baughan, '"Every Citizen of Empire Implored to Save the Children!" Empire, Internationalism and the Save the Children Fund in Inter-War Britain', *Historical Research* (2013), 86 (231), pp. 116–37.
74 See Sarah Roddy, Julie-Marie Strange and Bertrand Taithe, *The Charity Market and Humanitarianism in Britain, 1870–1912* (London, UK: Bloomsbury, 2018).
75 Mark R. Frost, 'Humanitarianism and the Overseas Aid Craze in Britain's Colonial Straits Settlements, 1870–1920', *Past & Present* (2017), 236, pp. 169–205; and Damousi, 'An Appeal from Afar'.
76 Michelle Tusan, 'Genocide, Famine and Refugees on Film: Humanitarianism and the First World War', *Past & Present* (2017), 237, pp. 197–235.
77 Klose, *The Emergence of Humanitarian Intervention*.
78 Jessica Reinisch, 'Internationalism in Relief: The Birth (and Death) of UNRRA', *Past & Present* (2011), 210, pp. 258–89.
79 Rachel E. Crowdy, 'The Humanitarian Activities of the League of Nations (Address given on April 12th, 1927)', *Journal of the Royal Institute of International Affairs* (May 1927), 6 (3), pp. 153–69.
80 Forclaz, *Humanitarian Imperialism*, p. 11.
81 Linda Mahood, *Feminism and Voluntary Action: Eglantyne Jebb and Save the Children, 1879–1928* (New York, NY: Palgrave Macmillan, 2009).
82 Forclaz, *Humanitarian Imperialism*.
83 Jean Allman, 'Making Mothers: Missionaries, Medical Officers and Women's Work in Colonial Asante, 1924–1945', *History Workshop* (1994), 38, pp. 23–47.
84 Andrew Thompson, 'Humanitarian Principles Put to the Test: Challenges to Humanitarian Action during Decolonization', *International Review of the Red Cross* (February 2016), 897/898, https://international-review.icrc.org/articles/

humanitarian-principles-put-test-challenges-humanitarian-action-during-decolonization, accessed on 21 August 2021.

85 Mandy Banton, 'Destroy? "Migrate"? Conceal? British Strategies for the Disposal of Sensitive Records of Colonial Administrations at Independence', *The Journal of Imperial and Commonwealth History* (2012), 40 (2), pp. 321–35; Mandy Banton, 'History Concealed, History Withheld: The Story of the Foreign and Commonwealth Office "Migrated Archives" and the Decades-Long International Search for Redress', *Archives: The Journal of the British Records Association* (2020), 55 (1), pp. 1–29; David M. Anderson, 'Guilty Secrets: Deceit, Denial, and the Discovery of Kenya's "Migrated Archive"', *History Workshop Journal* (2015), 80 (1), pp. 142–60; David M. Anderson, 'Mau Mau in the High Court and the "Lost" British Empire Archives: Colonial Conspiracy or Bureaucratic Bungle?', *The Journal of Imperial and Commonwealth History* (2011), 39 (5), pp. 699–716; Gregory Rawlings, 'Lost Files, Forgotten Papers and Colonial Disclosures: The "Migrated Archives" and the Pacific, 1963–2013', *The Journal of Pacific History* (2015), 50 (2), pp. 189–212.

86 Thompson, 'Humanitarian Principles Put to the Test', p. 50.

87 Ibid., p. 61.

88 Ibid., p. 53.

89 Ibid., p. 51.

90 Matthew Hilton, 'Charity and the End of Empire: British Non-Governmental Organizations, Africa, and International Development in the 1960s', *American Historical Review* (2018), 123 (2), pp. 493–517. See also Kevin O'Sullivan, 'A "Global Nervous System": The Rise and Rise of European Humanitarian NGOs, 1945–1985', in Marc Frey, Sönke Kunkel and Corinna R. Unger (eds), *International Organizations and Development, 1945–1990* (Basingstoke, UK: Palgrave Macmillan, 2014), pp. 196–219.

91 Patrick Kilby, *NGOS and Political Change: A History of the Australian Council for International Development* (Canberra, Australia: ANU Press, 2015), pp. 26–30.

92 For the wider context, see Paul Betts, *Ruin and Renewal: Civilizing Europe after World War II* (New York, NY: Hachette, 2020).

93 Barnett, *Empire of Humanity*; Samuel Moyn, 'Empathy in History, Empathizing with Humanity', *History and Theory* (2006), 45 (3), pp. 397–415; Moyn, *The Last Utopia*; and Barnett, *Humanitarianism and Human Rights*.

94 Samuel Moyn, 'Human Rights and Humanitarianism', in Barnett (ed.), *Humanitarianism and Human Rights*, p. 33.

95 Moyn, *The Last Utopia*.

96 Tehila Sasson and James Vernon, 'Practising the British Way of Famine: Technological Relief, 1770–1815', *European Review of History* (2015), 22, p. 861.

97 Quoted in Skinner and Lester, 'Humanitarianism and Empire'.

98 Allman, 'Making Mothers', p. 43.

Part I

Transatlantic humanitarianism, 1760–1838

1

Anthony Benezet: *A Short History of Guinea* and its impact on early British abolitionism

Trevor Burnard

One enduring question in the vast historiography of slavery and abolition is how the institution of Atlantic slavery, based on African slavery and the Atlantic slave trade, came under attack in Britain in the 1780s. Atlantic slavery was transformed from an institution that had the full support of Western European states, notably Britain and France – one that had brought considerable economic benefits to Europe, as well as forming the foundation for colonial prosperity in the plantation societies of British North America, and the French and British Caribbean – into one that was a focus of the greatest moral reform movement of modern times. This moral reform movement – abolitionism – hardly existed before the Seven Years War (1756–63), although it can be argued that the philosophical case against slavery had been established by Montesquieu and John Locke in the late seventeenth and through the early eighteenth centuries.[1]

That philosophical case, however, was theoretical and did little to stop the juggernaut that was the slave and plantation interest, focused in particular on the necessity to continue the slave trade to the Americas, especially to the West Indies, where it was an essential bulwark in a highly destructive plantation system. Criticisms of the slave trade and the plantation system on economic grounds – the grounds that mostly held in France until very late in the abolition process – also tended to have academic intentions rather than practical outcomes. The start of abolitionism as a problem within the small religious sect of Quakers during the Seven Years War, when a few marginal figures within Quakerism began to convince followers that being involved in the Atlantic slave trade was akin to violating the long-held Quaker concept of pacifism, did little to harm the slave trade. In both Britain and France, the trade expanded rapidly after the end of the Seven Years War and continued to expand until the 1790s, feeding the plantation system of the French and British Antilles, when the production of sugar and other tropical crops was increasing at a rapid rate.[2]

Abolitionism started in earnest during the Seven Years War, when a tiny number of religiously minded Quakers began to consider slavery and the slave trade as being not just morally indefensible and economically less desirable than wage labour, but also a sin, one that violated religious norms and stained the good name of Britain.[3] These Quakers, in both Britain and the British Empire, decided not just to make theoretical statements, but also to take decisive action, beginning with publishing polemical tracts against the evil of the slave trade and taking practical action to force Quaker organisations to disown slavery, including shaming Quaker slave owners into manumitting enslaved people.[4]

The two most important American Quakers initiating this historically significant process were John Woolman and Anthony Benezet.[5] It is the latter who is the focus of attention in this chapter. I pay special attention to a ground-breaking book that he wrote in 1762, which was republished in 1783: *Some Historical Account of Guinea, Its Situation, Produce, and the General Disposition of Its Inhabitants with an Inquiry into the Rise and Progress of the Slave Trade, Its Nature, and Lamentable Effects*. This book, in its second edition, included long and favourably treated extracts from a famous 1769 book by Granville Sharp, a High Church evangelical Anglican. Sharp was an early abolitionist, writing in 1769 *A Representation of the Injustice and Dangerous Tendency of Tolerating Slavery*, which was pivotal in shaping the thinking of the pioneering antislavery writer, Thomas Clarkson, in the 1780s.[6] Benezet's book proved to be highly influential in its second iteration, primarily as a source of information for Clarkson and William Wilberforce who were amassing as much data as they could about Africa, Africans, the slave trade and slavery in the Americas, in order to educate a public ignorant of the trade about the horror of Britain's involvement had been with Africa and with slavery.[7] Benezet's book is also worth studying as an early and impressive foray into the developing concept of humanitarianism. His book demonstrated a rare concern with seeing Africans as people worth considering in imperial calculations.[8]

Benezet's selective reading

Randy Sparks notes that when Thomas Clarkson began his landmark Cambridge prize essay on the slave trade in 1785, he recalled that he had no idea where to begin research on that topic, but 'when going by accident into a friend's house I took up a newspaper, then lying on the table; one of the articles which attracted my notice was an advertisement for Anthony Benezet's historical account of Guinea. I soon left my friend and his paper, and to lose no time hastened to London to buy it. In this precious book, I found almost all I wanted'. As Sparks notes:

Clarkson was only one of many thousands of readers who gained their first insights into Africa and the slave trade from Anthony Benezet's influential study of West Africa. At a time when much of Africa was unknown to Europeans and when a great deal of what was known about Africa was erroneous and coloured by European ethnocentrism, Benezet set out to collect reliable, first-hand accounts of West Africa and the conduct of the slave trade there. Influenced by his own encounters with Africans in Philadelphia and by insights gained from his knowledge of other Africans whose stories of their enslavement were reported to him, he was eager to correct many misrepresentations of West Africa that were used to defend the slave trade and to present as accurately as he could the rich cultural diversity in the region known to Europeans as Guinea.[9]

Benezet's account was based on a highly selective reading of accounts on West Africa produced by men mostly involved in the Atlantic slave trade. What was unusual about his work was that he systematically ignored evidence that Africans were savages in favour of positive descriptions of West Africa and the rulers and people of those realms. This interpretive approach was a radical departure from previous accounts of West Africa. It was an imaginative yet persuasive rethinking of the subject, all done from the comfort of his study, using books in local libraries, and without either first-hand experience of Africa or, more surprisingly, without interrogating some of the Africans who lived in Philadelphia – many of whom Benezet knew well.[10] His aim was to produce a book that stood up on scholarly grounds and used his opponents' words to condemn them. He was notably concerned with extensive footnoting so that readers could be directed to where he got his information from and so that he could not be accused of making things up. He was concerned about not just telling a good story but in providing hard evidence of the immorality of slave trading.[11] Consequently, the books he used and cited extensively were well-known works – what Philip Curtin has called 'a canon of West African knowledge' at mid-century, such as works by eighteenth-century commentators, William Snelgrave, Jean Barbot and Willem Bosman. These books had been published in London and were the first points of reference around 1760 for scholars who wanted to understand what was known about these supposedly savage lands.[12]

Benezet argued three things. First, he insisted that Africa was not an irredeemably savage place but one that bore comparison if not to Europe then at least to pre-Columbian North America. He sought to deny 'accounts we frequently hear or read of [Africans'] barbarous and savage way of living in their own country'. He insisted that it was wrong to think of Africans as 'incapable of improvement, destitute, miserable and indefensible of the benefits of life and that our permitting them to live amongst us, even on the most oppressive of terms is to do them a favour'. He gave lengthy descriptions of the climate, the agricultural fecundity of the soil and the nature of governance of West African societies, distinguishing neatly between various kinds of society in different geographical areas and arguing that much of the region had been Edenic in its pastoral harmony and beauty before Europeans arrived. West Africa, he admitted, was unhealthy for Europeans but not for native-born Africans. The climate was wonderful and crops could be grown with ease. Moreover, these were lands with both government and religion. In particular, he wanted to show that Africans were just as human as Europeans – 'Are they not Men as well as we, and have they not the same Sensibility?' It was all very well, he noted, to favour one's own countrymen but one should go beyond that to love all men. While a 'Patriot or lover of his own Country is a brave character, a lover of mankind is a braver Character'. Here he might have been having a none-too-subtle dig at his fellow Pennsylvanian Benjamin Franklin who, in the nearly contemporaneous *Observations on the Peopling of Mankind*, had famously justified his disgust for having Africans peopling Pennsylvania by stating that everyone was partial to their own countrymen and thus were willing to exclude other peoples from areas in which they lived. Franklin's argument was that Pennsylvania would be a better place if there were no Africans living there.[13]

In Benezet's rendering, Africans were made to exemplify a whole range of Quaker virtues, few of which they had been previously associated with. Africans, he argued, were generally honest, industrious and full of integrity. They were not naturally warlike, were not naturally libidinous, and were not poor parents of children and even worse husbands to wives (he cited strict laws on adultery and murder to prove this point), nor were they lacking in a religious sensibility. Unusually for the time and for a man of deep Christian conviction, Benezet spent a lot of time praising Africans for their religious practices. He noted that many Africans in the Congo were Catholics as a result of Portuguese colonisation, and he praised Africans in the northern regions of West Africa for their strong Islamist beliefs. He even excused those Africans who were animist pagans – the Africans usually most despised by Europeans for holding outrageous and beastly religious beliefs – for their lack of Christian understanding. He noted that 'some authors say, the wisest of these Negroes are sensible of their mistakes in this opinion but dare not forsake their own religion for fear of the populace rising and killing them'.[14] In short, Africans, like American Indians and by extension ancient Europeans, were capable of improvement and being assimilated into Christianity. It was a 'pretence', he argued, to portray Africans as 'savages unworthy of liberty and the natural rights of mankind'.[15]

Second, Benezet wanted to show that enslavement was not positive for Africans, but was a gross violation of their human rights. He argued that enslavement left Africans 'broken-spirited and dejected'.[16] He attempted to prove that Africans were not brutes and savages, as depicted in the writings on Africa that he studied, whose condition was improved by enslavement, but rather were equal members of the greater human family. This understanding of the human family, in what was the first example of the developing concept of human rights being applied by an English-language author to Africans, was innovative and, as Clarkson later testified, transformative in showing Europeans that Africans were part of humankind.[17] The concept of human rights was not new to Benezet, of course, but he was perhaps the first to apply it so concretely to Africans. Because Africans were human, they should not be enslaved, especially as that enslavement was so obviously contrary to their rights and likely to bring great unhappiness to the enslaved. In this respect, Benezet's book was a singular advance in racial thinking. Along with John Woolman, he challenged the casual coupling of race and slavery that had been a feature of the considerable literature on African capacity for several hundred years.[18]

Finally, Benezet wanted to prove that whatever was wrong with Africa came entirely from the ills of European colonisation. He insisted that any source of social disorder in Africa could be laid fully at the feet of avaricious European slave traders, who had corrupted the inhabitants' original innocence and persuaded them to enslave and sell their own countrymen for short-term pecuniary advantage. He made it very clear that the Atlantic slave trade was a uniquely disruptive force for evil in West Africa, and that Europeans were destroying Eden for the sake of money and because they were a naturally warlike people. It was a formulation of European actions in pursuit of Mammon and power that is remarkably similar to the idea of 'war capitalism' as enunciated today by practitioners of the New History of Capitalism in the United States.[19] War formed a large part of Benezet's analysis and he stressed that Europeans rather than Africans were the people more naturally disposed towards conquest, conflict and war for war's sake: Europe had destabilised Africa and then taken advantage of that destabilisation both ideologically and practically. He spent a lot of time writing about how Europeans fomented war in order to acquire slaves and then justified their taking of slaves by dint of Africa being a place that was naturally warlike – ignoring their own role in creating the circumstances that they used to benefit themselves.[20]

Influence on early abolitionism

How influential was Benezet's account in changing the terms of the debate on abolitionism and in sparking outrage among readers that one section of humankind was being treated so abominably? What role did the book play in the early stages of abolitionism?

Without denying the importance of Benezet's book in the long and often disgraceful representations of Africans in Western thought, and its honourable role in providing the first argument in favour of decoupling race from slavery and in stressing a unity of mankind in which Africans were included just as much as Europeans, I would like to stress one part of Benezet's book as contributing more to contemporary European discourse about the Atlantic slave trade than is usually noted. Benezet was insistent that it was Europeans, not Africans, who had transformed Africa from its Edenic state prior to European contact into its present state, in which tyranny and oppression existed. He argued, contrary to a considerable literature that posited Africa as a place of unredeemable darkness and sin, that Africa had been mostly good before Europeans arrived. European slave traders had, through their activities, despoiled what had been a more than tolerable place to live in. They had compounded their bad deeds by claiming that, as a result of the devastation they themselves had caused, they were doing a favour to the captives they took to enslavement in the Americas by removing them from places of savagery to places of civilisation. It was Europeans, not Africans, Benezet implied, who were the real savages.[21]

Central to the discourses on early abolitionism was concern about what the effects of imperial expansion and the Europeans' greater involvement in, and power over, the larger world was doing to European character and morals. Benezet was interested in reclaiming, or perhaps establishing, a view of Africans as being no worse than, and possibly better than, Europeans through seeing Africans as fellow human beings. This was an influential view, as the testimony of Thomas Clarkson proves. The founder of Methodism, John Wesley, also found this interpretation appealing, and used Benezet's book to shape his thinking on why slavery was a sin.[22]

Nevertheless, the argument that the slave trade was corrupting Europeans and showing Europeans to be inclined towards sin in their dealings with others was extremely important, especially in the works of early abolitionists such as Granville Sharp. Sharp's arguments against the slave trade and against Atlantic slavery were less concerned with establishing the moral equivalency of Africans and Europeans than in attacking the pretensions and tyranny of West Indian slave-holders and highlighting the danger to Britain from allowing too many Africans into the country. Abolitionism had a much more European-focused and xenophobic tinge than accounts that focus on Benezet's argument for a positive view of African morals and character would allow. Older and very racist accounts of Africa as a place of savagery, and Africans as an irredeemably savage people, continued to have considerable purchase in the thought and actions of early abolitionists, especially in England – a country enjoying, or enduring, what seemed to observers at the time an uncontrollable immigration of Africans, especially into London.[23]

This approach helps illuminate some of the themes that shaped the beginnings of abolitionism in Britain, themes that have been well outlined in a series of important books by historians from the 1930s to the present day.[24] Historians have created a minor industry in debating the causes of the sudden upsurge in interest in abolitionism between the 1750s and the 1780s in Britain and the northern colonies of British North America. The explanations, roughly speaking, fall into four interrelated groups, all of which consider three things: the rise of an industrial economy in Britain from about 1760; the development of a religiously inspired humanitarianism from about the same time; and the changes in imperial thinking that resulted from Britain's overwhelming victories over France in the Seven Years War, which led many Britons to think afresh about what Britons were doing in the wider world.[25]

One explanation emphasises Providence, taking seriously abolitionists' claims that they were extending the will of God in the world.[26] Abolitionism can be explained mainly by reference to religious change, especially the increasing importance in Enlightenment thought of the views on war, liberty and slavery held by dissenter groups such as Methodists and, especially, Quakers. A second explanation focuses on economic rather than religious change. It argues that the transformation of Britain into an industrial society, with an increasing belief in the doctrines of free trade as exemplified by Adam Smith, played an important role in convincing people that slavery was not only morally distasteful but also economically inefficient. Economics and morality thus went together to encourage people to attack slavery. A third explanation fuses these two views, suggesting that the increasing penetration of Enlightenment beliefs about human rights into British society, as well as changing views about what the possibilities were for activist Christians to effect moral reform at home and abroad, led people to think not only that slavery was wrong but, more importantly, that it could also be ended and should be ended, and that people who thought slavery was a sin had the tools to end it.[27]

The fourth explanation is that one reason for the sudden interest in Africa, the slave trade, the plantation system and the slave-holders who benefited from the slave trade is that Britain's victories in the Seven Years War led to both a massive expansion in the territories and peoples ruled by Britain, and to a sudden and intense interest in the doings of Empire and especially in what Britons were doing in the Empire by British people resident in Britain.[28] I focus on this explanation of the rise of abolitionism in discussing the impact of Benezet's work among early British abolitionists, notably Granville Sharp and his supporters in the Somerset case of 1772, where the question of the legality of enslavement in Britain was considered. What concerned the British most in the 1760s and early 1770s was how

Empire was being brought home to Britain in very disturbing ways. It led some people, like Sharp but also politicians like Edmund Burke, to take an interest in what was being done overseas by Britons in Britain's name in ways that had not been done before.[29] They did not like what they saw. What bothered them was not so much the things that bothered Benezet, who was concerned that Africans should be treated as fellow human beings. I see little of that impulse in the early stages of abolitionism, at least in Britain. Indeed, Granville Sharp admitted that he did not become an abolitionist from any concern about Africans, but because of his outrage at how badly West Indian planters living in London treated their enslaved property and because he feared that allowing this behaviour would eventually lead to the poor in Britain being treated in a similar manner to enslaved people.[30]

Benezet and Granville Sharp

Despite his many years as an abolitionist and his later advocacy of a free black colony in Sierra Leone, Sharp explained in 1772, 'I am far from having a particular Esteem for the Negroes'. But he did think that they were humans, and so should be treated in a Christian manner. He was perpetually horrified that planters thought of the 'Negro *as much private property as a horse or dog*'. Sharp concluded that he was '*obliged* to consider them *as men*' and thus also '*obliged* ... to use my best endeavours to prevent them from being treated *as beasts* by our unchristian Countrymen, who deny them the priviledges [sic] of *human nature*'.[31] If anything, his intellectual motivation for adopting antislavery well before it had become an issue of popular concern came from his belief, bolstered by extensive if eclectic reading, that slavery was both illegal in Britain due to longstanding assumptions that everyone was free as soon as they breathed British air, and also unchristian insofar as it violated a statement in Deuteronomy that 'Thou shalt not deliver unto his master the servant which is escaped from his master'.[32] Slavery was wrong under ancient theological law. Moreover, Sharp contended, based on his understanding of the medieval practice of villeinage, which allowed for a kind of slavery to exist in medieval England, that slavery had been outlawed in England for over two centuries.[33]

His anger over the reality of slavery existing in England as a result of slave-holders bringing African servants into the country was intensified by his concern for the poor and by a xenophobic belief that Britain was being overrun by blacks. Slavery was inherently dangerous, he argued, because it was hard to limit it to just one set of people. If Africans could be enslaved, so too could Britons. He noted that 'the practice of slaveholding is now only in its infancy among us', but it could easily spread, because if 'such practices are permitted much longer with impunity, *the evil will take root; precedent and custom will too soon be pleaded in its behalf* (emphasis in the original). The result eventually would be the introduction, once again, of the medieval institution of villeinage, which was thought a form of equivalency to enslavement. Sharp believed that new forms of villeinage would be hard to confine just to Africans, but would become institutions 'in which the poorer sort, even of the original English themselves, might in time be involved'.[34]

Sharp had larger objects in view than just the recognition in law that white West Indians could not force slavery upon England. He wanted a thoroughgoing moral and political reformation of the British nation. Included in this grand plan of reform was a strong xenophobic streak. It was foreigners, and foreign innovations, such as bringing colonial slavery to the metropolis, that, he argued, were corrupting the British people. Long before such views became commonplace during the American Revolution, Sharp believed that slave owners in the American South, and even more so West Indian planters, were not fellow countrymen as much as foreigners. He believed that they were determined to introduce their tyrannical and essentially un-British ways of life and their alien political beliefs into the nation in ways that would compromise the freedom of Britons, especially poor Britons.[35]

In this respect, Benezet had a more advanced and more sympathetic view of Africa and Africans than even such friends of the African race as Sharp. Benezet's views on Africans were but one view, and a heretical minority view at that, on Africans' capacity for improvement and their similarity to the rest of humanity. By the second quarter of the eighteenth century, European opinion about African character was largely fixed, as is clear in the texts in the 'West African canon' that Benezet used, but whose meaning and intention he deliberately subverted through extremely selective quotation.[36] One source that is particularly important is a 1703 work by Willem Bosman. It was a work, originally written in Dutch, which was extensively cited in English accounts of West Africa from the 1730s onwards. It is a curious work. William Pietz comments that it was simultaneously 'a triumph of scrupulous observation and the new scepticism and a bizarre phantasm wherein the new forces and categories of the mercantile world economy then reshaping African and European societies alike were read into a strange social order and locale'.[37] Bosman reported as follows on the moral character of Gold Coast Africans:

> The *Negroes* are all without exception, Crafty, Villainous and Fraudulent, and very seldom to be trusted; being sure to stop no opportunity of cheating an [sic] *European*, nor indeed one another. A Man of Integrity is as rare among them as a white Falcon, and their Fidelity seldom extends farther than to their Masters …

The degenerate Vices are accompanied with their Sisters, Sloth and Idleness; to which they are so prone that nothing but the utmost Necessity can force them to Labour: They are besides so incredibly careless and stupid, and are so little concerned at their Misfortunes, that 'tis hardly to be observed by any change in them whether they have met with good or ill success ...

Their government was licentious and irregular ... and frequent Wars are occasioned by their remiss Government and absurd Customs ... [while] the Priests, who are generally sly and crafty, encouraged by the stupid Credulity of the People, have all the opportunity in the World to Impose the grossest absurdities and fleece their Purses; as they indeed do effectively.[38]

Bosman's views on Africans were widely read and widely accepted. The thinking of the few English writers who gave much thought before the 1760s to the morality of slavery tended to be as follows. Enslaved Africans, it was reasoned, were better treated in America than in Africa and were offered the benefits of Christianity – benefits which made up for their servile condition. In short, slavery in this life in return for salvation in the next was the deal on the table for enslaved Africans. This was a self-serving argument, given that most planters refused to allow their slaves to get Christian instruction. More important was a belief that either enslaved Africans were treated better outside Africa than in it, or, more commonly, that violence was the only way they could be made to do as they were told and that Africans expected violence to be used against them.[39] Thomas Thompson, who served as a missionary on the Gold Coast (roughly equivalent to modern day Ghana) in the mid-eighteenth century, referred to Africans as 'pagans ... of as dark a mind as complexion'. The belief that slaves were treated with lenience had some support. As one eighteenth-century English economist wrote, 'Though the odious Appellation of *Slaves* is annexed to this Trade ... they are certainly treated with great Lenity and Humanity: And as the Improvement of the Planter's Estates depends upon the due Care being taken of their Healths and Lives, I cannot but think their Condition is much bettered to what it was in their own Country'.[40]

Most common was the view that Africans expected and deserved to be treated with violence. The English writer Daniel Defoe is a good guide to common thinking about Africans in the second quarter of the eighteenth century. Defoe never set foot in the Americas, or in Africa, but as the author of *Robinson Crusoe, Moll Flanders* and *Colonel Jack* – three highly influential and much-read accounts of life in the Americas – he had enormous authority among English audiences. He argued in his novel, *Colonel Jack*, that '*Negroes* cannot be mannag'd by Kindness, and Courtisy; but must be rul'd with a Rod of Iron, [and] beaten with *Scorpions*'.[41] Here Defoe follows the many statements of Jamaican writers that the essence of slavery was terror, from Edmond Hickeringill in 1661, to James Knight and Charles

Leslie writing in the 1730s and 1740s, when life for black Jamaicans was at its nadir. Knight argued that extreme violence was necessary against a people who were so 'sullen, deceitful, [with a] Refractory Temper'.[42] Leslie was certain that 'No country excels [Jamaica] in a barbarous Treatment of Slaves, or in the cruel Methods they put them to death', but insisted that such harsh usage was acceptable, owing to the nature of African character. Slavery in Jamaica was brutal 'given how impossible it were to live amongst such Numbers of Slaves, without observing their Conduct with the greatest Niceness and punishing their Faults with the utmost Severity'.[43]

Defoe concluded, after having his hero on a Virginia plantation begin to have human sympathy for Africans and then realise that the Africans laughed at him for his softness and weakness, that 'now I began indeed to see, that the Cruelty so much talk'd of, used in *Virginia* and *Barbadoes*, and other Colonies in Whipping the *Negro* Slaves, was not so much owing to the Tyranny of the English, as had been reported; the English not being accounted to be of a cruel disposition; and really are not so. But that it is owing to the Brutallity, and obstinate Temper of the *Negroes* who cannot be mannag'd by Kindness, and Courtisy'. Africans 'must be used as they do use them, or they would rise and murder all their Masters, which their Numbers consider'd, would not be hard for them to do, if they had Arms and Ammunition suitable to the Rage and Cruelty of their Nature'.[44]

These views continued to prevail after Defoe wrote them in the 1720s and were important in shaping the course of early abolitionism before the American Revolution. What was different was less that views on Africans changed than that views on Britain's role in the world changed dramatically during the Seven Years War, precisely when Benezet was writing on Guinea.

It is important to outline British views on the character of Africans and their suitability as slaves and how those views changed over time. The image of the African in the British and European mind is, of course, a subject of enormous interest, massive scholarship and wildly differing views.[45] Opinion roughly divides into two, which we might view through the lenses of two ways in which William Shakespeare wrote about Africans in Elizabethan and early Jacobean England. His most famous depiction of an African was Othello, a tragic hero even if a black Moor, and a character treated with sympathy and considerable respect for his humanity. This suggests that English views of Africans were malleable, open to change and that the English did not necessarily think, before the introduction of chattel slavery in Barbados in the 1640s, that Africans were ideally suited to be enslaved or that they deserved to be in that condition. Shakespeare, however, had another lesser-known black character in his plays, the Moor, Aron, in *Titus Andronicus*. Aaron was a consummate villain, without any redeeming features, implacably opposed to Europeans and condemned by Shakespeare to perhaps the most agonising death of anyone in his corpus. Shakespeare's depiction of Aaron places him as the natural slave and Africans as barely human and the least promising of God's creation. On balance, more Englishmen, especially those who ventured overseas, held views about black Africans that corresponded to what Shakespeare wrote about Aaron than about Othello. The view of Africans in England in the seventeenth and eighteenth centuries was generally extremely unfavourable, to the point of hostility and hatred. Africans should be enslaved because that was thought to be their natural condition. Benezet's views on African capacity thus were very different to commonly accepted opinion. Even abolitionists tended to share this highly negative opinion of Africans either in Africa or in the Americas or Europe.[46]

Somerset and xenophobia

We can see in the famous Somerset case of 1772 how existing views on Africans were more prominent in shaping early antislavery views than those put forward by Benezet in 1762. The advocates representing Somerset in court warmed to Sharp's xenophobic theme. Sergeant Davy, acting for the enslaved man, James Somerset, ominously declared that if the judge Lord Mansfield decided against Somerset, then nothing would stop a white West Indian owner of an English estate from 'stocking his farm with negroes' and that 'instead of the farmers who now drive his plough, he would say call out a hundred of my fellows and set them to the plough, and go to the ironmongers for half a score of tortures to make them do it better'. The day before the case started, Sharp had given Davy an iron muzzle used to discipline slaves in the West Indies to 'show that men are not to be entrusted with an absolute authority over their brethren'.[47] Davy made sure that he displayed it, somewhat gratuitously, to a shocked courtroom.

Even if allowing blacks to be held in slavery in England did not lead to the enslavement of the English poor, it was still a bad thing, as it introduced an alien presence into the country. This group of aliens were growing in numbers and contributing to growing levels of crime. Even worse, white West Indians were bringing in a group of lowly paid servants who were bound to displace white workers from their positions. There was already 'a dangerous increase of slaves in this Kingdom' and, since blacks were 'already much too numerous', Sharp thought that 'the public good seems to require some restraints on the unnatural increase of black subjects'.[48] Davy hinted that allowing more slaves into England to work for absentee planters would also lead to rapid population increase as a male slave might become a grandfather to ten others, which 'would occasion a great deal of heartburn'.[49] Sharp celebrated the result in *Somerset* as preventing the arrival of slave-holders from the West Indies 'bringing with them swarms of Negro attendants into this island'. Mansfield's decision in favour of the enslaved man, refusing his owner's intention to remove the slave from the island, meant that Britain was not 'overrun with a vast multitude of poor wretched slaves', who would inevitably 'engross the employment and subsistence of the free labourer and industrious poor'.[50]

Behind all these arguments lay a much simpler belief: that slavery was an innovation invented in the islands by tyrannical planters who wanted to bring a foreign experiment to Britain and in doing so make Britain 'as base, wicked and Tyrannical as our colonies'. Sharp did not become opposed to slavery because he had a philosophical objection to slavery – he became an antislavery advocate because he saw slave-holders in action and did not like what he saw. The episode that turned him against slavery was when he found Jonathan Strong, an enslaved man living in London in the early 1760s, badly hurt after his master had beaten him. Moreover, Sharp discovered, to his shock, that, after Strong had recovered, his owner reclaimed his property rights in Strong and decided to send his enslaved property out of the country. He could not believe that slave owners could be so cruel. The more that Sharp studied slavery and the more he knew about how West Indian planters behaved, the more he came to realise that violence maintained the system and that planters acted with the authority of arbitrary monarchs in order to treat enslaved people abominably.

Sharp's 1769 tract against slavery was full of condemnation of white West Indians as cruel and hypocritical tyrants. He exhaustively researched colonial law in order to show that the planters of Virginia, Barbados and Jamaica had illegally developed laws about slavery. He concluded that the Virginia laws were 'the most consummate wickedness, I suppose, that anybody of people under the specious form of legislature were ever guilty of'. Jamaican lawmakers, he asserted, 'do not scruple to charge the slightest and most natural offences with the most opprobrious epithets', and introduced barbaric punishments long discarded in Europe.[51] What they had done, he argued, made West Indian planters fundamentally un-British, because slavery by its very nature only enhanced malign characteristics like 'avarice, choler, lust, revenge, caprice and all other human infirmities'. It made ordinary men tyrants: 'every petty planter who avails himself of the service of Slaves, is an arbitrary monarch, or rather a lawless Basha in his own territories'.[52]

What should have been especially worrying to West Indian slave-owners was that the arguments that the prosecutors made on behalf of James Somerset were encased within a discourse in which Caribbean planters were compared with tyrannical Turks and Russian slave-owners. Sergeant Davy argued that Virginian law could not prevail in England, because otherwise a Turk could bring his Circassian slave to England and rape her with impunity. Behind Davy's argument was not only an explicit racism (what would happen if foreigners brought white slaves, possibly Englishmen enslaved in Barbary, to England?) and sexism (the comments about rape were intended to inflame), but was also an assumption that white West Indians were not proper Englishmen. White West Indians introduced into Britain not just alien Africans, who themselves were a source of corruption for the lower orders, but also themselves – people who could be compared with oriental Turks, vicious Russians or African barbarians. The one thing they were not was legitimate Britons.[53]

Francis Hargrave, a prosecutor who made a name for himself through his speeches in support of James Somerset in the *Somerset* case, made explicit English fears that colonial masters were corrupt foreigners. He argued that planters wanted to bring the laws of infant colonies and 'a barbarous nation, Africa', to the home country.[54] If West Indians were British, they were a 'disgrace to the British name'. They had no rights that a British court need recognise, because 'men who do not scruple to detain others in Slavery, have but a very partial and unjust claim to the protection of the laws of liberty'.[55] The only reason they wanted to have slaves in England, Sharp speculated, was that they needed people upon whom to exercise their tyranny and perhaps to deprive English people of opportunities. Moreover, he thought it strange and unpatriotic that slave-owners would insist on the service of their slaves in England 'whilst so many of our own free fellow-subjects want bread'.[56]

Sharp was also influenced by ideas promulgated after 1763 that the rights of all peoples in the Empire had to be considered, whether they be Native Americans, African slaves, Bengali peasants, Irish or Canadian Catholics or American and West Indian planters. Sharp did not accept the colonial settler argument that settlers were merely Britons abroad, with all the rights of Britons and, most importantly, the capacity to make their own laws, including laws over slavery. He did not so much concern himself with the political rights of British colonists than with what he called 'the natural rights of mankind'.[57] In short, American and West Indian settlers were nothing special: they were subjects of the Crown in the way that all other peoples in the Empire, including enslaved people, were subjects of the Crown.[58]

It was imperative, therefore, that British colonists recognised the sins they were committing against other subjects of the king, such as American Indians and especially enslaved people. Benezet's comments – that all the harm done in Africa came ultimately from European vice and insatiable desire for dominion and for money – was also taken up by Sharp in 1769 and in *Somerset*. Sharp challenged colonial settlers to right the wrong of slavery, arguing that 'it is a shame to this nation ... that the British constitution and liberties should be excluded from any part of the *British dominions*'. He thought that it was 'the grossest infringement of the *King's prerogative* that the *influence, benefit and protection of the King's laws and courts of justice* should not be extended *to all His Majesty's subjects* even in the remotest parts of the *British Empire*' (original emphasis). Slaves and Native Americans, he believed, 'are as much intitled [*sic*] to an equitable and reasonable freedom' as 'American provincials'.[59]

Indeed, Sharp believed that some of the problems that America faced in the years after 1772, as they tried to deal with an expanding prerogative power claimed by the Crown, were due to God's displeasure about how colonial settlers mistreated their slaves. Perhaps, he speculated, the imperial difficulties that many Americans experienced from the Stamp Act of 1765 crisis onwards in their relations with British imperial officials, who refused to properly understand constitutional issues, was in fact 'a just punishment from God for the enormous Wickedness which are openly avowed and practiced throughout the British Empire'. Among the sins exercising God were how colonial legislatures and people were committed to publicly encouraging the slave trade and allowing 'the open toleration of Slavery and Oppression in the Colonies abroad'.[60]

Concern about hybridity

At the bottom of the arguments about why Lord Mansfield should decide *Somerset* against West Indian interests was an intense concern over hybridity and its ills. And in the mid-eighteenth century British, British American and white West Indian mind, hybridity was associated overwhelmingly with Spanish America. Benezet's concern was to rehabilitate the position of Africans so they were thought of as members of humanity rather than as either property or savages. Sharp was sympathetic to such a project. What he was more concerned about, however, was what the Massachusetts clergyman Cotton Mather called in 1700 'creole degeneracy' – the view that being in America had made Britons barbarians, and that when they came to Britain, they brought that barbarism with them. West Indian colonists were intensely aware of this metropolitan disdain for their cultural standing because they realised that, as in Spanish America, one result of colonisation in British America had been the creation of a new type of people – people of mixed-race status – whether mestizo or mulatto, to use the terms then commonly employed.

Unlike Spanish America, which by the eighteenth century had recognised the Indian heritage of Latin America as part of the foundational history of the region, Britons wanted to imagine that Indians would disappear, and in Jamaica from 1760 they tried to put up strict legislative barriers to prevent people of mixed race being able to pass into white society. In short, they wanted to avoid what they considered to be the 'mongrel' hybridity of Spanish America, a hybridity that they believed made Spanish America lethargic, superstitious, slothful and in inexorable decline. Colonists were determined not to be viewed in that way in British America. They knew that Britons in the metropole thought that people of mixed-race status were illegitimate, subordinate, marginal or invisible, and that they associated people of mixed race directly with white people born in America – sometimes to the extent of calling white Americans 'Indians'.[61]

British concern about hybridity was longstanding and especially pronounced by European standards. In the Middle Ages, England expelled all Jews from the country under Edward I in 1290. Nearly seventy years later, England passed the Statute of Kilkenny, prohibiting marriage between Irish and English.[62] That concern over the 'purity' of the English race continued down the centuries and by the mid-eighteenth century became focused on America, especially on white West Indians, suspected of being too keen on African tendencies and capable of slipping into Spanish American habits of 'mongrelisation'.[63] Among the many coincidences that occurred around the end of the Seven Years War in regard to treatments of race and subjecthood in an expanded British Empire, the birth of early abolitionism was accompanied by a nearly simultaneous push by writers such as Edward Long of Jamaica to make the understanding of race a biological as well as a political construct.[64]

White West Indians were intensely aware that English observers could see that they were a hybrid people who were overly fond of fraternising with Africans, especially sexually. That hybridity made English observers compare white West Indians unfavourably with people in Spanish America – the very model of a nation that let hybridity destroy its essence. Edward Long in 1774 bundled together the fears and prejudices of Western Europeans about the dangers of racial mixing, especially in relation to questions of blood and lineage, into fantasies of minute categorisation of peoples according to their percentage of white heritage. Long praised 'the genuine English breed, untainted with those heterogeneous mixtures' of the Spanish Americans, while he unrealistically hoped that white Jamaicans would soon give up their devotion to 'rioting in the goatish embraces' of their enslaved mistresses.[65] He expressed the latter largely in hope because he knew that in a society such as Britain's, where racism against Africans was probably increasing rather than declining (no matter what came from Benezet, a rare non-racist voice), the biggest fault seen in white men by their erstwhile supporters was their enthrallment to sexually avaricious black women, often depicted in pornographic fashion as fat, smelly and physically repulsive. In contrast to what Long thought was the mixed and mongrel nature of Spanish America, British settlers in Jamaica, he argued, would raise 'in honourable wedlock a race of unadulterated beings'. We can note here the equation between legitimacy of birth and legitimacy of bloodlines, as well as the negative assessment of Spanish America as the fount of American evils.[66]

Conclusion

Comparing Sharp to Benezet and outlining the xenophobic reasoning behind the defenders of James Somerset's right to not be deported to Jamaica in the most pivotal early case in British abolitionism highlights how advanced Anthony Benezet was in making claims for a relativistic understanding of African culture and African society.[67] Benezet's sympathy for Africans and African culture as being varied, historical rather than ahistorical, and able to fit into an account of world historical change in which African development was not impossible but which was compared, often favourably, to the prehistoric past of Europeans, were revolutionary ideas. Indeed, they were so far advanced as to not have much influence on early abolitionism, with his principal influence coming after the second edition of his book was published in 1783, when it was taken up by Thomas Clarkson.[68] That story is reasonably well known. What is less well known is the reception of Benezet's book and sympathetic identification with Africans by Granville Sharp from the late 1760s.[69] Benezet was an important author for Sharp, as Brycchan Carey has shown. Sharp and John Wesley corresponded with Benezet and found in his writings a 'ready-made discourse on antislavery from which they could draw appropriate words, useful phrases and tested arguments'. Pro-slavers were not as rhetorically advanced, putting them at a great disadvantage to Sharp and other non-Quaker antislavers, who, until the 1780s, when public opinion was against them, did not have 'an equivalent set of shared and repeated statements'.[70]

What is especially remarkable about Benezet's work is that it was a work of reading in the silences of a corpus of material that not only did not support Benezet's arguments, but which argued precisely the opposite points. Benezet was not held back in his humanitarian approach to including Africans within rather than outside humanity by the hostility towards Africans held by racist slave traders who used their knowledge of West Africa to justify their exploitation of Africans in the slave trade.[71] Benezet's work was thus a signal early example of a later trend conspicuous in abolitionism and exemplified in the works of Thomas Clarkson: using other people's personal testimony, often hostile to the cause of abolitionism, directed against the intentions of the original authors into devastating critiques of the pro-slavery position.[72] Anthony Benezet's great work needs to be read not just for the new arguments against the slave trade and against anti-African diatribes that it provided – which in turn were very influential for shaping abolitionist argument – but also for its creation of a mode of discourse that did not require any personal testimony, but could be conducted from the confines of the writer's study.

Notes

1 For the foundations of abolitionism, see Christopher Leslie Brown, *Moral Capital: Foundations of British Abolitionism* (Chapel Hill, NC: University of North Carolina Press, 2006). There is a huge body of literature on abolitionism. For a selective bibliography, see Michael Guasco, 'The Abolition of Slavery', in *Oxford Online Bibliography in Atlantic History*, www.oxfordbibliographies.com/view/document/obo-9780199730414/obo-9780199730414-0001.xml?rskey=KvOAze&result=1, accessed 21 August 2021.
2 Brycchan Carey, *From Peace to Freedom: Quaker Rhetoric and the Birth of American Antislavery, 1657–1761* (New Haven, CT: Yale University Press, 2012); Srividhya Swaminathan, *Debating the Slave Trade: Rhetoric of British National Identity, 1759–1815* (Farnham, UK: Ashgate, 2009); Philip Gould, *Barbaric Traffic: Commerce and Antislavery in the Eighteenth-Century Atlantic World* (Cambridge, MA: Harvard University Press, 2003).
3 Jean R. Soderlund, *Quakers and Slavery: A Divided Spirit* (Princeton, NJ: Princeton University Press, 1985); David Brion Davis, *The Problem of Slavery in Western Culture* (New York, NY: Oxford University Press, 1988).
4 Soderlund, *Quakers and Slavery*.
5 Geoffrey Plank, *John Woolman's Path to the Peaceable Kingdom: A Quaker in the British Empire* (Philadelphia, PA: University of Pennsylvania, 2012); and Maurice Jackson, *Let This Voice Be Heard: Anthony Benezet, Father of Atlantic Abolitionism* (Philadelphia, PA: University of Pennsylvania Press, 2009). See also Gary B. Nash, *Warner Mifflin: Unflinching Quaker Abolitionist* (Philadelphia, PA: University of Pennsylvania Press, 2017).
6 Dee E. Andrews and Emma Jones Lapsansky-Werner, 'Thomas Clarkson's Quaker Trilogy': Abolitionist Narrative as Transformative History', in Brycchan Carey and Geoffrey Plank (eds), *Quakers and Abolition* (Urbana, IL: University of Illinois Press, 2014), pp. 194–208, and Emma Gibson Wilson, *Thomas Clarkson: A Biography* (London, UK: Macmillan, 1989).
7 For accounts of Benezet's life and career, see David L. Crosby, 'Anthony Benezet's Transformation of Anti-Slavery Rhetoric', *Slavery and Abolition* (2002), 23, pp. 39–58; Irv A. Brendlinger, *To Be Silent ... Would Be Criminal: The Antislavery Influence and Writings of Anthony Benezet* (Lanham, MD: Scarecrow Press, 2007); Jackson, *Let This Voice Be Heard*; and Jonathan D.

Sassi, 'With a Little Help from the Friends: The Quaker and Tactical Contexts of Anthony Benezet's Abolitionist Publishing', *Pennsylvania Magazine of History and Biography* (2011), 135, pp. 33–71.

8 Amanda B. Moniz, *From Empire to Humanity: The American Revolution and the Origins of Humanitarianism* (New York, NY: Oxford University Press, 2016), chs 1–2.

9 Randy J. Sparks, '"This Precious Book": Africa and Africans in Africa in Anthony Benezet's Account of Guinea', in Marie-Jeanne Rossignol and Bertrand Van Ruymbeke (eds), *The Atlantic World of Anthony Benezet (1713–1784)* (Leiden, Netherlands: Brill, 2016), p. 185; Thomas Clarkson, *The History of the Rise, Progress, and Accomplishment of the Abolition of the African Slave-Trade by the British Parliament* (London, UK: 1808).

10 In this respect, Benezet differed from his Quaker compatriot, John Woolman, who was also opposed to slavery. Benezet was shaped in his views by the oppression he saw enslaved people enduring in western New Jersey, where slaves were numerous, and even more by trips to the American South. Plank, *John Woolman's Path*, pp. 102–5.

11 Benezet did not use footnotes in his other published work. Sparks, '"This Precious Book"', p. 9.

12 William Snelgrave, *A New Account of Some Parts of Guinea, and the Slave-Trade* (London, UK: 1734); Willem Bosman, *A New and Accurate Description of the Coast of Guinea* (London, UK: 1705).

13 Benjamin Franklin, 'Observations Concerning the Increase of Mankind, Peopling of Countries etc. (1751)', in Alan Houston (ed.), *Franklin: The Autobiography and Other Writings on Politics, Economics, and Virtue* (Cambridge, UK: Cambridge University Press, 2004), pp. 215–22.

14 Anthony Benezet, *Some Historical Account of Guinea, Its Situation, Produce, and the General Disposition of Its Inhabitants with an Inquiry into the Rise and Progress of the Slave Trade, Its Nature, and Lamentable Effects* (London, UK: 1783), pp. 32–3.

15 Ibid., p. 54.

16 Ibid., p. 1.

17 For human rights in the Spanish Empire, see Bianca Premo, *The Enlightenment on Trial: Ordinary Litigants and Colonialism in the Spanish Empire* (New York, NY: Oxford University Press, 2017).

18 John Woolman, *Some Considerations on the Keeping of Negroes Recommended to the Professors of Christianity of Every Denomination* (Philadelphia, PA: 1754).

19 Trevor Burnard and Giorgio Riello, 'Slavery and the New History of Capitalism', *Journal of Global History* (2020), 15, pp. 225–44.

20 David L. Crosby, 'On War and Slavery: Benezet's Peace Testimony and Abolition', in Rossignol and Van Ruymbeke (eds), *Atlantic World of Benezet*, pp. 70–90.

21 Benezet, *Some Historical Account*, p. 54. For attitudes to Africa, see Toby Green and Jonathan D. Sassi, 'Africans in the Quaker Image: Anthony Benezet,

African Travel Narratives, and Revolutionary-Era Antislavery', *Journal of Early Modern History* (2006), 10 (1–2), pp. 95–130; George E. Boulukos, 'Olaudah Equiano and the Eighteenth-Century Debate on Africa', *Eighteenth-Century Studies* (2007), 40 (2), pp. 241–55; John Thornton, 'Africa and Abolitionism', in Seymour Drescher and Pieter C. Emmer (eds), *Who Abolished Slavery? Slave Revolts and Abolitionism: A Debate with João Pedro Marques* (New York, NY: Berghahn Books, 2010), pp. 93–102; David L. Crosby, *The Complete Antislavery Writings of Anthony Benezet, 1754–1783: An Annotated Critical Edition* (Baton Rouge, LA: Louisiana State University Press, 2013).
22 John Wesley, *Thoughts upon Slavery* (London, UK: 1774), pp. 18–22.
23 Gretchen Gerzina, *Black London: Life Before Emancipation* (New Brunswick, NJ: Rutgers University Press, 2005).
24 Surveys of abolitionism and its historiography include Seymour Drescher, *Abolition: A History of Slavery and Antislavery* (Cambridge, UK: Cambridge University Press, 2009); David Brion Davis, *Inhuman Bondage: The Rise and Fall of Slavery in the New World* (New York, NY: Oxford University Press, 2006); and Manisha Sinha, *The Slave's Cause: A History of Abolition* (New Haven, CT: Yale University Press, 2016).
25 Brown, *Moral Capital*; Davis, *Problem of Slavery in Western Culture*; and Adam Hochschild, *Bury the Chains: Prophets and Rebels in the Fight to Free an Empire's Slaves* (Boston, MA: Houghton Mifflin, 2005).
26 John Coffey, '"Tremble Britannia!": Fear, Providence and the Abolition of the Slave Trade, 1756–1807', *English Historical Review* (2012), 127, pp. 844–81.
27 In addition to the work noted above, see Thomas Bender, *The Antislavery Debate: Capitalism and Abolitionism as a Problem of Historical Interpretation* (Berkeley, CA: University of California Press, 1992); J. R. Oldfield, *Transatlantic Abolitionism in the Age of Revolution* (Cambridge, UK: Cambridge University Press, 2013); and J. R. Oldfield, *The Ties that Bind: Transatlantic Abolitionism in the Age of Reform* (Liverpool, UK: Liverpool University Press, 2020).
28 Jack P. Greene, *Evaluating Empire and Confronting Colonialism in Eighteenth-Century Britain* (Cambridge, UK: Cambridge University Press, 2013).
29 P. J. Marshall, *Edmund Burke and the British Empire in the West Indies* (Oxford, UK: Oxford University Press, 2019).
30 Trevor Burnard, *Jamaica in the Age of Revolution* (Philadelphia, PA: University of Pennsylvania Press, 2020), pp. 162–4.
31 Sharp to Jacob Bryant, 19 October 1772, Sharp MSS, cited in Brown, *Moral Capital*, p. 96; Granville Sharp, *A Representation of the Injustice and Dangerous Tendency of Tolerating Slavery or of Admitting the Least Claim of Private Property in the Persons of Men, in England* (London, UK: 1769), p. 13, emphasis original. Sharp was also strongly influenced by meeting black abolitionists. Vincent Caretta, *Equiano, the African: Biography of a Self-Made Man* (Athens, GA: University of Georgia Press, 2005).
32 Steven Wise, *Though the Heavens May Fall: The Landmark Case that Led to the End of Human Slavery* (Cambridge, MA: Harvard University Press, 2006).
33 Dana Rabin, '"In a Country of Liberty?": Slavery, Villeinage and the Making of Whiteness in the Somerset Case', *History Workshop Journal* (2011), 72, pp. 5–29.

34 Sharp, *Representation*, pp. 92, 110. See also Catherine Molineux, *Faces of Perfect Ebony: Encountering Atlantic Slavery in Imperial Britain* (Cambridge, MA: Harvard University Press, 2012).
35 For Sharp's attitudes to America see Sharp, *Representation*, pp. 81–2 and Brown, *Moral Capital*, pp. 161–82 (quote 170).
36 Green and Sassi, 'Africans in the Quaker Image'.
37 William Pietz, 'Bosman's Guinea and the Intercultural Roots of an Enlightenment Discourse', *Comparative Civilizations Review* (1982), 9, article 3.
38 Bosman, *New and Accurate Description*, p. 152, original emphasis.
39 Robert Robertson, *A Letter to the Right Reverend the Lord Bishop of London from an Inhabitant of His Majesty's Leeward-Caribee Islands* … (London, UK: 1730); Swaminathan, *Debating the Slave Trade*; and David Lambert, 'The Counter-Revolutionary Atlantic: White West Indian Petitions and Proslavery Networks', *Social and Cultural Geography* (2005), 6, pp. 405–20.
40 David Brion Davis, *The Problem of Slavery in Western Culture* (New York and Oxford: Oxford University Press, 1966), pp. 165–87; Winthrop Jordan, *White Over Black: American Attitudes Toward the Negro, 1550–1812* (Chapel Hill, NC: University of North Carolina Press, 1968), pp. 3–43; Alden T. Vaughan and Virginia Mason Vaughan, 'Before Othello: Elizabethan Representations of Sub-Saharan Africans', *William and Mary Quarterly* (1997), 3rd series, 54, pp. 21–44; William Hamlin, *The Image of America in Montaigne, Spenser, and Shakespeare: Renaissance Ethnography and Literary Reflection* (New York, NY: Oxford University Press, 1995), pp. 2, 9; Kim F. Hall, *Things of Darkness: Economies of Race and Gender in Early Modern England* (Ithaca, NY: 1995), pp. 211–26; Malachy Postlewayt, *The National and Private Advantage of the African Trade Considered* (London, UK: 1745), p. 4 (first quotation); Thomas Thompson, *The African Trade for Negro Slaves, Shewn to Be Consistent with Principles of Humanity, and with the Laws of Revealed Religion* (Canterbury, UK: 1772), p. 10 (second quotation). Thompson's pamphlet outraged Benezet, who wrote angry comments in his copy. See David Brion Davis, *The Problem of Slavery in the Age of Revolution, 1770–1823* (Ithaca and London, Cornell University Press, 1975), p. 532. On race and ideas of Africa and Africans, see Stuart B. Schwartz (ed.), *Implicit Understandings: Observing, Reporting, and Reflecting on the Encounters between European and Other Peoples in the Early Modern Era* (Cambridge, UK: Cambridge University Press, 1994); George Fredrickson, *Racism: A Short History* (Princeton, NJ: Princeton University Press, 2002); Benjamin Braude, 'The Sons of Noah and the Construction of Ethnic and Geographical Identities in Medieval and Early Modern Periods', *William and Mary Quarterly* (1997), 3rd series, 54, pp. 103–42; David Theo Goldberg, *Racist Culture: Philosophy and the Politics of Meaning* (Oxford, UK: Oxford University Press, 1993); Ivan Hannaford, *Race: The History of an Idea in the West* (Baltimore, MD: Johns Hopkins University Press, 1996); Reginald Horsman, *Race and Manifest Destiny: The Origins of American Racial Anglo Saxonism* (Cambridge, MA: Harvard University Press, 1981); and Audrey Smedley, *Race in North America: Origins and Evolution of a Worldview* (Boulder, CO: Westview, 1993).

41 Daniel Defoe, *Colonel Jack*, ed. Samuel Holt Monk (New York, NY: Oxford University Press, 1989), p. 128. The original publication date of this novel was 1722.
42 Jack P. Greene, *The Natural, Moral, and Political History of Jamaica ... by J[ames] K[night]* (Charlottesville, VA: University of Virginia Press, 2021). See also Edmund Hickeringill, *Jamaica Viewed ...* (London, UK: 1661).
43 Charles Leslie, *A New and Exact Account of Jamaica* (Edinburgh, UK: 1741), p. 41.
44 Defoe, *Colonel Jack*, p. 133.
45 See the works cited in Andrew Wells, 'Race and Racism', and Michael Guasco, 'The Idea of Race', in *Oxford Online Bibliography in Atlantic History*, www.oxfordbibliographies.com/browse?module_0=obo-9780199730414, accessed 21 August 2021.
46 Ania Loomba, *Shakespeare, Race and Colonialism* (Oxford, UK: Oxford University Press, 2002).
47 Gerzina, *Black London*, pp. 104–5; Wise, *Though the Heavens May Fall*.
48 Cited in Brown, *Moral Capital*, p. 94.
49 Cited in Wise, *Though the Heavens May Fall*.
50 F. O. Shyllon, *Black Slaves in Britain* (Oxford, UK: Oxford University Press, 1974), pp. 82–164.
51 Sharp, *Representation*, pp. 65, 68.
52 Ibid., pp. 82, 163.
53 Trevor Burnard, 'Powerless Masters: The Curious Decline of Jamaican Sugar Planters in the Foundational Period of British abolition', *Slavery & Abolition* (2011), 32, pp. 185–98.
54 George Van Cleve, '*Somerset's Case* and its antecedents in imperial perspective', *Law and History Review* (2006), 24, p. 627; Daniel J. Hulsebosch, 'Nothing But Liberty: "Somerset's Case" and the British Empire', *Law and History Review* (2006), 24, p. 656.
55 Sharp, *Representation*, p. 81.
56 Ibid., p. 75.
57 Cited in Brown, *Moral Capital*, p. 164.
58 Hannah Weiss Muller, *Subjects and Sovereign: Bonds of Belonging in the Eighteenth-Century British Empire* (New York, NY: Oxford University Press, 2017), ch. 4.
59 Sharp, *Representation*, p. 51.
60 Sharp to Benjamin Rush, 27 July 1774, in John A. Woods, 'The Correspondence of Benjamin Rush and Granville Sharp, 1773–1809', *Journal of American Studies* (1967), 1, p. 10.
61 Daniel Livesay, *Children of Uncertain Fortune: Mixed-Race Jamaicans in Britain and the Atlantic Family, 1733–1833* (Chapel Hill, NC: University of North Carolina Press, 2018); Linford Fisher, '"Dangerous Designes": The 1676 Barbados Act to Prohibit New England Indian Slaver Population', *William and Mary Quarterly* (2014), 71, pp. 99–124. For a theoretical perspective on hybridity, see Lauren A. Benton and John Muth, 'On Cultural Hybridity:

Interpreting Colonial Authority and Performance', *Journal of Colonialism and Colonial History* (2000), 1, DOI: 10.1353/cch.2000.0002, accessed 21 August 2021.

62 Dana Rabin, *Britain and Its Internal Outsiders, 1750–1800: Under Rule of Law* (Manchester, UK: Manchester University Press, 2017); Thomas Bartlett, *Ireland: A History* (Cambridge, UK: Cambridge University Press, 2010), pp. 57–61.

63 Trevor Burnard, 'White West Indian Identity in the Eighteenth Century', in John D. Garrigus and Christopher Morris (eds), *Assumed Identities: Race and the National Imagination in the Atlantic World* (College Station, TX: Texas A&M Press, 2010), pp. 71–87; and Trevor Burnard, '"A Compound Mongrel Mixture": Racially Coded Humor, Satire, and the Denigration of White Creoles in the British West Indies, 1780–1834', in Elizabeth Mansfield and Kelly Malone (eds), *Seeing Satire* (Oxford, UK: Voltaire Press, 2013), pp. 149–65.

64 Suman Seth, 'Materialism, Slavery and *The History of Jamaica*', *Isis* (2014), 105, pp. 764–72; Suman Seth, *Difference and Disease: Medicine, Race and the Eighteenth-Century British Empire* (Cambridge, UK: Cambridge University Press, 2018), pp. 208–40.

65 Edward Long, *History of Jamaica* ... (London, UK: 1774), vol. II, pp. 13, 281, 328, 331. Trevor Burnard, '"Rioting in Goatish Embraces": Marriage and Improvement in Early British Jamaica, 1660–1780', *History of the Family* (2006), 11, pp. 185–97.

66 Burnard, 'Rioting', p. 192; Brooke Newman, *A Dark Inheritance: Blood, Race, and Sex in Colonial Jamaica* (New Haven, CT: Yale University Press, 2018).

67 Richard S. Newman, 'From Benezet to Black Founders: Toward a New History of Eighteenth-Century Atlantic Emancipation', in Rossignol and Van Ruymbeke (eds), *Atlantic World of Benezet*, pp. 221–41.

68 Nina Reid-Maroney, 'Benezet's Ghost: Revisiting the Antislavery Culture of Benjamin Rush's Philadelphia', in Rossignol and Van Ruymbeke (eds), *Atlantic World of Benezet*, pp. 199–209.

69 For Sharp's ongoing interest in Africa, see Simon Schama, *Rough Crossings: Britain, the Slaves and the American Revolution* (New York, NY: Ecco/Harper Collins, 2006).

70 Carey, *From Peace to Freedom*, p. 218.

71 Green and Sassi, 'Africans in the Quaker Image'.

72 Andrews and Lapsansky-Werner, 'Thomas Clarkson's Quaker Trilogy'.

2

An incident at the Sun Tavern: Changing the discourse on Indigenous visitors to Georgian Britain

Kate Fullagar

On 4 March 1765 London's daily *Gazetteer* ran an advertisement for a fresh novelty in the city. 'Two Indian warriors of the Mohawk Nation', it declared, could be seen at the Sun Tavern on the Strand for the price of one shilling per person, 'from ten in the morning till six in the evening'.[1] The Mohawks had in fact been on display for a week. By the eighth day, however, the gig was up. Someone had complained of the spectacle to no less an establishment than the House of Lords. On the ninth day, both the proprietor of the Sun Tavern, John Schuppe, and the so-called chaperone of the Mohawks, Hyam Meyers, were standing before the scowling peers of Britain's upper parliamentary chamber.

After listening to a short, finger-pointing statement by Schuppe and a long, self-justificatory ramble by Meyers, the Lords agreed that the culprits must not 'shew the said Indians from this time'. Further, they decreed that Schuppe and Meyers needed to take 'proper care' of the Indians 'till a proper person should be sent by the commissioners for trade and plantations to receive them, in order to their being returned to America'. Finally, the Lords issued two general resolutions:

1. That the bringing from America any of the Indians who are under his Majesty's protection, without proper authority for doing so, may tend to give great dissatisfaction to the Indian nations, and be of dangerous consequence to his Majesty's subjects residing in the colonies.
2. That the making a public shew of Indians, ignorant of such proceedings, is unbecoming and inhuman.[2]

A contextualised history of the two Mohawks at the Sun Tavern reveals that the first of the Lords' resolutions reflected a longstanding approach towards Indigenous arrivals in Britain. From around the early 1700s, Britons had been particularly alert to the question of Indigenous satisfaction. They understood that the British presence in the American colonies especially – the lives of their settlers and the viability of their increasingly lucrative economic interests there – depended on Indigenous accommodation.³ Sometimes accommodation could come in the form of alliance, but at other times it could involve just the minimisation of outright hostility. This broad concern to achieve accommodation did not preclude hostility, of course, but it did ensure that Indigenous travellers to Britain at least were rarely made into degrading spectacles. Above all, concern with Indigenous envoys was a political, or diplomatic, anxiety that was articulated in a political register.

A wide-angle lens on the two Mohawks additionally shows, however, that the second of the Lords' resolutions was something new on the British discursive horizon. Few Britons had ever made statements about Indigenous American travellers, focussing on Indigenous rights, that were apparently unmoored from the formal politics or diplomacy of Empire. Here was a pronouncement that invoked the values of personhood rather than statehood. It was issued in a moral register. The alignment of the second resolution with extra-political rights, together with its gesture towards appropriate personal behaviour on the part of Britons to 'distant strangers', marks it as an early instance of modern humanitarian thinking.⁴ This kind of utterance appeared in much subsequent literature about Indigenous arrivals in Britain. Significantly, it also appeared alongside ever greater numbers of Indigenous human exhibitions in Britain.

This chapter does not claim to explain the causal link between increased moral admonishments against the 'public shewing' of Indigenous people and greater actual numbers of Indigenous people being displayed for profit in Britain. But it does outline the correlation between the new discursive moralising interest and the unsavoury practice of human commodification. It joins others in this volume that raise questions about the emancipatory effects of humanitarian speech into the nineteenth century. The chapter argues that there was a shift in the mode of discourse regarding Indigenous arrivals – a shift from political to moral, or from engagement with Empire to disengagement with Empire – that matched a change in the practical reception of such peoples. This was a change from fascinated though largely diplomatic responses to voyeuristic and increasingly privatised inclinations. The Lords' resolutions of 1765 neatly encapsulate this overall shift, even though it took another few decades to play out fully and it did so in a roundabout fashion.⁵

More broadly, this chapter demonstrates how the discursive shift regarding Indigenous envoys occurred against a background of growing British certainty in the inevitability of Empire. Where Britons had previously debated the merits of pursuing an expansionist trajectory, they began from the 1790s to debate merely which kind of imperialism was best in the circumstances. Humanitarians played an important role in these later 'fine-tuning' debates, but they did so at the cost of accepting the existence of Empire as an a priori fact. The certainty of Empire, it might be said, eroded the political nature of imperial discourse. It allowed for a variety of moral positions *about* expansion but diluted the radical questioning *of* expansion that had prevailed earlier.

The chapter begins with a brief survey of Indigenous individuals who journeyed to Britain before the two Mohawks' arrival. It then narrates in greater detail the series of events that led to the Mohawks' ignominious exhibition in 1765. The second half of the chapter traces the two distinct phases that followed the Lords' resolutions: the rest of the eighteenth century, which witnessed a mixed approach to the Indigenous traveller, as well as a change in British understandings of who exactly exemplified such a person; and then the early nineteenth century, which saw simultaneously a broadening of so-called Indigenous exemplars in Britain and a narrowing of ways to treat them. The larger story of the incident at the Sun Tavern illuminates an important arc in Britain's imperial history and the ways in which humanitarian impulses connected with the consolidation of Empire.

In terms of existing historiography, the chapter aligns with some recent scholars who highlight the paradox of increasing humanitarian rhetoric and increasing imperial violence. It provides the little-investigated prehistory of this paradox through one peculiar lens and connects some salient scholarly observations about imperial discourse in the eighteenth century with histories of empathy in the nineteenth century.[6]

Indigenous visitors before 1765

With its inextricable link to territory, the category of Indigeneity in the early modern British imaginary always attached to those non-Europeans whose land was the focus of most expansionist attention. Between 1500 and about 1770, the paramount exemplars of Indigeneity were unquestionably Indigenous Americans.[7]

The first recorded Indigenous American visitors to Britain were three Beothuk Indians, who arrived with some Bristol-based fishermen in 1501. 'This year were browght unto the king iii men takyn in the New Found Ile land', noted one chronicler.[8] Although these men reputedly gained an audience with Henry VII, they otherwise made very little impact on ordinary locals. Notwithstanding the scarcity of evidence on popular phenomena at this time, the Beothuks' relative inconsequence epitomised the general British response to Indigenous visitors through the sixteenth and seventeenth centuries. Delegates turned up about once every generation or so, mainly to secure political negotiations; many met with the monarch of the day and often the relevant minister for American affairs, but few made much of a splash on urban publics. Such muted interest in Indigenous Americans matched both the delayed response that most Britons had for the momentousness of American discovery and the general lack of public engagement with the early stages of British colonisation.[9]

This all changed as a newly stabilised and militarised Britain entered the eighteenth century. In 1710, four supposed Iroquois Kings arrived in London, repeating very well-worn tracks of Indigenous Americans travelling from recently threatened homelands to the heart of the Empire.[10] Only these travellers, however, encountered crowds of fascinated onlookers. Like their predecessors, the Iroquois met with the monarch and with Whitehall officials, but their far more notable exchanges were with the 'rabbles', 'throngs' and 'mobs' of ordinary Londoners following them, touching them, depicting them and discussing them. Newspapers recounted their every move. Artists produced dozens of images of them. Schoolchildren even laid on dinners in their honour.[11]

The mobbish interest in the Iroquois of 1710 was not wholly admiring, of course. Several commentators derided the visitors: the essayist Joseph Addison chuckled at their 'wildness'; a popular street ballad entitled *The Four Indian Kings* pitied their 'sad condition'.[12] But even derisive interest was notable, compared with the absence of attention in earlier centuries.

Significantly, amid all this fascination – both favourable and unfavourable – the Iroquois never faced the prospect of being turned into local commercial displays. Although they were known to have frequented entertainment venues such as alehouses, cockfighting pits, and puppet theatres, they participated as patrons rather than as the entertainment itself.[13] This was partly due to official anxiety about Iroquois opinion – their Whitehall hosts knew that they represented peoples of 'fatall consequence' in the current war against French colonists in North America.[14] It was also, though, in part due to the way the public saw them as ideal ciphers through which to discuss this war and its wider imperial implications. This utility overrode the idea that such arrivals could be instead generic exotics suitable for a freak show.

As I have argued elsewhere, the rise of popular fascination for Indigenous visitors from the early 1700s centred on their presumed association with the concept of savagery, and the subsequent value of this idea for a people coming to terms with their own imperialism.[15] Both admirers and detractors employed cognates of savagery to describe the Iroquois, and nearly every one of them did so in order to reflect on Britain's own expansionist trajectory. For example, Addison invoked their wildness solely to praise Britain's supposedly converse sophistication via imperial growth. Likewise, the *Four Indian Kings* ballad rendered them as 'humble ... heathens' as a way to condone British efforts as edifying and Christianising. Positive deployment of the Iroquois as savages worked similarly as a means to understand a burgeoning Empire. Addison's peer, Richard Steele, for example, explicitly called the visitors 'savage' because he thought they were people of 'natural justice', which was a state he, for one, found to be (re-)emerging in a more cosmopolitan Britain.[16] All commentators were, at core, analysing their own transforming society rather than Indigenous American society. They each found the supposed embodiment of stark social simplicity – or savagery – in visiting Indigenous Americans to be the most compelling means by which to do so.

The notion that Indigenous visitors appealed to early eighteenth-century Britons because they provided a way to debate Empire consolidates when comparing envoys across the early decades of the period. The pattern of the visit of seven Cherokee from the American southeast in 1730, for instance, bears striking resemblance to that of the four Iroquois. Like their predecessors, the Cherokees also attracted enthusiastic mobs: 'a numerous crowd of spectators', reported one newspaper; a 'vast concourse of people', noted another.[17] Also, like the Iroquois, these diplomats ventured often into the leisured world of London – the taverns and the parks, as well as, this time, the fairs and the spas. But not once did the envoys instigate tales of profiteering behaviour by local showmen.

The controversy that surrounded the seven Cherokees focused instead on the way their so-called savagery provoked discussion about Britain's imperialism. A writer for *Fog's Weekly Journal* exemplified how some used the latest Indigenous visitors to attack surging British expansionism. This writer thought the Cherokees showed a 'true copy of the primitive ... in a simple state of government'. Such a state was apparently dignified, wise, transparent, martial, fearless and abstemious. The analogy was deployed in the journal's article to show up, by contrast, Britain's current government, which was said to be run by secretive thieves who 'guttled [sic] the public purse' and surrounded themselves with 'cringing sycophants'.[18] Two weeks after the *Fog's* piece, on the other hand, the *Daily Post* ran an editorial on how the visitors, 'like worms out of the earth', showed up instead the 'good protocol', clockwork organisation and philanthropic instinct of a trading nation like Britain.[19] Early eighteenth-century Indigenous envoys spurred political debate about the effects of Empire far more than they instigated discussion of their 'human rights' or treatment in Britain.

A Creek delegation in 1734, also from the southeast, was similar again. They too were regaled with a 'prodigious' number of locals, who 'flock'd in to see them' wherever they went. Their destinations included the usual fairs, parks, clubs and theatres. They also attended hospitals and universities, and took a barge trip down the Thames.[20] Just as with the others, no gossip about undue commercialisation ever emerged from the flurry of discourse about them. As was now standard, that discourse focused instead on what the Creeks' so-called savagery said about Britain. While the *Monthly Intelligencer* thought that the delegation's base humility shone a light on 'the Power and Greatness' of the British nation, a popular street broadside rebutted that the Creeks' simplicity actually proved the opposite.[21] Referencing Indigenes from nearby Britain's new colony of Georgia, this broadside thought that the delegation reminded Britons of their recent imperial bloating:

> Wealth without End, from such Exploits as These,
> Crown'd our large Commerce, and extended Sway;
> And hence dissolv'd in soft luxurious Ease,
> Our ancient Virtue vanish'd soon away.

These were but two examples of how British people talked about the latest arrival from Indigenous America.[22]

In 1762 another group of Cherokees arrived in the imperial capital. On the whole, they continued behaviours now entrenched by previous Indigenous envoys. They toured many of the same venues and everywhere they met with 'a gaping multitude'.[23] As ever, some commentators wielded their apparently simple condition as a weapon against the 'dangerous ... luxury' that Britons now faced due to their over-extended commerce, while others countered that it instead only shone a light on the greater sophistication of British arsenals, governance and freedoms.[24]

Some aspects of the 1762 visit, however, in retrospect, signalled the beginnings of a change in the general reception of Indigenous Americans in Britain. For one thing, the reigning monarch, George III, took some convincing to meet with these envoys. All previous delegations had quickly secured royal attention, owing to ongoing British recognition that Indigenous American satisfaction was critical to imperial claims across the Atlantic. George III did eventually meet with the Cherokees, who had come over to resolve a recent peace treaty between them after a ferocious two-year war. Although the King may have felt that his army's victory made the visitors now unimportant, his advisors – specifically the Secretary of State for American affairs – knew that the Crown's struggle to maintain precedence in America was far from over. It would still need Indigenous assistance.[25]

More significantly, the 1762 envoys provoked a couple of instances of a new mode for discussing Indigenous American visitors. One involved the colonial chaperone of the Cherokees, Henry Timberlake. Commissioned by the Virginian Governor to escort and look after the Cherokees while in London, Timberlake found himself the focus of press rumours that he was charging a fee for people to view the visitors at their residence. Timberlake exploded with rage at the accusation, which was indeed probably untrue (it had been started by his landlord who was feuding with him for other reasons). The Secretary of State stepped in nonetheless at this point to forbid explicitly any such behaviour.[26]

The other instance happened that same week. In late July 1762, *Lloyd's Evening Post* published a letter by a publican complaining that his wife was advertising the presence of the Cherokees at their tavern as a lure for business. The publican was apparently disgusted at his wife for doing this: 'I think no man has a right to make a property of them', he protested.[27] This letter itself may or may not have been a cynical advertisement, and the proprietors may or may not have charged a direct fee for viewing rights. What is important here is that the publican's utterance joins the rumours over Timberlake in auguring a new theme in contemporary discourse about Indigenous visitors. This theme focused on the Cherokees' right to be free of a certain type of degradation. No earlier discussion had defended this right because no earlier envoy had ever faced overt threats of crude commodification. The stereotyping of such people as savages for productive meditation on Empire still dominated local discussions. But a new way of perceiving Indigenous arrivals – as simply 'distant strangers' disconnected from Empire though yet due some moral consideration – was starting to creep in as well.

Two Mohawks at the Sun Tavern

The tendency to moralise about Indigenous American visitors rather than politicise them emerged again three years later during the incident at the Sun Tavern. The two Mohawks at the centre of the incident were called Sychnecta and Trosoghroga, from the Canajoharie settlement of what the British then called their New York colony. The Mohawks had first arrived in Britain in the spring of 1764. They had been brought over by two entrepreneurial colonists from New York – Hyam Meyers, a New York City merchant, and Lawrence Blessius, a tailor from Canajoharie.[28]

One of the few scholars to have investigated this episode in Indigenous travel, George Hamell, speculates that Meyers and Blessius always intended to 'make money through the public exhibition of the two young Mohawks'.[29] Later events seem to support this hypothesis, but the earlier history of Indigenous visitors to Britain suggests otherwise. Neither colonist would have had heard many stories to indicate it could be a worthwhile gamble – overt Indigenous exhibiting was simply not prevalent enough before the 1760s. The wider colonial context of Sychnecta and Trosoghroga's journey points instead to a confluence of at least three factors to explain the journey.

First, most Indigenous American travellers in the eighteenth century travelled of their own volition. Hamell speculates that the Mohawks were victims of their escorts' determination, but this is chiefly because the escorts' enemies implied such a reading in some of the remaining documents. If the Mohawks shared anything in common with the Iroquois, Cherokees and Creeks before them, they were rather seeking a trip to London in order to acquire redress from at least one set of settlers' encroachments into their homelands. Like other members of the Iroquois federacy, and like most Indians further south, Mohawks had been battling imperial incursion for a long time, and understood by now that petitions to the heads of respective empires were a productive means of getting political attention. Sychnecta and Trosoghroga were probably central to the momentum behind their journey to Britain.

Second, Lawrence Blessius was probably a descendant of Palatine refugees at Canajoharie and an associate of another more famous Canajoharie Palatine, George Klock. Klock was well known to British officials for making fraudulent claims to Indian lands. In 1764 one British official complained to the New York Governor that Klock was sending Blessius off on a mission to London to bypass colonial rules about land grabs. Moreover, the official said that Blessius had 'inveigled two young Indians' to go with him to help support his case. Just as Indigenous Americans understood the power of petitioning an emperor directly for their needs, so too did some of the Empire's more marginal characters – and these people often co-opted Indigenous motivations in the process.[30]

Finally, Hyam Meyers represented a third probable force in the delegation. An urban trader, he may not have cared about land politics 300 kilometres north of his city. But he was said to have 'suffered by the Indian trade' and perhaps sought in a fresh connection to a few individual Mohawks some kind of inside deal that would circumvent both imperial and Indigenous officials.[31] All three factors were more likely to have figured in the rationale behind the quartet's mission than the little-tested practice of Indigenous exhibitionism.

Whatever its origins, the mission started to go terribly wrong upon arrival in Britain. Just as Timberlake had faced in 1762, unheralded envoys from the colonies after the Seven Years War were no longer guaranteed an immediate royal audience. With no official sanction – and perhaps even with some official forewarning against them – the party found itself blocked from the desired power source. In consequence, the partnership between Blessius and Meyers crumbled. At this point, Blessius absconded with 'one of the Mohawks' to Amsterdam – perhaps to a German-speaking contact there.[32] Meyers, in fury, pursued him, taking the other Mohawk along too. In his deposition to the House of Lords, Meyers related how, after many months, he managed to find Blessius 'but, notwithstanding all his endeavours, could not get [the accompanying Mohawk] again'. At this point, Meyers appealed to the British Ambassador at the Hague, demonstrating a telling knowledge of how the British State still viewed chaperoned Indigenous Americans. Ambassador Joseph Yorke had more success with Blessius, rescued his accompanying Mohawk, and ordered Meyers to take both Sychnecta and Trosoghroga back to America, via Britain. For assistance, 'he would write on [my] behalf', Meyers recounted, 'to the Secretary of State, to whom he directed [me] to apply upon ... arrival in England'.[33]

Meyers confessed later to the Lords that, for some reason, once back in Britain he 'made no application ... to the Secretary of State'. Instead, he decided to try to recoup his unexpected expenses by 'shewing' the Mohawks for money. The circumstances of this exhibition appear, then, to be unplanned, and conducted under a sense of impulsive subterfuge and knowing illegality.

Granted, Meyers's decision was not so extraordinary as to be incomprehensible to others. The proprietor of the Sun Tavern, John Schuppe, clearly recognised the viability of his idea when he consented to let a room to Meyers for the showing, as did the patrons who made the venture worthwhile financially for at least seven days. But the speed with which the House of Lords commanded an explanation, as well as the plaintive quality of the testimonies given, suggests that Indigenous exhibiting was far from mainstream and widely understood to be a problem.

It was probably an agent of Ambassador Yorke who caught Meyers.[34] Yorke had already alerted his fellow peers in Parliament of his order to the colonist, and seems himself to have hired, or asked another peer to hire for him, someone to track down Meyers in London. Both acts underscore how concerned officials were to ensure satisfactory experiences among any potential allies. The plainness of the Lords' first resolution confirms it: *do not physically interfere with any Indians connected to British colonial claims; British settler lives may be at risk.*

The wording of the Lords' second resolution, however, requires further reflection. Its proclamation against the commercialisation of Indigenous Americans was not tied to obvious political ends. Instead, the Lords invoked, through a negative formulation, the necessity for seemly and 'human' behaviour for its own sake. Inklings of this kind of moral sentiment had arisen during the last Cherokee visit three years before, but it had not otherwise featured in the voluminous and diverse discussions about previous Indigenous delegations. Those discussions had offered commentaries on Britain's imperial position in broadly political terms – sometimes they were defensive; sometimes they were critical; but they always invoked the core economic, social or governmental fallout of ambitious incursion. Such discussions had accompanied, on the whole, a similarly political mode of hosting them: Britons may not always have been respectful of Indigenous envoys, considering some of the usages of savagery imposed upon them, but they did usually award them the standard protocols of state diplomacy. These included a meeting with the imperial sovereign and a general acknowledgement that envoys were not commodities. The focus of the Lords' second resolution, on the other hand, was not obviously political. It was more about personal propriety: *do not behave in unbecoming or inhuman ways to Indians because this is neither nice nor fair.*

What was at stake in this shift from a political register to a moral one? And what were its effects? The evidence from the scandal surrounding Sychnecta and Trosoghroga is not enough on its own to address these questions. The only solid remaining source on these travellers comes from the New York Governor, Cadwallader Colden, who confirmed that the British Government did, within the month, secure a return for the Mohawks. 'You have by this', Colden reflected to an associate, 'a strong instance of the regard the King and House of Lords have to the honour of the Mohawk Nation that they would not suffer any of them to have the disgrace of being exhibited as a public shew'.[35] Colden's remarks reiterated the still prevailing official line that focused on Indigenous satisfaction. Colonists in America were the least likely Britons to forget the strategic significance of Indigenous people for Empire.

The meaning of the difference between the first and second resolutions is better gleaned if we situate the Mohawk incident among some of the proceeding visits by Indigenous envoys to Britain. These visits went through two phases. For the rest of the 1700s, Indigenous Americans continued to travel to Britain to achieve redress for their grievances, but they faced less and less recognition from both officials and the public. This granted them some freedom from the imposition of the savage ideal, but it also reduced their access to effective power. Britons were not entirely done, though, with using Indigenous visitors as ciphers to debate the increasing complexity of their Empire. During these decades, Britons instead came to see another group of people from another region of the world as the perfect examples of Indigeneity.

The persistence of the political mode for thinking about Indigenous people, via circuitous means, at least forestalled much indulgence in Indigenous exhibition. This situation changed into the 1800s. As the scholar Sadiah Quereshi has noted, 'the nineteenth century witnessed significant changes in the scale and nature of [non-European] human displays'. This increase coincided with a broadening out of British understandings of who counted as Indigenous as well as more, if ineffective, murmurings about the legality and propriety of putting them 'on shew'.[36] The register of the Lords' second resolution had come to outweigh that of the first.

Indigenous arrivals, 1765–1800

At least a dozen more Indigenous American envoys arrived in Britain between 1765 and the splintering of Britain's Atlantic Empire in 1783.[37] Almost all of them came for the same reasons as had motivated their predecessors: they sought an audience with those ultimately responsible for British encroachments into their land. Barely any of them, however, secured a meeting at Whitehall. Two Narragansett brothers, Tobias and John Shattock, for instance, arrived in 1768 to plead land rectification from Rhode Islander intruders. Tobias died of smallpox in Britain, while John failed to gain attention from anyone. A Wampanoag man from Massachusetts, Simon Porridge, was luckier in that he managed to have his case read by the Privy Council in 1773, but no Crown reimbursements or adequate redress followed. A delegation of seven Wappinger Indians from around the Hudson's River sought the King's help over a land claim, yet achieved nothing. An Inuit woman called Mikak from far-eastern Canada came to protest the British removal of her people westward from their homes, but also gained little purchase with officials.

Each of these arrivals left some mark on private citizens – personal letters testify to a certain level of intrigue – but this was notably less than the effect earlier Indigenous visitors had engendered. It was also less obviously marked with a political tone. One observing gentleman noticed how Mikak liked to eat nothing but salmon; William Pitt's wife recorded that her five children were delighted to encounter the Wappinger at the seaside.[38] At least it can be noted that, for these dozen or so envoys, during this brief period, avaricious interests did not rush in where political ones had fallen away. There is little evidence to suggest any of the envoys were degraded into commodities, nor even that anyone worried that they might be.

There were exceptions, of course. Samson Occom, a Mohegan Evangelical convert, visited Britain for over a year in 1766–67, famously preaching to many Presbyterian congregations in order to raise funds for an Indian school on his homelands. But while Occom did reach many Dissenters, and did raise a lot of money that became consequential in the founding of Dartmouth College, his fame was more limited than many historians now assume. King George III refused to meet him, as was now becoming standard for a monarch who believed that recent British victories in America meant that imperial diplomacy was over. And because Occom's religious mission was so strident, the press barely considered him in either political or moral terms.[39] Mohawk Joseph Brant was another exception. He visited Britain twice, in 1775 and 1785, and stirred a high-profile response on both occasions as a noted and eloquent ally of loyalist forces during the American Revolution. But, rather like Occom, Brant was so strongly linked to another cause, in his case loyalism, that there was no chance he would be understood as either a political cipher or a spectacle-worthy freak.[40] Occom and Brant were so different from the majority of Indigenous visitors to Britain that their travels hardly disprove overall patterns.

Despite Britain's waning regard for Indigenous American arrivals, this did not denote the coincident abandonment of 'savagery' as a productive foil for discussions of Empire. Britons were, if anything, more divided over this issue between the 1760s and the 1780s than they had ever been.[41] Their simultaneous victory over other European empires in 1763 and the recognition of potential ruin through the conduct of a civil war across a sea spurred fiercer rather than tamer debates. But in these debates, the figure of the Indigenous American – so closely associated with the source of all British tension – lost its appeal as an idealised type. Fortunately for a British public still puzzling over the pros and cons of imperial growth, another kind of Indigenous visitor now came along to fit the image of all that apparently opposed an expansionist society. This was the visitor from the South Pacific, which the British State was then exploring as a solution to Atlantic problems.

When the first Pacific Islander reached London in 1774, he appeared to rehabilitate the concept of savagery for local political discourse. Mai from Ra'iatea near Tahiti – who had arrived via James Cook's second Pacific voyage on his own mission to reconnoitre British resources, and often known as Omai – was instantly deemed a 'savage' in the press.[42] He gained easy admission to the King and all manner of social elites. Most of all he inspired exactly the kind of vociferous debate about British destiny that had earlier found so much use for Indigenous American envoys. A popular pamphlet, for example, conjured Mai as a noble savage come to show up the failings of British imperialism. The pamphlet imagined him viewing London 'with all her pilfer'd wealth', won from imperial wars that 'butcher ... kill [and] ravage distant realms'.[43] The poet William Cowper, on the other hand, depicted Mai as 'rude [and] ignorant' who could not help but put into relief 'sweets tasted here', including a sense of British 'virtue' that was 'gentle, kind, / By culture tamed'.[44]

A similar, if fainter, strain of discourse characterised the visit of the Palau Islander Lebuu in 1784. This visitor had arrived aboard an East India Company vessel that had accidentally chanced on Palau but saw advantage in forging relations with the islanders. Lebuu occasioned less intense interest than had Mai but enough to foment one bestseller and a meditation by the renowned poet Samuel Taylor Coleridge. The bestseller, George Keate's *Account of the Pelew Islands*, depicted Lebuu favourably as a savage who yet sees all the superior benefits of supposedly non-savage imperial Britain. Keate presented him as a 'natural man' whose uncorrupted eyes could plainly identify the excellence of Britain's refined urban spaces and hard-won worldly knowledge.[45] Coleridge, on the other hand, saw Lebuu's 'savagery' as an indictment of Britain's society. He also depicted the visitor as a natural man, but thought his qualities highlighted (and were ultimately consumed by) Britain's 'intolerable ... corruption'.[46]

Neither Mai nor Lebuu ever faced formal exploitation (though undeniably, as with all previous Indigenous travellers, they suffered an intense public gaze). But, in retrospect, the most significant aspect of Lebuu's visit may be that he inspired one other kind of commentary in addition to political critique. Six months into his visit, Lebuu unfortunately died from smallpox at his host's house in Rotherhithe. The mode by which observers discussed this event was qualitatively different from that seen before. The presiding doctor wrote in his report that it gave him a lesson in 'patience and fortitude ... I shall never forget', that all who attended, maidservant and all, were overcome with tears, grief and a personal resolve to be better souls. A children's book based on Keate's *Account* also focused on the 'affecting' nature of this moment.[47] Back in 1734, a member of the Creek delegation had also died from smallpox, but no one then had remarked upon it in a sentimental vein or with any reference to personal behaviour. Narratives of Lebuu's death signalled a turn towards a more moral tone when discussing Indigenous travellers, one that centred self over state.

The topic that would most attract moralising and sentimental reflections in Britain from the 1790s was, of course, not Indigeneity but slavery. The correspondence between the abolitionist movement and the development of humanitarian discourse is well known. All the same, as many recent scholars have shown, the relationship between humanitarian rhetoric and the actual ending of slavery is far more fraught than was once believed.[48] So too the rise of a moralising and sentimental attitude towards Indigenous people in Britain produced some unexpected and unintended effects.

Indigenous people in Britain into the 1800s

After Lebuu, the vogue for critical embodied savagery faded from British history forever. Plenty of other contenders for the dubious title arrived after him, but none again provoked the kind of fundamental debate about what Britain was in fact doing, to itself and to others, by expanding into foreign lands. The first Aboriginal Australian from Britain's newest 'New World' colony arrived in 1793, but his reception was negligible. Pacific Islanders turned up in 1806, 1807 and 1808, but once more to little comment.[49] This downturn did not reflect mere boredom with a novelty. It revealed something crucial about the status of the Empire for Britons at home. After the loss of the American Revolution, as historian Linda Colley long ago noted, Britons forged a much more consciously patriotic and determined society. Where before some Britons 'had been embarrassed by the weight of empire', after the revolution 'many of those scruples and uncertainties were gone'.[50] Fellow scholar Christopher Bayly put it another way when he argued that Britons from the 1780s found the 'ideological will' to create a 'much more vigorous empire'.[51] Britons may have carried on debating the best ways of managing their Empire from this date – how much to depend on missionaries, for example, or what were the best models of governance – but they stopped wondering if they should or should not have one. In this crucial but often overlooked transformation, Britons duly lost their use for a category of radical otherness that embodied savagery had once seemed to represent.

At the same time that Empire became more acceptable (or more accepted as inevitable), the specificity of the idea of Indigeneity also lost traction. Newly confident about the rightness of their place in a global hierarchy, Britons grew less and less concerned about the exact relationship between themselves and the people their Empire troubled. In consequence, peoples subjected by other empires came to be included in the loose concept of Indigeneity as often as did those under British subjugation. For this reason, the arrival in Britain of the Khoekhoe woman Sara Baartman in 1810 fitted as well with the tradition of 'New World' Indigenous travel as it did with any lineage of African presence. Evidently not enslaved, Baartman was designated simply a 'tribal person' or person of 'another race'.[52] By the 1800s, examples of such figures were all starting to converge for the British.

Baartman came from lands bordering first Dutch, then British, colonies at the African Cape. Brought against her will by a freed black entrepreneur and a colonial white doctor, she found herself displayed for profit to British audiences on and off for four years. While it is clear that Baartman's bosses, unlike Meyers half a century before, always intended this fate for their charge, the plan was nonetheless something of a risk. Just as in 1765, there was still little proof that Britons would get away with such 'unbecoming and inhuman' behaviour. The doctor, Alexander Dunlop, showed some understanding of the potential problem by arranging for a private showing to some powerful Londoners before opening up the 'show' to the public. Dunlop's first advertisement for Baartman assured that 'the value of the exhibit has been fully proved, by the approbation of some of the first Rank and chief Literati of the kingdom'.[53] If true, some of these may have included lords who sat in Parliament.

Even so, Baartman's 'shewing' was not without contention. The first person Dunlop approached to help him create the show, William Bullock, refused to do so on the grounds that it 'would not meet the countenance of the public'.[54] Bullock was an astute master of public taste, running the most popular museum of the day in London. Eventually Dunlop did find a venue, and promoted his charge as the 'Hottentot Venus'. It appeared to be an immediate, if modest, success. Within a month, however, the abolitionist Zachary Macaulay heard of the show, paid money to view Baartman, and decided to make it his cause to rescue her. He appealed to the highest court in the land to see if Baartman's display contravened the Mansfield ruling against slavery within the British Isles. Macaulay sprinkled his application with injured cries against Baartman's 'subjection', the way she was being treated like 'a wild beast', and the fact that she was utterly 'helpless' before the brutish impulses of her 'keepers'.[55]

While the King's Bench deliberated, other Londoners joined Macaulay's moral outcry. One went to see Baartman but sighed at how 'they ill-use that poor creature! Good God! How very shocking!' Another reported to his brother that 'some of the papers have written about the impropriety of shewing a poor unfortunate stranger ... Yet nobody prevents it!'[56] The language that disparaged Baartman's display resembled to a remarkable extent that used in the Lords' second resolution of 1765. The critics denounced the idea of Indigenous spectacle, but none linked it to any wider British activity in Baartman's homelands. They defended her rights solely as an individual 'stranger', not as an agent in some larger imperial machine.

In the end, the King's Bench, unlike the House of Lords, did not feel empowered to wade beyond legalities into moralities. Legally, they ascertained that Baartman was given some of the profits from her display, through a contract, and so her display did not disturb Britain's slavery laws.[57] Unlike in 1765, British censure against Indigenous commodification did not terminate the event.

After Baartman, despite the threat of bad publicity from legal investigations – or maybe because of it – more and more showmen took the gamble that displaying Indigenous people would pay off. William Bullock, who had refused to host Baartman in the 1810s, came up with a quickly-celebrated show of three Sámi just one decade later. Bullock kept careful track of the public tolerance for such things. In 1813 he had written to the Prime Minister to seek advice on displaying the supposed head of seventeenth-century republican leader Oliver Cromwell, 'still intire with the flesh having been embalmed'.[58] Cromwell was no Indigene and presumably Bullock was asking about the political rather than ethical implications of displaying his remains. But the Prime Minister's reply was telling. He thought that 'strong objections ... would naturally arise to the exhibition of *any human* at a Public Museum'.[59] By 1822, however, the Prime Minister's instincts were wrong and Bullock's were right.

Bullock's show of Nordic life, replete with live reindeers, a Sámi man, a Sámi woman, and a Sámi child, was a massive success. It earned over £100 a day and attracted nearly 60,000 viewers. As with Baartman, the Sámi show raised some concerns. One journalist wondered if it was 'injudicious' for customers to feed the child sweets. Another hinted that the exhibition made the host's manners look a bit graceless.⁶⁰ But a consensus emerged more quickly than in 1810: the show's moral problems were more than compensated for by the 'very interesting' insight the show afforded Britons into a 'pure' race 'imperfectly known'.⁶¹

That same summer, former abolitionists were successfully galvanising the government to order a royal commission into European rule over Indigenous people in various hotspots of the world. They sought to investigate any signs of 'degradation' or 'brutal harshness' against Indigenous populations in the Cape Colony, Ceylon or Mauritius. The Commission of Eastern Inquiry of the 1820s, as historian Zoë Laidlaw has shown, helped spark a 'strident' decade of humanitarian activity.⁶² But this growing focus on protecting Indigenous people abroad failed to translate into any programmatic vigilance against Indigenous degradation at home. Because Britons no longer understood Indigenous people as being significant to the success of Empire, they no longer felt particularly sensitive to Indigenous arrivals on their own front step.

Entrepreneur George Catlin's exhibition of nine Ojibwe from in 1843 summarised the state of Indigenous exhibition in Britain in the early nineteenth century. After eight years spent with Indigenous Americans of various nations, Catlin was not the average London showman. Although deeply paternalistic and frankly pessimistic about Indigenous American culture, Catlin had been motivated from an early age to document and celebrate Indigenous life before, as he feared, it was assimilated entirely by settler colonialism. He had tried to stage a show in London of Indigenous American artefacts in 1840, but this had largely flopped. Catlin realised this was because the 'Vivants Indiennes' he included in the show were in fact just working-class British actors. Audiences wanted the real thing. By extraordinary fortune, he came across nine Ojibwe in Britain three years later, brought over by a young Canadian would-be showman. He substituted the fake with the genuine, and the show boomed.⁶³

As ever, amidst the mostly glowing reviews, there existed some criticism. Catlin addressed them directly in his memoir. 'Do you think it right, Sir', one audience member asked of him, 'to bring these poor ignorant people here to dance for money?' Another then apparently shouted, 'I think it is degrading to those poor people ... to be shown like wild beasts, for the purposes of making money'. Catlin dismissed the accusations. He explained how he was personally revolted by the idea of bringing Indigenous people over for show, but since these Indians were already here and since they shared some of the profits, the performance he created was completely different.⁶⁴ The huge profits and lasting impression of Catlin's Indian show indicated that most Britons felt the same way.

One of the giants of scholarship on British popular culture, Richard Altick, once mused that 'Catlin's charges proved to be the advance guard of a veritable invasion of [Indigenous exhibitees]'. The growing taste for displaying Indigenous arrivals after the 1850s, he thought, matched 'what was becoming a more and more openly and aggressively displayed aspect of the English character, its complacent assumption of racial supremacy'.[65] Like most scholars, Altick did not notice the humanitarian critique that had accompanied Indigenous exhibits from the late eighteenth to at least the mid-nineteenth centuries. Few scholars indeed have ever connected the growth of humanitarian discourse with the rise of Indigenous display, and certainly not with late-Victorian aggressive racism. But pondering the afterlife of the Lords' resolutions of 1765 suggests some disconcerting associations.

The 1760s witnessed the gradual development of the moralising tone of the Lords' second resolution when it came to discussing Indigenous visitors to Britain. From the 1800s, Britons often deployed the outright condemnation of the 1765 pronouncement in conjunction with Indigenous 'shewing'. Before the visit of Sychnecta and Trosoghroga, little evidence exists of public Indigenous exhibitionism at all and so neither the need for moralising or for condemnation. Earlier Indigenous visitors had faced plenty of damaging stereotypes, but the political utility of these idealised notions had precluded the visitors' degradation into commodities.

Humanitarian discourse may not have caused increased Indigenous exhibition, and certainly it is hard to draw a direct line to later full-blown racist aggression. But the changed tone is no doubt an effect of the same critical transformation in British imperial history. This was a transformation from an age that entertained radical debate about the fundamental principle of Empire to one that accepted it as inevitable. Where once Indigenous people from the edges of Britain's Empire had triggered division because they were so keenly recognised as a core part of an unsettled destiny, they came to signify not much at all in an Empire that was now taken for granted. In the place of a politicised notion of savagery, Indigeneity became a broad, exotic, but ultimately static category in British discourse. The suffering of Indigenous people became something that was personally affecting and sadly general, but mostly happened elsewhere. The gross commercialisation of such people into the 1800s could always raise some ire, but decreasingly in any way that inspired its prohibition.

Notes

1 *Gazetteer and New Daily Advertiser*, 4 March 1765, cited in William Cobbett, *The Parliamentary History of England, from the Earliest Period to the Year 1803*, vol. XVI (London, UK: T. C. Hansard, 1806–20), p. 50.
2 Cobbett, *The Parliamentary History of England*, pp. 16, 51.

3 This period saw a convergence of greater British activity in North America and greater everyday recognition, in Britain, of its significance. Insightful narratives of heightened British incursion range from Michael A. McDonnell, *Masters of Empire: Great Lakes Indians and the Making of America* (New York, NY: Farrar, Strauss, and Giroux, 2005) for the Great Lakes region to Tom Hatley, *The Dividing Paths: Cherokees and South Carolinians through the Era of Revolution* (Oxford, UK: Oxford University Press, 1995) for the southeast. The most influential history of increased British interest in imperial matters is Kathleen Wilson's *The Sense of the People: Politics, Culture and Imperialism in England, 1715–1785* (New York, NY: Cambridge University Press, 1995).

4 My definition of early humanitarianism derives from Thomas W. Laqueur, 'Bodies, Details, and the Humanitarian Narrative', in Lynn Hunt (ed.), *The New Cultural History* (Berkeley, CA: University of California Press, 1989), on its personal and othering nature; Michael Barnett, *Empire of Humanity: A History of Humanitarianism* (London, UK: Cornell University Press, 2011), on its extra-political nature; and Rob Skinner and Alan Lester, 'Humanitarianism and Empire': New Research Agendas', *Journal of Imperial and Commonwealth History* (2012), 40 (5), pp. 729–47, for clarifying its concern with distant strangers.

5 In this way, the chapter follows the lead of recent scholars who emphasise the paradox of increasing imperial violence running alongside the growth of humanitarianism: for example, Alan Lester and Fae Dussart, *Colonization and the Origins of Humanitarian Governance: Protecting Aborigines across the British Empire* (Cambridge, UK: Cambridge University Press, 2014), and the special issue edited by Penelope Edmonds and Anna Johnston, 'Empire, Humanitarianism and Violence in the Colonies', *The Journal of Colonialism and Colonial History* (2016), 17 (1). Unlike these scholars, I aim here to provide some sketch of the oft-neglected prehistory to this paradox as well as the way that it played out through the relatively small topic-lens of Indigenous spectacle in Britain.

6 For scholars on the paradox, see those cited in note 5, and especially Elizabeth Elbourne, 'Violence, Moral Imperialism and Colonial Borderlands, 1770s–1820s: Some Contradictions of Humanitarianism', *Journal of Colonialism and Colonial History* (2016), 17 (1), online. Salient commentators on eighteenth-century imperial discourse include Linda Colley, *Britons: Forging the Nation 1707–1837* (London, UK: Pimlico, 1994) and Christopher A. Bayly, *Imperial Meridian: The British Empire and the World 1780–1830* (London, UK: Longman, 1989), while an exemplary work on historical empathy is Zoë Laidlaw's 'Investigating Empire: Humanitarians, Reform and the Commission of Eastern Inquiry', *The Journal of Imperial and Commonwealth History* (2012), 40 (5), pp. 749–68 – each are discussed later in this chapter.

7 For definitions of Indigeneity, see Kate Fullagar and Michael A. McDonnell, 'Empire, Revolution, and Indigeneity', in their *Facing Empire: Indigenous Experiences in a Revolutionary Age* (Baltimore, MD: Johns Hopkins University Press, 2018), pp. 8–10; and Ravi de Costa, 'Fifty Years of Indigeneity: Legacies

and Possibilities', in Jane Lydon and Jane Carey (eds), *Indigenous Networks* (London, UK: Routledge, 2014), pp. 273–85. This chapter acknowledges that the word was almost entirely unused as a reference to people in the British eighteenth century, but after some recent works, especially Coll Thrush, *Indigenous London: Travellers to the Heart of Empire* (New Haven, CT: Yale University Press, 2016), 'Indigenous' appears the most useful and sensitive label at the current moment to describe the original inhabitants of Britain's settler colonies.

8 Richard Fabyan, *Great Chronicle of London* (1502), reproduced in David Quinn, *New American World: A Documentary History of North America to 1612*, vol. I (London, UK: Arno, 1979), p. 103.

9 Further explicated in Kate Fullagar, *The Savage Visit: New World Peoples and Popular Imperial Culture in Britain, 1710–1795* (Berkeley, CA: University of California Press, 2012), pp. 14–36. See also Peter Burke, 'America and the Rewriting of World History', in Karen O. Kupperman (ed.), *America in European Consciousness 1493–1750* (Chapel Hill, NC: University of North Carolina Press, 1995), pp. 33–51; and David Armitage, 'The New World in British Historical Thought', in Kupperman (ed.), *America in European Consciousness*, pp. 52, 61.

10 The four delegates were not, of course, kings, nor were all of them Iroquois (Haudenosaunee). One was a *sachem* (chief) of high status, but the other three were middling leaders. Three were Mohawks, who were then part of the Haudenosaunee confederacy, while the fourth was a Mohegan, which was a group only nominally under the thumb of the Haudenosaunee in 1710. Londoners preferred to simplify the details and elevate the reputation of their Indigenous guests in order to make them fit more neatly into idealised political discourse.

11 See *Spectator*, 27 April 1711; *Dawks's News Letter*, 29 April 1710; *Gray's Inn Journal*, 10 August 1710. The public reactions to this visit are more fully recounted in Fullagar, *The Savage Visit*, ch. 2; Richmond Bond, *Queen Anne's American Kings* (Oxford, UK: Oxford University Press, 1952); and Eric Hinderaker, 'The Four Indian Kings and the Imaginative Construction of the First British Empire', *William and Mary Quarterly*, 3rd Ser. (July 1996), 53, pp. 487–526.

12 Addison in *Spectator*, 19 May 1711; *The Four Indian Kings Garland in Two Parts* (London, UK: J. Baker, 1710).

13 As recounted, for example, in *Dawks's News Letter*, 22 April 1710 and 29 April 1710; *Dublin Intelligence*, 6 May 1710; *Evening Post*, 2–4 May 1710.

14 As explained by the Iroquois's colonist host to the Secretary of State: Vetch to Sunderland, 9 January 1710, Vetch Letter Book cited in Bond, *Queen Anne's*, p. 42.

15 Fullagar, *The Savage Visit*.

16 Steele in *Tatler*, 13 May 1711.

17 See *Daily Journal*, 12 August 1730; *Daily Courant*, 7 August 1730; *Daily Post*, 10 September 1730; *Grub Street Journal*, 10 September 1730; *Universal Spectator*, 12 September 1730. On this visit, also see Fullagar, *The Savage Visit*,

ch. 3, as well as Alden Vaughan, *Transatlantic Encounters: American Indians in Britain* (Cambridge, UK: Cambridge University Press, 2006), ch. 8.
18 *Fog's Weekly Journal*, 22 August 1730.
19 *Daily Post*, 10 September 1730.
20 See *Edinburgh Caledonian Mercury*, 18 August 1734; *London Magazine*, September 1734, p. 494; *Daily Journal*, 6 August 1734. For this visit, see also Julie-Anne Sweet, '"Bearing Feathers of an Eagle": Tomochichi's Trip to England', *Georgia Historical Quarterly* (2002), 87, pp. 339–71.
21 *Monthly Intelligencer*, August 1734, p. 447. *Tomo-Chi-Chi: An Ode*, reprinted in C. C. Jones, *Historical Sketch of Tomo-Chi-Chi* (Albany, NY: J. Munsell, 1868), pp. 59–63.
22 The most comprehensive survey of these arrivals is Vaughan, *Transatlantic Encounters*, which built on the pioneering account of Carolyn T. Foreman, *Indians Abroad 1493-1938* (Norman, OK: University of Oklahoma Press, 1943). For the best insight into the Indigenous experiences of these visits, see Thrush, *Indigenous London*.
23 *St James' Chronicle*, 31 July 1762. See also *London Chronicle*, 27 July 1762; *British Magazine*, 6 July 1762.
24 *London Chronicle*, 31 August 1762; *Public Register*, 20 July 1762. See also Kate Fullagar, *The Warrior, the Voyager, and the Artist: Three Lives in an Age of Empire* (New Haven, CT: Yale University Press, 2020), ch. 3.
25 See Henry Timberlake, *The Memoirs of Lieut. Henry Timberlake* (London, UK: J. Ridley etc., 1765), p. 117. The two-year war has since been called the Anglo-Cherokee War of 1760–61, a particularly gruesome theatre of the Seven Years War.
26 Timberlake, *Memoirs*, pp. 119–21.
27 *Lloyd's Evening Post*, 28 July 1762. For a cynical reading of this notice, see John Oliphant, 'The Cherokee Embassy to London, 1762', *Journal of Imperial and Commonwealth History* (1999), 27, p. 20.
28 George R. Hamell, 'Mohawks Abroad: The 1764 Amsterdam Etching of Sychnecta', in Chrisian C. Feest (ed.), *Indians and Europe* (Lincoln, NE: University of Nebraska Press, 1999), pp. 175–94.
29 Hamell, 'Mohawks Abroad', p. 182.
30 See William Johnson (Letter, 1764), in James Sullivan, *The Papers of William Johnson*, vol. IV (Albany, NY: SUNY Press, 1921), pp. 316–17. See also Vaughan, *Transatlantic Encounters*, pp. 182–3, and Hamell, 'Mohawks Abroad', p. 181.
31 Johnson in Sullivan, *The Papers of William Johnson*, vol. IV, p. 342.
32 Meyers's deposition in Cobbett, *The Parliamentary History of England*, vol. XVI, pp. 50–1.
33 Ibid.
34 Ibid.
35 Johnson in Sullivan, *The Papers of William Johnson*, vol. XI, p. 754.
36 Sadiah Qershi, *Peoples on Parade: Exhibitions, Empire, and Anthropology in Nineteenth-Century Britain* (Chicago, IL: University of Chicago Press, 2011).

37 See, for further details on those mentioned in this paragraph, Fullagar, *The Savage Visit*, pp. 113, 227 n. 12; and Vaughan, *Transatlantic Encounters*, pp. 179–32.
38 Letter from Earl of Bathurst to the Reverend Joshua Parry, 1769, quoted in A. Savours, 'Early Eskimo Visitors to Britain', *Geographical Magazine* (1963), 36 (6), pp. 336–43. See also M. P. Stopp, 'Eighteenth Century Labrador Inuit in England', *Arctic* (2009), 62 (1), pp. 45–64. Lady Chatham to E. Wilson, 29 July 1766, in E. G. Ashbourne, *Pitt: Some Chapters of his Life and Times* (London, UK: Longmans, 1898), p. 3.
39 Many historians cite Occom's description of George III, but this was only given while Occom was a spectator himself. The King refused a formal meeting: see Vaughan, *Transatlantic Encounters*, p. 198.
40 On Brant, see Thrush, *Indigenous London*, pp. 121–9.
41 For the uptick on imperial debate during this period see especially Wilson, *Sense of the People*, chs 4–5; Jack P. Greene, *Evaluating Empire and Confronting Colonialism in Eighteenth-Century Britain* (Cambridge, UK: Cambridge University Press, 2013), ch. 3; and Kate Fullagar, 'Popular Contests over Empire in the Eighteenth Century: The Extended Version', *History Australia* (2016), 13 (1), pp. 67–79.
42 *London Chronicle*, 19 July 1774 and 21 July 1774.
43 Anon., *An Historic Epistle from Omiah to the Queen of Otaheite* (London, UK: T. Evans, 1775), pp. 3, 11, 42–4.
44 William Cowper, *The Task, A Poem* (Boston, MA: WSB Store, 1833), pp. 23–4. (Originally published in 1785.)
45 George Keate, *An Account of the Pelew Islands* (Paris, France: J. J. Tourniesen, 1789), pp. 340–1, 342, 350. (Originally published in 1788.)
46 See citations and discussion in James C. McKusick, '"That Silent Sea": Coleridge, Lee Boo, and the Exploration of the South Pacific', *Wordsworth Circle* (1993), 24 (2), pp. 102–6, esp. 104.
47 Physician cited in Keate, *An Account*, 354–5; Anon., *The Interesting and Affecting History of Prince Lee Boo* (London, UK: Newbery, 1789).
48 See for examples Selwyn H. H. Carrington, *The Sugar Industry and the Abolition of the Slave Trade 1775–1810* (Gainesville, FA: University of Florida Press, 2002); Brown, *Moral Capital*; and Seymour Drescher, *Abolition: A History of Slavery and Antislavery* (New York, NY: Cambridge University Press, 2009).
49 For the Australian Bennelong, see Kate Fullagar, 'Bennelong in Britain', *Aboriginal History* (2009), 33, pp. 31–51. On the Islanders – Māori travellers Moehanga and Matara, and the Tahitian Tapioi – see Vincent O'Malley, *Haerenga: Early Māori Journeys Across the Globe* (Wellington, New Zealand: Bridget Williams Books, 2015) and Sujit Sivasundaram, *Nature and the Godly Empire* (Cambridge, UK: Cambridge University Press, 2005), pp. 110–11.
50 Colley, *Britons*, p. 145.
51 Bayly, *Imperial Meridian*, p. 99.

52 See Clifton Crais and Pamela Scully, *Sara Baartman and the Hottentot Venus* (Princeton, NJ: Princeton University Press, 2009), p. 83, citing both National Archives, King's Bench 1/36/4: Statement of Z. Macaulay, 17 October 1810 and Statement of W. Bullock, 21 November 1810.
53 Cited in Crais and Scully, *Sara Baartman*, p. 78.
54 National Archives, King's Bench 1/36/4: Statement of W. Bullock, 21 November 1810.
55 National Archives, King's Bench 1/36/4: Statement of Z. Macaulay, 17 October 1810.
56 John Kemble and Henry Grimston, cited in Crais and Scully, *Sara Baartman*, p. 93.
57 E. H. East, 'The Case of the Hottentot Venus', in *Reports of Cases Argued and Determined in the Court of King's Bench* (Hartford, CT: Hudson and Goodwin, 1816), pp. 195–6.
58 Cited in E. P. Alexander, 'William Bullock: Little-Remembered Museologist and Showman', *Curator* (1985), 28 (1), p. 124.
59 Cited in Alexander, 'William Bullock', p. 125, my italics.
60 *Literary Gazette*, 19 January 1822; *Times*, 21 January 1822. And see Richard Altick, *The Shows of London* (Cambridge, MA: Harvard University Press, 1978), p. 274.
61 *Literary Gazette*, 19 January 1822.
62 Laidlaw, 'Investigating Empire'.
63 See Altick, *Shows of London*, pp. 275–9.
64 George Catlin, *Catlin's Notes of Eight Years' Travels*, vol. I (London, UK: G. Catlin, 1848), pp. 153–5. See also Stephanie Pratt, 'Objects, Performance, and Ethnographic Spectacle', *Interventions* (2013), 15 (2), pp. 272–85.
65 Altick, *Shows of London*, p. 279.

3

Humanity amidst calamity: Humanitarian discourse in New South Wales, 1788–1830

Jillian Beard

In July 1791 the colony of New South Wales was in distress. Rations were short and the drought long. Convicts continued to work, despite evidence of starvation, but the rise in crime and petty theft led Governor Arthur Phillip (1738–1814) to chain the offending convicts together or have them wear an iron collar with protruding spikes to restrict their movement. This would have been the limit of their punishment, observes marine lieutenant Watkin Tench (1758–1833), if they had refrained from also stealing spears and fishing tackle from the local Indigenous peoples, an offence that they had been repeatedly warned about. If not for that, he claims, 'humanity would have been anxious to plead in their defence'.[1]

This account is one of many which Tench included in his two volumes related to his time in the colony: *A Narrative of the Expedition to Botany Bay* (1789) and *A Complete Account of the Settlement at Port Jackson* (1793). Tench was an educated man who had read the philosophers and historians of the period. Anticipating the interest the expedition would garner, and with the aim of both informing and entertaining his potential readers, he contracted with a London publisher to provide an account of it, before sailing for Botany Bay.[2] The first volume proved particularly popular, running to three English editions. It was also translated into French, Dutch German and Swedish for an interested European market. By the time the *Complete Account* was published in 1793, demand for details about New South Wales had ebbed, but Tench's work remained widely read.

In these volumes, Tench ponders the limits of humanity in the early years of the New South Wales colony, often making his evaluations by juxtaposing the conduct of his compatriots with the behaviour of the Indigenous peoples he interacted with. In the case of the convicts, Tench knew that their interference with Indigenous peoples' possessions disrupted efforts to enact the policy of conciliation Governor Phillip was commanded to pursue in the Instructions he received from the British Admiralty:

You are to endeavour by every possible means to open an Intercourse with the Savages Natives and to conciliate their affections, enjoining all Our Subjects to live in amity and kindness with them. And if any of Our Subjects shall wantonly destroy them, or give them any unnecessary Interruption in the exercise of their several occupations. It is our Will and Pleasure that you do cause such offenders to be brought to punishment according to the degree of the Offence. You will endeavour to procure an account of the Numbers inhabiting the Neighbourhood of the intended settlement and report your opinion to one of our Secretaries of State in what manner Our Intercourse with these people may be turned to the advantage of this country.[3]

Conciliation, and Governor Phillip in his performance of it, have been lauded as exceptional. Anthropologist and historian Inga Clendinnen credits him as a visionary in his willingness to understand cross-cultural issues and integrate Indigenous Australians into the emergent colony and society.[4] Others have gone so far as to label him a humanitarian in his handling of the relationship.[5] Such claims raise Phillip's stocks as a hero of Empire, but, as historian Claire McLisky has convincingly argued, applying this term to the late eighteenth century is anachronistic and unhelpful.[6] I argue that the false equivalence applied to conciliation and humanitarianism (and Phillip's performance of it) have obscured our understanding of perceptions of humanity in the earliest period of the colony. In this chapter I will argue that before the 1830s, when Britain was reforming 'everywhere and all at once',[7] those in the colony who concerned themselves with the idea of humanity explored its limits by observing the conduct of the Indigenous peoples they interacted with and comparing it with their own, paying particular attention to their emotional responses. If their conduct and emotions aligned with European norms, those Indigenous people were treated as exceptional – exemplars of the potential for those regarded as 'savage' to become 'civilised'.

This potential for 'improvement' was founded upon Enlightenment stadial theory that explained differences between peoples in terms of how they provided for themselves. In this schema, social groups passed through four stages from 'savage' hunting and gathering to pastoralism, before developing agricultural practices and then finally progressing to commercial society – the stage which became equated with 'civilisation'. While some in the colony looked for this potential for 'improvement' in the conduct of Indigenous people, many more construed their behaviour as problematic, reinforcing notions of the intractability of their 'savage' humanity. Examining Europeans' perceptions of Indigenous humanity in the colony before the 1830s reveals the fluidity of these judgements. It marks a time before institutionalised humanitarianism evaluated humanity not on the basis of individual conduct, but by the attainment of Christianisation and civilisation.

Understanding humanity

Recent scholarship has enlivened us to various conceptualisations of humanity and savagery as they were understood in the late eighteenth and early nineteenth centuries. In particular, the connections between Enlightenment thought and the work of naturalists, ethnographers, anthropologists and botanists in colonial contexts have been explored, revealing shifts in the definitions of humanity and the application of its cognate concepts.[8]

Historians working at the intersection of colonial and intellectual history have captured the ways in which these ideas evolved in colonial contexts and became integrated into Enlightenment discourses of humanity in Europe. Silvia Sebastiani has shown how 'the humanization of the orangutan went hand in hand with the animalisation of the savage' after advances in anatomical dissection prompted some to argue for the inclusion of the apes into the lower rungs of a hierarchy of humanity in order to facilitate the idea of their equivalence with slaves, enabling the justification of the use of unfree labour.[9] Gunlög Fur's work on the divergent approaches of Swedish naturalists Andreas Hesselius (1677–1733) and Pehr Kalm (1716–79), has identified that the trend towards using a taxonomic approach to impose order on naturalists' observations of Indigenous peoples evacuated those observations of their social elements, leading to non-Europeans being represented in a similar manner to those of flora and fauna. She identifies that these practices were part of a globalised network of knowledge creation that posited the diversity of humanity as a problem to be investigated and understood by way of 'observation, classification and taxonomy'.[10] Bruce Buchan and Linda Andersson-Burnett trace the contributions of naturalists to the development of new criteria for the categorisation of humanity. They argue that observable physical differences became racialised, leading to these new racial categories being reinscribed onto older ideas of savagery.[11] The work of these and other historians continues to challenge assumptions about the trajectory of conceptualisations of humanity across time and space.[12]

As part of the broader 'emotional turn' in historical enquiry that has been developing since the late twentieth century, historians of emotions have gleaned valuable insights into understandings of Indigenous peoples' humanity by considering colonial encounters through the lens of emotions. Jacqueline van Gent reminds us that colonial narratives often focused on the 'appropriateness' of Indigenous peoples' emotions and that the control of those emotions was also scrutinised and often perceived as deficient. She notes that this perception often resulted in Europeans characterising Indigenous peoples as child-like, immature or uncivilised.[13] In Susan Broomhall's examination of the Dutch East India Company's seventeenth-century encounters with Indigenous peoples along the western coastline of

Australia, then known to the Dutch as the South Land, she has convincingly shown how cross-cultural readings of emotion could be driven by commercial concerns and efforts to maintain European pride, rather than ethnographic observation. Nevertheless, these readings contributed to narratives in which Indigenous people were characterised as 'destructive and belligerent'.[14] Indigenous emotions historian Shino Konishi has shown how European explorers seeking to understand the Indigenous peoples they encountered in the Australian colonies in the eighteenth century read both the physiognomy and the countenance of Indigenous Australian men. She argues that the tone of their evaluations strongly correlated with the spirit of their first contact but evolved in line with the shifting dynamics of cross-cultural relations.[15] The work of these historians of emotion captures the impact that the expression, reading and understanding of emotions have had on shaping relations between Europeans and Indigenous Australians beyond the point of their first contact.

In the first part of this chapter I will also use the lens of emotion to consider observations in Tench's journal and analyse the ways in which he related his perceptions of Indigenous Australians' emotions to conceptions of their humanity. As an educated British officer who engaged regularly with the Indigenous peoples of the colony in a variety of circumstances, Tench's observations constitute a valuable resource to discern whether these evaluations changed over a sustained period of time. The latter part of the chapter also considers the ways in which readings of Indigenous Australians' emotions contributed to representations of their humanity. It does so by analysing how those representations were expressed in the colony's first newspaper, the *Sydney Gazette*, which commenced publication a little over a decade after Tench had departed. Through the *Gazette*'s pages we gain access to a variety of local perspectives that both align with and differ from those of distant metropolitan elites engaged in more scientific approaches to the question of humanity.[16]

Humanity in the colony

The distress of the colony that had so troubled Tench was relieved early in July 1791 when the arrival of the transport ship *Mary Anne* furnished the colony with supplies. But it was not the supplies that were foremost in Tench's mind when describing the *Mary Anne*'s arrival. Instead, he praises 'the effect of humanity and justice' on the wellbeing of the passengers. Only three of the 144 women on board the *Mary Anne* had died during the journey from England. The remainder had arrived in 'perfect health' and sang the praises of the Master, Munro, upon landing in Sydney. Tench adds to their praise, explaining that Munro's benevolent treatment of his human cargo should be widely known since 'the advocates of humanity are not yet become numerous: but those who practise its divine precepts, however humble and unnoticed be their station, ought not sink into obscurity, unrecorded and unpraised, with the vile monsters who deride misery and fatten on calamity'.[17]

Tench's reference to the survival rates on the successful voyage presents a deliberate comparison with the extensive loss of life on the tragic Second Fleet of 1789. Unlike the successful but expensive First Fleet, the Second Fleet had operated on a fixed-price per head basis, with the contract for transportation being awarded to the lowest bidder, regardless of the number of convicts who survived the voyage, or what physical state they were in when they arrived in the colony. In fact, in the spirit of 'economy', the Master was permitted to sell any remaining provisions at the end of the voyage. In conditions akin to the infamous middle passage of Atlantic slavery, the outcome was bleak. Of the approximately 1,000 prisoners who sailed from Portsmouth, 267 died en route, and another 150 or more died soon after disembarking in Sydney.[18] Tench's obvious disdain for those who engaged in such profitable, government-sanctioned misery and mortality raises questions about the means by which colonial actors judged themselves and others to be humane or 'advocates of humanity' at a time when the boundaries of humanity were not clearly defined.

Tench gives an account of the settlement at the time of his departure in December 1791 replete with tales of the progress of gardens and harvests and the burgeoning built environment that typify the concerns of the late eighteenth-century colonial project. But, as always, it was the people he pondered more deeply. He reflects on the behaviour of Boladaree, an Indigenous man who had regularly travelled with Tench and his companions, exploring the Hawkesbury region. Boladaree had 'prudently' fled the settlement, and all the people he knew, after his retaliatory spearing and wounding of a convict who had destroyed his canoe. Careful to place the assault in its broader context, Tench observed that 'if they sometimes injured us, to compensate they were often of signal benefit to those who needed their assistance'.[19] Willingness to render assistance would become a fundamental element of humanitarian discourse in the decades that followed. In the meantime, Tench's curation of anecdotes around this theme provides useful insights into some of the means by which British colonisers configured the idea of humanity at the close of the eighteenth century.

To illustrate the redeeming helpfulness of the Indigenous peoples he knew, Tench describes two episodes where they rendered assistance to the colonisers. In the first, Bennelong, the colony's primary intermediary, and his countrymen, witnessed a British boat capsizing on the harbour and swam out to save the crew. Not only did they prevent the drowning of the sailors, but they also returned them to shore, made them a fire, dried their clothes and prepared a meal for them, before escorting them, unharmed, back to Sydney.[20] In the second story, a soldier, lost and distressed, and a long way from the settlement, was fortunate enough to encounter some local Indigenous people who assured his passage home provided he was willing to surrender his weapon. The disoriented soldier did so with some reluctance and when he surrendered his weapon, the entire party of Indigenous people laid down their spears and escorted him unharmed back to the fringes of the settlement. At this point his weapon was returned to him, and Tench remarks, with an element of wonder, that 'they took their leave without asking for any remuneration, or even seeming to expect it', clearly distinguishing this approach from those who would expect payment for services rendered.[21]

The proximity of these anecdotes to Tench's remarks about those who would 'fatten on calamity' is instructive. The willingness shown by Indigenous people to risk their own lives to save Europeans, despite their inclination to steal or damage Indigenous peoples' possessions, is starkly juxtaposed against the selfish behaviour of the 'vile monsters' who 'fatten on calamity'. Readers are implicitly challenged to question the superiority of European morality and rationality as Tench's narrative attempts to make sense of the evidence that might prove otherwise.

Mixed emotions

Bennelong, a year after his capture in late 1789, was regarded as a vital intermediary – a man who had been quick to absorb and adhere to some of the manners and customs of the British people he interacted with. He had formed 'an unlikely friendship' with the governor, whom he addressed as *Beanna* (father).[22] Phillip had recently had a home built for him.[23] However, it was at this time, when relations between Bennelong and the British appeared to be at their best, that his conduct astonished them the most. In November 1790 Bennelong declared to the governor his intention to kill an Indigenous woman – a threat made all the more real since he brandished a hatchet and threatened to cut off her head. As Bennelong set off to find her, Governor Phillip and Judge Advocate David Collins (1756–1810) followed, along with a sergeant. Along the way, Bennelong spoke 'wildly and incoherently' of his 'fury and revenge' and he was relieved of the hatchet and offered a walking stick in its place. Undeterred, when he encountered the woman, Bennelong snatched up a 'sword of his country' and managed to inflict two severe wounds on her head before the British officers could intervene effectively. Phillip tried to both soothe and censure Bennelong. The sergeant threatened him with a musket. Tench records that it was all to no avail: 'he seemed dead to every passion but revenge; forgot his affection to his old friends; and, instead of complying with the request they made, furiously brandished his sword at the governor, and called aloud for his hatchet to dispatch the unhappy victim of his barbarity'.[24] Onlookers were bewildered to know the cause of Bennelong's 'inveterate inhumanity'. Eventually, Bennelong revealed that in a recent battle with the woman's father, she had joined her father in the assault. The humiliation had invoked the resentment of the young warrior.

After placing the injured woman under guard in hospital, the governor advised Bennelong that he would be shot if he harmed her. He was not dissuaded, and it was only the persistent resistance of the guards that finally defeated his attempts at further violence. A few days later the governor ordered Bennelong to be taken to see the woman he had threatened and assaulted to see 'if feelings of compassion towards an enemy, could be exerted by an Indian warrior'. It appears that after what Tench describes as a brief struggle, his resentment was ended, and he spoke to his countrywoman 'with kindness', expressing sorrow for his actions and promising future protection so tenderly as to raise the ire of his wife, Barangaroo, who had accompanied him on the visit.

The British had witnessed this type of violence in the colony before and had rarely interfered. The shock they registered at the incident did not relate to the violence as such, but the fact that with these actions Bennelong had departed from the norms they thought they had instilled in him. When Bennelong's action caused them to question his humanity, they used the opportunity to ascertain what feelings he might display beyond that moment. Having regressed to 'inveterate inhumanity' could he return to exhibiting the 'civilised' norms he had previously attained? Having shocked them once, he surprised them again. His 'inappropriate' violent resentment was quickly followed by entirely appropriate contrition, baffling Tench and other onlookers. The boundaries of Bennelong's humanity remained questionable.[25]

A year later Tench's views of the instability of the Indigenous peoples' emotions had not changed. He describes their behaviour as 'sudden and quick in quarrel', but adds, 'if their resentment be easily roused, their thirst of revenge is not implacable ... Their attachment and gratitude to those among us, whom they have professed to love, have always remained inviolable, *unless effaced by resentment*, from sudden provocation: then, like all other Indians, the impulse of the moment is alone regarded by them'.[26] Politesse, it seems, was possible, but remained precarious.

With or without feeling: the fluidity of humanity

More than a decade after Tench departed New South Wales, the colony's first newspaper was established. The accounts of cross-cultural contact expounded in the pages of the *Sydney Gazette* from March 1803 were more constrained by time, space and the interests of a colonial readership than Tench's journal had been. Nevertheless, the immediacy of their narratives provides insights into the ways in which colonial readings of Indigenous emotions were mediated to explicate humanity in the colony. The interest in these boundaries of humanity was a regular feature of the *Gazette*. An 1804 account describes how Yaranibi, an Indigenous man well known to the colonists, was speared by his countrymen for having 'inhumanely forsaken' his female companion, whom he left at a time of sickness, resulting in her 'grief and famine' and death. The punishment of Yaranibi in accordance with custom was described as 'particularly interesting to honour and to humanity'. The writer considered the act a credit to the 'feelings of a barbarous people'. The positive attribution of 'feelings' to a 'barbarous people' indicates how intrinsic to conceptions of humanity appropriate feelings were. The desire to exact retribution on Yaranibi was considered not only justified, but laudable, since it accorded with British notions of justice premised on what Indigenous historian Shino Konishi refers to as British 'presumptions of the brutal gender inequalities of "savage societies" and their own superior sense of chivalry, sexual allure and self-control'.[27]

While still considered barbarous, the assailants in the spearing are viewed as having acted *humanely*.[28] This bifurcated evaluation of Indigenous peoples' humanity was not unusual in the early nineteenth century, as the following examples also show. There was a variability in the assessments of Indigenous peoples' humanity that exceptionalised those whose emotional responses accorded with British expectations and values, while reinforcing appraisals of the majority of Indigenous society as lacking the appropriate feelings to meet the requirements of humanity.

This variability allowed for the enfolding of 'barbarity' and 'unfeelingness' into the most unlikely of circumstances. In May 1804, James Bevan was to be executed, having confessed to and been convicted of the rape of an eight-year-old Indigenous girl – a crime the newspaper reports repeatedly described as 'heinous'[29] and 'unpardonable'.[30] On his approach to the gallows for execution, Bevan declared that another suspect, who had given evidence at the trial, was also guilty. The *Gazette* reporter suspended judgement on Bevan's claim, leaving it to 'the Great Avenger of injured innocence' to decide, despite the fact that this might expose others in the colony to potential harm. Instead the writer focused on how 'the criminal appeared insensitive to the awfulness of his condition, and betrayed no evident anxiety as to his future state', suggesting that the lack of feeling on Bevan's part was caused by 'long reference to the society and an extraordinary habit of intimacy with the natives, [during which] he seemed to have imbibed their natural depravity of inclination and total want of human feeling'.[31] The concern for Bevan's soul is not unusual for the time. However, blaming Bevan's 'unfeeling' indifference to divine judgement on his association with Indigenous peoples reveals the degree to which appropriate feelings were considered markers of humanity, and how their 'inhumane' absence is conflated with the supposed lack of humanity of Indigenous Australians. The need to maintain a hierarchy of humanity that configured Europeans as superior, whatever their behaviour, is evident.

In an episode that underscores the exceptionalisation of those Indigenous peoples whose conduct appears to conform to European norms, readers of the *Gazette* in October 1804 are offered a glowing assessment of the character and humanity of Grewin, an elderly Aboriginal man from Mullett Island, on the Hawkesbury River. The *Speedwell*, a schooner that regularly plied the Hawkesbury, had run aground in a creek and, despite the efforts of the crew and onlookers, remained stuck fast. Having abandoned the schooner to find further assistance, the crew returned and were about to renew their salvage attempt when Grewin stepped in and cautioned them that the boat might contain 'a banditti of fugitive desperadoes'. He swam out to assess the situation and, finding only an acquaintance of his in distress, the signal was given for the safe return of the crew. For this act, Grewin is described as engaging in 'very humane, friendly, and precautionary conduct' that would 'reflect the highest credit to a polished member of civilized society ... from the contrast it affords to the manners of a race so strongly characterised *by the want of common feeling*' (emphasis added). The writer goes on to assure readers that, although Grewin's cautionary actions revealed all was well, this did not diminish him as 'a subject of admiration', and indicated that his friendship towards the crew and his concern for their property made him indignant at the thought that any should 'presume to menace their [Indigenous people's] property or safety'.[32]

Grewin was considered to have acted with appropriate 'feeling' in contrast to the generalised 'want of common feeling' ascribed to Indigenous peoples as a whole. This exceptionalisation operated as a means by which Indigenous peoples might be portrayed as capable of reaching European standards of 'feeling' and therefore humanity, while the generalisations (so often used for contextualising the exceptional) served to reinforce diminished versions of their humanity.

The connections between humanity and property also play out in an incident in December 1804 in which an Indigenous boy's boat was stolen by a group of settler's children, whom the *Gazette* categorises as delinquents.

Making off with the canoe, the 'mischievous' group held their chosen 'driver' aloft in the canoe, when they were set upon by the 'exasperated native' from whom they had stolen it, at which point the canoe bearers fled, causing their friend in the canoe to 'fall dangerously into the hands of an enemy'. 'Up flew the waddy', the journalist writes, noting that a single stroke might have killed the culprit, were it not for a 'certain something' that suspended the blow mid-air and spared him. That 'certain something' that curtailed the blow, the writer quizzically suggests, is 'perhaps humanity!' Having tentatively ascribed this quality to the Indigenous boy, the writer remarks that he sought no immediate justice and assumes that he 'left the duty of correction to those whose province nature has decreed it'.[33] The theft of Indigenous people's property, as has been shown elsewhere in this chapter, was considered problematic by those who thought it jeopardised the potential for conciliatory relations between colonists and the Indigenous inhabitants. Various colonial administrators recognised that such thefts resulted in retaliation that was not always visited directly upon the thief. This increased the chance of acts of random violence, which the authorities struggled to punish, given that the thefts transgressed British norms regarding the paramount importance of property. The restraint shown by the boy, in whose hands rested the capacity for mortal retaliation, failed to place him unreservedly in the ranks of humanity. Instead, in keeping with colonists' bifurcated assessment of Indigenous peoples' humanity, the writer reminds us that the Indigenous boy had not attained sufficient humanity to proceed with 'correction' through the established norms presided over by those who are 'naturally' capable of enforcing them – the settlers who understand that property is to be defended and that justice is a hallmark of 'civilisation'.

Indigenous children increasingly became a locus of attention with respect to conceptions of humanity. The 2 December 1804 edition of the *Gazette* suggested that the only way Indigenous peoples could achieve humanity was to fully reject their heritage. Detailing the experience of the 'first of the savage inhabitants of this colony introduced to civil society', the writer recounts how an Indigenous boy, who went by the name of James Bath, was 'adopted as a foundling' after both his parents were shot in a raid at Toongabbie. James was raised by a succession of male convicts and colonists, and according to the *Gazette* account, abhorred his origins and had an 'unconquerable aversion to all of his own colour'. As proof of the benefit of his upbringing, he was said to have undergone a 'total change of disposition ... as he was docile, grateful, and even affable; he took much pride in cleanliness of dress'.[34] Added to these advantages were the observations that he spoke only English and was a pious Christian firmly attached to the British, so that at his untimely death at sixteen 'it cannot be supposed that he lived friendless or died unregretted'. James Bath's 'transformation' from 'savage' to pious Christian is considered complete when he is simultaneously able to exhibit the refined feelings of docility, gratitude and affability, and *unfeeling* towards his ancestors, exemplifying historian Bronwen Douglas's assertion that conformity to European norms led to positive appraisals of Indigenous people's behaviour.[35]

Instilling and institutionalising humanity

During the eighteenth century, ideas about a person's capacity for feeling and ability to sympathise with the pain and suffering of others became intrinsic to the development of humanitarian discourses in Britain.[36] By the early nineteenth century, nascent humanitarian sentiment in the New South Wales colony focused on the wellbeing of settler children. The Female Orphan Institution opened in 1801 in response to Governor Philip Gidley King's (1758–1808) concerns about the welfare of young girls on the brink of 'ruin and prostitution'.[37] By the time Lachlan Macquarie (1762–1824) became governor in 1810, the Orphan Institution had enlarged and, in accordance with King's plans, Macquarie moved the Institution to Parramatta in 1818.

At the same time, concerns were also being raised as to how to go about 'humanely rescuing the natives from their deplorable state of barbarism'. The idea that educating Indigenous children might 'civilise' them was gathering momentum, but for at least one correspondent to the *Gazette*, in July 1810, this was a vain hope. Some Indigenous children had learnt to 'read, write, and converse with tolerable fluency' when they had been separated from their families and schooled by settlers, but the writer observed that a lack of curiosity and 'the wish of enquiry' hindered any further progress.[38] He adds that their failure to engage in agriculture or defend themselves against the weather, 'which they nevertheless acutely feel', by building a home reflected this lack.

This evaluation borrowed from stadial theories of progress and civilisation that posited that humanity moved through four historical stages of human societal development.[39] In the first, and supposedly most primitive and barbarous stage, hunter-gatherers lived a wholly opportunistic mode of existence, making no plans for their future wellbeing. Like the boy who felt the loss of his stolen canoe but failed to formally pursue justice, those who could feel their own deprivation, but failed to make an effort to remedy it, were thought to inhabit this stage of human progress. In her exposition of this period in New South Wales, historian Grace Karskens suggests that the colony was a place where all stages of stadial development jostled simultaneously, meaning there could be no 'distinctive history' of the Indigenous peoples there. In the colony, she suggests, they transcended particularities and peculiarities and 'simply fitted in with the grand historical narratives of European expansion'.[40]

It was expected that elevating Indigenous children to the next stage of this stadial hierarchy, where they would engage in pastoralism, would require some education. William Shelley, who had settled in Parramatta in 1814 after various ventures as a missionary and trader, speculated that previous attempts had failed because Indigenous children had not learnt the 'industrious habits' that would allow them to make a living after their schooling.[41] In a letter to Governor Macquarie in April 1814, Shelley proposed a public institution where Indigenous children would be schooled in religious education, reading and writing.[42] Beyond this, boys would be trained for manual labour in the mechanical arts and agriculture, and girls taught to pursue domestic skills, such as sewing, spinning and knitting.[43]

Macquarie agreed to Shelley's plan and made arrangements for an institution to be established near the Parramatta Church. In consultation with Shelley, Macquarie drafted fifteen rules and regulations for what became known as the Parramatta Native Institution. He encouraged the enrolment of the children, hosting a public conference and feast in December 1814, which was attended by sixty Indigenous adults, but resulted in just eight enrolments when the Institution officially opened in 1815.[44] Despite promises to grant land and farming tools to the families of the children who graduated,[45] few pupils attended diligently, and, as a result, the Institution closed in 1829.

Even before the closure of the Institution there were suggestions that more needed to be done to ameliorate the 'miserable and perishing condition' of the Indigenous people in the colony. In this letter to the *Gazette* of 20 May 1820 'Philanthropus', a regular contributor, writing under a pseudonym, appealed to the Christians in the colony to manifest their 'sympathy or tender compassion' for those that are 'men and brethren' that were 'suffering fellow-creatures, without habitation, without clothing, without food, without comfort, without hope, without God'. In an effort to follow Christian rhetoric with action Philanthropus implores the *Gazette*'s readers to consider:

> We have heard of a projected charitable design to promote the improvement of all the aborigines in these Settlements, by endeavouring to lead them to a knowledge of Christianity, and its benign influence and happy effects on mankind. But where now are its friends and supporters? Who among us will assist, by speech or beneficence, in the pious work of attempting to instruct and Christianize the sable tribes of New Holland?[46]

An influx of missionaries into the colony during the 1820s would attempt to execute this 'charitable design', and Indigenous peoples' emotional responses to religious overtures became yet another locus for the colonial gaze to scrutinise their humanity.

In September 1822 an 'interesting ceremony' facilitated one such evaluation. Dickey, the son of Bennelong (who had died in 1813 when his son was just ten years old), was baptised Thomas Walker Coke in the Wesleyan Methodist Chapel in Parramatta. The young minister, William Walker (1800–55), took the opportunity to relate to the gathering, the character of the young man he had befriended and converted and was now about to adopt.[47] Walker's 'judiciously guarded' remarks were thought to show just how suitably 'qualified the young person was, to be initiated into the visible Church of Christ'. If readers required further proof, they could be assured that 'The aboriginal displayed considerable feeling during the ceremony, and wept much'. While no remarks were made as to whether Dickey's tears were borne out of sadness or happiness, their plenitude appears sufficient to indicate that Thomas Walker Coke entered the ceremony with appropriate good faith. The novelty of a young Indigenous man undergoing such a ceremony, and the hope that it might be the first of many, is reflected in the journalist's acknowledgement that many of 'his brethren' attended and that the congregation was 'unusually large, were very attentive and highly interested'.[48] The account is pregnant with the question as to who exactly Dickey/Thomas's 'brethren' were – his flesh and blood relations, or those of the spiritual brotherhood that he had been baptised into.

No doubt there was some hope placed in the capacity of Bennelong's son to embrace the faith and act as an intermediary between the Church and his people, as his father had once done between the British and his countrymen in the colony. Instead, just a few short months later young Thomas's obituary described how the 'once poor friendless black boy amply compensated his master, friend and brother for the sedulous attention that was paid to his interest' and that he was baptised and honoured with the '*humanising* name of the immortal Dr. Coke'.[49] Having made the connection between the elevation of Indigenous peoples to humanity through their embrace of Christianity, the *Gazette* writer seizes the opportunity to make an appeal, the echoes of which would crescendo through the remainder of the century with the advent of more organised attempts at humanitarianism. The writer concludes the obituary by soliciting financial contributions, suggesting that if readers could sight a letter written by the young convert, they would understand that 'nought but circumscribed effort, arising from the absence of pecuniary resources', precludes the 'aborigine from the sweet enjoyments of civilization, and deprives him of the Heaven-born rights of Christianity'.[50] This call for funds, and their expenditure to bring 'humanity' and 'civilization' to the Indigenous peoples of New South Wales, would usher in an era of humanitarian effort, premised on readings of Indigenous emotions that continued to exceptionalise those whose 'feelings' accorded with British expectations and to render 'inhumane' the lives of those who did not.

The interplay of an array of late eighteenth- and early nineteenth-century discourses contributed to understandings of the humanity of the Indigenous peoples in the colony of New South Wales. Some were metropolitan, scientific and elite, relying on the accounts of returned travellers, the observations of the naturalist, the ethnographer, the botanist and the trader. Each rendered their estimation of these non-Europeans from a blend of reflections on interactions with them (either personal or related by other writers), the boundaries of their own life experience, the demands of their occupation or the paradigms of their emerging scientific disciplines. A significant body of scholarship continues to reveal the meaningful particularities of these encounters across the temporal and spatial dimensions of Britain's Empire.

This chapter adds to that scholarship by providing insights into how the calibration of Indigenous peoples' emotions against those of the settler colonial population informed understandings of their humanity in New South Wales before the 1830s, when more concerted and self-consciously humanitarian efforts began in earnest. From Tench's journal, written during the earliest 'conciliatory' period in the colony, we gain the sense that, in scrutinising the countenance and behaviour of the Indigenous peoples, Tench was also prompted to evaluate those of his own countrymen. Among them, he lamented those who would disrupt attempts at conciliation by purloining Indigenous property (his conception of property was limited, however, to the tools they used and the boats they made, it did not include the theft of their land), and he was disturbed by those who would for the sake of personal gain, 'fatten on calamity'. He offered his readers a contrast when recounting instances of Indigenous people's humanity – their willingness to put their own lives at risk to assist those who counted as friends and brethren, the grasping and the greedy.

While those excerpts of Tench's accounts might seem effusive in their praise of Indigenous humanity, there were equally moments where their humanity was called into question as Indigenous people defied the norms to which colonial administrators attempted to acculturate them. In their emotional responses, colonial agents like Tench encountered both the shared humanity of Indigenous peoples and their profound 'otherness'. This supposed inconsistency was repeated in emotional evaluations by other colonial actors.

From the pages of the colony's first newspaper, the difficulty of coming to a singular understanding of Indigenous humanity through encounters with their emotionality was writ large. When embodying what were reckoned to be appropriate emotional responses, individual Indigenous people could be recognised, and even lauded, for their humanity. Yet, these accounts would also be quick to exceptionalise this behaviour by applying generally negative stereotypes to Indigenous peoples as a whole. This bifurcation in understandings of humanity allowed for both the valorisation and the condemnation of Indigenous agency.

As attempts to harness this agency to Enlightenment ideas of progress and Christianity were made in the early nineteenth century, commentators were able to focus evaluations of Indigenous humanity onto emotional responses to those concepts. In the emergent educational and religious institutions colonists saw the potential for their own benevolent feelings and hopeful emotions to catalyse the 'sweet enjoyments of civilisation' in Indigenous lives. In the forty years since Tench had decried a dearth in the 'advocates of humanity' in New South Wales, they arrived – first in a trickle, and then in a steady stream, engaging variously in the 'politics of empathy'.[51] Conciliation and acculturation gave way to education and Christianisation at the hands of those who would come to be labelled as humanitarians.[52]

Notes

1 Watkin Tench, *A Complete Account of the Settlement at Port Jackson in New South Wales* (London, UK: G. Nicol and J. Sewell, 1793), p. 77.
2 Isabelle Merle, 'Watkin Tench's Fieldwork: The Journal of an "Ethnographer" in Port Jackson, 1788–1791', in Margaret Jolly, Serge Tcherkézoff and Darrell Tryon (eds), *Oceanic Encounters: Exchange, Desire, Violence* (Canberra, Australia: Australian National University Press), p. 203.
3 'Governor Phillip's Instructions', in F. Watson, *Historical Records of Australia* (hereafter *HRA*), 33 vols (Sydney, Australia: Library Committee of the Commonwealth Parliament, 1914), Series I, vol. I, p. 13.
4 Inga Clendinnen, *Dancing with Strangers* (Cambridge, UK: Cambridge University Press, 2005), p. 23.
5 Gary L. Sturgess, 'Commodore of the Fleet', *Sydney Journal* (2015), 5 (1), p. 31; J. H. Thomas, 'Close Encounters of a Different Kind: Arthur Phillip and the Early Opening of Australia', *Terra Incognitae* (2012), 44 (1), p. 51.
6 Claire McLisky, '"Due Observance of Justice, and the Protection of Their Rights": Philanthropy, Humanitarianism and Moral Purpose in the Aborigines Protection Society circa 1837 and Its Portrayal in Australian Historiography, 1833–2003', *Limina* (2005), 11 (1), p. 57.
7 Kate Boehme, Peter Mitchell and Alan Lester, 'Reforming Everywhere and All at Once: Transitioning to Free Labour across the British Empire, 1837–1838', *Comparative Studies in Society and History* (2018), 60 (3), pp. 688–718.
8 On the 'dramatic flux' of conceptualisations of humanity see Bronwen Douglas, 'In the Event: Indigenous Countersigns and the Ethnohistory of Voyaging', in Jolly, Tcherkézoff and Tryon (eds), *Oceanic Encounters*, p. 176.

9 Silvia Sebastiani, 'A "Monster with Human Visage": The Orangutan, Savagery and the Borders of Humanity in the Global Enlightenment', *History of the Human Sciences* (2019), 32 (4), p. 92.
10 Gunlög Fur, 'Different Ways of Seeing "Savagery": Two Nordic Travellers in 18th-Century North America', *History of the Human Sciences* (2019), 32 (4), pp. 43–62.
11 Bruce Buchan and Linda Andersson-Burnett, 'Knowing Savagery: Australia and the Anatomy of Race', *History of the Human Sciences* (2019), 32 (4), pp. 115–34.
12 See also Kate Fullagar and Michael McDonnell, *Facing Empire: Indigenous Experiences in a Revolutionary Age* (Baltimore, MD: Johns Hopkins University Press, 2018); Silvia Sebastiani, *The Scottish Enlightenment: Race, Gender and the Limits of Progress* (New York, NY: Palgrave Macmillan, 2013).
13 Jacqueline Van Gent, 'Rethinking Savagery: Slavery Experiences and the Role of Emotions in Oldenorp's Mission Ethnography', *History of the Human Sciences* (2019), 32 (4), p. 29.
14 Susan Broomhall, 'Emotional Encounters: Indigenous Peoples in the Dutch East India Company's Interactions with the South Lands', *Australian Historical Studies* (2014), 45 (3), p. 366.
15 Shino Konishi, *The Aboriginal Male in the Enlightenment World* (Abingdon, UK: Pickering & Chatto, 2012), p. 53.
16 These views, while varied in voice, should be considered in light of the monopoly the *Sydney Gazette* had on news until William Wentworth launched the *Australian* in 1821. For a more detailed discussion, see Melodee Beals, 'The Role of the *Sydney Gazette* in the Creation of Australia in the Scottish Public Sphere', in Catherine Freely and John Hinks (eds), *Historical Networks in the Book Trade* (Abingdon, UK: Routledge, 2017), pp. 148–70; Anna Johnston, *Paper War: Morality Print Culture and Power in Colonial New South Wales* (Perth, Australia: University of Western Australia Press, 2011), pp. 106–8.
17 Tench, *A Complete Account*, p. 92.
18 Ibid., p. 39.
19 Ibid., p. 91.
20 Ibid.
21 Ibid.
22 Keith Smith, 'Bennelong among His People', *Aboriginal History* (2009), 33, pp. 7–30.
23 Clendinnen, *Dancing with Strangers*, pp. 137–8.
24 Tench, *A Complete Account*, p. 61.
25 Ibid.
26 Ibid., p. 127.
27 Konishi, *The Aboriginal Male in the Enlightenment World*, p. 5.
28 *Sydney Gazette*, 16 Dec 1804, p. 4.
29 Ibid., 20 May 1804, p. 4.
30 Ibid., 27 May 1804, p. 2.
31 Ibid.

32 *Sydney Gazette*, 21 October 1804, p. 2.
33 Ibid., 23 December 1804, p. 2.
34 Ibid.
35 Douglas, 'In the Event', p. 179.
36 Karen Haltunnen, 'Humanitarianism and the Pornography of Pain in Anglo-American Culture', *American Historical Review* (1995), 100 (2), pp. 303–34.
37 John Ramsland, *Children of the Backlanes: Destitute and Neglected Children in Colonial New South Wales* (Sydney, Australia: New South Wales University Press, 1986), p. 5.
38 *Sydney Gazette*, 14 July 1810, p. 3.
39 John Pocock, *Barbarism and Religion: Volume 4, Barbarians, Savages and Empires* (Cambridge, UK: Cambridge University Press, 2005), pp. 41, 176.
40 Grace Karskens, *The Colony: A History of Early Sydney* (Crows Nest, UK: Allen and Unwin, 2009), p. 70. On the intellectual history of stadial theory, see Mark Hickford, '"Decidedly the Most Interesting Savages on the Globe": An Approach to the Intellectual History of Maori Property Rights, 1837–1853', *History of Political Thought* (2006), 27 (1), pp. 122–67.
41 Karen Laughton, 'Children and Empire: The Institutionalisation of Children and British Colonisation in New South Wales, 1750–1828' (PhD thesis, Griffith University, Brisbane, Australia, 2017), p. 144.
42 William Shelley, 'William Shelley to Governor Lachlan Macquarie', Enclosure No. 1, 8 April 1814, *HRA*, Series I, vol. VIII (Sydney, Australia: Library of the Committee of the Commonwealth Parliament, 1916), pp. 370–1.
43 Joanna Cruikshank, '"To Exercise Beneficial Influence over a Man": Marriage, Gender and the Native Institutions in Early Colonial Australia', in Amanda Barry-Hirst, Joanna Cruikshank, Andrew Brown-May and Patricia Grimshaw (eds), *Evangelists of Empire?: Missionaries in Colonial History* (Melbourne, Australia: eScholarship Research Centre, University of Melbourne, 2008), p. 116.
44 Laughton, 'Children and Empire', p. 146.
45 'Proclamation', 8 June 1816, *HRA*, Series I, vol. IX (Sydney, Australia: Library of the Committee of the Commonwealth Parliament, 1917), p. 144.
46 *Sydney Gazette*, 20 May 1820, p. 4.
47 Meredith Lake, *The Bible in Australia* (Sydney, Australia: University of New South Wales Press, 2018), p. 49.
48 *Sydney Gazette*, 27 September 1822, p. 2.
49 Ibid., 6 February 1823, p. 2 (my italics).
50 Ibid.
51 Jane Lydon, *Imperial Emotions: The Politics of Empathy Across the British Empire* (Cambridge, UK: Cambridge University Press, 2020).
52 Jillian Beard, 'Conciliation at the Margins and Peripheries of British Empire: 1788–1815', in M. Gillespie, P. LaPlace and M. Savaric (eds), *Marges et périphéries dans les payes de langue anglaise* (Paris, France: L'Hartmann, 2014), pp. 215–25.

4

'Nor do they harbour vermin': Material culture approaches to exploring humanitarian exchanges

Amanda B. Moniz

Conditions were intolerable in New York Hospital's upper wards at the beginning of the nineteenth century. Scraps of food were strewn around and 'dirty cups' piled up. The 'beds and bedding [were] in a very filthy state', charged attending physician David Hosack, because of the nurses' 'gross neglect' in cleaning up the 'discharges and excrements of the patients'. Hosack's disgust is still palpable in the report he submitted to the governors in June 1805, and he spent only several hours each week in the wards.[1] The hospital's records do not say what the nursing staff or patients thought or felt about the state of the space they worked in every day, or lived in, often for months at a time. Yet exploring the doctors' and New York Hospital governors' views on the beds and bedding in the wards offers insights into nurses' attitudes to care-work across lines of disease and race. It also offers hints of patients' bodily experiences in the individual space assigned them for their care in this overcrowded charitable institution. Moreover, examining the mundane, essential material objects of patient care illuminates how New Yorkers' relationships across the wide Atlantic and within the hospital's confined spaces intersected either to advance or hinder the institution's humane mission. Because hospitals were prominent philanthropic institutions during the Age of Benevolence (1750–1850), they are key sites for the study of transnational humanitarianism. They provided contemporaries with experience collaborating with far-flung associates to develop practices, including bureaucratic control, bodily supervision, human-subject research, logistical management, fundraising and sentimental storytelling critical in the expansion of philanthropy's reach. The Atlantic material community that underlay hospitals' capacity to develop humanitarian expertise touched everyone within these complex institutions without, however, fostering a similarly inclusive imagined community of sympathy.[2]

Historians have long studied the economic, political, intellectual and emotional dimensions of colonial and early-national Americans' humanitarianism in transatlantic and transnational contexts, but have generally overlooked the material culture of this philanthropic activity.[3] By contrast, the managers of eighteenth- and nineteenth-century charities paid a great deal of attention to the objects they needed to operate their institutions. They regularly discussed beds and bedding, medical supplies, books, garments and much more. Focusing on these objects tells stories both about the expansive international trade networks that helped supply charitable institutions and about the limits of managers' power to shape the lives of their putative beneficiaries, as the managers of New York Hospital discovered. In the early 1800s, the managers, influenced by the latest European practice, imported up-to-date hygienic iron bedsteads and new bedding from Britain. This port city hospital served a heterogeneous population, including many foreign immigrants, African-Americans and sojourning mariners, and its patient population lent credence to the managers' proclaimed intention of providing 'Charity … to All'.[4] Conflicts between doctors and nurses over the cleanliness of beds and bedding in venereal disease and African-American wards, however, reveal the lack of control managers and doctors had over patients' lives on a day-to-day basis.

Material culture analysis and the historiography of philanthropy

Relationships structured by gifts define philanthropy. The gifts donors make to institutions are often, although certainly not always, financial, but for charitable institutions to pursue benevolent agendas requires an enormous range of objects. In other words, organised philanthropy takes material form when it moves from idea to program. Meanwhile, charities routinely attract and laud supporters by proffering all manner of goods – such as tote bags, mugs, umbrellas and more – in return for donations.

So fundamental is the connection between philanthropy and objects that the field of material culture has roots in the debate conducted by twentieth-century scholars Bronislaw Malinowski and Marcel Mauss in their studies of gift relationships.[5] They probed the way in which people in various societies, Pacific Islands in Malinowski's work and a range of 'archaic' societies such as ancient Rome and early twentieth-century Melanesia in Mauss's analysis, cultivated status, displayed power and structured social bonds through the exchange of objects and the attendant performative practices in gift relations. In spite of that connection, scholarship on American giving has not paid much attention to the stuff of philanthropy. The social control approach that long reigned in the historiography of humanitarianism distracted scholars from the material focus in the study of gift-giving. Historians in that influential school examined the way rising classes in the Anglo-American world used their charitable activity to establish class identity and discipline, more or less overtly, the lower sorts into the pliant workers sought by industrial capitalists.[6] Historians in the social control vein have explored ceremonial displays of philanthropic power and the social relations developed through gifts of time, money and moral concern. Yet their emphasis has been on benevolent activists' aims and attitudes rather than the material objects through which philanthropy's relationships were experienced or challenged. More recently, historically oriented scholars, including Philippa Koch and Hillary Kaell, have begun turning their attention to the material culture of religious philanthropy. Their interest has been largely in the objects, such as medicines branded by a charitable enterprise, and mite-boxes used for collecting funds for missionary work, that help donors imagine and feel themselves to be part of far-flung communities of faith. Likewise, historian Hannah Robb has examined poor purses used for dispensing alms, and through the wearing of which early-modern Englishwomen displayed their generosity and piety.[7] Less attention has been devoted to the objects employed in charitable institutions' day-to-day programmatic work.

Charities' minutes as a source

While historians of philanthropy have paid relatively little attention to material culture, quite the opposite has been true for people active in benevolent institutions. Charity leaders and their clients bought, managed, used and appropriated all sorts of objects – medical equipment, furniture, cooking implements, apparel and much more – and the written sources from their institutions are rife with discussions of all this stuff. Charity meeting minutes are especially rich sources for exploring the stories of the goods crucial to the workings, or failings, of philanthropy. Month after month, charity leaders and staff considered their material needs; made decisions about what to purchase, from whom and at what price; kept track of those orders; and discussed any problems with equipment or supplies – and then recorded all of this information of humanitarianism as a day-to-day, tangible operation.

The practice of keeping minutes, those essential sources for exploring philanthropy's material culture, grew with the development of associational life in the eighteenth century. As middling white men on both sides of the Atlantic founded a huge range of voluntary organisations to pursue their priorities, they carefully established protocols for managing their institutions.[8] Minuting meetings was one of those. Early in the creation of a new voluntary association, its leaders typically decided, often with a formal vote, to buy books for recording 'the proceedings of each Meeting'. It fell to the secretary to 'take Minutes' in a rough form during the meeting and then, before the next meeting, to 'transcribe the same into the book assigned for that purpose'. The business of subsequent meetings depended on the accurate record of previous discussions.[9] Secretaries entered details, such as the time, place and attendance of meetings, and summarised discussions of all the matters that came before the managers, from high-level programmatic questions to sometimes difficult personnel and facilities issues, to routine orders for goods and services, to the ever-important concerns about raising and spending money that undergirded all their plans.

As sources, minutes both obscure and reveal. Terse notes hide the details of sensitive problems, as did the Philadelphia Dispensary secretary's entry in April 1791 on the sudden departure of the charity's apothecary for 'very reproachful behavior'.[10] Yet, in spite of the ways bland bureaucratic minuting could suppress, potentially forever, the exposure of difficult situations, these records illuminate the messy realities of humanitarian activity through their comprehensive chronicling of both the significant and the ordinary. These records bare divergences between organisations' stated policies and their actual practices, as a 1797 New York Hospital minute about two African-American patients showed. Although the hospital's rules called for patients to be discharged once they had recovered, the managers found that 'John Johnson a black man both legs off and Joseph also a black man one leg off & both Cured are Still remaining in the Hospital'. Staff, perhaps concerned about the men's welfare, had evidently violated policy and continued housing them after the hospital could no longer provide medical care. When the managers learned of the situation, the minutes show, they too allowed Johnson and Joseph to remain while a committee tried to arrange for the men's admission to the almshouse.[11] Charities' printed materials, such as annual reports, conveyed the stated rules. Minutes offer insight into what actually happened.

While minutes shed light on the goings-on in charitable institutions generally, it is often with issues around objects that these sources are most revealing. In the case of the Philadelphia Dispensary, repeated references in the minutes to glass vials tell a story of the conflicting priorities of managers and patients of the charity. Established in 1786, the dispensary was a charity providing free outpatient medical care to working people. Patients received their medicines in custom-made glass vials that had the words 'Philadelphia Dispensary' on them. After finishing the medicine, patients were supposed to return the vials. Instead, the patients often sold the containers, to the consternation of the managers, who saw working Philadelphians' appropriation of the goods as a drain on the charity's funds.[12] Managers' and patients' different expectations about the disposition of the vials highlights their different expectations about the dispensary's purpose. The managers saw providing medical care to the working poor as a way to preserve the health and lives of breadwinners and thereby prevent families from sliding deeper into poverty. The charity, as they saw it, protected both families and public resources.[13] The patients may well have valued the access to health care. They also found in the vials a way to make some money and, evidently, to gain a modicum more control over their own lives. Not directly, but through the managers' complaints about the disappearing vials, the patients help us understand how they found the dispensary useful in their survival strategies.[14] Like their counterparts in Philadelphia, the managers and elite doctors leading New York Hospital would complain about social inferiors' inadequate care for essential items. Their frustration shows the limit of their power in a complex charitable institution where the successful realisation of its stated goals required leaders, donors, staff and beneficiaries to share common understandings of equipment and supplies necessary to its operations.

Atlantic world connections at New York Hospital

New York Hospital's origins lie in the transatlantic community of doctors that had been nurtured by the British Empire. Before American independence, young American men pursuing university medical education went abroad, typically to Edinburgh, for their doctors' degrees. They developed relationships with other members of the republic of medicine from the British Isles, North America, the West Indies and Europe, and they often maintained these relationships over their careers. American doctors also became familiar with the latest developments in medicine and medical philanthropy across the Atlantic, and they increasingly contributed to those conversations. Through participation in this strong medical network, New York doctors in 1769 instigated the founding of New York Hospital. A charity and teaching institution, it was the city's first stand-alone hospital and second only to the hospital within the almshouse. Under the leadership of merchants and city officials, New York Hospital was chartered in 1771. The Revolutionary War (1776–83) disrupted the work of setting up the hospital, but finally, in early 1791, New York Hospital admitted patients and began operations.[15]

During its first decades, the strong transatlantic connections New Yorkers had both before and after the Revolution shaped much about the hospital, from the architecture and the patient population to resources for caring for the patients. The building's design had been based on plans of British hospitals, with the information coming to New York through American and British collegial relationships. Funds too came from overseas. In the early years, governors solicited donations for the hospital from British, Irish and Caribbean business associates. Commercial ties not only contributed to fundraising, but also, and to a much greater extent, shaped the hospital's patient population and the governors' understanding of the hospital's value. By caring for New Yorkers, American mariners and other 'distressed Strangers', the hospital, they believed, 'contribute[d] to the prosperity' of the port city and, as a result, the whole state. Indeed, the patient population reflected the city's position as a thriving commercial port. About half the patients were foreign-born, with Irish and British predominating, but patients also hailed from across Europe, the West Indies and occasionally Asia. Medicine, medical books and journals, and other supplies necessary for tending to the hospital's diverse patients also sometimes came from overseas.[16]

Beds and bedding, patient care and the work of caring

Among the supplies that were fundamental to patient care were beds and bedding. The Hospital, of course, provided medical services thanks to the skills of a full roster of doctors. The city's 'eminent' physicians and surgeons served as attending doctors '*gratis*' on a rotating basis, although the doctors earned fees from the medical students they taught at the hospital. Each of the attending physicians and surgeons visited, or was supposed to visit, several times per week. In addition, each year the institution appointed an apothecary, house physician and house surgeon, typically young men starting out in their professions, who 'resided constantly' at the hospital, with room and board their compensation.[17] The doctors examined patients, prescribed medicines, which were dispensed by the apothecary, and performed surgeries. For much of patients' stays, though, they were convalescing. In addition, the charity periodically housed some destitute patients after they had recovered. The rules did not allow patients to stay beyond when they could benefit from medical care, but, as they did with John Johnson and Joseph, the pragmatic governors and staff typically tolerated the situation until they could find other institutions to take distressed individuals. So, for much of patients' time at the hospital, their experience of care was having a bed to sleep in, food to eat and shelter. Patients did not simply lie in bed all day. They might go out during the day, but were expected to be in bed by 'Ten O'Clock at Night'. Those who were healthy enough were expected to assist with care work, such as nursing other patients, and with chores, including washing and ironing linens and cleaning the rooms, as directed by the matron or steward. Nonetheless, patients spent much time in bed, and beds and bedding were central to their experience of care and comfort.[18]

Doctors' expectations about patient care reflected developments both in beds as a social tool and in comfort as a cultural ideal. In the centuries before the establishment of New York Hospital, the function of beds had changed in the European and then American world. In the late Renaissance era, elite Europeans socialised in bedchambers, and beds were designed for that use, with space for seating around the mattress. Over the next century, the design of beds changed as Europeans came to think of sleep as key to preventing disease. Rather than being open and suitable for entertaining, beds were enclosed with curtains to promote, as contemporaries saw it, healthful sleeping conditions. Not only did the purpose of beds narrow over the early-modern period, but this piece of furniture also became more widespread, as the eighteenth-century consumer revolution brought more goods to more people and changed attitudes towards material surroundings. People in this era were increasingly likely to have beds in their homes, and as beds became common in homes, philanthropists came to see the furniture as important in the humane, healthful care of the unfortunate. That view reflected changes in the idea of comfort. Once a concept associated with a meaning similar to 'moral support', 'comfort' came to refer to physical well-being as Britons and Americans developed a language to explain the pursuit of their desires in the expanding consumer market. Later in the century, as a sign of the era's burgeoning moral sensibility, philanthropists embraced comfort as a priority for the objects of their concern.[19] New York Hospital's leaders shared that moral sentiment and noted in a 1794 fundraising appeal that from the hospital's founding 'comfortable lodging' was essential to patient care.[20]

As the hospital matured after its first, fledgling years in operation, the attending doctors turned their attention to beds and blankets. They first raised the issue of beds in 1796, when they recommended to the governing board that wooden bedsteads be replaced with metal ones. Although they responded positively, the governors seem not to have followed through on acquiring new furniture. Starting in 1805, the doctors gave sustained attention to the issue of bedsteads. The hospital's finances had improved, they noted in a formal report to the governors, and so the doctors felt they could now suggest improvements. Among various other issues, they recommended that the hospital not 'purchase any more wooden bedsteads'. The hospital should start by introducing iron bedsteads into the fever wards and other wards housing patients with contagious diseases. Moreover, the institution should switch to sacking bed-bottoms in place of the wooden bed-bottom. Over the years, doctors returned to the issue of bedsteads in their efforts to improve sanitary conditions. They also repeatedly emphasised the importance of clean bedding and clothes for promoting the patients' health.[21]

The doctors' views on the materials used for making bedsteads were shaped by their participation in transatlantic networks and reflected the latest thinking on hygiene. '[M]any European hospitals' used iron bedsteads, the doctors explained. After independence, and building on pre-revolutionary practices and networks, American medical men maintained strong ties to their overseas brethren. They went abroad for some medical training, corresponded with far-flung colleagues and circulated medical literature, including the reports of medical charities widely. Through all these channels, doctors kept abreast of developments elsewhere, and American doctors had corresponded with their European counterparts for some time on preventing the spread of infectious disease. Because iron bedsteads '[did] not retain dirt' and were 'not apt to retain infection', they were more sanitary and therefore preferable for contagious wards. Moreover, iron bedsteads, the doctors pointed out, did not 'harbour vermine [sic]' – namely, bedbugs – 'like wood' beds did.[22]

Bedbugs and fevers had each emerged as a significant concern as globalisation both changed ideas about bodily comfort and posed risks to public health. People of African descent, especially, faced great dangers to health, as Europeans, Americans and Africans built the deadly and debilitating transatlantic slave trade, and Europeans and white Americans created an economy exploiting the labour of enslaved people of African descent to produce the goods making life more comfortable for some. Not until late in the 1700s did significant numbers of white Britons and Americans focus on the afflictions caused by the slave trade.[23] Earlier in the century, white Britons noticed new threats to their own wellbeing, bedbugs included. As historian Lisa Sarasohn has explained, early-modern Englishmen and women were well familiar with bedbugs and took the tiny creatures in their stride. Attitudes changed with growing global connections, both exhilarating and disquieting in their effects. As Britain expanded its military and commercial reach, many English people not only boasted of national pre-eminence, but also came to believe in their bodily superiority over other peoples. Moreover, well-off English people now imagined bedbugs as foreign in origin. Starting in the early 1700s, enterprising Britons founded extermination businesses, while those with tighter wallets relied on do-it-yourself methods of bug eradication. If, as Sarasohn writes, 'bedbugs were a canary in the coalmine' for changing ideas of the body and the environment, they signalled the widespread concern with fever that emerged later in the century.

From around the mid-eighteenth century, doctors focused on the risk of fever, particularly in congregate institutions such as barracks, ships, workhouses, jails or cramped urban quarters, as they developed ideas about the impact of environmental conditions on health. Based on experienced doctors' recommendations, leaders of charitable hospitals designed or redesigned buildings to promote airflow and enhanced their cleaning regimen, and more. Many doctors and municipal leaders worried, too, about the potential for travellers or cargo to transmit infections. That concern was an old one, and lazarettos, or quarantine hospitals, were familiar Mediterranean institutions for preventing travellers from introducing disease, especially plague, to port cities. Building on these ideas, Britons and Americans in the late eighteenth and early nineteenth centuries, debated or established lazarettos or other quarantine practices as they sought to keep communities safe from imported diseases.[24]

As part of their increasing emphasis on public health conditions, doctors and others trained their attention on bed technology for institutional settings. As with various other innovative approaches to hygiene and welfare, Italy was a source of inspiration. Like other reformers in the era, English surgeon Samuel Sharp gathered ideas about eleemosynary institutions during his travels, and, in a 1767 book on his experience in Italy, he advocated that English hospitals follow the Italian example and adopt the use of metal bedsteads.[25] About two decades after Sharp's book was published, London furniture-maker Thomas Waldon developed a novel, vermin-free bedstead. Patented in 1785, Waldron's iron bedsteads were built using sliding metal fitments, instead of screws and nuts, to join parts. His method appealed to contemporaries because it eliminated, as they understood it, the spots where bedbugs dwelled.[26] Furniture-makers were not the only ones developing new, more sanitary bedsteads. Doctors too were inspired to improve bedsteads to lessen exposure to bedbugs, with Doctor John Redman Coxe of Philadelphia receiving a patent for his invention of a bedstead that reduced lodging options for the creatures.[27]

New York Hospital's doctors were familiar with the current trends in hygienic bed technology and believed that this up-to-date furniture would enhance patient care. But they knew also that, in spite of the advantages the bedsteads offered, budget would be a factor in acquiring them. Acknowledging that buying iron bedsteads would be expensive, the doctors pointed out to the cost-conscious governors that iron was more 'durable' than wood and would save money in the long run. While the governors declined for several years to invest in the expensive furniture, they acknowledged the advantages and eventually appointed a committee to procure them.[28]

Just as transatlantic networks shaped doctors' knowledge about the benefits of iron bedsteads, so too did international commerce shape the governors' management of the hospital, including their purchases of blankets and other hospital supplies. Blankets were one of the items the hospital bought most often. By 1810 the institution had around 200 patients at any time and with their bodily fluids soiling their bedding, blankets needed to be replaced often. Many of the hospital's governors were merchants, and they used their commercial knowledge to buy the goods the charity needed at the best prices possible, whether the items came from a local or overseas business. It fell periodically to merchant Gilbert Aspinwall to import blankets from England or Europe in lots of several hundred. The 250 blankets and twelve pieces of flannel he ordered in 1805 cost the hospital $352.94. New York merchants and their faraway associates made money from the hospital's and other charity spending, but merchants also sometimes declined to profit from supplying the charity. In 1811 the governors were pleased to find that a London merchant had filled an order for 300 blankets without charging a commission. Just as far-flung networks shaped charitable endeavours, philanthropy helped strengthen both local and overseas commercial relationships.[29]

Prominent attending doctors' and merchants' participation in transatlantic communities influenced decisions about who the hospital admitted, what it was furnished with, and more. But it was decisions by nurses and other staff in intimate, institutional quarters where care-work took place that affected patients' experience. Care-work was familiar to many women, but paid nursing in an institutional setting was a fairly new development in the United States and nursing itself as a profession was in its infancy in the early 1800s. Until the late eighteenth century, the British American colonies and the early United States had few congregate welfare institutions where women (or men) might find employment. In some places, such as colonial Massachusetts, which had a robust social safety net, women could work in their own home, caring for eligible sick or disabled strangers who boarded with host families compensated by the province's poor relief system. Women did much of the caregiving work, although married women lacked legal control over the money they earned from their labour. While authorities exercised some control over the work through the power of their purse, the women – and in some cases men – tending to the sick or disabled managed their own daily labour much as women doing piecework at home did.[30] In the late eighteenth and early nineteenth centuries, managers in institutions, such as the Philadelphia Almshouse, relied on both the pauper inmates and hired women to provide nursing, though they had some misgivings about both.

New York Hospital, likewise, had patients assisting with nursing as well as paid nurses. The hospital's hired nurses worked under the supervision of the hospital matron, who '[w]ith the consent' of a committee of governors, 'ha[d] full Liberty to employ or discharge' female staff.[31] Tending to patients and cleaning wards, beds and linens occupied the nurses' days. The hospital records shed little light on how the women experienced that work, with one exception that suggests how onerous their labour could be. In 1792, the year after the hospital had opened its doors to patients, the governors considered raising nurses' wages, but ultimately rejected the idea. One nurse, they determined, did merit extra pay. 'Eleanor Lock, one of the Nurses', they noted, 'had had, for several Months past, extraordinary Trouble', and so in recognition of her 'extraordinary Services', the board voted her a 'small Gratuity' of eight dollars.[32]

The governors' recognition of Lock's outstanding work was unusual. For their part, the doctors repeatedly criticised the nurses. Dr David Hosack was harshest in his 1805 denunciation of the state of patients' bedding. But over the years other governors and doctors also complained. '[T]he Nurses [are] seldom in the Wards at the hour of Medical attendance', one doctor reported, while another objected that 'the administration of remedies was neglected & that due attention was not given to the Condition of the Patients'.[33] In 1809 the members of the hospital's inspecting committee added details that illuminated at least part of the problem. The men identified four wards where the bedding was inadequately maintained and conditions were generally unsanitary. Two 'were Syphilitic', while the other two were 'black wards'. Unclean bedding had medical implications. '[I]ts influence on the air of the wards is so obvious',[34] wrote two governors. In an era when many believed miasmas caused disease, insalubrious air was considered dangerous to health. The upshot of the dirty bedding was that patients suffered in filth and the doctors avoided the wards – inevitably in the medical men's view because conditions were so offensive. As a result, the patients were denied adequate medical care as contemporary physicians saw it.[35]

To the doctors, the squalor in venereal and African-American wards betrayed the nurses' negligence and poor character, while for historians, it is but one chapter in a long, disturbing history of African-Americans' unequal access to medical care. The terrible conditions of the beds and bedding may also tell a story of conflict between the nurses and some or all their superiors at the hospital – the governors, doctors and matron. Scholars have long pointed to the breaking or taking of tools, machinery, supplies or food as means by which labourers, whether enslaved or not in bondage, resisted their masters.[36] Like their counterparts in business enterprises, staff in charitable institutions used objects to challenge maltreatment. Personnel at the Philadelphia Almshouse, historian Monique Bourque has argued, continually appropriated supplies to register their discontent.[37] The disorder at New York Hospital suggests that the nurses may have been exercising what little power they had to protest low pay for work they saw as undesirable. A major reason for the failures to keep the Black quarters properly, the governors' inspecting committee explained, was 'the difficulty in procuring nurses for the wards'.[38] Caring for venereal patients and, in a racist society, African-Americans may have bothered the evidently white nurses and made it harder to fill those positions. Beyond the challenges of finding staff for those wards, the nurses' pay was a persistent issue. On occasion, a nurse spoke up about it, as Johannah Winall did in 1805 when she wrote to the governors about her wages.[39] Similarly, both doctors and the committees of governors made the case from time to time for 'raising [nurses'] wages' and, relatedly, hiring more of them so that their workload was manageable. Higher wages for nurses, several of the governors noted, might 'induce persons of good character and sober habits to engage in that capacity – unfortunately, many of the Nurses in times past', they felt, 'having been of a different description'.[40] The records are unclear, but perhaps the governors eventually heeded their colleagues' advice and increased compensation. By the early 1810s, the doctors typically praised the nurses for being 'attentive to the wants of the Sick', with two women, Mrs Patterson and Mrs Campbell, commended in particular.[41] The Reverend Ezra Stiles Ely, who visited the hospital regularly between 1810 and 1813 to minister to patients, likewise approved of the nurses. The nurses and the physicians, he found, were 'ever-watchful'. 'Servants of colour', he therefore believed, were better off there than in their masters' home.[42]

The Bible, speech and sound at New York Hospital

Doctors interpreted patients' experiences through beds, blankets and the sights and smells they associated with them. For Ely, a different type of object, the Bible, led to oral and aural engagement with patients, including African-Americans. In addition to John Johnson and Joseph, patients in the Black wards included 'Richard Neal, a native of Delaware, aged twenty-eight years, who is blasted with the rheumatism', and J— J—, a man said to be thirty but who looked fifty. Another was a woman who, explained Reverend Ely, had been stabbed by her deranged husband. She did not, he added, cry out during the attack out of fear of the husband being executed while an 'impenitent sinner', though perhaps a concern about unequal justice explains her reticence.[43] Ely, or his assistant, orated, read to and talked with the almshouse residents and hospital patients, and found the unfortunates were listening. Focused on book, speech and sound, Ely observed and conveyed a more positive impression of the wards and the patients' experience in them.

Conclusion

As a minister and an author, Ely performed his benevolence. In person, he used a book as a prop, as he sought to bring the gospel to his hospital and almshouse audiences. In print, he used the Good Book as an avatar to win support from evangelical readers. Just as it was for Ely, the hospital was a site of a philanthropic performance for the governors, doctors, nurses and other paid staff, and patients. Leading the hospital, providing medical services for free, buying blankets from business associates and participating in conversations about the best furnishings to promote health allowed merchants and doctors to present their humanity to local and distant audiences. Referring to activity in a charitable institution as a performance does not diminish the hard work and dedication those men put into managing finances and overseeing operations, evaluating and treating patients, and ministering to distressed souls. Yet they also put effort into exhibiting their benevolence, not least because effective fundraising required (and continues to require) displays of humanity, probity and gratitude. Beyond burnishing their reputations and fundraising, acting on their philanthropy at a major port city institution, in conjunction with overseas associates, helped men in these networks achieve a goal among many in elite circles to expand their humanitarian reach. They provided charity locally in no small part thanks to their access to intellectual and material resources from far and wide. But for the governors, doctors and funders, successful achievement of the Hospital's goals also relied on nurses. The same material objects that allowed governors and doctors to display their humanity and expertise on an international stage exposed nurses to close contact with patients and their bodily discharges. In response, the nurses evidently sometimes refused to play their roles.

The conflicts over bedding reveal nurses' views, in spite of their silence in the records. The doctors' and governors' comments suggest that the nurses felt anxiety about or antipathy to syphilitic patients and African-Americans. But the foul state of the bedding in those wards also reveals something else. Here, in decisions about beds and bedding, all the various hospital players' concerns intersected: the governors with finances, management and hiring; the doctors with the latest medical developments and patient care; the nurses with their own demanding work and preferences; and the patients with their bodies and experiences. When they did intersect, the governors and doctors found their authority was limited. Exploring humanitarian expansion through bedsteads suggests the potential effectiveness of doctors' exchanges: the iron bedsteads were more hygienic and had the potential to improve patient care materially by lessening exposure to vermin and mitigating the spread of disease. Focusing on the bedding, however, shows the staff's power and the doctors' and governors' impotence. New York philanthropists' robust networks spanned the Atlantic, but could not necessarily reach the hospital wards.

Notes

1 Report by David Hosack on the state of the hospital during his tour as attending physician, New York Hospital Board of Governors' Meeting, 4 June 1805,

New York Hospital Minutes, vol. II, New York-Presbyterian-New York Weill Cornell Medical Center Archives (hereafter NYH Minutes). On the rules for attending physicians and surgeons, along with those for the house-physician and house-surgeon, see *A Brief Account of New-York Hospital* (New York, NY: n.p., 1804), p. 8. On David Hosack, see Victoria Johnson, *American Eden: David Hosack, Botany, and Medicine in the Garden of the Early Republic* (New York, NY: W. W. Norton, 2018) and Christine Chapman Robbins, *David Hosack, Citizen of New York* (Philadelphia, PA: American Philosophical Society, 1964).

2 On the development of a philanthropic hospital movement in the eighteenth century, see, for example, John Woodward, *To Do the Sick No Harm: The British Voluntary Hospital Movement to 1875* (London, UK: Routledge and Kegan Paul, 1974); Karen Sonneliter, *Charity Movements in Eighteenth-Century Ireland: Philanthropy and Improvement* (Woodbridge, Suffolk: Boydell and Brewer, 2016); Susan Lawrence, *Charitable Knowledge: Hospital Pupils and Practitioners in Eighteenth-Century London* (Cambridge, UK: Cambridge University Press, 1996); Roy Porter, 'The Gift Relation: Philanthropy and Provincial Hospitals in Eighteenth-Century England', in Lindsay Granshaw and Roy Porter (eds), *The Hospital in History* (London, UK: Routledge, 1989), pp. 149–78. For an exploration of the role of material culture in creating an imagined Atlantic community, see Zara Anishanslin, *Portrait of a Woman in Silk: Hidden Histories of the British Atlantic World* (New Haven, CT: Yale University Press, 2016).

3 The rich literature on this topic includes David Brion Davis, *The Problem of Slavery in the Age of Revolution, 1770–1823* (Ithaca, NY: Cornell University Press, 1975); Thomas L. Haskell, 'Capitalism and the Origins of the Humanitarian Sensibility, Parts 1 & 2', *American Historical Review* (1985), 90, pp. 339–61, 547–66; Christopher Leslie Brown, *Moral Capital: Foundations of British Abolitionism* (Chapel Hill, NC: Published for the Omohundro Institute for Early American History and Culture, Williamsburg, VA, by the University of North Carolina Press, 2006); Rachel Hope Cleves, *The Reign of Terror in America: Visions of Violence from Anti-Jacobinism to Antislavery* (Cambridge, UK: Cambridge University Press, 2009); Ashli White, 'The Dangers of Philanthropy', in Ashli White (ed.), *Encountering Revolution: Haiti and the Making of the Early American Republic* (Baltimore, MD: Johns Hopkins University Press, 2010); Margaret Abruzzo, *Polemical Pain: Slavery, Cruelty, and the Rise of Humanitarianism* (Baltimore, MD: Johns Hopkins University Press, 2011); Thomas W. Laqueur, 'Mourning, Pity, and the Work of Narrative in the Making of "Humanity"', in Richard Ashby Wilson and Richard D. Brown (eds), *Humanitarianism and Suffering: The Mobilization of Empathy* (Cambridge, UK: Cambridge University Press, 2009), pp. 31–57; Conrad Edick Wright, *The Transformation of Charity in Postrevolutionary New England* (Boston, MA: Northeastern University Press, 1992); Sarah Knott, *Sensibility and the American Revolution* (Chapel Hill, NC: Published for the Omohundro Institute of Early American History and Culture, Williamsburg,

VA, by the University of North Carolina Press, 2009); Emily Conroy-Krutz, *Christian Imperialism: Converting the World in the Early American Republic* (Ithaca, NY: Cornell University Press, 2015); Nicole K. Dressler, '"Enemies to Mankind": Convict Servitude, and Authority in the British Atlantic World', *Early American Studies* (2019), 17 (3), pp. 343–76.

4 New York Hospital, *Charity Extended to All. State of the New York Hospital for the Year 1797* (New York, NY: n.p., 1797).

5 Leonie Hannan and Sarah Longair, *History through Material Culture* (Manchester, UK: Manchester University Press, 2017), pp. 18–19; Bronislaw Malinowski, *Argonauts of the Western Pacific: An Account of Western Enterprise and Adventure in the Archipelagoes of the Melanesian New Guinea* (London, UK: Routledge, 1922); Marcel Mauss, *The Gift, Forms and Functions of Exchange in Archaic Societies* (Glencoe, IL: Free Press, 1954). On gift relationships, see also Natalie Zemon Davis, *The Gift in Sixteenth-Century France* (Madison, WI: University of Wisconsin Press, 2000).

6 Works exploring American philanthropy from a social control perspective include, among many others, John Alexander, *Render Them Submissive: Responses to Poverty in Philadelphia, 1760–1800* (Amherst, MA: University of Massachusetts Press, 1980); Davis, *The Problem of Slavery in the Age of Revolution*; Charles I. Foster, *An Errand of Mercy: The Evangelical United Front, 1790–1837* (Chapel Hill, NC: University of North Carolina Press, 1960); Clifford S. Griffin, *Their Brothers' Keepers: Moral Stewardship in the United States, 1800–1865* (New Brunswick, NJ: Rutgers University Press, 1960); David J. Rothman, *The Discovery of the Asylum: Social Order and Disorder in the New Republic* (Boston, MA: Little Brown, 1971). The famous debate among David Brion Davis, Thomas L. Haskell and John Ashworth over the self-interested class dimensions of the antislavery movement are collected in Thomas Bender, *The Antislavery Debate: Capitalism and Abolitionism as a Problem in Historical Interpretation* (Berkeley, CA: University of California Press, 1992). This scholarship was deeply influenced by Michel Foucault, *Discipline and Punish: The Birth of the Prison*, trans. Alan Sheridan (New York, NY: Vintage Books, 2nd edn, 1995).

7 Philippa Koch, 'Marketing Missions: Material Culture, Theological Convictions, and Empire in Eighteenth-Century Christian Philanthropy', *Religions* (2018), 9 (7), pp. 207–24; Hillary Kaell, 'Evangelist of Fragments: Doing Mite-Box Capitalism in the Late Nineteenth Century', *Church History* (March 2017), 86 (1), pp. 86–119; Hannah Robb, 'Purses and the Charitable Gift', *Journal of Social History* (2015), 49 (2), pp. 387–405. In addition to Koch's and Kaell's studies, works that explore the material culture of American philanthropy include Teresa A. Goddu, *Selling Antislavery: Abolition and Mass Media in Antebellum New York* (Philadelphia, PA: University of Pennsylvania Press, 2020); Beverly Gordon, *Bazaars and Fair Ladies: The History of the American Fundraising Fair* (Knoxville, TN: University of Tennessee Press, 1998). See also Anne M. Boylan, *Sunday School: The Formation of an American Institution, 1790–1880* (New Haven, CT: Yale University Press, 1988).

8 On the development of the voluntary association form and associated practices in the British Atlantic world, British American colonies, and early United States, see Peter Clark, *British Clubs and Societies, 1580–1800: The Origins of an Associational World* (Oxford, UK: Oxford University Press, 2000); Johann Neem, *Creating a Nation of Joiners: Democracy and Civil Society in Early National Massachusetts* (Cambridge, MA: Harvard University Press, 2008); Jessica Choppin Roney, *Governed by a Spirit of Opposition: The Origins of American Political Practice in Colonial Philadelphia* (Baltimore, MD: Johns Hopkins University Press, 2014); Kevin Butterfield, *The Making of Tocqueville's America: Law and Association in the Early United States* (Chicago, IL: University of Chicago Press, 2015).

9 New York Hospital Board of Governors' meetings, 24 July 1771; 2 June 1794, New York Hospital Minutes, vol. I.

10 Philadelphia Dispensary Managers' Meeting, 7 April 1791, Philadelphia Dispensary Minute Book 1786–1806, Pennsylvania Hospital Archives, Philadelphia.

11 NYH Board of Governors' Meeting, 2 May 1797, NYH Minutes, vol. I; on the African-American experience in eighteenth- and early nineteenth-century New York City, see Leslie Harris, *In the Shadow of Slavery: African Americans in New York City, 1626–1863* (Chicago, IL: University of Chicago Press, 2003); Shane White, *Somewhat More Independent: The End of Slavery in New York City, 1770–1810* (Athens, GA: University of Georgia Press, 1991).

12 Philadelphia Dispensary Managers' Meetings, 19 January 1789, 9 April 1804, Philadelphia Dispensary Minute Book 1786–1806. On the dispensary movement, see I. S. L. Loudon, 'The Origins and Growth of the Dispensary Movement in England', *Bulletin of the History of Medicine* (1981), 55, pp. 322–42; Robert Kilpatrick, '"Living in the Light": Dispensaries, Philanthropy and Medical Reform in Late Eighteenth-Century London', in Andrew Cunningham and Roger French (eds), *The Medical Enlightenment of the Eighteenth Century* (Cambridge, UK: Cambridge University Press, 1990); Charles E. Rosenberg, *Caring for the Working Man: The Rise and Fall of the Dispensary Movement* (New York, NY: Garland Publishing, 1989).

13 *Plan of the Philadelphia Dispensary for the Medical Relief of the Poor* (Philadelphia, PA: n.p., 1787), pp. 1–2.

14 An example of Philadelphia's working poor valuing the dispensary for the access it provided to medical care comes from Philadelphia's Mother Bethel Church's subscription to the charity. See Richard S. Newman, *Freedom's Prophet: Bishop Richard Allen, the AME Church, and the Black Founding Fathers* (New York, NY: New York University, 2008), p. 172. On the ways in which the poor used charitable institutions in their survival strategies, see Tim Hitchcock, *Down and Out in Eighteenth-Century London* (London, UK: Hambledon, 2004), esp. ch. 7; Seth Rothman, *Scraping By: Wage Labor, Slavery, and Survival in Early Baltimore* (Baltimore, MD: Johns Hopkins University Press, 2009).

15 On the medical community and on the origins of the hospital, see Eric Larabee, *The Benevolent and Necessary Institution: An Informal History of a Great*

'Nor do they harbour vermin'   115

Teaching Hospital and the People Who Created it (New York, NY: Doubleday, 1971); Charles E. Rosenberg, *The Care of Strangers: The Rise of America's Hospital System* (New York, NY: Basic Books, 1987), pp. 15–46; Amanda B. Moniz, *From Empire to Humanity: The American Revolution and the Origins of Humanitarianism* (New York, NY: Oxford University Press, 2016), pp. 39–41, 56–5.

16 On the architecture, see the NYH Board of Governors' Meeting, 10 March 1773; 2 July 1773; 6 June 1794, NYH Minutes, vol. I; on donations of funds and books from overseas, see 13 November 1771, 2 February 1774, 6 May 1800. For snapshots of the origins of hospital patient, see *A Brief Account of New-York Hospital*, p. 65; *An Account of the New-York Hospital* (New York, NY: 1811), p. 56.

17 *An Account of the New-York Hospital*, p. 9; NYH Board of Governors' Meeting, 1 November 1796, NYH Minutes, vol. I, 1 November 1796.

18 This paragraph draws on the analysis of the hospital's minutes from 1791 to 1817. NYH Board of Governors' Meetings, New York Hospital Minutes, vols. I–III. On patients' convalescing, see, for example, Board of Governors' Meeting, 7 March 1808, NYH Minutes, vol. II. On patients who stayed beyond when they could benefit from medical care, see NYH Board of Governors' Meeting, 2 May 1797, NYH Minutes, vol. I. For the rules, see NYH Board of Governors' Meeting, 18 September 1792; 27 August 1793, NYH Minutes, vol. I.

19 Sandra Cavallo, 'Invisible Beds: Health and the Material Culture of Sleep', in Anne Gerritsen and Giorgio Riello (eds), *Writing Material Culture* (London, UK: Bloomsbury, 2015), pp. 143–9. John E. Crowley, 'The Sensibility of Comfort', *American Historical Review* (June 1999), 104 (3), pp. 749–82, 752, 776–9; John E. Crowley, *The Invention of Comfort: Sensibilities and Design in Early Modern Britain and Early America* (Baltimore, MD: Johns Hopkins University Press, 2003).

20 NYH Board of Governors' meetings, 6 June 1794, NYH Minutes, vol. I.

21 NYH Board of Governors' Meeting, 7 June 1796; 8 July 1796, NYH Minutes, vol. I; NYH Board of Governors' Meeting, 2 April 1805; 4 June 1805; 4 April 1809; 2 December 1806, NYH Minutes, vol. II.

22 On transatlantic medical networks, including doctors' attention to fever hospitals, see Moniz, *From Empire to Humanity*, pp. 89–96. NYH Board of Governors' Meeting, 2 April 1805, NYH Minutes, vol. II.

23 On the horrifying effects of transatlantic voyages on captive Africans' health, see Stephanie Smallwood, *Saltwater Slavery: A Middle Passage from Africa to American Diaspora* (Cambridge, MA: Harvard University Press, 2008); works on the health of enslaved people include Sharla M. Fett, *Working Cures: Healing, Health, and Power on Southern Slave Plantations* (Chapel Hill, NC: University of North Carolina Press, 2002); Londa Schiebinger, *Secret Cures of Slaves: People, Plants, and Medicine in the Eighteenth-Century Atlantic World* (Stanford, CA: Stanford University Press, 2017). On the impact of a notorious health crisis on African-Americans, see J. Worth Estes and Billy G. Smith, *A Melancholy Scene of Devastation: The Public Response to the 1793*

Philadelphia Yellow Fever Epidemic (Canton, MA: Published for the College of Physicians of Philadelphia and the Library Company of Philadelphia by Science History Publications, USA, 1997). While people of African descent suffered the worst health consequences of the colonial project in the Caribbean, white arrivals in the region also faced high rates of mortality from tropical diseases. A starting point for exploring the topic is Philip D. Curtin, *Death by Relocation: Europe's Encounter with the Tropical World in the Nineteenth Century* (Cambridge, UK: Cambridge University Press, 1989). An important recent book on the topic is Mark Harrison, *Medicine in an Age of Commerce and Empire* (Oxford, UK: Oxford University Press, 2010). On the role of medicine in the construction of race, see Suman Seth, *Difference and Disease: Medicine, Race, and the Eighteenth-Century British Empire* (Cambridge, UK: Cambridge University Press, 2018); Rana A. Hogarth, *Medicalizing Blackness: Making Racial Difference in the Atlantic World, 1780–1840* (Chapel Hill, NC: University of North Carolina Press, 2017). The literature on antislavery is vast. Recent works include Manisha Sinha, *The Slave's Cause: A History of Abolition* (New Haven, CT: Yale University Press, 2016); J. R. Oldfield, *Transatlantic Abolitionism in the Age of Revolution: An International History of Anti-Slavery, c. 1787–1820* (Cambridge, UK: Cambridge University Press, 2013).

24 Lisa T. Sarasohn, '"That Nauseous Venomous Insect": Bedbugs in Early Modern England', *Eighteenth-Century Studies* (Summer 2013), 46 (4), pp. 513–30, quotation on 513; on the history of vermin as a category, see Mary Fissell, 'Imagining Vermin in Early-Modern England', *History Workshop Journal* (Spring 1999), 47, pp. 1–29. On eighteenth-century concerns about and responses to fever and infection, see Guenter B. Risse, '"Typhus" Fever in Eighteenth-Century Hospitals: New Approaches to Medical Treatment', *Bulletin of the History of Medicine* (Summer 1985), 59 (2), pp. 176–95; David S. Barnes, 'Cargo, "Infection", and the Logic of Quarantine in the Nineteenth Century', *Bulletin of the History of Medicine* (Spring 2014), 88 (1), pp. 75–101; Kevin Siena, *Rotten Bodies: Class and Contagion in 18th-Century Britain* (New Haven, CT: Yale University Press, 2019); Erica Charters, *Disease, War, and the Imperial State: The Welfare of the British Armed Forces during the Seven Years' War* (Chicago, IL: University of Chicago Press, 2014); Mark Harrison, *Contagion: How Commerce Has Spread Disease* (New Haven, CT: Yale University Press, 2012); Simon Finger, *The Contagious City: The Politics of Public Health in Early Philadelphia* (Ithaca, NY: Cornell University Press, 2012).

25 Sarasohn, 'That Nauseous Venomous Insect', p. 526.

26 Pat Kirkham, *The London Furniture Trade 1700–1870*, *Furniture History*, vol. XXIV (1988), pp. 47, 129.

27 For Coxe's innovation, see 'Improvement in the Common Bestead', *The (Philadelphia) Emporium of Arts and Sciences* (February 1813), 2 (10), p. 283.

28 NYH Board of Governors' Meeting, 2 April 1805 ('durable'), NYH Minutes, vol. II; NYH Board of Governors' Meeting, 4 June 1811, NYH Minutes, vol. III.

29 NYH Board of Governors' Meeting, 5 February 1811, NYH Minutes, vol. III; NYH Board of Governors' Meeting, 3 December 1805; 3 March 1807; 2 May 1809, NYH Minutes, vol. II; NYH Board of Governors' Meeting, 6 June 1794, NYH Minutes, vol. I; NYH Board of Governors' Meeting, 5 September 1815, NYH Minutes, vol. III; Board of Governors' Meeting, 4 February 1800, NYH Minutes, vol. I. On the patient population, see *A Brief Account of New-York Hospital*, p. 65; *An Account of the New-York Hospital*, p. 56.

30 Laurel Daen, '"To Board & Nurse a Stranger": Poverty, Disability, and Community in Eighteenth-Century Massachusetts', *Journal of Social History* (Spring 2020), 53 (3), pp. 716–41. On Massachusetts's social-safety net, see also Cornelia H. Dayton and Sharon V. Salinger, *Robert Love's Warnings: Searching for Strangers in Colonial Boston* (Philadelphia, PA: University of Pennsylvania Press, 2014); Carl L. Hammer, '"Being Old and Dayly Finding the Symptoms of Mortality": The Troubled Last Years of Hannah Beamon of Deerfield and the Law of 1726', *Early American Studies: An Interdisciplinary Journal* (2019), 17 (2), pp. 151–82. While Northern cities had a more extensive welfare infrastructure, philanthropists and municipal leaders in Southern cities likewise participated in contemporary transatlantic trends in the establishment of poor relief institutions. On the Charleston case, see Barbara L. Bellows, *Benevolence among the Slaveholders: Caring for the Poor in Charleston, 1670–1860* (Baton Rouge, LA: Louisiana University Press, 1993); on the emergence of medical charities contemporaneously in Barbados and the United States, see Moniz, *From Empire to Humanity*, 117–18.

31 NYH Board of Governors' Meeting, 2 June 1794, NYH Minutes, vol. I.

32 NYH Board of Governors' Meetings, 11 September 1792; 18 September 1792, NYH Minutes, vol. I.

33 NYH Board of Governors' Meetings, 5 March 1811; 6 August 1811, NYH Minutes, vol. III.

34 NYH Board of Governors' Meeting, 7 March 1809, NYH Minutes, vol. II.

35 NYH Board of Governors' Meeting, 4 June 1805; 4 April 1809; 6 June 1809, NYH Minutes, vol. II.

36 Classic works exploring this topic include E. P. Thompson, *The Making of the English Working Class* (New York, NY: Vintage, 1966); Eugene D. Genovese, *Roll, Jordan, Roll: The World the Slaves Made* (New York, NY: Pantheon Books, 1974).

37 Monique Bourque, 'Women and Work in the Philadelphia Almshouse, 1790–1840', *Journal of the Early Republic* (2012), 32 (3), pp. 383–413, see esp. 400–2.

38 NYH Board of Governors' Meeting; 2 May 1809; NYH Minutes, vol. II.

39 NYH Board of Governors' Meeting, 3 September 1805, NYH Minutes, vol. II.

40 NYH Board of Governors' Meetings, 2 April 1805; 5 April 1808 ('induce'), NYH Minutes, vol. II.

41 NYH Board of Governors' Meetings, 5 November 1811; 6 September 1814, NYH Minutes vol. III.

42 Ezra Stiles Ely, *Visits of Mercy: Being The Journals of Ezra Stiles Ely, D.D. Written while He Was Stated Preacher to the Hospital and Alms-house in the City of New York*, vol. I (London, UK, 1813; reprinted from the New York, 1811, edition), p. 160 ('ever-watchful', 'Servants of colour').
43 Ely, *Visits of Mercy*, vol. I, p. 156 ('Richard Neal'), pp. 111, 43.

5

The realpolitik of emancipation in the British Empire, 1833–38

Alan Lester

The translation of humanitarian concern into governmental action is never straightforward. Humanitarians' mobilisation of empathy tends to be selective and made for particular purposes. It is propelled in particular geographical directions and towards certain kinds of precarious people rather than others.[1] The journalists, activists and lobbyists who mobilise and popularise concern do not generally want or need to consider the social and economic relations that have generated precarity, which can be affected in turn by humanitarian interventions. Yet the trade-offs between the privileges and advantages of differently positioned subjects, both domestic and overseas, are intrinsic to governance. Governments act on humanitarian concerns both to sustain their legitimacy and to ameliorate disorder.[2] The realpolitik of humanitarian interventions involves balancing the welfare of the precarious groups identified by humanitarians at any one time with the maintenance of social order – which means, broadly, the current distribution of privilege. This ameliorative function is a characteristic of humanitarianism which has, since the late eighteenth century, distinguished it most starkly from the coeval and potentially more revolutionary discourse of human rights.[3] If we are to understand the effects of humanitarianism in the world, we need to take these broader governmental imperatives and the compromises and limitations which they compel into account.[4]

This chapter focuses on what many have regarded as a foundational moment in the history of modern Western humanitarianism: the abolition of slavery within the British Empire.[5] It develops a holistic analysis of the governance of a process celebrated by imperial apologists as an unprecedented mobilisation of British compassion for distant strangers.[6] As well as being the product, at least in part, of a humanitarian campaign, the Slavery Abolition Act of 1833 was one component of a much broader restructuring of the British Empire as a whole. When chattel slavery was abolished in the Caribbean colonies, the Cape Colony within modern South Africa and Mauritius as the Act came into effect in 1834, many other forms of unfree labour were allowed to persist or, indeed, were innovated, there and elsewhere. The context for these changes included both the restructuring of the East India Company and a government-sponsored surge in British emigration to the settler colonies, especially in modern day Australia. As Britons' opportunities in the West Indies were curtailed by the abolition of slavery, so the government provided new outlets for investment elsewhere, including in a Company-governed India, branded as free from slavery, yet reliant on bonded labour.

This chapter highlights the much broader shift in British domestic and imperial governance of which the Abolition Act, or to give it its full title, the Act for the Abolition of Slavery throughout the British Colonies, for Promoting the Industry of the Manumitted Slaves, and for Compensating the Persons Hitherto Entitled to the Services of Such Slaves 1833, was one part. This shift marked the culmination of what historian Christopher Bayly called the Second British Empire, with its centre of gravity lying in the Indian and Pacific oceans rather than along a transatlantic axis. Largely unremarked by imperial historians, who tend to focus either on abolition to Britain's west or the East India Company restructuring to its east, the transition was completed with a flurry of legislation affecting Britain and its colonies equally in the years immediately following the 1832 Reform Act.[7] After prolonged and intense agitation, the 1832 Reform Act, cautiously opening the franchise to more commercially and professionally minded electors, was swiftly followed by a gamut of legislation to improve conditions in schools, factories, prisons and municipal government. Parliamentarians were debating the Board of Control's renegotiation of the East India Company's charter at the same time that they considered the Abolition Act in 1833, and the government was simultaneously implementing legislation to free up trade and promote British emigration to Australasia.[8] These processes were not just concurrent, they were also complementary elements of a new, more liberal governmental dispensation, which in turn reflected Britain's shifting political economy, at a time when longstanding humanitarian concern for the enslaved in British colonies was translated into emancipation.[9]

Different British government departments, with their own priorities and agendas, were involved in effecting emancipation between the passage of the Abolition Act in 1833 and the end of the apprenticeships that it mandated in 1838. Emancipation was a far more long-winded, complex and geographically variegated process than is often imagined, with governing men constantly adjusting their calculations of, and negotiating, the weighting that it should be accorded relative to other priorities in Britain and across more than thirty colonies. This chapter examines this process: highlighting continued forms of coerced labour, the restrictions imposed on the rights of freed people of colour and the accelerated invasion of Indigenous peoples' land in Australasia, it shows how the conditions of imperial realpolitik redefined and delimited emancipation.

Emancipation in context

When people from other countries apply for citizenship or 'indefinite leave to remain' in the United Kingdom today, they are required to learn about British history for a 'Life in the UK Test'. In the official version of that history, which they have to memorise for the test, the abolition of slavery is credited to 'people in Britain who opposed' it. William Wilberforce and other abolitionists, new Britons are told, 'succeeded in turning public opinion against the slave trade'. It was then a logical step from the abolition of the trade in 1807 to the emancipation of the enslaved in 1833. In the meantime, 'the Royal Navy stopped slave ships from other countries, freed the slaves and punished the slave traders'.[10] Although historians of the British Empire have recently objected to this account's erasure of the agency of the enslaved and its overlooking of economic factors (and might also object to its omission of the subsequent fate of 'liberated' Africans taken from other countries' slave ships, or 'recaptives' as they are more accurately known), scholars still widely acknowledge that the antislavery lobbying campaign undermined the legitimacy of slavery and contributed to a modern humanitarian sensibility within Britain.[11] This sensibility contributed vitally to the passage of the Abolition Act.[12]

The historian and first Prime Minister of independent Trinidad and Tobago, Eric Williams, first analysed the affinities between the antislavery movement and the claims of Britain's rising industrial and commercial classes. At its heart, the debate that he launched sought to understand and explain the coincident emergence of 'humane' solutions to problems of crime, poverty and other social ills and the de-legitimisation of the institution of slavery as inhumane.[13] The historian Thomas Haskell suggested that the contractual rules and practices of the capitalist market provided a precondition for involvement in the plight of others, which enabled the emergence of abolitionist sentiment. Grounded in abolitionism, humanitarianism relied on the ability to recognise both moral responsibility for, and causal connections with, distant strangers.[14] As historian Christopher Leslie Brown points out, antislavery activities were conducted with an eye to national atonement for British actions in the Caribbean, which were successfully orchestrated and represented in the new media of antislavery and missionary press as sinful in the wake of the loss of the American colonies.[15]

Following the abolition of the slave trade in 1807, the focus of antislavery campaigners turned to the ending of slavery itself. This second antislavery campaign would continue for nearly thirty years and occupy much of the evangelical Colonial Office official James Stephen's attention. By the time Stephen drafted the bill which abolished slavery in the British Empire in 1833, he was the Colonial Office's permanent under-secretary, widely credited with knowing more about the British colonies than any other person alive. For more than two decades he had played a leading role in trying to implement amelioration measures in the face of resistance from Caribbean slave-owner assemblies.[16] The antislavery campaign, which Stephen supported and saw through to its final realisation, had been bolstered after the abolition of the slave trade by long-term insecurities over the future profitability of the Caribbean slave plantations once the transatlantic trade was illegal and by the resistance and activism of enslaved people themselves. When enslaved people rebelled in Barbados in 1816, Demerara in 1823, and especially Jamaica in 1831–32, the costs of maintaining their subjection increased and their actions provided more ammunition for antislavery activists, who pointed to the extreme violence that colonial governments were obliged to use to maintain the institution.[17] The abolition of slavery was primarily but not solely a Caribbean issue. The capture of new colonies during the Revolutionary and Napoleonic Wars of the preceding forty years meant that the British were now responsible for many of those people held in slavery by the French, Dutch and Spanish in and beyond the Caribbean.

Enslaved people from South and Southeast Asia and eastern Africa undertook the most arduous and lowest-status jobs in the recently acquired Cape Colony, Ceylon and Mauritius. India and Ceylon also had indigenous forms of slavery which the East India Company and Colonial Office respectively now administered. From the 1780s to the 1820s, the antislavery campaign had focused on the icon of an enslaved man of African descent in chains proclaiming 'Am I Not a Man and a Brother?'. The campaign had tended to ignore these forms of enslavement beyond the Caribbean plantations, but in the early 1830s, Stephen would have the task of disentangling them to see whether they fitted with the primary project of emancipation in the Caribbean for which much of the new electorate, and now Parliament, had called.[18]

When Stephen drafted the antislavery bill, he knew that a price would have to be paid for Parliament's assent. The MPs representing the pro-slavery West Indies interest had been weakened by the election following the 1832 Reform Act as more antislavery MPs were elected, but not displaced.[19] The price for the MPs' compliance was compensation for the confiscation of the slave owners' human property. The rate of compensation, set by commissioners in London, would vary according to the colony and the estimated productivity of each enslaved person. Enslaved people were worth the most in Honduras, where owners were paid £195 per slave, and least in the Bahamas, where they were 'worth' only £35. Owners of enslaved people in Demerara and Berbice demanded a considerable portion of the compensation payout. The total compensation required was £20 million, which equated to 40 per cent of Treasury revenue. Rather than increasing taxation to pay off the slave-owners, the Treasury raised a loan from a syndicate led by financiers Nathan Mayer Rothschild and Moses Montefiore. Fifteen million pounds was borrowed for the Caribbean slave owners, and a further £5 million was raised later for owners in the Cape and Mauritius.[20]

The Abolition of Slavery Act was a complex piece of legislation. It was the result of Stephen's decades of familiarity with the diverse legal codes of the various slave-holding colonies. It abolished the institution of slavery with effect on 1 August 1834 throughout the British Empire, with the exceptions of Ceylon and St Helena, and the territories in India and Southeast Asia governed by the East India Company.[21] Children below the age of six were freed from their owner's control immediately. On the advice of Evan MacGregor, governor of Antigua, full emancipation came into immediate effect there, and also in Bermuda.[22] Elsewhere, those freed from slavery in 1834 were not allowed to leave their owners' estates. They would continue working for their employers, no longer as their property but as 'apprentices'. If the former slaves were considered to provide domestic labour in households, they were to be allowed to leave their employers on 1 August 1838. If they were classed as field labourers, however, their final emancipation would be delayed a further two years to 1 August 1840. Under-Secretary of State George Grey described apprenticeship as 'an intermediate system of modified coercion', in which former slaves would continue to work for most of their time for former owners without pay but have their welfare safeguarded by local officials known as Protectors of Slaves.[23]

Stephen set this period of apprenticeship alongside the payment of compensation to owners as the inducement necessary to ensure the compliance of West Indies interests in Parliament. He justified it with the belief that people held for much or all of their lives as chattel would require a period of instruction before they could become self-sufficient. Four years of apprenticeship for domestic servants and six for field labourers would be sufficient to prepare them for newfound responsibilities when they entered the workforce as freely contracting men and women. In practice, the measure delayed transition on behalf of colonial elites, who feared the drastic repercussions of enslaved people abandoning the plantations en masse and seeking revenge on 1 August 1834.

Plantation owners could also use this period to secure future labour supplies. As John Gladstone (father of the future Prime Minister William Ewart Gladstone), a shipping owner, merchant and planter in Demerara (soon to be part of British Guiana), complained, 'it is a matter of doubt and uncertainty how far [the freed slaves] may be induced to continue their services on the plantations after their apprenticeship expires in 1840'.[24] Gladstone, who was engaged in 'a rearguard action to fashion an ameliorated and reformed slavery that maintained the still-enormous profits generated by the plantation economy', was one of the first to devise a practical solution on behalf of plantation owners.[25] At the beginning of 1836 he asked the Liverpool shipping company Gillanders, Arbuthnot and Co. if they could divert some of the indentured Bengali workers they were already transporting to Mauritius to Demerara instead. Through this means, Gladstone organised the transportation of 396 Indian workers between 1836 and 1838, with James Stephen obliging him by issuing an order in council legalising five-year, rather than just three-year contracts.[26] The false pretences under which recruiters secured these labourers in India and their abysmal conditions of transport and employment, however, led to the suspension of this experimental indenture scheme in 1839 and forced Gladstone 'to divest himself of most of his Demerara holdings' and, along with many others with a stake in slavery in the Americas, 'invest in India and in British railways' instead.[27] It was only after a new system of recruitment was governed more effectively from the early 1840s that a diaspora of some half a million indentured Indians would partially replace slave labour in both old and new British colonies.[28]

Between 1833 and 1838, Stephen's personal imperative as an antislavery evangelical reformer, or what we might today call a humanitarian, was finding opportunities for formerly enslaved apprentices to join the ranks of a reformed, post–slave-holding, Christian society, ideally on the same terms as Britain's colonists. His aim as the Colonial Office's chief administrator, and effectively its key adviser on colonial affairs, however, was to oversee the Empire's transition to free labour in as orderly a fashion as possible, with minimal disruption to established British interests and the imperial economy. Within these constraints, Stephen developed the most immediate objectives for emancipation. The first was to distinguish exactly who was to be freed and from what kind of relationship. This was more complicated than it seemed. The Colonial Office's instruction from Parliament seemed reasonably clear: bring an end to slavery and the apprenticeship system which had succeeded it. But during the course of the year, Stephen and his colleagues became entangled in the complexities of distinguishing slavery from the Empire's other coercive labour relationships, which were vital to sustaining colonists' productivity in tropical and subtropical plantations.

Defining emancipation

Britain itself still had apprenticeship regulations and legal codes that were weighted heavily in favour of masters over servants and enforced by punitive magistrates. 'Free' labour, especially in agricultural regions, was protesting its subjugation to criminal punishment and incarceration, rather than just the withholding of wages, when employers found workers' performance or behaviour deficient. Such issues had fuelled the Swing Revolts of rural southern and eastern England, which targeted agricultural mechanisation and worker impoverishment in 1830, and helped propel the electoral reform of 1832. Both pro- and antislavery activists had highlighted perceived similarities between the conditions of enslaved and then apprenticed people in the Caribbean, and those of the poorest workers in Britain and Ireland. Defenders of Caribbean slavery used the analogy to assert that charity should begin at home rather than on overseas plantations, while abolitionists drew attention to dire local working conditions as part of a broader reformist agenda.[29]

Across the Empire overseas there were many more varieties of forced labour. Transported British convicts were made to work without pay, either for the government or for free settlers in the Australian colonies. Indian, Ceylonese, Mauritian, Aboriginal, Khoisan and other convicts were serving sentences by labouring either within their own colonies or in exile in other parts of the Empire.[30] Even the African captives liberated from other nations' slave ships by the Royal Navy following the abolition of the slave trade in 1807 were assigned as unpaid apprentices for colonists in the Caribbean, Sierra Leone and St Helena – if they were not forcibly recruited into the West India or West Africa Regiments of the British Army.[31] Meanwhile, the East India Company directors' attention was now being drawn to the slave-like conditions of its Indian subjects, recruited, as we have seen, on contracts of labour indenture for Mauritius since the early 1830s and from 1836 for the Caribbean. Of much greater numerical significance were those subjected to indigenous forms of slavery under East India Company rule in India itself. The British Empire of 1838 was sustained by many shades of labour relations in between Adam Smith's alternatives of wages and the whip.

The Act of 1833 had indicated that, within this varied palette of employer subjection, the chattel slaves of the Caribbean were the primary target of British benevolence. Those originally transported from West Africa to the West Indies and their descendants had been the focal point for the preceding decades of antislavery campaigning. These were the people to whom the British public and its government acknowledged a moral debt, represented by that powerful image of the kneeling man on countless pamphlets, embroideries, posters, medallions and even Wedgwood china. In early 1838, James Stephen received an address that appeared to come from precisely this kind of idealised subject for emancipation. It was from apprentices in the Bahamas who wished to exclaim their delight at Queen Victoria's coronation. Secretary of State Lord Glenelg replied on behalf of the monarch, assuring them that there 'is no class of persons whose welfare is more dear to Her Majesty ... than those who ... were raised ... from the condition of slaves to free subjects of the British Crown'.[32] These were the kind of people – directly traded in and then owned by Britons, abused by British planters, and now grateful and loyal members of British colonial society – who campaigning Britons at home most wanted to be freed. It was in respect of this group that Stephen's instructions were clearest.

The waters were muddied, however, by the inclusion in the 1833 Abolition Act of some further variants of slavery, and the exclusion of others, in different parts of the Empire. The 1833 Act also promised freedom to enslaved people in Mauritius and the Cape Colony, who had been traded and owned, not by Britons, but by French and Dutch colonists. It explicitly excluded enslaved people in St Helena, India and Ceylon. In St Helena, the Colonial Office inherited administration from the East India Company only as a result of the 1833 Charter renewal and found that local Company officials were already phasing out slavery, while in Ceylon an established process of gradual emancipation on the plantations of the coastal belt was being accompanied by a tentative undermining of indigenous Kandyan forms of enslavement.[33] The most significant single omission from the act, therefore, was India.[34]

Long before the East India Company became the pre-eminent authority in the subcontinent, African, Southeast Asian and Indian people had been trafficked across the Indian Ocean. By the 1830s, an illegal trade supplied African chattel slaves to wealthy Indian families, but their households also contained Indian women and children who had been kidnapped or sold by destitute family members. People continued to be sold openly at slave markets in the Company-supervised Princely States of India. Beyond these practices, which the British might well identify as akin to Caribbean chattel slavery, there was a complex spectrum of labour bondage in the Indian countryside. Whole communities were tied hereditarily to the owner of the land they worked, their inferior status reinforced by caste distinctions, with Company officials understanding that most, but not necessarily all, enslaved people were also 'untouchables'.[35] Landowners might not have bought and sold these agricultural labourers, but they inflicted physical punishment and limited their movement. Other Indians were obliged to serve those to whom they were indebted. Data on such practices are imprecise, but it has been estimated that between one and sixteen million in a population of over one hundred million people lived in some such kind of servitude under the Company's administration.[36]

However, the British public's attitude to Indian slavery was more ambivalent than that towards its Caribbean variant. In these early days of humanitarian campaigning, it was not so much a case of compassion fatigue as compassion concentration. In the 1790s, and again in the 1820s, the British antislavery campaign had organised a boycott of slave-grown sugar in order to render Caribbean slavery unprofitable. Gleefully, the importers of East Indies sugar promoted it as the consumer's ethical alternative. Smith and Leaper of Bishopgate Street advertised 'East India Sugar made by Free People'. The Peckham Ladies' African and Anti-Slavery Association published *Reasons for Using East India Sugar* in 1828, claiming that buying Indian sugar undermined slavery in 'the safest, most easy, and effectual manner in which it can be done'.[37] The West India interest, including John Gladstone, furiously contested these claims, pointing out that the sugar imported from Company territories was itself grown by enslaved people.[38] It was not just pro-slavery interests who identified abolitionist inconsistency. After reading the popular Indian travel narrative of Frances Buchanan, the radical writer William Cobbett complained that 'East India sugar is raised by slaves; by slaves who are property, by slaves who are bought and sold, by slaves who are mortgaged, by slaves who are let out like cattle'.[39]

With the East India Company's charter being up for renewal and revision at the same time that the Abolition Act was being debated, the President of the Board of Control, Lord Glenelg (who would be James Stephen's political boss as Colonial Secretary at the time of emancipation in 1838), raised the issue of slavery with the Company directors. The Government of India Act 1833, which gave the Company its charter for the next twenty years, placed Indian government more firmly into the hands of the Governor General in Bengal, stripped the Company of its commercial functions and its monopoly on trade with China, and transferred the governance of St Helena to the Crown. One thing it did not do was insist on abolishing slavery in Company territories. All that the Company was enjoined to do was 'adopt measures to mitigate the state of slavery' at some point before the next charter renewal. The directors had convinced Glenelg that the governance of India itself would be jeopardised if they pressed on with abolition against the wishes of slave-holding Indian elites.

Four years later, as former slaves elsewhere in the Empire were being emancipated from apprenticeship, the Company directors and the Board of Control were faced once again with the need to justify leaving Indian slavery intact. Although the British public's attention was still focused almost exclusively on the Caribbean, there were some dissenting voices still arguing for abolition in India, regardless of how impractical it may seem. Among them were missionaries in Travancore in southern India, backed by the London Missionary Society. They reported that there was no domestic slavery in the region since higher castes would consider themselves defiled by the proximity of slaves. Rather, 'the slaves were condemned to remain in the rice fields where they carried out the most arduous tasks, and when not required for labour they were left to starvation or to resort to theft ... By few are they comforted, pitied or relieved; none seek to remove their distresses, and no man cares for their souls'.[40] William Adam, a former missionary who had worked with Ram Mohan Roy on the Bengali translation of the New Testament and now lived in the United States of America, was a particularly vocal enemy of British hypocrisy on the issue. In 1840 he complained to the leading antislavery campaigner in the House of Commons, Thomas Fowell Buxton, that:

> The people of England have just paid twenty million sterling to emancipate eight hundred thousand slaves in the British West Indies; and while they are congratulating themselves that now at length every British subject is a free man, and insultingly reproaching republican America with her slavery, they are to be told that their congratulations are premature; that their reproaches may be retorted; that there are probably 800,000 slaves more, British subjects, in the East Indies.[41]

For all Adam's zeal though, as Stephen pinned down questions of who was actually to be freed, where and when, abolitionist campaigners' concern over Indian slaves receded once again.

As Andrea Major points out, Zachary Macaulay (the historian and father of Thomas Babington Macaulay, Secretary of the Board of Control) spoke for many when distinguishing between West and East Indian slaves' entitlement to freedom. As a teenager, Macaulay had managed the books on a Jamaican sugar plantation, evincing little sympathy for its enslaved workforce. He developed evangelical sympathies after his return to Britain, where he befriended William Wilberforce. Once he became part of the inner circle of British abolitionists, Macaulay's horizons were further broadened when he visited the great abolitionist colonial experiment of Sierra Leone. Macaulay had been a leading figure in the campaign to abolish the transatlantic slave trade in 1807. Yet, in the 1820s he helped allay concern for the fate of India's slaves. Pointing out that Cobbett and others' information on slavery in India had been swayed by Buchanan's travel narrative, Macaulay insisted that Buchanan had travelled only in Mysore, from where little sugar was grown and none exported. The relative cheapness of Indian sugar, compared with Jamaican, could be attributed, he argued, to better soils and the use of ploughs rather than hoes, not to an equally enslaved workforce. As emancipation became a practical project to be managed from London, Macaulay's thinking epitomised its concentration on western slavery and Britons' reluctance to extend it eastwards. 'There is a difference', he maintained, 'between the slavery of the East and West, that of the latter we ourselves are the sole authors, and are chargeable, therefore, with its whole guilt and turpitude. In the East whatever slavery exists we found there; we did not create it ourselves'.⁴²

Macaulay, then, was concerned to delimit this foundational humanitarian intervention by attributing compassion for precarious subjects solely to direct responsibility for their plight. As a result, and as John Gladstone appreciated, up to late 1837 and again in the early 1840s, India's bonded labour force was considered available for indentured service in other colonies as the 'free labour' alternative to enslaved labour. Indian slave-owners would only lose their right to control labourers during the following decade and the East India Company would not criminalise slave-holding until 1862.

For varying reasons, then, enslaved people in St Helena, Ceylon and India had all been excluded from the liberation offered by the 1833 Abolition Act. While the Act was focused mainly on the Caribbean, however, it did include two other, relatively new, British colonies: the Cape Colony at the southern tip of Africa, and Mauritius in the Indian Ocean. Both had variants of slavery that were different in many respects from the West Indies system that conditioned the abolitionist imagination. Stephen was relatively unconcerned about the process of emancipation in the Cape Colony. The 1833 Act applied to 30,000 people owned as chattel slaves, mainly in the western half of the colony. The Dutch East India Company had been trading in these chattel slaves for the Cape's primarily Dutch-speaking colonists from what is now Malaysia and Indonesia since the late seventeenth century. These enslaved people worked mainly in wheat and wine production. Their emancipation, promised in the 1833 Act, would ultimately incite the mass emigration of Afrikaner colonists in the Great Trek to establish new republics on the Highveld and in Natal, which would bring its own problems for the Colonial Office. Nevertheless, in early 1838 Stephen saw the process of ending their apprenticeship itself as relatively unproblematic, not least because of the promise of £3 million compensation to the colony's slave-owners.⁴³ This money 'enabled planters and farmers to ride out emancipation with far fewer changes to the wider societies and economies of the former slave colonies than humanitarians and abolitionists had hoped'. The Bank of South Africa, founded in 1838, had 2,050 shareholders of whom at least 951 were slave-owners, investing some of the £2.6 million in compensation for the 11,896 slaves they had owned.⁴⁴

In Mauritius, too, enslaved people were included in the freedom offered by the 1833 Act. Here, Stephen foresaw greater difficulty. French governments and settlers in Mauritius had traded in slaves from Africa and Madagascar long before the British seized the colony in 1810. These people, referred to as 'Creole', worked on the island's sugar plantations and now constituted two-thirds of its population. The 1833 Act abolished slavery in Mauritius with effect six months after its demise in the Caribbean, on 1 February 1835. Two million pounds of compensation went to the island, intended to appease the French-speaking slave-owners, around a fifth of them free people of colour, some of whom were still threatening rebellion against continued British occupation. In early 1835 the formerly enslaved Creole workforce was apprenticed for three years to former owners. Both James Stephen and the Governor knew that the Creoles would face particular difficulty from indentured Indian workers' competition when they entered the island's free labour market.

From 1825 the Colonial Office had encouraged sugar production in Mauritius by granting tariff equality on the same favourable terms as West Indian sugar. By 1830 Mauritian acreage under sugar cane had doubled and slave prices had quadrupled. Even before they received their compensation money, slave-owners were organising the recruitment of Indian migrant labourers on contracts of indenture as the cheaper alternative, and companies like Gillanders and Arbuthnot and Co. in Liverpool were shipping them across ever more efficiently using the new steam ships. Over the previous five years, the number of Indians brought to the island had increased from 8,600 to 19,700 per year. The trouble for the Creole apprentices was that, even before they were freed, the Indian immigrants had already undermined the Creoles' position in the local labour market.

Many Mauritian apprentices were being 'literally pushed off estates' to make way for the guaranteed low-wage Indian workforce. James Stephen sympathised with them. He warned that the introduction of more indentured labourers from India could undermine the former slaves' ability to acquire profitable employment. He refuted the charge made by Mauritian employers that the Creole workforce had broken the terms of their apprenticeships by abandoning their plantations since 1833, insisting they had been forced to leave. However, Stephen and his Secretary of State Lord Glenelg were at odds on this issue. The patrician Glenelg believed that the fierce competition for paid employment with indentured migrants 'at this critical period' would have a 'most useful influence on the conduct of the apprenticed population'.[45]

Mauritius's Governor, William Nicolay, believed that he had enough experience to compare the predicament of apprentices in the Caribbean and Mauritius, having been the Governor of Dominica from 1824 to 1831, and of St Kitts from 1832 to 1833. Four months before emancipation, he drew on this experience to agree with Glenelg: the apprentices, 'becoming accustomed to labour in the same fields with men in a state of entire freedom, will, on their final emancipation, betake themselves more willingly to their accustomed employments'. In the same dispatch, he could not contain his enthusiasm about the effect of the compensation payments to the 7,000 former slave-owners on the island:

> The increase of Revenue in 1836, is stated at £31,308.4.6¼. The principal increase of Revenue has been ... the increased capital from the indemnity to Slaves ... The Registration fees, in the Internal Revenue Department, have also afforded considerable augmentation in 1836: chiefly arising from the transfers of property, attributable also, in a great measure, to the altered circumstances of the Colonial Society from the emancipation of the Slaves ... From the introduction of Indian labourers in 1836, the produce of the soil should show an augmentation in 1837.[46]

Stephen may have feared that the colonial government had failed to give Mauritius's apprentices sufficient support in their transition to free labour, but in the face of this boon to the colonial economy and the availability of cheap Indian labour, his disquiet was not enough to convince either the Colonial Secretary or the island's Governor that the former slaves needed protection.

By the middle of 1838, Stephen's correspondence with governors around the world was allowing him to develop a mental map of emancipatory priorities. This map informed the imperial government's interventions in labour relations as enslaved people were freed. Stephen's primary concern was to ensure a smooth transition from apprenticeship to free labour in the Caribbean. Despite his reservations about the fate of Creoles and news of the first Dutch-speaking trekkers leaving the Cape Colony, the alteration in status from apprentice to free labour seemed less problematic in Mauritius and the Cape Colony, both of which were included in the terms of the 1833 Act. In the meantime, Britons could rest assured that the kind of chattel slavery that they had in mind had, to all intents and purposes, already been phased out in St Helena and Ceylon. In India, there were concerns about forms of Indigenous slavery, which British administrations continued to tolerate, if not condone. However, this consideration could be set to one side while still fulfilling the humanitarian mandate for emancipation.

Emancipation and civil rights

The planters represented in Jamaica's Legislative Assembly viewed emancipation with the greatest anxiety in 1833. Since 1664 this body, elected on a restricted property franchise, had shared legislative responsibility with governors appointed from London. In 1833 the Governor was the Marquess of Sligo. As he had inherited two plantations in Jamaica, the island's planters had expected him to be sympathetic to their struggle against abolition. However, he had objected vehemently to planter cruelty and, after the 1833

Act, made it clear that he wanted Jamaica to be 'absolved forever from the reproach of Slavery'.[47] Well aware of the continuing abuses of the apprenticeship system, he sought out sixty special magistrates to ensure that the promised protections for former slaves would be enforced. Planters mocked him and set about vilifying him in Britain. The Assembly's vote to withhold his salary gave the Colonial Secretary, Lord Glenelg, no choice but to remove Sligo from office in September 1836.[48] For James Stephen, the episode was a salutary lesson in the realpolitik of emancipation.

One of Stephen's greatest dilemmas in 1838 was the extent to which he could afford to mollify Jamaica's slave-owners without negating the benefits of emancipation for former slaves. Aside from trying to stop planters abusing apprenticeship, Sligo had earned their wrath by fostering a 'Coloured Party' for free black representatives within the Assembly, encouraging men of colour to run for membership as a counterweight to planter influence. In late 1837, as the end of apprenticeship and a drastic increase in the free black population neared, the last election to the Jamaican Assembly had returned five more 'Coloured Party' members and a corresponding reduction in the proportion of white representatives. Despite his liberal reputation, Sligo's successor, Lionel Smith, whose father had been a West Indies trader, was concerned that any further increase in black political representation would undermine the stability of the colony. He wrote to Glenelg privately with the sensitive suggestion that the franchise property qualification be raised upon emancipation so as to prevent even more 'Coloured members being elected'. '[T]wo more general elections', he wrote, 'would, I am persuaded, throw every white member out of the House under the present law'. Smith feared that free people of colour, and especially former slaves, 'are not yet qualified by education and property to command the respect of the country'. The consequence of allowing further black representation in these circumstances 'must be the rapid sale of property and abandonment of the Island by the few influential white Gentlemen who now reside in it'.[49]

Glenelg and Stephen conferred over Smith's covert strategy to maintain white political dominance. Although it might well buy the co-operation of Jamaica's planters, Stephen replied that such franchise manipulation would smack of explicit racial discrimination against those whom Britain wished emancipated. It could not be allowed. Normally such a discussion might have been kept between the Governor and Colonial Office. Unfortunately for Smith, however, the correspondence that he had sought to keep secret leaked. The Assembly's free people of colour came to hear of it from correspondents in Britain. An outraged Smith blamed a leak from within the Colonial Office, earning the haughty reply from Stephen that such indiscretion among his staff was inconceivable. By the time the apprentices were freed in August, Smith was mistrusted almost in equal measure by the 'Coloured

Party' for his covert attempt to undermine them, and by planters resisting his efforts to rein in their abuses of apprenticeship. The ensuing legislative deadlock meant that Smith had to be recalled while the planter-dominated Assembly managed, in the years after emancipation, to raise the franchise qualification so as to exclude the vast majority of people of colour after all.[50]

Smith's next posting was to Mauritius, where he confronted precisely the same issue that had caused his downfall in Jamaica: how far should the British obligation to former slaves extend beyond emancipation to include the same civil rights enjoyed by propertied white colonists? In 1838, while Stephen was preventing Smith from limiting black representation in Jamaica's Assembly, he was simultaneously instructing William Nicolay, the current Governor of Mauritius, to open his advisory Council of Government to the newly freed 'Creoles'. Stephen was optimistic that free men of colour everywhere would ultimately prove themselves worthy to participate in representative institutions on the same terms (generally a property-based franchise) as white men.

In reality, Governor Nicolay's plan for Mauritius was more modest. In March 1838 Stephen received a dispatch that Nicolay had sent in September the previous year: 'Were I called upon to give an opinion as to when an extensive system of representative legislature could be safely introduced, founded on the consideration of the equality of legal rights which will be enjoyed by all classes on the expiration of the Apprenticeship, my answer must be that the period is far – very far – distant'. Rather, Nicolay would 'bring into effect the desire formerly expressed by His Majesty's Government, of granting to the [Creole] inhabitants, a more free participation in the legislative affairs of the colony, by admitting a certain number (under various restrictions with regard to eligibility) into the Council of Government'.[51]

Whatever Stephen's long-term ambitions, Glenelg noted that the management of post-emancipation transition required the co-operation of Mauritius's French-speaking elites, who were already expressing their discontent with the Anglicisation of their island's administration. Glenelg took Nicolay's warnings about rebellion seriously. He agreed that the rights of Creole former slaves should be circumscribed as the governor saw fit. Disaffected British planters in Jamaica were one thing – a rebellion against British sovereignty itself was another. As ever in government, even in this celebrated year of British altruism, security and economic and moral concerns were weighed against each other, with differing outcomes in different places.

Emancipation and colonisation

As well as being the product, at least in part, of a humanitarian campaign, the Abolition Act was one component of a much broader restructuring of the British Empire. This included both the renewal and reorientation of the East India Company's charter and the far more vigorous promotion of British emigration to the settler colonies. As Britons' opportunities to obtain privileges through slavery in the West Indies were curtailed, so the government provided new opportunities to invest in the East Indies and in the settler colonies of Australasia.

The Legacies of British Slave Ownership database, developed at University College London, has exposed the slave-owners, especially those living in Britain who received compensation from 1834, to scrutiny.[52] But the guarantee of dividends for East India Company shareholders, negotiated at the same time, is less well known outside the Indian historiography. The previous renewal of the Company's charter, in 1813, had pushed the organisation away from being a commercial entity by abolishing its monopoly on trade between India and Britain, while respecting its monopoly on the trade, mainly in opium and cotton, between India and China. The 1833 renewal removed that vestigial monopoly, opening up the China and East Indies trade to new competitors. Under terms approved by Parliament at the same time that the abolition bill was being debated, the East India Company was obliged to repay long-term loans, and award compensation and pensions to former employees in its trading arm.[53] Historian Thomas Babington Macaulay was the Board of Control's Secretary and its spokesman in the House of Commons at the time. Considering the simultaneous abolition of slavery and the dissolution of the East India Company's commercial role prompted him to write:

> The N*****s in one hemisphere
> The Brahmins in the other
> Disturb my dinner and my sleep
> With 'Ain't I a man and a brother'?[54]

In June–July 1833 Parliament was preoccupied with the issue of compensation for vested interests in both the West and East Indies, with Company shareholders facing the loss of profits from commerce just as slave-owners were losing their 'property'. The interests of the tens of thousands of slave-owners and 1,700 East India Company shareholders – between them representing a significant proportion of both moderately and extravagantly propertied British families – would, however, be safeguarded as far as possible.[55] Any opposition that the East India Company shareholders and directors (those with 4,000 or more shares) may have mounted to the loss of revenue from trade was swiftly deflected by Macaulay's promise that they would continue to receive an annual dividend of 10.5 per cent. This was 'precisely the same dividend which they have been receiving for forty years, and which they have expected to receive permanently'.[56] Rather than being derived in part from trade, the shareholders' dividends would from now on be extracted exclusively from the rent paid by the Company's Indian subjects in return for the privilege of being governed by it, and from the profits of the Company-grown opium sold in China. Between 1834 and 1837 the dividends paid to the roughly 2,000 Company proprietors continued to amount to over £600,000 per annum.[57]

The compensatory mechanisms overseen by the Colonial Office, the Board of Control and the Treasury in 1833 helped secure the passage of East Indies traders and shareholders into the reoriented Second British Empire, by and large with status and wealth intact, as well as paying slave-owners. This government safeguarding is easily overlooked if we examine each facet of the mid-1830s transition, such as emancipation, in isolation. So, too, is the provision of opportunities for new investments, including in settler colonialism. These compensatory mechanisms enabled a reorientation of people, investment and expertise to the intensified colonisation of Australia, in particular.[58]

At the same time that James Stephen was seeking to manage the transition from slavery to apprenticeship in some parts of the Empire, the Cabinet expected him to help effect a large-scale demographic transfer, from an apparently overpopulated Britain to the colonies of settlement in North America, southern Africa and Australia. Edward Gibbon Wakefield's and the colonial reformers' agitation for systematic colonisation was at its height during the debates over Stephen's Abolition Act, and the new government's support for British emigration was manifested in the South Australia Colonization Act in 1834.[59] Seizing the opportunity of the reformed Parliament, Wakefield followed up swiftly, chairing the first meeting of the New Zealand Association, which would later become the New Zealand Company, the following year. While managing the fate of apprentices, Stephen was obliged to accede to plans for more 'systematic' colonisation.[60] In 1834 he appointed the Colonial Office official Thomas Elliot to oversee emigration schemes to Australia. By 1840, thanks in no small part to Elliot's co-ordination, more than 50,000 Britons had emigrated to the Australian colonies.[61]

The majority of emigrants forming this invasion were not the sort of people who benefited from slave-owner compensation payments, new trade opportunities or guaranteed dividends from the East India Company's restructuring. However, the government sales of Aboriginal people's land that funded their migration and their opportunities for employment in Australia were bolstered by those who were. Two such examples were the East India trader Charles Robert Prinsep and the West India merchant and ship owner George Fife Angas.[62]

Like many other East India Company officials, John Prinsep, father of Charles Robert Princep, had repatriated a generous salary, then invested it through agency houses 'in India to develop private ventures under the Company's monopoly'.⁶³ Having invested in sugar cultivation in India, John Prinsep, after his return to London, had joined the lobby from the East Indies against slavery in the West Indies. In a series of pamphlets, he argued that 'the Jamaican sugar trade ... was entirely underwritten by the "detestable traffick" in slave labour', whereas the Indian sugar trade could provide a more economical industry based on 'mild and liberal principles of government over the natives'.⁶⁴ With his own competitive advantage established under the Company's auspices, by 1813, Charles's father was lobbying for the end of the Company's monopoly.

Charles Prinsep's own legal practice in Calcutta also enabled him to accumulate funds to invest in passenger shipping and trading ventures between India, Singapore and Van Diemen's Land. After the 1833 charter renewal, the loss of the East India Company's remaining monopoly on the Indian Ocean and South China Sea trade persuaded Charles Prinsep and others 'to diversify their holdings and business interests'. He saw Australia in particular as a place to invest.⁶⁵ By 1837 he had recruited other British and Indian investors to back an Australian Association of Bengal. Utilising the new technology of steam shipping, they sought to enrich themselves and fuel settler expansion in Australia, integrating it with the Company's new economy of governance and rent extraction in India. Together with thirteen Britons, his ship carried one 'Chinaman and 37 Lascars' to work his newly purchased farm on the western bank of the Leschenault Estuary in Western Australia. Prinsep named the estate, described by one visitor as a 'droll sort of East India establishment', Belvidere, after his home in Calcutta.⁶⁶ By 1850, still never having actually visited the property, he was employing Indian workers on contracts of indenture as a cheap and controllable workforce on his 9,300 hectares.

At the same time, some of those who were compensated by the 1833 Act for the loss of their enslaved workforce in the Caribbean were founding Australia's latest colony. Nick Draper has noted the role of the antislavery nonconformist George Fife Angas in facilitating transfers of much of the capital required to colonise South Australia. Angas was one of a number of beneficiaries who did not directly own slaves, but acted as London-based agents claiming compensation on behalf of those who did.⁶⁷ In May 1835 he became a member of the South Australian Colonization Commission, established by Wakefield's South Australian Company, which had the role of managing emigration and the sale of land, while the colony's governor assumed all the other functions of government. When the Commission struggled to fulfil the government-set pre-requisite of £35,000 of colonial land sales before the first emigrants could be transported, it was Angas who 'came to the rescue by offering to form a [separate] joint-stock company'. He and two partners bought two-thirds of the unsold land, transferring it all to the South Australian Company from 1836. His own trading company then equipped and sent out two whalers, a store ship and a coastal trader to help get the settlement established; the cost of the crews and labourers recruited in Britain was charged to the Commission's emigration fund. 'In 1840 the South Australian Company paid its first dividend, only because Angas had saved its bank from competition for four years'.[68] Despite the Company's and the British government's promises of protection, the consequences for South Australia's Aboriginal people would be dire.[69]

Conclusion

The act of emancipation, so often celebrated as both a foundation in the history of modern, Western humanitarianism and a matter of British national pride, was shaped and delimited by the realpolitik of imperial restructuring in the 1830s. James Stephen drafted the Slavery Abolition Act as part of an extensive restructuring of the Empire, which is overlooked when, as is conventional, colonial and imperial historians focus only on one part of the Empire at any one time. That partial focus means that the contestation between humanitarian campaigning and realpolitik remains partially obscured. Only by looking everywhere and all at once do we appreciate that Stephen had to think through emancipation at the same time as he was being pressed to develop settler societies, that parliamentarians were debating the end of slavery at the same time as the restructuring of the East India Company, and that these processes became interlinked.[70]

As humane concern in Britain contributed to the freeing of 800,000 enslaved people, primarily in the Caribbean, enslavement and other forms of coerced labour remained untouched in other colonies, the rights of newly freed people of colour were restricted so as to maintain white supremacy, and Aboriginal Australians, in particular, suffered accelerated invasion from those deflected from both slavery in the Caribbean and Company-protected trade in the East Indies. These processes were not just simultaneous, they were inextricably connected by the trade-offs in which Stephen and his contemporaries engaged as they sought to manage emancipation alongside imperial regrowth and restructuring.

The British Empire was transitioning in many ways all at once between 1833 and 1838. The basis of its economy was changing, from slave-produced tropical commodities towards emigrant-produced temperate products (although East India Company-produced opium remained a constant); its geography was shifting, from twin circuits of trade in the West and East Indies towards new centres of gravity in the Indian Ocean and the Southern Hemisphere; and its mode of governance was altering, from the autocratic military elite that had seized new colonies from Britain's enemies towards a bureaucracy more accountable to settlers overseas and an expanded electorate at home. This transition was packaged in part as a move away from slavery, as evangelical humanitarian campaigners had demanded. Among other things, that move entailed the rebranding of Indian and other forms of slavery as not really slavery at all.

These multiple transitions were all connected to an imperial political economy increasingly attuned to the needs of Britain's rising and newly enfranchised commercial, financial and manufacturing classes. The task of the men governing the British Empire and effecting emancipation was to manage this wide-ranging transformation with due regard to those who had invested heavily in the Empire's earlier form and who were now admitting the nouveau riches into their ranks. By the end of 1838, Britons who had owned slaves in the Caribbean had been compensated for their emancipation and assured of continued labour supply through indenture, while those who had bought East India Company stock had been assured of continued dividends as the Company became exclusively the government of India, overseeing millions of unfree labourers.

Fortunately for planters in Ceylon, Mauritius, the Caribbean and the Pacific, the East India Company's governance provided a means to persuade Indian peasants to leave their homes and work for them under indenture. Not entirely, but almost, free from the scrutiny that antislavery activists afforded to those enslaved in the Caribbean, the Colonial Office itself could allow Indians, 'Creoles' and convicts in other parts of the Empire to persist in various states of coerced labour for some time to come. As for the post-emancipation civil rights of people of colour, James Stephen and the Colonial Office may have been committed to 'colour blindness' as a principle, but tended to concede it when governors expressed concern about colonists' resistance.

Emancipation was implemented only because the compensation shielded slave owners from its most deleterious economic effects. It was one component of a broader drive to restructure domestic and imperial political economies towards freer trade, which also saw the East India Company reoriented from commerce to governance and its shareholders protected by guaranteed dividends. New outlets for 'surplus' people and capital in the colonisation of Australia, in particular, at this time, were another, closely related component of the realpolitik of this 'emancipatory' restructuring.

Notes

1 David Lambert and Alan Lester, 'Geographies of Colonial Philanthropy', *Progress in Human Geography* (2004), 28 (3), pp. 320–41; Gary Jonathan

Bass, *Freedom's Battle: The Origins of Humanitarian Intervention* (New York, NY: Knopf, 2008); Brendan Simms and David J. B. Trim, *Humanitarian Intervention: A History* (Cambridge, UK: Cambridge University Press, 2011).

2 As ex-British Prime Minister Tony Blair made clear in his Chicago speech of 1999, intervention in Kosovo was as much about sustaining the global interdependence upon which Britain's national economic interest relied as it was about human rights abuses perpetrated by Milosevic's regime: 'We are all internationalists now, whether we like it or not': Oliver Daddow, '"Tony's War"? Blair, Kosovo and the Interventionist Impulse in British Foreign Policy', *International Affairs* (2009), 85 (3), p. 549. See also Simon Reid-Henry, 'Humanitarianism as Liberal Diagnostic: Humanitarian Reason and the Political Rationalities of the Liberal Will-to-Care', *Transactions of the Institute of British Geographers* (2014), 39 (3), pp. 418–31.

3 Alan Lester, 'Humanitarian Governance and the Circumvention of Revolutionary Human Rights in the British Empire', in M. Barnett (ed.), *Humanitarianism and Human Rights* (Cambridge, UK: Cambridge University Press, 2020), pp. 106–26. See Samuel Moyn, *The Last Utopia: Human Rights in History* (Cambridge, MA: Harvard University Press, 2012), for the betrayal of human right's revolutionary potential in practice.

4 While the more political science- and international relations-oriented literature on international humanitarian intervention has tended to analyse competing, simultaneous governmental priorities (see Bass, *Freedom's Battle*, and Simms and Trim, *Humanitarian Intervention*), that on British imperial policies of emancipation has tended to focus mainly on a Caribbean–British axis, overlooking concurrent governmental preoccupations both there and elsewhere. Exceptions include Andrea Major, '"The Slavery of East and West": Abolitionists and "Unfree" Labour in India, 1820–1833', *Slavery and Abolition* (2010), 31 (4), pp. 501–25.

5 See Michael Barnett, *Empire of Humanity: A History of Humanitarianism* (Ithaca, NY: Cornell University Press, 2013).

6 Although earlier emancipations were announced in revolutionary France in 1794 (revoked in 1802) and brought to costly fruition by formerly enslaved people themselves in Haiti, the British Parliament's act of abolition is popularly conceived as a ground-breaking act of national selflessness. See, for example, Jeremy Black, *Imperial Legacies* (New York, NY: Encounter, 2019); Niall Ferguson, *Empire: How Britain Made the Modern World* (London, UK: Penguin, 2018).

7 Christopher A. Bayly, *Imperial Meridian: the British Empire and the World, 1780–1830* (London, UK: Routledge, 1989). For an exception to the neglect of furious legislative reform within Britain and its effects on imperial governance, see Miles Taylor, 'Empire and Parliamentary Reform: The 1832 Reform Act Revisited', in Arthur Burns and Joanna Innes (eds), *Rethinking the Age of Reform: Britain 1780–1850* (Cambridge, UK: Cambridge University Press, 2003), pp. 295–311.

8 The Board of Control was the government-appointed body which oversaw the activities of the East India Company Directors, and could overrule them if necessary.

9 John Oldfield, *Transatlantic Abolitionism in the Age of Revolution: An International History of Anti-Slavery, c.1787–1820* (Cambridge, UK: Cambridge University Press, 2014). Taylor, 'Empire and Parliamentary Reform'; Alan Lester and Nikita Vanderbyl, 'The Restructuring of the British Empire and the Colonization of Australia, 1832–8', *History Workshop Journal* (2020), 90, pp. 165–88.

10 Life in the United Kingdom: Guide for Immigrants, 3rd edn, https://lifeintheuktests.co.uk/study-guide/?chapter=3&section=4/#start10, accessed 28 September 2020.

11 For historians' protest, see https://historyjournal.org.uk/2020/07/21/historians-call-for-a-review-of-home-office-citizenship-and-settlement-test/, accessed 20 August 2021. For the fate of 'recaptives', see Bronwen Everill, *Abolition and Empire in Sierra Leone and Liberia* (London, UK: Palgrave Macmillan, 2013), and Suzanne Schwarz, 'Reconstructing the Life Histories of Liberated Africans: Sierra Leone in the Early Nineteenth Century', *History in Africa* (2012), 39, pp. 175–207.

12 Roger Anstey, *The Atlantic Slave Trade and British Abolition, 1760–1810* (London, UK: Macmillan, 1975); David Brion Davis, *The Problem of Slavery in Western Culture* (Ithaca, NY: Cornell University Press, 1966) and David Brion Davis, *The Problem of Slavery in the Age of Revolution, 1770–1823* (Ithaca, NY: Cornell University Press, 1975); Seymour Drescher, *Econocide: British Slavery in the Era of Abolition* (Pittsburgh, PA: University of Pittsburgh Press, 1977). Manisha Sinha, *The Slave's Cause: A History of Abolition* (New Haven, CT: Yale University Press, 2016).

13 Eric Williams, *Capitalism and Slavery* (Chapel Hill, NC: University of North Carolina Press, 1944).

14 Thomas L. Haskell, 'Capitalism and the Origins of the Humanitarian Sensibility, Part 1', *American Historical Review* (1985), 90 (2), pp. 339–61 and 'Capitalism and the Origins of the Humanitarian Sensibility, Part 2', *American Historical Review* (1985), 90 (3), pp. 547–66.

15 Christopher Leslie Brown, *Moral Capital: Foundations of British Abolitionism* (Chapel Hill, NC: University of North Carolina Press, 2006).

16 As Prime Minister, the conservative Duke of Wellington objected to government reports authored by this 'partisan of abolition': Paul Knaplund, *James Stephen and The British Colonial System 1813–1847* (Madison, WI: University of Wisconsin Press, 1953). On amelioration, see J. R. Ward, *British West Indian Slavery, 1750–1834: The Process of Amelioration* (Oxford, UK: Oxford University Press, 1988); Mary Turner, 'Planter Profits and Slave Rewards: Amelioration Reconsidered', in Roderick A. McDonald (ed.), *West Indies Accounts: Essays on the History of the British Caribbean and the Atlantic Economy in Honour of Richard Sheridan* (Kingston, UK: University of the West Indies Press, 1996), pp. 232–52; Alvin O. Thompson, *Unprofitable*

Servants: Crown Slaves in Berbice, Guyana, 1803–1831 (Kingston, UK: University of the West Indies Press, 2002), pp. 36–44; Christa Dierksheide, *Amelioration and Empire: Progress and Slavery in the Plantation Americas* (Charlottesville, VA: University of Virginia Press, 2014); and Caroline Quarrier Spence, 'Ameliorating Empire: Slavery and Protection in the British Colonies, 1783–1865' (PhD dissertation, Harvard University, 2014).

17 Gelien Matthews, *Caribbean Slave Revolts and the British Abolitionist Movement* (Baton Rouge, LA: Louisiana State University Press, 2013); Emilia Viotti da Costa, *Crowns of Glory, Tears of Blood: The Demerara Slave Rebellion of 1823* (Oxford, UK: Oxford University Press, 1994); Dierksheide, *Amelioration and Empire*; David Turley, *The Culture of English Antislavery, 1780–1860* (London and New York: Routledge, 1991).

18 These conditions are treated in more detail in Alan Lester, Kate Boehme and Peter Mitchell, *Ruling the World: Freedom, Civilisation and Liberalism in the British Empire* (Cambridge, UK: Cambridge University Press, 2020).

19 Turley, *The Culture of English Antislavery*; Taylor, 'Empire and Parliamentary Reform'.

20 Nicholas Draper, *The Price of Emancipation: Slave-ownership, Compensation and British Society at the End of Slavery* (Cambridge, UK: Cambridge University Press, 2010).

21 Bill for Abolition of Slavery throughout the British Colonies, for Promoting the Industry of the Manumitted Slaves, and for Compensating the Persons Hitherto Entitled to the Services of Such Slaves: https://parlipapers.proquest.com/parlipapers/docview/t70.d75.1833–014099, accessed 28 September 2020.

22 See Natasha Lightfoot, *Troubling Freedom: Antigua and the Aftermath of British Emancipation* (Durham, NC: Duke University Press, 2015); James Smith, *A New Dawn. An Analysis of the Emancipation Experience in Bermuda* (Bermuda: Ministry of Cultural Affairs, 1991).

23 Hansard, House of Commons Debate, 'Abolition of Negro Apprenticeship', 29 March, 1838, vol. XLII, cols 40–108.

24 In the event, all apprentices, whether domestic or agricultural were freed on 1 August 1838, in part owing the emotive force of the Jamaican apprentice James William's *Narrative of Events since the First of August, 1834*, promoted in Britain by the campaigner Joseph Sturge: see James Williams (ed. Diana Paton), *A Narrative of Events since the First of August, 1834, by James Williams, an Apprenticed Labourer in Jamaica* (Durham, NC: Duke University Press, 2001). See also Kate Boehme, Alan Lester and Peter Mitchell, 'Reforming Everywhere and All at Once: Transitioning to Free Labor across the British Empire, 1837–1838', *Comparative Studies in Society and History* (2018), 60, pp. 688–718.

25 Trevor Burnard and Kit Candlin, 'Sir John Gladstone and the Debate over the Amelioration of Slavery in the British West Indies in the 1820s', *Journal of British Studies* (October 2018), 57, p. 761.

26 Jonathan Connolly, 'Indentured Labour Migration and the Meaning of Emancipation: Free Trade, Race and Labour in British Public Debate, 1838–1860', *Past and Present* (2018), 238 (1), pp. 85–119.

27 Burnard and Candlin, 'Sir John Gladstone', p. 781.
28 See Madhavi Kale, *Fragments of Empire: Capital, Slavery, and Indian Indentured Labor Migration in the British Caribbean* (Philadelphia, PA: University of Pennsylvania Press, 1998).
29 Turley, *The Culture of English Antislavery*.
30 Clare Anderson, *Subaltern Lives: Biographies of Colonialism in the Indian Ocean World, 1790–1920* (Cambridge, UK: Cambridge University Press, 2012), and Clare Anderson, 'Transnational Histories of Penal Transportation: Punishment, Labour and Governance in the British Imperial World, 1788–1939', *Australian Historical Studies* (2016), 47 (3), pp. 381–97.
31 Everill, *Abolition and Empire*.
32 The National Archives (TNA), Colonial Office Records (COR) CO 23/100, *Bahamas: Despatches*, no. 28, Cockburn to Glenelg, 15 January 1838.
33 See Boehme, Lester and Mitchell, 'Reforming Everywhere and All at Once', from which much of this section is taken.
34 As Hazel Petrie shows, the Treaty of Waitangi signed on behalf of the Colonial Office in 1840 neatly sidestepped the issue of ongoing Māori forms of slavery: *Outcasts of the Gods?: The Struggle Over Slavery in Maori New Zealand* (Auckland, New Zealand: Auckland University Press, 2015).
35 Dharma Kumar, *Land and Caste in South India: Agricultural Labour in the Madras Presidency During the Nineteenth Century* (Cambridge, UK: Cambridge University Press, 1965).
36 Major, 'The Slavery of East and West', p. 506, and Andrea Major, *Slavery, Abolitionism and Empire in India, 1772–1843* (Liverpool, UK: Liverpool University Press, 2012).
37 Major, 'The Slavery of East and West', pp. 508–9.
38 Burnard and Candlin, 'Sir John Gladstone'.
39 Major, 'The Slavery of East and West', p. 514.
40 Dick Kooiman, 'Conversion from Slavery to Plantation Labour: Christian Mission in South India (19th Century)', *Social Scientist* (1991), 19 (8/9), pp. 57–71.
41 William Adam, *The Law and Custom of Slavery in British India, in a Series of Letters to Thomas Fowell Buxton, Esq.* (London, UK: Weeks, Jordan & Company, 1840), pp. 10–11.
42 Quoted in Major, 'The Slavery of East and West', p. 503.
43 Lester, Boehme and Mitchell, *Ruling the World*.
44 Aaron Graham, 'Slavery, Banks and the Ambivalent Legacies of Compensation in South Africa, Mauritius and the Caribbean', *Journal of Southern African Studies* (2021), 47 (3), pp. 473–87.
45 Quoted in Marina Carter, 'The Transition from Slave to Indentured Labour in Mauritius', *Slavery & Abolition* (1993), 14 (1), p. 120.
46 TNA COR, CO 167/198, *Mauritius: Despatches*, no. 125, W. Nicolay to Lord Glenelg, 5 March 1838.
47 See Thomas Holt, *The Problem of Freedom: Race, Labor, and Politics in Jamaica and Britain, 1832–1938* (Baltimore, MD: Johns Hopkins University Press, 1992), pp. 97–100.

48 Anne Chambers, *The Great Leviathan, The Life of Howe Peter Browne, 2nd Marquess of Sligo, 1788–1845* (Dublin, Ireland: New Island, 2017).
49 TNA, COR. CO 137/221, *Jamaica: Despatches*, no. 216, L. Smith to Glenelg, 20 December 1837.
50 Holt, *The Problem of Freedom*.
51 TNA, COR, CO 167/198, 123, Miscellaneous, Nicolay to Glenelg, 18 November 1837.
52 *Legacies of British Slave-Ownership*: www.ucl.ac.uk/lbs/, accessed 28 September 2020.
53 For the directors' attempts to negotiate these terms, see 'Copy of Correspondence between the Directors of the East India Company and the Board of Control Respecting the East India Charter', House of Commons Parliamentary Papers online, 1833–014326_01–08, accessed 28 September 2020; and Board of Control, 'Papers Respecting the Negotiation with His Majesty's Ministers on the Subject of the East India Company's Charter and the Government of His Majesty's Indian Territories for a Further Term …', 1833, British Library, IOR/V/27/220/11.
54 Catherine Hall, *Macaulay and Son: Architects of Imperial Britain* (New Haven, CT: Yale University Press, 2012), p. 206.
55 In 1834 some 300 families both owned enslaved people and had close personal or financial connections with the Company: Christopher Jeppesen, 'East Meets West: Exploring the Connections between Britain, the Caribbean and the East India Company, c.1757–1857', in Katie Donington, Ryan Hanley and Jessica Moody (eds), *Britain's History and Memory of Transatlantic Slavery* (Liverpool, UK: Liverpool University Press, 2016), pp. 102–28.
56 Hansard, House of Commons Debate 10 July 1833, vol. XIX, cols 479–550.
57 'Accounts Respecting the Annual Territorial Revenues and Disbursements of the East India Company for the Years 1833/4, 1834/5 and 1835/6', House of Commons Parliamentary Papers Online, 1839–018481_01–26, accessed 28 September 2020.
58 Catherine Hall, 'Writing History, Making "Race": Slave-Owners and Their Stories', *Australian Historical Studies* (2016), 47 (3), pp. 365–80; Draper, *Price of Emancipation*.
59 An Act to empower His Majesty to erect South Australia into a British Province or Provinces and to provide for the Colonization and Government thereof: https://parlipapers.proquest.com/parlipapers/docview/t70.d75.hol_00567 –000056, accessed 28 September 2020.
60 See Jane Lydon, 'Mr Wakefield's Speaking Trumpets': Abolishing Slavery and Colonising Systematically', *Journal of Imperial and Commonwealth History* (2021) DOI: 10.1080/03086534.2021.1956834, accessed 20 August 2021.
61 Eric Richards, 'How Did Poor People Emigrate from the British Isles to Australia in the Nineteenth Century?', *Journal of British Studies* (1993), 32 (3), p. 254.
62 These and other cases are examined in further detail in Lester and Vanderbyl, 'The Restructuring of the British Empire'.
63 Malcolm Allbrook, *Henry Prinsep's Empire: Framing a Distant Colony* (Canberra, Australia: ANU Press, 2014), p. 7.

64 Ibid., p. 50.
65 Ibid., p. 38.
66 Angela Woollacott, *Settler Society in the Australian Colonies: Self-Government and Imperial Culture* (Oxford, UK: Oxford University Press, 2015), p. 57.
67 Draper, *Price of Emancipation*, p. 242.
68 'Angas, George Fife (1789–1879)', Australian Dictionary of Biography, National Centre of Biography, Australian National University, http://adb.anu.edu.au/biography/angas-george-fife-1707/text1855, published first in hardcopy 1966, accessed online 28 September 2020; Lester and Vanderbyl, 'The Restructuring of the British Empire'.
69 Robert Foster, Rick Hosking and Amanda Nettelbeck, *Fatal Collisions: The South Australian Frontier and the Violence of Memory* (Adelaide, Australia: Wakefield Press, 2010); Robert Foster and Amanda Nettelbeck, *Out of the Silence: The History and Memory of South Australia's Frontier Wars* (Adelaide, Australia: Wakefield Press, 2018). The Colonial Frontier Massacres in Australia, 1788–1930 project at the University of Newcastle Australia has identified forty-four recorded massacres in South Australia between 1788 and 1930: https://c21ch.newcastle.edu.au/colonialmassacres/map.php.
70 For a more extensive approach to British imperial governance everywhere and all at once, and a review of the historiography, see Lester, Boehme and Mitchell, *Ruling the World*.

Part II

Humanitarianism and Indigenous peoples, 1838–c. 1950

6

Humanitarianism in a genocidal age: The tragic story of the Aboriginal prison on Rottnest Island, Western Australia, 1838–1903

Ann Curthoys

Governor John Hutt, a man strongly influenced by British humanitarian thought, played a crucial role in the early 1840s in establishing an Aboriginal prison on Rottnest Island, known to local Whadjuk Noongar as Wadjemup, eighteen kilometres to the west of Perth on the coast of Western Australia.[1] For Hutt, the 'improvement and instruction' of the prisoners mattered more than their punishment, and he appointed a Protector to keep watch. Yet during the sixty-five years the prison operated, it became a feared and hated place for Aboriginal people, with approximately 3,700 prisoners subjected to regimes of hard labour and harsh physical punishment – and 10 per cent of them died in custody. The island is now a place of great sadness for Noongar and other Aboriginal groups in Western Australia, and modes of recognition and remembrance of this history are under continuing discussion. In this chapter, I explore the prison as a startling case study in the failure of humanitarian principles and policies to translate into humanitarian action on the ground. I use the term 'humanitarians' broadly, to indicate those in the colony of Western Australia who sought the protection of Aboriginal people from frontier violence and advocated policies ensuring their survival either within or alongside settler society.[2] I build on the work of historians Alan Lester and Fae Dussart in *Colonization and the Origins of Humanitarian Governance*, which drew attention to the ways in which humanitarians sought to shape colonial governments' dealings with Indigenous peoples and ultimately to govern Indigenous peoples themselves, and of Amanda Nettelbeck, who has emphasised that, in the Australian context, government-appointed Protectors, initially conceived as mediators and advocates for Aboriginal people, often became agents of the state, overseeing and administering punishment.[3]

In exploring the history of the prison on Rottnest Island, I draw out the contradictory nature of humanitarian ideas in a colonising context, especially in the humanitarian involvement in the punishment of Indigenous people. On the one hand, humanitarians in the settler colony of Western Australia wished to minimise death and injury to the Aboriginal peoples whose lands the colony was taking and developing for settler purposes. Colonists often had a genuine interest in aspects of Aboriginal culture and tradition, as Governor Hutt had in Aboriginal connections to their own country. Their language and discourse were not those of the settler, who, in his rage against Aboriginal men who stole food, sheep and cattle and sometimes attacked settler families or servants, could see only a violent savage who must be destroyed. On the other hand, humanitarians, both within and outside government, wished to ensure the smooth path of colonisation itself, the securing of the land for settlers and their descendants, and the imposition of English law and order. Many of them became ardent assimilationists, seeking to destroy Indigenous culture and replace it with a version of Britishness. In seeking to impose the rule of English law, sometimes immediately, at other times more gradually, they aimed to undermine Indigenous law and the wider Indigenous cultures of which it was a crucial part. If we think of Polish Jurist Raphaël Lemkin's founding definition of genocide as having 'two phases: one, destruction of the national pattern of the oppressed group; the other, the imposition of the national pattern of the oppressor', we can understand the history of the Rottnest Island Aboriginal Prison as a vital part of a project of cultural genocide.[4]

The humanitarians I consider here were a diverse group of men brought together by a distinctive British colonisation project. The Swan River Colony, founded in 1829 and renamed Western Australia in 1832, was government-controlled and sponsored by private investors. Based on a land grant system underpinning private settlement, the small isolated settlement consisted of government officials, a military detachment, landed settlers, some professionals, such as lawyers and newspaper editors, and a small labouring class, many of whom had arrived from Britain with their employers as indentured servants. These were largely British people, who brought with them a range of ideas concerning their rights as settlers and the rights (or lack of rights) of the existing Indigenous population, who in the early years were the Noongar people of the south-west. Some of these officials and settlers were humanitarians, and some have attracted historical attention.[5] They are not the only people in Western Australia, however, who might attract the label 'humanitarian'. What connects the men discussed here is that all had some involvement in the public discussions concerning the Aboriginal prison on Rottnest Island.

Humanitarians: the first wave, 1832–49

The early humanitarians who considered the possibility of island detention for Aboriginal offenders include Robert Lyon, a well-educated early colonist; Francis Armstrong, the colony's English-Noongar interpreter and for a while mission superintendent; George Fletcher Moore, a wealthy farmer, leading legal figure and prolific writer; William Nairne Clark, a lawyer and newspaper editor; Louis Giustiniani, an Italian-born Anglican missionary; and Governor John Hutt, governor of the colony from 1839 until 1846. These were all very early settlers and officials in Western Australia, Lyon and Armstrong arriving in 1829, Moore in 1830, Clark in 1831, Giustiniani in 1836 and Hutt in January 1839. They came from various parts of the stratified social spectrum that characterised the early years of the colony. Hutt and Moore were part of the small colonial elite, while Lyon, Armstrong, Giustiniani and Clark were all, despite their access to granted or purchased land, outside that elite. Though very different in their social position and backgrounds, these men shared an interest in Aboriginal people and a concern for their welfare in the wake of British settlement. We could say they formed an early colonial intelligentsia, able to draw on classical examples to develop their arguments and often beset by fractious relations among themselves.

The story of the prison on Rottnest begins in mid-1832 under the regime of James Stirling, the first governor of the colony. As conflict between Noongar and settlers escalated, several officials and settlers considered how best to suppress Aboriginal resistance and secure the persons and property of the settlers. Some were attracted to a solution like that adopted in January 1832 in Van Diemen's Land (Tasmania), where after several years of bloody frontier violence the government had persuaded the surviving Aboriginal people to move to Flinders Island, lying off the north coast of the colony; one prominent settler, William Shenton, suggested they follow suit and remove troublesome Noongar to Rottnest Island.[6] Rottnest, however, was not then available, Governor Stirling having opened it for settlement the previous year.[7] One of those receiving a land grant on the island was Robert Lyon. While he left the colony in 1835, before the prison was established, Lyon is important in this story for his role in suggesting that offshore islands could be used as places of conciliation with Noongar resisting settlement. In October 1832, two months after Stirling had gone on extended leave to England and Frederick Irwin had become Acting Governor, frontier conflict was at a height. When Irwin and the Executive Council (consisting of several leading government officials whose tasks included advising the governor) were considering how best to punish captured outlaw and rebel leader, Yagan, and his two companions, Lyon urged against execution. They should be regarded, he urged, not as criminals but as prisoners of war with whom one would attempt conciliation. As Lyon later commented in a letter to the Secretary of State, 'to put prisoners of war to death, in cool blood, was contrary to the law of nations and usages of war'.[8] His alternative suggestion in

October 1832 was that the men, accompanied by Lyon, be taken to nearby Carnac Island, where he could learn their language, teach them English and some aspects of Christianity, and perhaps he and they could reach some negotiated agreement.[9] In making this suggestion, Lyon was perhaps influenced by a long history of Europeans establishing missions for Indigenous people on islands in order to keep out settler and other influences that might undermine missionary work.

Concerned that putting the three men to death could provoke Noongar reprisals, Irwin and the council agreed with Lyon's proposal. Accordingly, Lyon and two military guards lived on Carnac Island with Yagan, Dommera and Ningena for five weeks, he learning their language and they learning English, before the three men escaped by boat on 15 November 1832.[10] Although disappointed, Lyon observed that the experiment had at least shown 'the practicability of teaching them to work and maintain themselves by their own industry'.[11] Lyon continued to advocate conciliation as an advantage to the colony. 'Can a people be governed without a knowledge of their language and their manners?', he asked in the *Perth Gazette* in March 1833. 'Can there be any safety for the properties and lives of settlers unless a friendly intercourse be established between them and the Native Tribes?'[12] In a subsequent letter to the *Perth Gazette*, he urged the importance of teaching Noongar to work, warning that 'those who would have them to work, must treat them like men, not like brutes'. Ideally, the government should place them on a farm by themselves, where they could be instructed in 'the arts of civilized life' and even more importantly, the 'principles of Christianity'.[13] In a long impassioned speech in June 1833, criticising settler and government violence, he urged conciliation and respect: 'They have all along shown themselves ready to be reconciled, desirous to make peace and amity with you, and even willing to be taught your manners, laws, and polity'.[14]

One of Lyon's supporters was George Fletcher Moore, who for a time helped fund his work among Aboriginal people, so that he could 'try what he can to effect an understanding or arrangement with them'.[15] Moore came from a comfortable Irish background, and had practised law in Ireland for six years before arriving in Western Australia in October 1830 with four indentured servants from his father's farm.[16] His biographer, James Cameron, describes Moore's wide range of occupations and interests. He was 'a successful landowner, small scale merchant, explorer and land evaluator, accomplished lawyer and legislator, a more than adequate poet, songster and amateur musician, and a pioneer recorder and interpreter of Aboriginal language and custom. He was a major contributor to the colonial press on a range of subjects'.[17] In 1834, Moore became Advocate-General, a position requiring him to advise the governor on questions of law, prosecute offenders and conduct all Crown cases. He was a member of the colony's elite, being also prominent in the Anglican Church, the Western Australian Bank, the Agricultural Society and a local agent for the Western Australian Missionary Society.

Moore's respect for Aboriginal people grew with contact. 'Within months of arrival', Cameron notes, 'he declared that Aborigines were "not as despicable" as he "first supposed" but were, in fact, "active, bold and shrewd"'.[18] His appreciation deepened as he learned more about their customs and as he developed friendships with older men like Weeip, Tomghin, Doorbup and Geear. Like Lyon, he began publishing in the newly established *Perth Gazette* in 1833 on Aboriginal customs and his views on policy. He wanted to find a way to protect both Aboriginal people and settler society. On 13 July 1833, he urged settlers to attempt reconciliation rather than confrontation. It could guarantee the amelioration of the condition of Aborigines and at the same time 'our lives and property may be secure from hazard – so that their procurement of subsistence may be compatible with our enjoyment of the soil'.[19]

Moore's hopes for effective conciliation were not to be realised. Two months after Stirling returned from England and resumed his role as governor, he turned in November 1834 to a military solution, leading to an infamous massacre at Pinjarra, at the southern edge of the settlement. For a while afterwards, colonial authorities turned to programmes of education and welfare, though without the assistance of Robert Lyon, who had abandoned all hope of conciliation and left the colony for Mauritius in early 1835, where he became professor of Latin and Greek at the College of Port Louis.[20] Instead, Stirling placed the young Francis Armstrong, who had arrived as a sixteen-year-old with his family in 1829 and had befriended Noongar and learnt their language, in charge of an Aboriginal institution on Mt Eliza and appointed him native interpreter for the colony.[21] In addition, the Western Australian Missionary Society, formed in London in September 1835 with colonial support, in 1836 sent an Anglican missionary, Dr Louis Giustiniani, and two catechists to establish a mission in the colony.[22] The mission was much closer to the colonial settlement than originally planned, and within six months Giustiniani began to express strong opposition to the settler culture he encountered, which sought to crush Aboriginal stealing of food and other attacks on the settlement through whatever means available.[23] In a letter to the *Swan River Guardian* newspaper (which, incidentally, he financially supported),[24] he alluded to the fact that the courts had begun sentencing Noongar to long prison sentences for stealing, and was appalled that it had now become common to 'condemn a Native to seven years imprisonment for having stolen Grapes in a fenced portion of his land, where he, from his childhood, was accustomed to dig roots for his own support'.[25] Giustiniani also attempted to revive Lyon's idea of accompanying Aboriginal people to a nearby island, having offered himself for 'a voluntary transportation to one of the islands nigh to our shores with the Natives whom the Governor might think proper to Civilize and to Christianize without any additional emolument from the Government, or even thanks from the Settlers'. According to Giustiniani, Governor Stirling and his Executive Council had refused on the grounds that 'the natives are British subjects and it would be an infringement of their liberty to force them to leave their Native Land'.[26]

While the government did not accept Giustiniani's offer of voluntary transportation, it nevertheless began to take seriously the idea of transporting Aboriginal prisoners to an offshore island. With the greater use of courts to punish theft, and sometimes assault, the number of Noongar men incarcerated in Fremantle Gaol, the colony's main prison, was rapidly increasing.[27] So, too, were the number of escapes by Noongar from gaol. Administrators sought a form of punishment consistent with British practice and yet specific to Aboriginal offenders who were proving difficult to manage in the usual way. One solution attracting their attention was that traditional British punishment, transportation beyond seas, which underpinned the colonies of New South Wales and Van Diemen's Land and formed a crucial component of British imperial expansion and power.[28] In October 1837 William Mackie, as Chairman of the Perth Court of Quarter Sessions of the Peace, sentenced two men, Dur-gap and Go-gool, to seven years 'transportation beyond seas' for stealing food in the Upper Swan.[29] The *Swan River Guardian* asked, quite reasonably, 'to what Colony are these Natives to be transported?' Aware that New South Wales and Van Diemen's Land would refuse to receive them, the *Guardian* suggested that the best solution for Western Australia was 'to form a penal Establishment on the Island of Rottenest [sic] and point out to the Natives that all those who commit offences against whites, and those who spear other natives, will be sent there for a very long time'.[30] It is telling to see this suggestion coming from the relatively sympathetic *Guardian*, edited by William Nairne Clark, a lawyer from Scotland. Clark knew Rottnest well, having attempted, and failed, to make a living from a fishery there when the island was opened to settlers in 1831.[31] Now he favoured using it as a site for Aboriginal offenders, including those practising their own law.

The *Swan River Guardian* returned to the issue on 1 February 1838, commenting that the best response to a recent tribal killing in a Perth street would have been 'the formation of the Island of Rottenest into a penal Settlement, for the reception of notorious offenders'.[32] Forced to close by new government regulations, the *Guardian* ceased publication later that month, but debates over what to do about the colony's growing Aboriginal prison population continued in the pro-government *Perth Gazette*. Commentators came to prefer Rottnest Island to Carnac Island, since it was further away from the mainland and therefore more secure against escapes, and in addition thought to be large and fertile enough to become self-sufficient.[33] As the *Gazette* put it, on Rottnest Island the prisoners could continue hunting and fishing, as well as being profitably employed in 'collecting salt, curing fish and gathering firewood and in other occupations'.[34] The opportunities for both maritime employment and subsistence farming suggested an island prison could be run cheaply and at the same time assist in transforming Noongar from 'savages' into a useful source of labour for the colony as a whole. The presence of settlers was no longer a serious problem, since the island's settlers, other than Robert Thompson and his family, had all left when their ventures failed for want of capital, labour or sufficiently productive land.

Prompted by an outbreak of disease in Fremantle Gaol, the colony's gaoler, Henry Vincent, in mid-1838 urged the governor to establish a prison on Rottnest Island. Not only would the island be a good site for an Aboriginal prison, he suggested, but he, Vincent, would be the ideal person to be its superintendent. When Stirling took the plan to the Executive Council on 14 June 1838, it approved Vincent's proposal, though it appointed Laurence Welch, the sheriff's officer for Perth, rather than Vincent as superintendent.[35] After a false start (the first group of Noongar prisoners taken to the island escaped using Thompson's boat, and it took some time to persuade Thompson to leave as agreed), Welch managed to establish the prison in the final few months of 1838, setting the prisoners to work at burning stones for lime, hewing firewood, sawing sandstone and starting a garden.[36]

The prison was thus barely in existence when a new governor, John Hutt, arrived in January 1839. John Hutt is an excellent example of governors in the British Empire in the 1830s and 1840s who attempted to govern according to certain humanitarian principles. His approach was informed in part by his education. As legal historian Ann Hunter describes, he came from a family with a strong background in the East India Company navy. In 1809 at the age of fifteen, he studied at the Company's Haileybury College in Hertfordshire, and from 1813 served as a business agent and court registrar in Madras, India. While a civil servant in Madras, he gained further education for a year in 1813 at the recently founded College of Fort St George, which, under the leadership of Francis Whyte Ellis, emphasised the importance for British governors and officials of learning local Indian languages and culture.[37] On his return to England in 1821, Hutt had become involved in schemes to encourage British emigration to the Australian colonies.[38] With his better-known brother, William, he was a follower of influential colonial promoter and author, Edward Gibbon Wakefield, and was a member of the parliamentary committee appointed to investigate the disposal of colonial wastelands, whose report in August 1836 advocated the Wakefieldian scheme for colonial expansion – the sale of land in the colonies to fund emigration. After working as superintendent of emigration for South Australia from 1835 to 1838, he sought appointment as the colony's governor, but in April 1838, was appointed to Western Australia instead. [39]

Before leaving England, Hutt was briefed by the Aborigines Protection Society on the new imperial policy of protection, and he brought with him to Western Australia a copy of the influential 1837 Report of the House of Commons Select Committee on Aboriginal Tribes in British Settlements.[40] The report emphasised the importance of protection of Aboriginal people from settler aggression, the application of British law to Aboriginal people, and the need for compensation for Aboriginal peoples' loss of land in the form of religious instruction and education. Hutt was aware that the Aboriginal people he would meet in Western Australia might differ substantially from those in New South Wales and Van Diemen's Land, mentioned in the report, and determined to learn local languages and culture. He was especially concerned to understand Aboriginal peoples' political structures and ideas of land proprietorship, and in the early years of his governorship assisted in the production of Aboriginal vocabularies by both George Moore and another local official, resident magistrate George Grey, who later rose to prominence as a governor in South Australia, New Zealand and Cape Colony.[41] Hutt developed a good relationship with Moore on many matters, and the two men agreed that the long-term future for Aboriginal people lay in employment, education and Christianisation.[42] Shortly before Hutt arrived, Moore had given a major speech to the Western Australian Church Missionary Association on 17 November 1838,[43] opposing the idea that Aboriginal people were different and inferior, saying we are all of one stock, 'all endowed with the same human nature'.[44]

It quickly became clear that Hutt had a programme of assimilation in mind and thought settler employment of Noongar was an excellent way to encourage inclusion. He saw three options for Noongars' future in the colony: death, slavery or absorption into settler society. A few months after taking office, he wrote to the Secretary of State arguing that the only answer was absorption, with its key elements being education, Christianisation and, above all, employment. For assimilationists like Hutt, a major question was how to respond when Aboriginal people obeyed their own laws but broke British ones, for example carrying out a killing mandated by tribal law. Moore strongly opposed punishing Noongar for crimes among themselves, commenting in the *Perth Gazette* on 6 July 1839, that it was 'imprudent and unadvisable to make their quarrels our own'.[45] Hutt agreed to an extent, believing that Noongar in unsettled areas could practise their own laws, and only gradually have British law applied to them. He was emphatic, however, that where settler protection was concerned, British law should be imposed immediately, a position that led him directly to the task of devising effective punishment for Noongar who broke British law. To this end, he established a locally funded civil police force and appointed interpreter Francis Armstrong as Constable of Police for Perth.[46] He would also involve the two men who had been appointed as Protectors of Aborigines – Charles Symmons (from December 1839) and Rivett Henry Bland (from October 1841) in overseeing punishment.[47]

The prison on Rottnest Island became an important part of Hutt's policy on punishment. He saw it as an effective deterrent and at the same time an opportunity for assimilation. His instructions to the superintendent in August 1839 stated: 'The Superintendent is to understand that the improvement and instruction of the natives, more than their punishment, is the object which the Government have in view in placing them on the island'.[48] He was also to 'teach them the arts and wants of civilized life', conduct Divine service every Sunday and employ the men in such a way that the establishment was self-supporting, such as fishing, erecting buildings, collecting salt and cultivating the ground. Given the colony's desperate need for agricultural labour, Hutt hoped also that the island prison could train Aboriginal people for farm employment; those who acquired farming skills could receive early parole and return to perform seasonal work in their districts.[49] It was important to Hutt that the prison not become a place of 'severe punishment': as he told the Legislative Council on 4 May 1840, 'the loss of their wild freedom and being subjected to regular labor ... may be considered to carry with them ... quite sufficient terror, without any additional pains or penalties'.[50] Hutt's use of the word 'terror' here is revealing, indicating a firm resolve to terrorise Aboriginal people into submission to the new British order. In July 1840 he presented to the Legislative Council a bill to constitute the Island of Rottnest a legal prison, which stated that Rottnest had been chosen as a place both secure and allowing them some liberty, since 'ordinary modes of restraint have been found insufficient to insure their safe keeping in any gaol', and confinement was 'particularly prejudicial to their health'.[51] Hutt realised that while he had dual aims for the prison – reformation and deterrence – many settlers were interested only in deterrence. In November 1841 he used his casting vote to ensure the Legislative Council passed the amended act, which formally established the prison and pronounced that Aboriginal prisoners would be 'instructed in useful knowledge and gradually trained in the habits of civilised life'.[52]

Hutt's ideas for the prison were developed at a time when there was extensive discussion and debate within the British Empire over Aboriginal policy and penal policy. His approach was influenced in part by the ideas that had coalesced around the Aborigines Report of 1837 and the Aborigines Protection Society, based in London. Instead of wholesale destruction in the course of colonisation, both the report and the society argued, Aboriginal people should be offered protection and, through education, the benefits of 'civilisation' and Christianity. Hutt's vision seems also to have drawn, eclectically, on the debates over penal policy that swirled around the Empire through the 1830s concerning the relative merits of transportation and incarceration in a penitentiary in terms of their effectiveness in deterring crime and reforming the convict. Transportation as a system, which had operated in the eastern colonies since 1788, was coming under attack and indeed nearing its end in New South Wales. Its critics saw it as unable to reform the convicts it managed and thought the penitentiary could achieve reform much more efficiently, being better able to make punishment more reliably proportionate to the crime and thus shape convict behaviour.

In the long run, transportation would be phased out and penitentiaries built in Britain and the colonies. In the late 1830s, when Hutt was considering the question of punishment, however, transportation was still a serious option. One penal thinker and administrator who sought to combine the two ideas – transportation and prison reform – was Alexander Maconochie, formerly a naval officer and then Professor of Geography at the University of London. Maconochie arrived in Van Diemen's Land as Governor John Franklin's personal secretary in 1837 and wrote a report on the state of the colony's prison discipline in 1838 in which he suggested replacing physical punishment (flogging) with moral training through employment on public works.[53] Unlike many advocates of the penitentiary at this time who praised the benefits of silence and solitary confinement, he favoured group activities and social bonds.[54] In 1839, having lost his position with Franklin and living in Hobart, he wrote a series of pamphlets advocating less focus on punishment and more on rewards for good behaviour, and providing improving influences, such as religion, music and gardening. In 1840, he began a four-year experiment as superintendent of the penal settlement on Norfolk Island, a small Pacific island over 1,100 nautical miles east of Sydney, applying these ideas, until he lost Colonial Office support for excessive leniency and expense, even though his claim to have 'found the island a turbulent, brutal hell, and left it a peaceful, well-ordered community' seems to have had some validity.[55] Hutt was developing his ideas about the fledgling prison on Rottnest Island at around the same time as Maconochie was developing his penal theory and putting it into practice on Norfolk Island. His vision was parallel to Maconochie's, especially in the notion of well-regulated labour as a key to moral reform, and may have been influenced by it, but its application to an Indigenous population reacting to the destruction

What the prison became

Hutt's complex vision for the prison gradually came undone.[56] First, he made an appointment that would undermine its 'improvement' and inclusion dimensions. After a second escape from the island by Noongar prisoners in August 1839, he removed Welch as superintendent and appointed Henry Vincent in his place.[57] Vincent, however, had little interest in Christianisation and education, and a great deal in the prison's building programme. During his first year as superintendent, he forced the prisoners to work, erecting several substantial stone buildings, which still stand today, as well as tending the gardens and harvesting and transporting salt from the island's abundant salt lakes for export to the mainland.[58] Like other prison warders, Vincent used violence to ensure the men worked, perhaps to a greater degree than the government expected. When Governor Hutt visited in early 1840, he expressed concern at the use of the cat-o'-nine-tails, since 'the common lash is quite sufficient'.[59]

Next, Hutt appointed Charles Symmons, Protector of Aborigines, as Visiting Magistrate of the island, whose task would be to ensure that the conduct of the prison conformed to the thinking expressed in the Act and the superintendent's instructions. This appointment also undermined the humanitarian aspects of Hutt's vision for the prison. Although a Protector, Symmons was also, as Furphy points out, a government official whose role was to assist in effectively policing Noongar. To make matters worse, Symmons had achieved his appointment through family patronage rather than aptitude for the position and would display little concern for Aboriginal rights and survival.[60] Over the next two and a half decades, Symmons would praise Vincent wholeheartedly, and defend him against the frequently recurring charges of cruelty. It was Symmons, as much as anyone, who allowed Vincent's violent regime to last as long as it did.

During the 1840s, the number of prisoners on Rottnest was rarely above fifty. People continued to be sentenced there for crimes such as stealing, and also for crimes amongst themselves, as the authorities strove to impose British law and undermine the operation of Noongar law. Throughout the decade charges of brutality were made against Henry Vincent by settlers and officials who heard stories from returned prisoners or on one occasion former military guards on the island. Each time, the government instituted an inquiry and each time concluded that the charges were unfounded. During these years, several men with humanitarian leanings either chose or were called upon to comment on events at the prison. In October 1840, Hutt sent George Fletcher Moore, along with Protector Symmons, to investigate the deaths of three prisoners on the island.[61] Their report was mixed, approving of the prisoners' working hours, but criticising the food, poor provision of blankets and clothing, lack of medical inspections and lack of visits from friends and people interested in their welfare.[62]

On one occasion, in 1842, Hutt became concerned after 'conversations with the natives themselves, who had been at Rottnest' that some prisoners thought they had been treated very harshly. After making private inquiries and concluding that Henry Vincent may have charges to answer, he handed the matter over to the Advocate General, Richard West Nash, 'with strict injunctions to take such steps as might ensure the speediest and utmost punishment the law allowed, should Mr. Vincent be found guilty'. Accordingly, on 26 December 1842, the chair of the Court of Quarter Sessions and a bench of four magistrates tried Vincent, accused of behaving with 'undue severity' and inflicting such a degree of chastisement upon a native [Kun-di-bang], as occasioned his death. The magistrates were unanimous in dismissing the charge.[63] Hutt made two more attempts to investigate the nature of disciplinary punishment on the island, sending first a senior military officer and then Armstrong to investigate.[64] The military officer reported there was no problem, but after his two-week stay on the island, Armstrong wrote, 'I can say nothing in favour of the apparent severity with which the natives are treated at Rottnest'. In particular, he recommended that the maximum number of stripes (lashes) allowed be halved, from thirty-six to eighteen.[65]

Armstrong was not Vincent's only critic from within settler society. Another was William Nairne Clark, whose thinking on Aboriginal matters was expressed in some detail in an essay published in three parts in the *Inquirer* in February 1842. This is a remarkable text, which echoes some of Lyon's thinking, expressed ten years before. In her 'excessive zeal' to acquire colonies, Great Britain, Clark argues, had infringed the rights of the colony's Aboriginal inhabitants, and in thus taking possession of the land *'without obtaining the consent of the natives'*, it now had a 'fearful responsibility'.[66] To emphasise his point, Clark quoted from Roman historian Quintus Curtius Rufus, who in his biography of Alexander the Great includes a speech purportedly given by the Scythian ambassador to Alexander the Great on the latter's threatened invasion of Scythia. In the first half of the nineteenth century, this speech had been printed in various religious and educational texts, but this is the only occasion I have found in which it was used to address the question of settler–Indigenous relations.[67] Clark quotes the Scythian ambassador, who says: 'you must expect that the nations you conquer will endeavour to shake off the yoke as fast as possible. *For what people chooses to be under foreign domination? It is in vain that confidence is reposed in a conquered people. There can be no sincere friendship between the oppressor and the oppressed*'.[68]

Clark could have quoted much more from this text, so apposite is it to the settler colonial situation, with its insatiable desire for conquest of other peoples' lands. Great Britain, said Clark, had learnt through experience the truth of many of the ambassador's remarks. He then imagines what an ambassador for the Aboriginal peoples of Australia might say to the British Court:

> White fellow say, this our land, that our land – ALL country our land. Black fellow say no! my country no white fellows' country, and black fellow take spear.
> White fellow say, black fellow take spear – soldier men shoot him black fellow ...
> Black fellow say, white fellow take land, white fellow take kangaroo – black fellow take sheep; white fellow then kill him black fellow.[69]

Angry at Governor Hutt's rejection of his request to be appointed Protector of Aborigines at King George's Sound, Clark attempted to take revenge by alerting British authorities to events at the prison on Rottnest. His letter to the Aborigines Protection Society in London, written in December 1842, alleged cruel behaviour by Vincent towards the island's Aboriginal prisoners, and was soon referred to the Secretary of State, Lord Stanley.[70] Although Hutt had his own suspicions concerning Vincent, in his reply to a query from Lord Stanley in February 1844 he vigorously defended him, pointing to the outcome of the public examination before the magistrates in December 1842, which had exonerated Vincent of all charges.[71] Stanley accepted Hutt's account of events, and the matter dropped.[72] Clark's connection with Rottnest appears to have ended at this point, and he left the colony in November 1848; he worked as a journalist in Hobart, where he died in 1854. Hutt also departed when his term as governor ended on 19 February 1846.

The prison was entering a difficult phase. After the death in office of Hutt's successor, Governor Andrew Clarke, on 11 February 1847, Frederick Irwin was again Acting Governor from 12 February 1847 until 11 August 1848, when the new governor, Charles Fitzgerald (1848–55) arrived. Perhaps in an effort to bring the prison more into alignment with its original purpose, in June 1847 Irwin appointed Armstrong to a multi-role position on the island entitled 'Interpreter and Moral Agent for Aboriginal People, Accountant and Storekeeper'.[73] Armstrong's first report as Moral Agent on 10 February 1848 made it clear that Vincent had provided him with no appropriate place and little time to conduct his instruction in Christianity.[74] The two men clashed, and in September 1848, Vincent evicted the Armstrongs from their cottage in the settlement and sent them to live near the lighthouse, a long walk away from the prisoners. Unable to carry out his duties satisfactorily, Armstrong left with his family in December 1848.[75] It seemed in any case that the prison might close, as the numbers were dwindling and the government needed Aboriginal labour on the mainland for infrastructure projects, such as road building. Governor Fitzgerald decided he needed the island for his own leisure and closed the near-empty prison in July 1849. It would remain closed for six years.

While the colony benefited from the deployment of Noongar prisoners for road building on the mainland, the government still needed a system of punishment to deter attacks on settlers' property and to continue the project of destroying Aboriginal law. Men with humanitarian credentials and leanings played a role in reshaping punishment in this period. Particularly zealous in his desire to stamp out Aboriginal law was Walkinshaw Cowan, Protector of Aborigines in York, a settlement 100 kilometres to the east of Perth, from 1848 and York's Resident Magistrate from 1863. Cowan had arrived in 1839 from Scotland, aged thirty, as Hutt's private secretary and had subsequently served as private secretary to Acting Governor Irwin, Governor Clarke and Governor Fitzgerald.[76] Historian Paul Hasluck describes Cowan as a man who 'retained Hutt's general conception of duty towards the natives', and he strongly objected when the prison was closed in 1849.[77] Putting prisoners to work on the roads, Cowan wrote, lacked the advantages of Rottnest – useful farm operations, security from escape and, above all, deterrence: confinement on the mainland did not 'fill them with the same vague and infinite terrors' as Rottnest.[78] A few years later, he would also object to the closure of the Native Institution (a mission school) at York, commenting in his annual report that, 'We have taken possession of the country of a savage people: our settlers are now realising large fortunes from the occupation, and the community likewise derives large sums annually from the sale of their lands, surely some portion of this should be devoted to their Christian instruction'.[79]

When the Rottnest prison closed in July 1849, the authorities had to decide what alternative punishment they should impose to prevent tribal killings. Where Hutt had wanted to apply British law to intra-Aboriginal relations gradually, Cowan followed those like George Grey, mentioned earlier, who had been a magistrate in the colony in 1839 and subsequently became one of the Empire's best known and most influential governing officials, and Colonial Secretary, Richard Madden, who had both advocated the immediate and full application of British law. In part, as Ann Hunter suggests, Cowan was influenced by the strong demand for Aboriginal labour in the York district and saw intertribal quarrels and punishments as interfering with the labour supply.[80] In December 1849, Cowan recommended to Governor Charles Fitzgerald that in order to deter future killings, the government ought to execute the three men who had killed a man named Yadupwert in the York district in revenge for the death of a relative. The Executive Council agreed, though not unanimously; after considerable public debate and a petition, Governor Fitzgerald decided at the last minute, as the men stood on the scaffold on 12 April 1850, to execute just one man – Kanyin – and sentence the other two, Mongeen and Ngolungoot, to transportation for life.[81] Kanyin was executed on 12 April 1850, and his body taken to York and hung in chains as an example.[82] The last-minute reprieve on the scaffold of Mongeen and Ngolungoot and the hanging of Kanyin's body in chains remind us of historian and theorist Michel Foucault's comments in *Discipline and Punish* concerning the role of physical punishment and spectacle in terrorising a population.[83] Foucault suggests, however, that by 1850 these forms of punishment had almost ceased, and in fact in Western Australia the public hanging of Kanyin would prove too much for many. Soon afterwards, the authorities turned against execution for intra-Aboriginal killings, preferring gaol sentences instead, although executions for such crimes did occasionally occur. Cowan thought this amounted to a dual system of law and commented in his 1856 report to the Colonial Secretary that while executions may be revolting to the public, the native killings themselves were worse.[84] Nevertheless, for intra-Aboriginal crimes, authorities remained wary of execution and continued to prefer gaol sentences, especially after the prison reopened on Rottnest Island in October 1855.

The prison grows, 1855–83

From 1850 to 1868, Britain transported approximately 9,400 convicts to Western Australia, a colony starved of labour and thus receptive to convict transportation. Governor Arthur Kennedy (1855–72), who had replaced Governor Fitzgerald in July 1855, reopened the prison three months after his arrival. As Hutt and others had done earlier, Kennedy justified the move in the name of freedom and survival. In Perth, he wrote, it had been necessary to keep Aboriginal prisoners 'chained and manacled in the most inhuman manner to prevent them from making their escape which in defiance of all vigilance they frequently effected'. Imprisonment of this kind, he wrote, 'is equivalent to a sentence of death'.[85] He was concerned with the rising cost and poor security of imprisonment on the mainland, and shared Hutt's earlier vision of a prison that could be largely self-supporting. The prison officially reopened on 23 October 1855 and Henry Vincent, now in his late fifties, was reappointed superintendent in December.[86] In his annual report for 1855, the ever-supportive Symmons praised the reopening of the prison on 'reformatory, sanitary, humane and pecuniary grounds'.[87] In press discussion of the reopening it was the last of these, the cost of imprisonment, that was most frequently mentioned.

For the next thirteen years, the Aboriginal prison on Rottnest operated alongside the British transportation system. There were significant changes in these years. On the one hand, the Noongar population in the Swan River area had declined, and on the other, as the colony expanded, mainly through pastoralism, hundreds of kilometres to the north, south and east of the Swan River settlement, more Aboriginal people from other regions were being convicted of offences ranging from stealing to assault to intra-Aboriginal homicide. In its second incarnation, the prison on Rottnest would affect many Aboriginal populations, often from far away, from the south-east to the north-west of the colony. At the same time, prison management in Western Australia became generally harsher. When Governor John Hampton (1862–68) replaced Kennedy as governor in February 1862, he turned to a much more punitive approach for the British convicts, reintroducing dark cells, flogging and chain gangs.[88] In this environment, the Aboriginal prison on Rottnest Island would drift even further away from Hutt's original notion of a relatively open prison. From 1862 to 1864, under Vincent's influence, a substantial prison building, featuring cells built around a central yard, was constructed on the island. It became known as the Quod, an English slang term for prison, and the cells intended for four men each would soon be required to house many more. The Quod is now one of the most hated aspects of the prison in Noongar and other Indigenous people's memory.

In 1867 William Dockwrey Jackson replaced Vincent as superintendent. Jackson had been for ten years the pilot on the island, and until 1870 occupied both positions.[89] He had few qualifications for the role of superintendent, and in the early 1870s, some concerned citizens suggested to the colony's most successful missionary that he take on the position.[90] This was Bishop Rosendo Salvado, leader for decades of a Benedictine mission based at New Norcia, north of Perth. Since the mid-1850s, the mission had been slowly growing, based on what historian Tiffany Shellam describes as 'a fine balance between Christian instruction, agricultural training, physical exercise, Aboriginal culture and "patience"' – in other words an approach that both respected Aboriginal culture and sought to inculcate, slowly, Christian values and the skills needed in settler society.[91] As Salvado put it in a letter to the Colonial Secretary on 19 February 1864, 'Surely, if the aborigines are left to themselves, they cannot but follow their forefathers' traditions and customs, but if properly and timely trained, I, for one, do not see the impossibility of their being truly civilised'.[92] Since his arrival in 1846, Salvado had realised the importance of learning the local language, and in a memoir published after three years in the colony had shown his considerable knowledge and understanding of the ways of life of the people living around the mission.[93] The Benedictines placed a high value on physical labour generally as a source of spirituality, and Salvado particularly valued Aboriginal labour, not only as a means of the mission becoming self-sufficient but also as a mode of assimilation into settler society. As he informed the Colonial Secretary, his emphasis on physical labour had three aims: to prevent sickness, to 'have them busy in doing something useful' and to 'introduce them by degrees into the habits of civilized and industrial life'.[94]

As the mission continued to flourish, now drawing its members from further afield, from 1870 Salvado began taking in juvenile offenders sentenced to gaol terms on Rottnest Island.[95] Intrigued by the suggestions he would make a good prison superintendent, Salvado decided to investigate.[96] On 16 January 1873, he called on Governor Frederick Weld (1869–75), who was from an English Catholic family and with whom Salvado had struck up a friendship, at the governor's summer residence on Rottnest. He stayed for five days, gathering information, at the end of which he decided not to pursue the matter further. In his 1883 report to the Propaganda Fide (the Catholic institution in Rome responsible for missionary work), he commented:

> After all that, however, I decided not to have anything to do with the establishment; since it was entirely dependent on the Government I could not have achieved anything good permanently, because the Governor and the main leaders of that Government would be replaced from time to time, and what some had decided could be annulled by others, and all our labours would be lost.[97]

For Salvado, there was also a larger problem: a missionary project on the island, he thought, was bound to fail. Imparting education to the prisoners would have little long-term effect, since on release they would go back to their people and their former ways:

> if they began to be a little educated, once the short time of their detention had been completed, they would go free, each one to their respective country in the Australian continent since the idea of leaving the island prison and going to the continent to see their relatives and friends again is foremost in their thoughts: they would not stay on the island for all the gold in the world, and once they returned to their friends, if they are left alone and, despite the education received during their short detention, they would go on with their nomadic and uncivilised life as before; so that, after years and years of toil on our part, the result could not but be insignificant, to say the least.[98]

More than anyone else, Salvado seems to have recognised the futility of the prison as a humanitarian or assimilationist project. He saw how unlikely it was that detention could ever effect the cultural shift Hutt and the others desired, and was deeply aware of the inherent fickleness of government policy, dependent as it was on the appointment of a seemingly endless succession of short-term governors chosen in London.

With Salvado not interested in governing the prison, Jackson continued as superintendent for another ten years. During the 1870s, visits to the prison by interested observers, such as writers and men of science, became increasingly common. When the famous English novelist, Anthony Trollope, visited the island in 1873, nine months after Salvado, he gave a fairly positive report, noting there were sixty-five prisoners in reasonable health who appeared to 'work cheerfully' and had Sundays off to fend for themselves, bringing home 'wallabies, and birds, and fishes'.[99] As the colony expanded north and settlers and authorities sought to stamp out sheep stealing, prison numbers rose. By the time Alexander Milne Robertson, Scottish-born colonial surgeon at Fremantle, visited for scientific research into circumcision and other cultural practices in August 1879, the number of prisoners had risen to 170. Robertson had a more critical view than Trollope: 'All the time', he wrote of the prisoners on Rottnest, 'they are fretting and longing for their old bush life. Prison life and hard labour are in their case other names for death'.[100] Both observers noted how many were there for intra-Aboriginal killings, as courts continued to sentence many men to death for such killings and then commute the sentence to life imprisonment on Rottnest.

Crisis at the prison, 1883–86

Rottnest proved to be a powerful tool in support of the colonisation of the north-west. After settler complaints, Governor William Robinson (who served three separate terms, the middle one from 1880 to 1883) in 1882 authorised an increase in the presence of magistrates and police in the northern Gascoyne and Murchison districts and appointed Charles Foss, former pastoralist and sheep-scab inspector, as itinerant Stipendiary Magistrate for the area.[101] For the frequency and length of the gaol sentences he imposed, Foss became known as an especially draconian magistrate, one newspaper describing his approach as one of 'transporting the whole of the native inhabitants to Rottnest'.[102] In November 1882, the liberal *Inquirer* raised concerns about the wholesale deportation by Foss and other magistrates in the district of Aboriginal people to Rottnest Island and the consequent overcrowding in the prison.[103]

Continuing press stories of overcrowding and disease on Rottnest confronted the Administrator, Chief Justice Henry Thomas Wrensfordley, during the interregnum between the departure of Governor Robinson in mid-February 1883 and the arrival in June of the next governor, Frederick Broome (1883–90). In addition, there were some individual humanitarian voices. The earlier group of humanitarians had disappeared from public life (all but Armstrong and Salvado had left the colony, and most had died) and now key figures included the Catholic missionary Duncan McNab and Anglican missionary John Gribble.[104] Both came from missionary work in other colonies, McNab from Queensland and Gribble from New South Wales. First to arrive was McNab, in March 1883. He had worked as a parish priest in Scotland and Victoria, before a tumultuous seven-year period as a missionary in Queensland, where his advocacy of land rights and equal treatment for Aboriginal people aroused hostility from settlers and the church; he left in disgust in 1882. On the invitation of Martin Griver, Bishop of Perth, he came to Western Australia, but before travelling north to establish a mission, he served for some months as a visiting chaplain to the prisoners on Rottnest Island.[105]

Two months after his arrival, McNab wrote on 11 May 1883 to Chief Justice Wrendsfordsley about what he had observed on Rottnest and made several recommendations for change. It is clear from his letter that any attempt to provide education and training had long been abandoned. Both, he suggested, should be provided on Rottnest. 'Even in Queensland', he wrote, 'when natives are imprisoned for a considerable time, they are taught some trade, at which they can employ themselves when released'. They could be profitably occupied in making fishing nets, boatbuilding, cooperage, shoemaking, tailoring and saddlery, rather than the 'hoeing or scratching the soil practiced here'. They should also be taught to read and write, and 'the leading truths and morals of the Gospel'. In a second letter two weeks later, McNab addressed questions of Aboriginal policy more broadly, stressing the importance of protecting Aboriginal people from extermination: 'In newly occupied districts the natives should be treated as men and not shot down as vermin'. They should be compensated for their loss of land, provided with assistance and education, and protected by law from 'slavery, or being forcibly abducted to perform unremunerated labour'.[106] With Wrensfordley merely a temporary administrator and the Legislative Council unsympathetic to such suggestions, McNab's proposals predictably met little response. Suppressing resistance now took precedence over education and conversion. Accordingly, on 18 June 1883, two Aboriginal men from the Gascoyne, Wangabiddi and Guerilla, each convicted of murdering a white man, were hanged on Rottnest in front of 175 prisoners. Authorities hoped that the numerous prisoners from the Gascoyne, who soon returned home, would warn their countrymen against killing white men.[107] At the time, McNab was already on his long journey northwards along the western Australian coast to King Sound, approximately 1,000 nautical miles north of Rottnest Island, where, in 1885, accompanied by an assistant priest and an Aboriginal interpreter called 'Knife', he established a short-lived mission at Goodenough Bay.[108]

The executions took place just after Frederick Broome had begun his term as governor, on 2 June 1883. While it would be a stretch to class Broome as a humanitarian, he did share some humanitarian ideas concerning Aboriginal protection and education. When, on Broome's orders, the Colonial Surgeon, Alfred Waylen, investigated the situation on Rottnest Island, he reported on 3 August that Rottnest was overcrowded and that a recent influenza epidemic had led to many deaths.[109] While the average number of prisoner deaths on the island during its existence was a little over six per year, it peaked at sixty-two in 1883.[110]

In an attempt to prevent further overcrowding on Rottnest, Broome introduced an Aboriginal Natives Offenders Bill that reduced the length of a prison sentence that a magistrate could impose from three years to two.[111] Finding the Legislative Council resistant to any restraint on magistrates' sentencing powers, Broome appointed John Forrest, Surveyor General and at age thirty-six new to the Legislative Council, to head a committee of inquiry into the treatment of Aboriginal prisoners and into other matters of Aboriginal policy. The commission met in October and November 1883, interviewing both Aboriginal and non-Aboriginal witnesses concerning conditions at Rottnest, and after considerable delay presented its report in September 1884, which among other things recommended improved training, hygiene, food and clothing.[112]

Matters had become desperate on Rottnest Island. After another outbreak of influenza in October 1884, Broome appointed a new Acting Superintendent, William Henry Timperley, and instructed him to act on the report's recommendations.[113] Broome also wrote a long minute to the Colonial Secretary about how the prison at Rottnest ought to be conducted.[114] His orders were extraordinarily detailed, many dealing with matters of hygiene, food, space, ventilation, clothing and blankets. He suggested provision of some practical training: 'One or two natives (to begin with) might be selected for instruction in carpentering at the Reformatory Workshop'. Importantly, he recommended that men convicted of intra-Aboriginal killings be considered for release after five years. Soon after, Broome left the colony for England (in part to press for British Government loans for infrastructure projects), where, in May 1885, he spoke about the colony to the Colonial Institute in Piccadilly. In his lecture, he expressed ideas about Rottnest very similar to those that Hutt had articulated forty years or so earlier. He began by referring to the island as the 'site of a prison or rather a reformatory for aboriginal natives', and explained that 100 or so men were there from all parts of the colony for offences such as 'stealing flour, spearing and eating settlers' sheep, killing each other out of tribal custom'. The inmates, he explained, 'are allowed a considerable amount of liberty, as they cannot escape' and are occupied in 'gardening and farming operations, saltmaking, etc. &c'. He pointed out that 'though Rottnest is a place of very lenient confinement, natives do not like it, as it removes them from their own people and their tribal life'.[115]

While Broome was away, Chief Justice Alexander Onslow acted as administrator. On 2 February 1885, in comments that also echoed Hutt, he wrote in response to Timperley's annual report for the prison for 1884:

> The establishment upon this island ought not to be treated purely as a prison in which offenders against the law are to be punished but as a school in which some elementary ideas of civilisation may be imparted to the prisoners. The constant endeavour on the part of the warders should be to impress upon the natives that though punishment will be meted out against offenders it will always be accompanied with justice and above all kindness should be shown in all dealings with savage races. It will effect a more lasting victory over them than force and punishment.
>
> I feel that under Mr Timperley's wise and experienced supervision Rottnest will be a good prison and a good school and will be a source of much good to its inhabitants and to the tribes to which they may eventually return.[116]

Onslow's letter is a reminder that notions of prisons as sites for moral reform were still alive in British debates over prison policy and reform, despite a general swing in Britain itself away from ideals of reform and back to an emphasis on deterrence.[117]

In August 1885, soon after Broome's return to the colony in June, Onslow, now back in the role of Chief Justice, took an ocean voyage from Fremantle to Geraldton on the *Otway*, on which ship he met and conversed with the recently arrived Reverend John Gribble. Like McNab, Gribble had hopes of obtaining missionary work in the north of the colony.[118] The Church of England had appointed Gribble, who had previously successfully set up and managed a mission in New South Wales, to establish a mission on the 150,000 acres of land in the Gascoyne granted to it for this purpose. In Western Australia, however, Gribble's missionary enterprise collapsed when his outspoken criticisms of the treatment of Aboriginal people aroused so much settler hostility that the Church withdrew his missionary licence in July 1886. In public lectures, newspaper articles, and a book entitled *Dark Deeds in a Sunny Land*, Gribble spoke of the abuses he had observed against Aboriginal people, including forced slave-like labour and sexual exploitation.[119] Especially important in his denunciations was the system of punishment, especially the use of chains over long distances to bring men to a magistrate for trial, keep them there, and then, once convicted, transport them to Rottnest. There are innumerable mentions of chains in *Dark Deeds in Sunny Land*, closely aligned with charges of slavery in the north. For example:

> In January of this year I saw between 30 and 40 natives chained together and enclosed within the narrow bounds of a corrugated iron enclosure not more than 30 feet square, and there they lay day after day and week after week under the rays of an almost vertical sun, while the perspiration poured from their naked bodies as though they had just been sluiced with bucketsful of water. These natives, most of whom had been brought down from the Peedong country, more than 300 miles, were accused of having speared cattle. I was present when, on the evidence of a very young white man, they were sentenced to two years' banishment on Rottnest Island.[120]

This description reminds us of Lemkin's list of methods used in genocide. Lemkin writes, for example, of the deportation from Spain of Moriscos (Spanish Muslims forcibly converted to Roman Catholicism) in 'unbearable sun'.[121] Gribble's account of what he saw was also, as Jane Lydon shows, strongly influenced by antislavery discourse, especially the lectures and rhetoric he had heard on his recent visit to London.[122] Subsequently, Gribble was effectively hounded from the colony; facing a large bill for legal costs when he lost his libel case against the *West Australian*, he left the colony forever in June 1887.[123]

In contrast, Salvado continued to have a connection to Rottnest, and the colony, of a very different kind. In the mid-1880s, New Norcia was reaching the height of its success, a success which lasted to the end of the century. The numbers of Aboriginal people attending the mission rose from forty in 1868 to eighty-four in 1883, 117 in 1887 and 163 in 1904.[124] Since the 1870s, the mission had been increasingly able to gather people displaced by settlement and impart occupational training, literacy, cricket and other skills.[125] While Salvado continued to stand aloof from the prison, and never regarded it as a potentially humanitarian project in the way Hutt, Broome and Onslow did, his visit to Rottnest in 1873 proved to have a long-term effect. During that visit, he encountered two men he already knew, Malònga and Pritagià, who implored him to ask the governor to grant them pardon and freedom, which Salvado did. After some correspondence between the bishop and the governor, the latter granted them pardons and in February both men left for their own country.[126] While these men were released to their own country, later interventions by Salvado appear to have depended on the men being sent to New Norcia. When seeking release for a man known as Harry in 1886, Salvado wrote to the Colonial Secretary that if Harry were 'allowed to be under my care and control at my Mission of New Norcia he would comport himself well (as it has been the case with others situated in similar circumstances and whose release from Rottnest I obtained)'. On this occasion, Salvado's request was refused, though it appears Harry was released to an employer later that year. After the creation of the Aboriginal Protection Board in 1887, both Salvado and Duncan McNab were appointed Protectors of Aboriginals. While McNab left the colony that year, his mission in the north having closed, Salvado continued his work, including rescuing convicted juvenile offenders from Rottnest. In November 1889, when an eleven-year-old boy known as Bagpipe Peter was sentenced to six months on Rottnest, he was released after a month to Salvado's custody at New Norcia.[127]

The prison closed in 1903, but a small section of the island continued to be used as an annexe of Fremantle Gaol until 1931, leading to both Aboriginal and white prisoners being sent there to maintain the island's buildings and infrastructure.

For Noongar and other affected Aboriginal groups, Rottnest remains a place of great sadness. Noongar especially have waged campaigns for many years now to ensure that the burial grounds are protected and that visitors (and there are many – Rottnest is now a popular tourist destination) understand the history of what happened there. As a result of these campaigns, the Quod, which for years had been operated as a hotel for tourists, was finally closed in June 2018, and discussions continue as to how such a hated place should be preserved and remembered.

Conclusion

When we learn this history of inculcating terror through isolation from kin, community, culture and country, the subjection of prisoners to forced labour, the use of chains and whips and the poor hygiene, food, clothing, medical care and shelter provided, we realise how far the daily practices of settler colonialism had travelled from the almost utopian island idyll of Hutt's imagination. There were several reasons for this disjunction. Prison superintendents had high levels of discretionary power and most did not share humanitarian visions for the prison. Financial considerations helped produce a harsh regime of forced labour secured through physical punishment. Most of all, the failure of the prison as a humanitarian project was a product of the nature and purpose of punishment in a colonising situation. It is hard to see how a punishment explicitly designed to terrorise people into submission could make the cultural values of an alien settler society attractive to prisoners. As Salvado perceptively noted, the prisoners hated the island with a passion and when they left returned whenever possible to their country and community.

In the genocidal context of settler colonialism, then, humanitarianism had become profoundly paradoxical. At times it seems inaccurate to describe the men I have discussed as humanitarians at all, so readily did many of them – the governors and figures like Moore, Clark and Cowan – see effective punishment as essential for colonisation and settlement. Yet when we look at what they said and wrote, they shared ideas with humanitarians elsewhere, with recognition of rights, a notion of common humanity, a belief that Aboriginal people deserved compensation for their loss of land, and often an interest in and respect for the Aboriginal people their colony was attempting to displace.[128] Despite their diversity – some were in government while others became vocal critics of government – they shared a hope that the prison on Rottnest Island could be a place of learning as well as punishment.

Perhaps the Rottnest Island prison was a place of learning for its inmates after all, but not in the sense the humanitarians intended. Rather than learning what humanitarians believed to be the values of British civilisation, prisoners learnt the power and cruelty of the invaders who were taking their land, removing their freedom and exploiting their labour. Of the seven prisoners who gave evidence at the Commission of Inquiry in 1883, three mentioned they had been brought to the island over very long distances with a chain around the neck. They all hated Rottnest, Bob Thomas commenting: 'I am not the same as if I was in my own country', and Harry, 'I would rather be on the mainland, even in chains, than over here. This is not a good place, natives get ill here and die'. They all longed to go home, Charlie Yadthee saying, 'I expect to go to my country soon, and shall be very glad'. Widgie Johnny commented, 'I do not know when I am going back, but I shall be very glad to go. I expect to go by and by'.[129]

Notes

1 There are several acceptable spellings, including both Noongar and Nyungar. See www.noongarculture.org.au/language/, accessed 30 September 2020.
2 For earlier treatments of humanitarians in this sense in Australian colonial history, see Henry Reynolds, *This Whispering in Our Hearts* (Sydney, Australia: Allen and Unwin, 1998); Claire McLisky, '"Due Observance of Justice, and the Protection of Their Rights": Philanthropy, Humanitarianism, and Moral Purpose in the Aborigines Protection Society circa 1837 and Its Portrayal in Australian Historiography, 1883–2003', *Limina* (2005), 11, pp. 57–66; Alison Holland, 'Aboriginal Affairs: Humanitarian Intervention Then and Now: Dis/connections and Possibilities', *Australian Journal of Politics and History* (2017), 63 (4), pp. 524–39; Jane Lydon, *Photography, Humanitarianism, Empire* (London, UK: Bloomsbury, 2016).
3 Alan Lester and Fae Dussart, *Colonization and the Origins of Humanitarian Governance: Protecting Aborigines across the Nineteenth-Century British*

Empire (Cambridge, UK: Cambridge University Press, 2014); Amanda Nettelbeck, *Indigenous Rights and Colonial Subjecthood: Protection and Reform in the Nineteenth-Century British Empire* (Cambridge, UK: Cambridge University Press, 2019).

4 Raphael Lemkin, *Axis Rule in Occupied Europe: Laws of Occupation, Analysis of Government, Proposals for Redress* (Washington, DC: Carnegie Endowment for International Peace, 1944), p. 79.
5 See Reynolds, *This Whispering in Our Hearts* for discussion of Robert Lyon, Louis Giustiniani, Duncan McNab and John Gribble.
6 W. Shenton to G. F. Moore, 16 June 1832, State Records Office of Western Australia (SROWA), Colonial Secretary's Office Inward Correspondence (CSR), Acc 36, vol. 21, pp. 170–2; Ann Hunter, *A Different Kind of Subject: Colonial Law in Aboriginal-European Relations in Nineteenth Century Western Australia 1829–61* (Melbourne, Australia: Australian Scholarly Publishing, 2012), pp. 28, 245.
7 Edward Jack Watson, *Rottnest: Its Tragedy and Its Glory* (Perth, Australia: D. L. Watson, 1998), pp. 10–11.
8 Lyon to Secretary of State, 1 January 1833, CO 18/9, cited by Reynolds, *This Whispering in Our Hearts*, p. 73. See also Bob Reece, '"A Most Singular Man": Robert Lyon Milne', *Early Days: Journal of the Royal Western Australian Historical Society* (2011), 13 (50), pp. 585–606.
9 Hunter, *A Different Kind of Subject*, p. 19; Minutes of the Executive Council, 4 October 1832, CO 20/1, Reel 1117–18, p. 100; Irwin to Secretary of State, 26 January 1833, SROWA, WAS 1180 Cons 42/1, pp. 212, 222; Lyon to Editor, *Perth Gazette*, 9 March 1833, p. 39.
10 *Perth Gazette*, 9 March 1833, p. 39; Reece, 'Robert Lyon Milne', p. 7.
11 Robert Lyon to His Honor the Lieutenant Governor in Council, 26 November 1832, printed in *Perth Gazette*, 9 March 1833, p. 39.
12 *Perth Gazette*, 2 March 1833, p. 35.
13 *Perth Gazette*, 9 March 1833, p. 39. Christianity spelled in lowercase in the original.
14 Printed in Robert M. Lyon, *Australia: An Appeal to the World on Behalf of the Younger Branch of the Family of Shem* (Sydney, Australia: J. Spilsbury and J. M'Eachern, 1839), p. 86.
15 James Cameron, 'George Fletcher Moore', *Studies in Western Australian History* (2000), 20, pp. 21–34.
16 Cameron, 'George Fletcher Moore', p. 22.
17 Ibid., p. 21.
18 Ibid., p. 26.
19 *Perth Gazette*, 13 July 1833, p. 111. This essay was followed by another a week later advocating generous compensation to Aborigines for loss of land and livelihood; *Perth Gazette*, 20 July 1833; Cameron, 'George Fletcher Moore', p. 27.
20 Reece, 'Robert Milne Lyon', p. 11.
21 Hunter, *A Different Kind of Subject*, pp. 37, 44.
22 Its colonial agents were George Fletcher Moore and William Mackie Cameron, see Hunter, *A Different Kind of Subject*, p. 54.

23 Giustiniani had both a classical education and a medical degree. Lesley Borowitzka, 'The Reverend Dr Louis Giustiniani and Anglican Conflict in the Swan River Colony, Western Australia 1836–1838', *Journal of Religious History* (September 2011), 35 (3), p. 355. See also Reynolds, *This Whispering in Our Hearts*, pp. 84–90; Michael Gladwill, 'A Journalist in the Rectory: Anglican Clergymen and Australian Intellectual Life, 1788–1850', *History Australia* (2010), 7 (3).

24 Borowitzka, 'The Reverend Dr Louis Giustiniani', p. 363.

25 Ibid., p. 112.

26 *Swan River Guardian* (Perth), 4 May 1837, p. 112. See also *Perth Gazette*, 13 May 1837, p. 901. Giustiniani continued to publish letters in the *Guardian* critical of government policy and settler actions towards Noongar. Having alienated most of settler society, the Society in London had dismissed him from his post in late 1837. He left the colony permanently in February 1838; Borowitzka, 'The Reverend Dr Louis Giustiniani', pp. 368–9.

27 Hunter, *A Different Kind of Subject*, pp. xxiv–xxv, 239 n. 49.

28 Clare Anderson, 'Transnational Histories of Penal Transportation: Punishment, Labour and Governance in the British Imperial World, 1788–1939', *Australian Historical Studies* (2016), 47 (3), pp. 381–97.

29 Dur-gap was also charged with breaking and entering; *Swan River Guardian* (Perth), 5 October 1837, p. 229.

30 Ibid.

31 Watson, *Rottnest*, pp. 10, 11. Clark letter to the editor, *Inquirer* (Perth), 20 August 1842, p. 3.

32 *Swan River Guardian*, 1 February 1838, p. 304.

33 Minutes of Executive Council, Western Australia, 14 June 1838; *Perth Gazette*, 16 June 1838, p. 94; Eversley Ruth Mortlock, *An Island Solution: Rottnest Reveals Our Colonial Secrets* (Subiaco, Australia: Livelihood Creative Spaces Press, 2016), p. 26.

34 *Perth Gazette*, 16 June 1838, p. 94; Neville Green and Susan Aguiar, *Far from Home: Aboriginal Prisoners of Rottnest Island, 1838–1938* (Cottesloe, Western Australia: Focus Education Services, 2018), p. 14. First edition is Neville Green and Susan Moon, *Far from Home: Aboriginal Prisoners of Rottnest Island, 1838–1938* (Nedlands, Australia: University of Western Australia Press, 1997).

35 Executive Council WA, *Minutes*, 11 July 1838, SROWA, p. 195.

36 Watson, *Rottnest*, p. 20; Prue Joske, Chris Jefferey and Louise Hoffman, *Rottnest: A Documentary History* (Nedlands, Australia: Centre for Migration and Development Studies, University of Western Australia, 1997), p. 28.

37 See Ann Hunter, 'Towards Amalgamationist Governance: Governor Hutt and Contradiction in British Colonial Policy Regarding Aboriginal People in Western Australia', *law&history* (2019), 5 (1), p. 92; Ann Hunter, 'John Hutt: The Inconspicuous Governor', *Early Days* (2009), 13 (3), p. 311. See also Thomas R. Trautmann, *The Madras School of Orientalism, Producing Knowledge in Colonial South India* (New Delhi, India: Oxford University Press, 2009), ch. 2.

38 Hunter, 'Towards Amalgamationist Governance', p. 92.
39 Ibid., pp. 92–7.
40 Peter Cowan, *A Colonial Experience: Swan River 1839–1888, from the Diary and Reports of Walkinshaw Cowan, Secretary to Governor Hutt – Clerk of the Councils, Perth, Guardian of Aborigines, Resident Magistrate, York* (Perth, Australia: the author, 1978), p. 5. Quoted by Ann Hunter, 'Towards Amalgamationist Governance', p. 98.
41 Hunter, *A Different Kind of Subject*, pp. 95–6. See Cameron, 'George Fletcher Moore', p. 28; George Grey, *Vocabulary of the Dialects spoken by the Aboriginal Races of South-Western Australia* (London, UK: T. & W. Boone, 1839); George Fletcher Moore, *A Descriptive Vocabulary of the Language in Common Use Amongst the Aborigines of Western Australia* (London, UK: William S. Orr and Company, 1842).
42 Cameron, 'George Fletcher Moore', p. 25.
43 *Perth Gazette*, 17 November 1838, p. 182.
44 In his speech, Moore strongly opposed the phrenological arguments expressed in George Combe, *The Constitution of Man Considered in Relation to External Objects*, first published in 1828 by John Anderson, Edinburgh, and reprinted many times. Moore described the indigenous people of Western Australia as 'acute and intelligent', well able to understand the principles of religion; *Perth Gazette*, 17 November 1838, p. 183.
45 *Perth Gazette*, 6 July 1839, p. 106.
46 Neville Green, *Broken Spears: Aborigines and Europeans in the Southwest of Australia* (Perth, Australia: Focus Education Services, 1984), p. 138.
47 Hunter, *A Different Kind of Subject*, p. 107; Nettelbeck, *Indigenous Rights and Colonial Subjecthood*, pp. 130–3.
48 Hutt to Russell on 15 May 1841, *Papers: Aborigines, Australian Colonies*, ordered to be printed 9 August 1844, House of Commons, *British Parliamentary Papers*, p. 387.
49 Neville Green, 'Aborigines and White Settlement', in Tom Stannage (ed.), *A New History of Western Australia* (Nedlands, Australia: University of Western Australia Press, 1981), p. 92; Green and Aguiar, *Far from Home*, p. 16.
50 Legislative Council, 4 May 1840, reported in *Perth Gazette*, 9 May 1840, p. 2. James Kerr notes that other colonial officials also recognised the exceptional feelings of terror that imprisonment held for Aboriginal people: James Kerr, *Out of Sight, Out of Mind – Australia's Places of Confinement, 1788–1988* (Sydney, Australia: S. H. Ervin Gallery, 1988), pp. 99–100.
51 *Perth Gazette*, 25 July 1840, p. 2. See Mark Finnane and John McGuire, 'The Uses of Punishment and Exile: Aborigines in Colonial Australia', *Punishment and Society* (2001), 3 (2), pp. 285–7.
52 Legislative Council, 19 November 1841, reported in *Perth Gazette*, 20 November 1841, p. 3.
53 Hilary Carey, *Empire of Hell: Religion and the Campaign to End Convict Transportation in the British Empire, 1788–1875* (Cambridge, UK: Cambridge University Press, 2019), pp. 161–2; John V. Barry, 'Maconochie, Alexander

(1787–1860)', *Australian Diction of Biography Online*, http://adb.anu.edu.au/biography/maconochie-alexander-2417, accessed 30 September 2020.
54 Carey, *Empire of Hell*, pp. 163–6.
55 John Gascoigne, *The Enlightenment and the Origins of European Australia* (Cambridge, UK: Cambridge University Press, 2002), p. 143.
56 For a more detailed account of these early years of the prison, see Ann Curthoys, 'The Beginnings of Transportation in Western Australia: Banishment, Forced Labour, and Punishment at the Aboriginal Prison on Rottnest Island before 1850', *Studies in Western Australian History* (2020), 34; *The Carceral Colony*, pp. 59–77.
57 *Perth Gazette*, 10 August 1839, p. 126.
58 *Perth Gazette*, 14 September 1839, p. 198; Watson, *Rottnest*, p. 24. Hutt to Secretary of State, 19 August 1840, 'Aborigines: Australian Colonies', p. 375.
59 Green and Aguiar, *Far from Home*, p. 18.
60 Sam Furphy, 'Philanthropy or Patronage? Aboriginal Protectors in the Port Phillip District and Western Australia', in Sam Furphy and Amanda Nettelbeck (eds), *Aboriginal Protection and Its Intermediaries in Britain's Antipodean Colonies* (New York, NY: Routledge, 2020), p. 67.
61 *Perth Gazette*, 7 November 1840, p. 2; Mortlock, *An Island Solution*, p. 21.
62 *Perth Gazette*, 7 November 1840, p. 2.
63 *Perth Gazette*, 31 December 1842, p. 2.
64 Hutt to Russell on 15 May 1841, 'Aborigines: Australian Colonies', p. 433.
65 Armstrong to Symmons, 6 October 1843, CSO 124/100–105, SROWA; Watson, *Rottnest*, p. 25; Kevin James Moran, *Rottnest: Ghosts of Wadjemup*, vol. 1 (Perth, Australia: Horizon Syndicate Pty Ltd, 2001), pp. 48–9.
66 William Nairne Clark, 'An Inquiry', *Inquirer* (Perth), 16 February 1842, p. 5.
67 The translation Clark uses is the same as that used in Vicesimus Knox, *Elegant Extracts: Or, Useful and Entertaining Passages in Prose Selected for the Improvement of Young Persons: Being Similar in Design to Elegant Extracts in Poetry* (London, UK: C. and J. Rivington, 1924) p. 392. See Book 3, section 7, 'The Scythian Ambassadors to Alexander'.
68 Clark, 'An Inquiry', p. 5. Italics in the original.
69 Clark, 'An Inquiry', p. 5.
70 Stanley to Hutt, 26 July 1843, 'Aborigines: Australian Colonies', p. 427.
71 Hutt to Stanley, 9 February 1844, 'Aborigines: Australian Colonies', p. 433.
72 Stanley to Hutt, 31 July 1844, 'Aborigines: Australian Colonies', p. 433.
73 *Inquirer*, 9 June 1847, p. 3.
74 Printed in the *Perth Gazette*, 26 February 1848, p. 3.
75 Watson, *Rottnest*, p. 32.
76 In addition, he had served as Clerk to the Executive Council for many years; *West Australian*, 26 January 1888, p. 2.
77 Paul Hasluck, *Black Australians: A Survey of Native Policy in Western Australia 1829–1897* (Melbourne, Australia: Melbourne University Press, 1970), p. 73.
78 Ibid., p. 83.
79 He made these comments in 1855; Cowan, *A Colonial Experience*, p. 67.

80 Hunter, *A Different Kind of Subject*, p. 183.
81 With the prison on Rottnest closed, the two reprieved men appear to have been gaoled on the mainland. *Inquirer* (Perth), 2 August 1854, p. 3.
82 Hunter, *A Different Kind of Subject*, p. 190. Something similar had been done after the Appin massacre in New South Wales in 1816; as Captain James Wallis recorded, 'I detached Lieut Parker with the bodies of Durell and Kinnahygal, to be hanged on a conspicuous part of a range of hills near Mr Broughton's', New South Wales State Archives and Records, Massacre at Appin, 17 April 1816, www.records.nsw.gov.au/archives/collections-and-research/guides-and-indexes/stories/massacre-appin-17-april-1816, accessed 30 September 2020. I thank Shino Konishi for alerting me to this source.
83 Michel Foucault, *Discipline and Punish: The Birth of the Prison* (London, UK: Penguin, 1991).
84 Cowan, *A Colonial Experience*, p. 69.
85 Moran, *Rottnest*, p. 57.
86 *Perth Gazette*, 26 October 1855; Watson, *Rottnest*, p. 34.
87 Hasluck, *Black Australians*, p. 84.
88 Carey, *Empire of Hell*, p. 284.
89 *Perth Gazette*, 7 August 1868, p. 2.
90 Rosendo Salvado, *Report of Rosendo Salvado to Propaganda Fide in 1883* (Eugene, OR: Wipf and Stock Publishers, 2016), p. 124.
91 Tiffany Shellam, '"A Mystery to the Medical World": Florence Nightingale, Rosendo Salvado and the Risk of Civilisation', *History Australia* (2012), 9 (1), p. 117.
92 Rosendo Salvado to the Colonial Secretary, 19 February 1864, printed in Western Australia Legislative Council, 'Information respecting the habits and customs of the Aboriginal inhabitants of Western Australia, compiled from various sources', Western Australia Legislative Council, *Votes and Proceedings* (Perth, Australia: Government Printer, 1871), p. 7.
93 Ronald Berndt, 'Salvado: A Man of and before His Time', in Rosendo Salvado, *The Salvado Memoirs: Historical Memoirs of Australia and Particularly of the Benedictine Mission of New Norcia and of the Habits and Customs of the Australian Natives*, translated and edited by E. J. Stormon, SJ (New Norcia, Australia: Benedictine Community of New Norcia, 2007), Appendix II, pp. 267–8. The memoirs were first published as Rosendo Salvado, *Memorie storiche dell' Australia* (Rome, Italy: Society for the Propagation of the Faith, 1851).
94 Salvado to the Colonial Secretary, 19 February 1864, p. 5.
95 Tiffany Shellam, '"On My Ground": Indigenous Farmers at New Norcia 1860s–1900s', in Ramón Máiz and Tiffany Shellam (eds), *Rosendo Salvado and the Australian Aboriginal World* (Santiago de Compostela, Spain: Consello da Cultura Galega, 2016), p. 164.
96 Salvado to Propaganda Fide, p. 124.
97 Ibid., p. 125.
98 Ibid., p. 125.

99 *Inquirer*, 24 September 1873, p. 3.
100 Alexander Milne Robertson, 'Anthropological Account of the Aborigines of Western Australia, Together with the Climate, the Diseases & the Productions of the Country', MD thesis, University of Edinburgh, 1883, available online, p. 83. On the basis of this visit, Robertson wrote a pamphlet on Aboriginal customs for the Sydney Exhibition of 1879, which subsequently attracted attention in Europe, and also used his findings in his MD; 'News in Brief', *Inquirer*, 17 October 1883, p. 5.
101 Kay Forrest, *The Challenge and the Chance: The Colonisation and Settlement of North West Australia 1861–1914* (Carlisle, Australia: Hesperian Press, 1996), p. 143.
102 Forrest, *The Challenge*, p. 142.
103 *Inquirer* (Perth), 8 November 1882, p. 5. Katherine Roscoe, '"Too Many Kill 'Em, Too Many Make 'Em Ill": The Commission into Rottnest Prison as the Context for Section 70', *Studies in Western Australian History* (2016), 30, p. 45.
104 Armstrong had retired from government service a few years before and lived in Perth. Now aged eighty-five, Moore had returned to England and was living in London. Giustiniani's life after his departure in 1838 is unknown. The others had died – Clark in 1854 in Hobart, Lyon in 1874 in Adelaide and Hutt in 1878 in London.
105 *West Australian*, 11 May 1883, p. 3.
106 Rev D. McNab, Rottnest, to Acting Governor, 25 May 1883, copied in 'Letters from the Rev. D. McNab relative to the settlement and civilisation of Aborigines of Western Australia', Western Australia Legislative Council, *Votes and Proceedings*, Second Session, 1883, p. 5. See also letter of 11 May 1883, pp. 3–4.
107 *The Herald* (Fremantle), 23 June 1883, p. 2; *Victorian Express* (Geraldton), 27 June 1883, p. 3.
108 See Brigida Nailon, 'Champion of the Aborigines: Father Duncan McNab 1820–1896: Part 3: His W. A. Mission', *Footprints* (August 1982), 4, pp. 5–8. After closing the mission, McNab returned to Melbourne, where he died in 1896.
109 *Inquirer and Commercial News* (Perth), 27 June and 4 July 1883; Western Australia Legislative Council, *Report by the Colonial Surgeon on the Condition of the Sick Native Prisoners at Rottnest Prison*, Parliamentary Paper A11.
110 Green and Aguiar, *Far from Home*, p. 52.
111 Western Australia Legislative Council, Debate on 13 August 1883 concerning draft legislation entitled 'An Act to Consolidate and Amend the Laws Providing for the Summary Trial and Punishment of Aboriginal Native Offenders in Certain Cases', *Parliamentary Debates* (Perth, Australia: Government Printer, 1883), pp. 207–17, esp. p. 209.
112 Western Australia Legislative Council, 'Report of a Commission Appointed by his Excellency the Governor to Inquire into the Treatment of Aboriginal Native Prisoners of the Crown in this Colony: and also into Certain Other Matters Relative to Aboriginal Natives', *Votes and Proceedings*, Parliamentary Paper

no. 32 (Perth, Australia: Government Printer, 1884), p. 9. Available at www.nla.gov.au/apps/cdview/?pi=nla.aus-vn1057351–5x-s9-e, accessed 22 May 2020.
113 Western Australia Legislative Council, 'Report on Rottnest Prison for the Year 1886', *Votes and Proceedings*, Parliamentary Paper no. 5 (Perth, Australia: Government Printer, 1887), p. 3. See Roscoe, '"Too Many Kill 'Em"', p. 53; Green and Aguiar, *Far from Home*, pp. 29–30.
114 Frederick Broome, 'From His Excellency to Governor to the Honourable the Colonial Secretary', 28 October 1884, attached to 'Superintendent Rottnest – Report on Rottnest Prison 1884', SROWA, S675 Cons527 1885/0445, pp. 23–39.
115 Governor Napier Broome, 'Western Australia', *West Australian* (Perth), 2 May 1885, p. 6.
116 Onslow to Colonial Secretary, 2 February, attached to 'Superintendent Rottnest – Report on Rottnest Prison 1884'.
117 Carey, *Empire of Hell*, pp. 299, 305.
118 J. M. Bennett, *Sir Alexander Campbell Onslow: Third Chief Justice of Western Australia, 1883–1901* (Sydney, Australia: Federation Press, 2018), p. 109; *Victorian Express* (Geraldton), 29 August 1885, p. 2.
119 *Daily Telegraph* (Melbourne), 6 and 9 July 1886.
120 John Gribble, *Dark Deeds in a Sunny Land, or Blacks and Whites in North-West Australia* (Perth, Australia: University of Western Australia with Institute of Applied Aboriginal Studies at the Western Australian College of Advance Education, 1987), p. 51, first published in 1886. It is not clear what Gribble meant by 'Peedong country', but it appears to apply to a northern Aboriginal group. For an examination of the impact in the early twentieth century of images of men in chains in Western Australia, see Lydon, *Photography, Humanitarianism, Empire*, pp. 102–7, and Jane Lydon, *The Flash of Recognition: Photography and the Emergence of Indigenous Rights* (Sydney, Australia: NewSouth Books, 2012), ch. 2.
121 John Docker, 'Are Settler-Colonies Inherently Genocidal?', in Dirk Moses (ed.), *Empire, Colony, Genocide: Conquest, Occupation, and Subaltern Resistance in World History* (New York, NY: Berghahn Books, 2008), p. 93. Docker is referring to Raphael Lemkin, 'Revised Outline for Genocide Cases', in Lemkin Papers, New York Public Library, Box 8, Folder 11.
122 Jane Lydon, 'Christian Heroes? John Gribble, Exeter Hall and Antislavery on Western Australia's Frontier', *Studies in Western Australian History* (2016), 30, pp. 59–72.
123 Su-Jane Hunt, 'The Gribble Affair: A Study in Colonial Politics', *Studies in Western Australian History* (1984), 8, pp. 62–73. Hunt's essay is also reprinted as an appendix to Gribble, *Dark Deeds in a Sunny Land*, reissued in 1987.
124 Hasluck, *Black Australians*, pp. 98, 219.
125 Ibid., pp. 98–9.
126 Report of Rosendo Salvado to Propaganda Fide in 1883, pp. 124–6.
127 Green and Aguiar, *Far from Home*, p. 98.

128 On the humanitarian belief in compensation in the Australian context, see Anne O'Brien, 'Humanitarianism and Reparation in Colonial Australia', *Journal of Colonialism and Colonial History* (2001), 12 (2), https://muse-jhu-edu.ezproxy1.library.usyd.edu.au/article/448310, accessed 30 September 2020.
129 'Report of a Commission Appointed by His Excellency the Governor to Inquire into the Treatment of Aboriginal Native Prisoners', pp. 12–13.

7

From humanitarianism to humane governance: Aboriginal slavery and white Australia

Amanda Nettelbeck

In 1896, as Australia's self-governing colonies prepared to unite as a federated commonwealth, a press editorial called attention to the evils of Aboriginal indenture as 'slavery under a convenient name', and argued that its solution lay in a stronger 'humane and practical native policy'.[1] The editorial reflected a much larger public commentary that peaked between the 1880s and the 1910s. This commentary circulated widely to condemn a system akin to Aboriginal slavery in the booming economies of northern Australia, and lobbied for stronger forms of government intervention. These decades also coincided with the period when all of Australia's mainland jurisdictions introduced a suite of new laws designed to bring Aboriginal people within the state's powers of protection.[2] Settler governments rationalised these laws as humanitarian measures that held a number of practical capacities: to regulate the labour relationships between Aboriginal workers and unprincipled employers, to prevent the sexual exploitation of Aboriginal women, and to safeguard Aboriginal interests more broadly. This folding of a settler humanitarian discourse into a statutory programme of humane governance endowed the settler state with new powers to intervene in race exploitation. It did so just at the moment when an idea of white Australian sovereignty was being shored up in other areas of law and policy.[3]

A growing body of scholarship has revisited humanitarianism's historical entanglements with nation-building projects to unpack how humanitarians' long-term objectives, so often grounded in values of universal humanity, allowed new sovereign powers to flourish in ways that perpetuated rather than dismantled structural inequalities.[4] A rich seam of this work has considered how a fluid humanitarian politics accommodated itself in various ways to colonising agendas.[5] Such work has helped to map humanitarianism's nineteenth-century transitions from an abolitionist focus on civil rights to more conservative forms of governmentality, and to disentangle the sometimes contradictory agendas of colonial humanitarianisms across place and time.[6] This chapter addresses one place and time in the history of this symbiosis between humanitarianism and colonialism – Australia at the turn to Federation around 1900 – to ask how an ambivalent settler humanitarianism manifested as concern about Aboriginal slavery, and how government responses to that concern helped to consolidate the priorities of the settler state. More particularly, it explores how settler uses of humanitarian vocabularies to protest the sexual enslavement of Aboriginal women by predatory male employers – a longstanding and largely unspoken problem on Australia's remote frontiers – contributed to an emergent system of humane governance that enabled the stronger policing of racial borderlines in a social climate of 'white ascendency'.[7]

Humanitarian debates about states of un-freedom had a complicated trajectory after the legal end of chattel slavery in the British Empire, as social unease took root about enslavement of other kinds.[8] Arguments that slavery was tolerated under another name plagued the vast system of indentured labour that replaced slavery in Britain's plantation colonies.[9] In the settler colonies, the violence and exploitation associated with indigenous dispossession also generated concern that slavery was reborn in other forms.[10] These post-abolition uses of slavery talk had their roots in older humanitarian anxieties about the fate of the Empire's non-white peoples, but they did not remain focused there. From the 1880s, as workers' rights and gendered codes of respectability became more scrutinised around the industrialised Victorian world, the language of enslavement expanded further to encompass the perceived economic threat of white men's wage exploitation and the moral threat of a 'white slave' traffic in prostitution.[11] As historians Fiona Paisley and Jane Lydon note, the language of slavery was enlisted to describe social ills even in settings where a formal history of slavery had never existed.[12] By the end of the nineteenth century, a diversified discourse of slavery was circulating on a global scale, aligning local concerns with international campaigns to protect the rights of varied groups.[13]

Settler humanitarianism and Aboriginal slavery in multiracial Australia

The diversified talk of modern slavery had some complex expressions in Australia on the cusp of the twentieth century. At the same time as the concept of 'white slavery' was being deployed to articulate perceived threats to the moral integrity of white women and the economic entitlements of white men, the abduction and forced indenture of Aboriginal and Pacific Islander workers continued to feed settlers' labour needs on the continent's northern frontiers, where pastoral stations, fisheries and sugar plantations flourished through the last decades of the nineteenth century. Queensland was the Australian colony most vigorously charged with toleration of slavery, reflecting its complex dependence upon the indenture of Pacific Islanders to work its sugar plantations, the exploitation of unwaged Aboriginal workers to build its pastoral and sea frontiers, and the violence of the Native Police Force to protect thriving pastoral hinterlands.[14]

Besides Queensland, Western Australia was the other Australian colony most persistently accused of modern slavery, particularly from the 1880s, as the colony's northern industries became ever more reliant upon Aboriginal workers who were paid only in rations and bound by written contracts without clear consent.[15] Unlike Queensland, Western Australia did not engage in the large-scale recruitment of Pacific indentured labour and, despite the opaque violence of its paramilitary policing strategies, did not formally employ a native police force on Queensland's model.[16] Nonetheless, the abusive labour practices and casual violence of the colony's northern frontiers, including the abduction of Aboriginal women, were all sufficiently well known to make these reputational differences just a matter of degree.[17] By the time Australian Federation arrived in 1901, reports of slavery across the northern half of the continent had been broadcast for more than a generation (see Figure 7.1).[18]

From the late 1860s onward, Australian colonial governments turned to legislation as the means of checking such abuses, particularly kidnapping

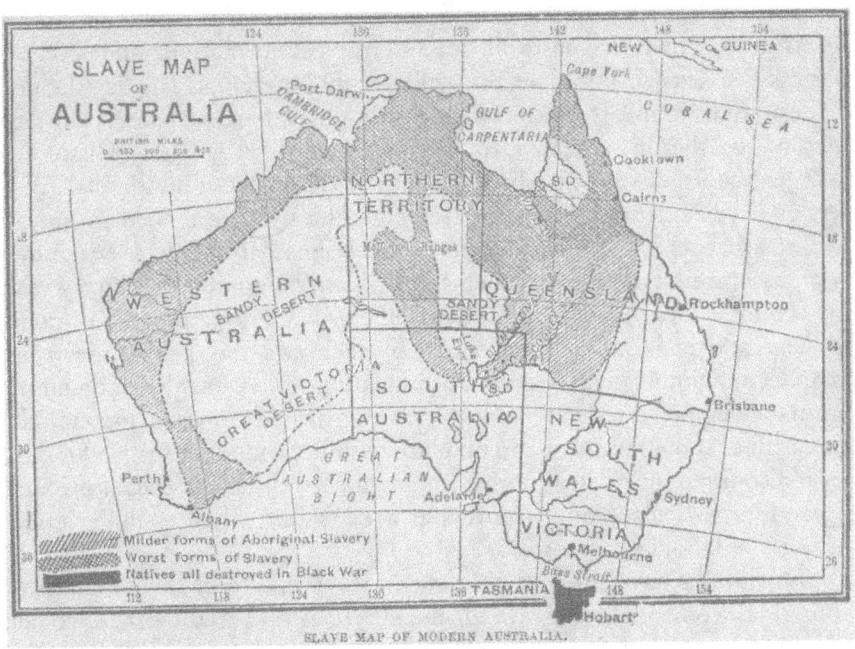

Figure 7.1 Slave map of Australia. Source: courtesy of the National Library of Australia.

in the indentured labour trade and the captivity of Aboriginal women in the pearling sector. Local interventions – beginning with Queensland's Polynesian Labourers Act 1868 and Western Australia's Pearl Shell Fishery Act 1871 – were boosted by the British imperial government's Pacific Islanders Protection Act 1872. These legal responses to modern slavery in northern Australia were part of a larger trend towards addressing labour abuses within the indentured labour system that spanned the British world. Through the 1870s, commissions of inquiry into the Indian indenture system and the passage of new laws to regulate it reflected the translation of humanitarian concern into a globalised legal framework of humane governance.[19] As historians have often argued, however, this sequence of government investigations and laws did little to repress widespread practices of abduction, violence and colonial exploitation. Indeed, the creation of a late colonial legal bureaucracy as the proxy for humane policy actually allowed labour abuses to escape punishment more often than not because their successful prosecution demanded such a high level of proof.[20] In this way, the juridification of humane governance – its accumulation of laws into a regulatory framework – contributed to the 'shrinking of humanitarian space'.[21]

In late colonial Australia, the scope of settler humanitarian space was circumscribed not only by the available channels of this growing legal bureaucracy but also by the racially porous nature of the regional north. On Australia's lucrative pastoral, sea and tropical northern frontiers, settler masters coexisted in intimate proximity with Aboriginal, Pacific Islander, Chinese and Southeast Asian workers, the last of whom were routinely bundled together in settler vocabulary as 'Malays' or 'Asiatics'. Historians have mapped the ways in which life and work on these multiracial frontiers evolved under conditions of closer familiarity than tended to prevail in the earlier-settled southern regions.[22] Labour relations were structured by an assumption of white entitlement, but also by domestic intimacy with and economic dependency upon racial others.[23] The layered codes of racial privilege and racial anxiety generated by such everyday proximities were complex and ambivalent. A publicly circulating voice of settler humanitarianism condemned the slave-like status of non-white workers in the multiracial north as something that had no place within the modern British Empire, but it also often included a more pointed anxiety about interracial proximity, and in particular about Aboriginal women's sexual accessibility under the guise of labour contracts.[24]

As historians have shown, white men's presumption of sexual access to Aboriginal women, especially in the northern pastoral sector where women were widely employed in multiple capacities, was so established that it was common practice to keep women on pastoral stations as a form of labour enticement. It was also well known, though largely unspoken, that such arrangements led to the birth of 'half-caste' children whose fathers responded with anything from acceptance or tolerance to denial.[25] The mutually uncomfortable visions of Aboriginal women's exploitation and allure produced an equivocal kind of settler humanitarian sentiment. It was 'a reproach to our civilisation' and an 'everlasting shame to think that this slavery should exist in a British community', ran one editorial in 1904, but so too was it 'a menace to the future development of the country'.[26]

Commentaries such as these were infused with an element of the antislavery rhetoric that had fuelled humanitarian arguments in the pre-abolition era. However, they were framed by a more specific settler colonial philosophy. By the late nineteenth century, faith in Indigenous peoples' future capacities for colonial citizenship had all but vanished in the British settler world. Retained was an earlier nineteenth-century belief in the state's role of trusteeship over Indigenous interests through humane oversight.[27] But largely dispensed with was a once-anticipated promise of Indigenous 'improvement' through access to legal rights, education and ameliorative labour. In its place was acceptance of a fixed racial hierarchy that invested the settler state with moral responsibility to check exploitation of the most vulnerable, but not to activate their rise to fuller rights.[28]

A parallel shift in the race politics of the late nineteenth-century settler world was the diversification of slavery discourse itself to envisage new forms of 'white slavery' that were exacerbated by the proximity of racial others. The lost status of racial entitlement supposedly exposed white women to the risk of slavery when they entered into intimate relationships with non-white men.[29] The adoption of white children into non-white families also raised fears about child slavery, prompting state rescues by settler states even as those states were removing Indigenous children from their families to be apprenticed as workers in settler homes.[30] This self-conscious racial ranking was apparent in the way that settler humanitarian arguments against Aboriginal enslavement at the end of the nineteenth century often included a level of distaste toward interracial contact that was much more pronounced than it had ever been within an earlier nineteenth-century philosophy of colonial amalgamation.[31] As one press editorial put it, the 'dusky handmaid' was both 'slave' and 'siren', and she posed a constant 'problem' for government officials.[32]

This conception of Aboriginal slavery as a twin problem – one of widespread abuse within the colonial labour sector and a more morally complex one of employers' presumed entitlement to Aboriginal women's bodies – brought scandal upon north-west Australia in 1886. In a series of widely circulated protests and a published pamphlet, the missionary John Brown Gribble alleged that Aboriginal people across the north-west were contracted to abusive masters on the shallowest pretence of consent, making them 'slave[s] in effect', and that an equal 'sign of slavery' was the assignment of Aboriginal women on labour contracts 'for purposes of immorality'.[33] Gribble's allegations were transmitted not only through the colonial press but also in direct appeals to the Aborigines' Protection Society and Colonial Office.[34] Obliged to respond, Western Australia's Governor, Frederick Napier Broome, reassured the Colonial Office that his government was doing everything possible to prevent abuses against Aboriginal people, and that the anticipated passage of new legislation – the Aborigines Protection Act 1886 – would encircle all Aboriginal labour arrangements with 'every possible precaution'.[35] Yet, as he readily acknowledged, sexual relations with Aboriginal women was a matter difficult to regulate through the law.[36] This continued to be true as the years passed. In 1901, the year of Australian Federation, one press report speculated that '99 out of every 100 white men' in the pastoral north-west kept Aboriginal women as their 'exclusive property'.[37]

If the image of the Aboriginal woman as 'slave' and 'siren' carried ambivalent messages about the moral failures and risks of settler governance, intimate relations between Asian men and Aboriginal women produced the strongest moral disapprobation in contemporary discourse. As historian Regina Ganter has shown, the prospect of Aboriginal–Asian intimacy was 'tendentially immoral' and inherently 'pernicious' in settler sentiment because 'Asian men were seen as such'.[38] The greatest level of settler suspicion was reserved for the Chinese who constituted a substantial percentage of the population in the multiracial north. Chinese workers and entrepreneurs were key contributors to the development of local economies and were rival employers of Aboriginal workers in ways that challenged a settler presumption of economic and racial entitlement. The investment of Chinese and other Asian migrants into northern economies also led to intermarriage and familial ties with Aboriginal communities in ways that further undermined 'officially sanctioned notions of home and nation'.[39]

Anti-Chinese sentiment played out in the press not only in reports about their 'heathen' activities and 'salacious' appetites, but in the adoption of an anti-slavery discourse that posed the Chinese as slave drivers. Chinese men sold their own wives and daughters as sex slaves, ran such accounts, and turned their Aboriginal workers into slaves.[40] Particularly abhorrent, because it subjected the most vulnerable people on the social ladder to slavery, was an alleged Chinese trade in Aboriginal women and children. This was the 'most terrible scandal in Australia', stated a press commentary in 1906, one able to proliferate in the north because the 'white population is so sparse'.[41] This construction of the Chinese as slavers – something supposedly given greater rein in the north by the insufficient presence of white settlement to check it – had a parallel in broader arguments that 'Asiatics' were the worst traffickers of women for prostitution, to a degree that overshadowed white settler abuses.[42] Although 'consorting with black women' was an unfortunate practice by white men in some remote regions, wrote a press correspondent in 1901, 'friends of the natives would be working more to the point if they were to interest themselves in removing their protégés from Asiatic degradation'; there would be opportunity 'to reform the lesser abuse practised towards the blacks by the whites when the graver evils resulting from Asiatic corruption are put an end to'.[43]

Settler arguments about saving vulnerable Aboriginal women from enslavement, prostitution and other moral evils did not only target Chinese and other 'Asiatics'; Aboriginal men were also widely blamed for prostituting and ill-using their women.[44] As historian Jessie Mitchell points out, this settler construction of Aboriginal men as 'deviant' and violent was as old as colonisation itself. Indeed, it had its roots in the civilising agendas of early missionaries and protectors, the appointed saviours of Aboriginal people whose views carried influence in wider humanitarian circles.[45] In these ways, a self-referential settler discourse of moral authority helped to shift the larger weight of responsibility for Aboriginal women's bondage from white men to 'yellow' and 'black' men, and by virtue of racial privilege, settler society became less the source of Aboriginal women's enslavement than its solution.

Intimate indenture and state intervention

Conditions in the first decade of the twentieth century illustrate how global, national and local influences came together in a system of humane governance that sought to address Aboriginal exploitation through the legal reinforcement of racial borderlines. On the global stage, the amalgamation of the British and Foreign Anti-Slavery Society and Aborigines Protection Society in 1909 reflected the continuation of an internationalised humanitarian agenda to expose twentieth-century forms of enslavement disguised within modern labour practices.[46] At the national level, the Federation of the Australian Commonwealth in 1901 exacerbated already-existing tensions between an aspirational, urbanised white Australia to the south and a multiracial north still shaped by a fluid frontier culture.[47] From state to state, the bureaucracy of Aboriginal protection that rolled out across Australia between the 1880s and 1910s demonstrated how legal interventions supposed to prevent the mistreatment of Aboriginal people served to strengthen the powers of modern settler governments. At the local level, all these concerns found a focal point in north-west Australia with the establishment in 1904 of a Royal Commission to inquire into 'the condition of the natives', led by Queensland's Protector of Aborigines, Walter Roth.[48]

Roth's report was scathing about the lack of legal checks to prevent violence against Aboriginal people in north-west Australia. It described a labour indenture system devoid of measures to guarantee Aboriginal workers' consent or access to minimum entitlements, a system of policing Aboriginal people that was irregular if not illegal, and a lingering culture of settler entitlement that tolerated Aboriginal women's 'defilement'.[49] The report helped to ensure the passage of Western Australia's Aborigines Act 1905, a stronger piece of protective legislation than its predecessors, which granted the Chief Protector or his proxies greater legal powers, among other things, to monitor Aboriginal employment arrangements and to remove Aboriginal women from the company of non-Aboriginal men.[50] In his role as Northern Protector in Queensland, Roth had already worked to support the introduction of similar legal provisions in that jurisdiction.[51]

Western Australia's Chief Protector of Aborigines, Henry Prinsep, had been arguing for several years for such capacities of intervention, having felt frustrated since the creation of his office by its lack of legal leverage.[52] No specific laws allowed him to prosecute those who abducted Aboriginal women, and when asked what could be done to prevent men from 'forcing the [Aboriginal] women against their will', he could only respond that he was trying to have the laws amended.[53] Reports continued to filter through to his office about the 'barbarous treatment' of Aboriginal workers in the north, and Prinsep hoped that the passage of the Aborigines Act 1905 would 'put a stop' to such injustices, as well as help 'to regulate the conduct of the blacks themselves so as to prevent them becoming willing victims of debauchery'.[54]

The Roth Inquiry and its influence in creating a stronger protective bureaucracy did not eradicate public commentary about the existence of Aboriginal slavery, however. Had recent government action 'ameliorated the tortures of slavery that existed in the pre-Roth days?', asked one editorial in 1905. 'No, slavery flourishes like a green bay tree. The black is as much the helot of the squatter as ever he was'.[55] A 1906 press editorial entitled 'Australian Slave Trade: Some Tales from the Far-Off North' queried the efficacy of the latest protective legislation and of the Chief Protector himself.[56] The 'Nor-West Horrors' of slavery were even put to verse.[57] Yet, as historians have often argued, moral concern about modern forms of slavery rarely triggered a revision of labour practices.[58] Instead of seeking to overhaul the colonised labour system, the approach of settler governments was to fortify their avenues of legal oversight. Accordingly, Prinsep's response to continuing reports of Aboriginal slavery and ill-treatment in the north was to forward them to the relevant local police for further inquiry.[59]

In November 1906, while the Chief Protector was fielding ongoing allegations of Aboriginal slavery in the north-west, a police investigation into conditions at Minderoo station was unfolding. Owned by the powerful family company of the Forrest brothers, Minderoo was a large pastoral property located forty kilometres inland from Onslow, a pearling town at the heart of the north-west coastal frontier. Gazetted only in 1885, Onslow and its pastoral surrounds had a strongly multiracial composition and a relatively small white male settler population. The region's pearling and pastoral economies were heavily dependent upon Aboriginal and Asian labour, which was widely available and readily exploitable.[60] Police attention alighted on Minderoo when the station's Chinese cook, Chi Coon, came forward to state that the manager, George Burrows, compelled an Aboriginal servant, Nellie, to remain at night with him at the homestead rather than return to the 'native camp' with her husband, Dicky Dad, and the station's other Aboriginal workers. Chi Coon said that Burrows refused to release Nellie even when confronted by Dicky Dad, who had left the station as a result. Questioned by the local policeman, Constable Barry, Nellie confirmed Chi Coon's account, saying that Burrows 'catch me, he catch me a long time' and 'no let me go'. Nellie's statement was corroborated by the depositions of two other Aboriginal station workers.[61]

Burrows's conduct was not unusual in a frontier setting where often only the station manager permanently occupied the pastoral homestead. Three months before the Burrows investigation, J. Bailey, manager of the Nannatharra station in the mid-west, was investigated for the same reason. According to the police report, Bailey admitted to keeping a young Aboriginal servant with him at the homestead at night but claimed 'he took her there for protection' from the risk of being beaten by another Aboriginal station worker. Despite her rightful husband coming 'several times to Nannatharra to get [her], Mr Bailey would not allow her to go'. The police held 'not the slightest doubt' that Bailey kept the young woman 'for immoral purposes', and otherwise considered him of bad character 'as regards his action to the natives'; but the matter did not on face value yield 'sufficient evidence to convict'.[62]

But although the case at Minderoo station was not especially remarkable, it is notable for what official responses to Nellie's circumstances revealed about the settler politics of humanitarian intervention. This was a politics driven by the state's belief in its obligation to redress Aboriginal exploitation, including the longstanding problem of women's sexual exploitation when bound by labour contracts. But this obligation did not extend to investing in Aboriginal people's larger civic freedoms, in the sense once imagined by anti-slavery campaigners. Rather it furnished the state with moral authority – an authority bolstered by legal capacity – to better regulate the indenture system and its unsanctioned intimacies. In exemplifying this concern, the police investigation at Minderoo station highlights how an ambivalent settler project of humane governance undertook to 'rescue' Aboriginal women from sexual bondage by more forcefully patrolling racial boundaries.

When the investigation into Minderoo station took place in late 1906, the district of Onslow had three 'fit and proper persons' to serve as Protectors of Aborigines, as was mandated by the Aborigines Act 1905.[63] The government practice of appointing Protectors was to bestow the role on local officials such as stipendiary magistrates, policemen and Justices of the Peace (JPs), the last of whom were usually pastoralists.[64] This mix of officials was represented in the district's three serving Protectors of Aborigines: the Resident Magistrate Dr Gurdon, Police Constable Barry, and a local JP and station manager, George Burrows himself. Just a few months earlier, Burrows had written to the Chief Protector in his capacity as a JP and Aboriginal Protector to relay that he had brought Nellie and another Aboriginal woman from Onslow to Minderoo station because they were being prostituted there by 'Malays' and other men. The women properly belonged under the protection of Minderoo station, he wrote. He would guarantee their employment there and he would look after them as the Aborigines Act directed.[65] As a JP and Protector, Burrows was empowered to remove the women from Onslow and to place them under his protection, but as a pastoral station manager he was part of the culture of Aboriginal exploitation.

Based on the depositions of Chi Coon, Nellie and the two other Aboriginal station workers, the Resident Magistrate, Dr Gurdon, charged Burrows with a suspected breach of section 43 of the Aborigines Act 1905, which prohibited non-Aboriginal men from 'cohabiting' with Aboriginal women. Countering the charge, Burrows presented himself as Nellie's rescuer from exploitation by the Asian and Aboriginal men around her. The Chinese cook Chi Coon was habitually drunk and unreliable, he said, and as a consequence Burrows had now dismissed him. Chi Coon himself wanted to sell Nellie to 'travellers & teamsters on the road' in exchange for grog, Burrows stated.[66] In addition to protecting her from Chi Coon, Burrows claimed to be protecting Nellie from her Aboriginal husband, Dicky Dad, who would otherwise prostitute her to 'teamsters and others for grog'. Dicky Dad was so dangerous that Burrows was periodically compelled to have him 'chained up' for his own and others' protection. Finally, appealing to the word of his settler neighbours, Burrows asserted the 'opinion of other right thinking men' that 'there was no justification' for the case against him.[67] Apart from this statement by Burrows, the only other European evidence came from Kimberley Forrest, the twenty-four-year-old son and nephew of the Forrest brothers who owned Minderoo station. Forrest's deposition was equivocal but not damning. He stated that he did not know if there was truth in the allegations, although he hinted that he thought it likely.[68]

Sifting through these claims and counterclaims, the magistrate Dr Gurdon felt 'no doubt in my own mind of the defendant's guilt'. Despite this, he dismissed the charge against Burrows, and did so on grounds that 'I did not feel justified in finding him guilty' on the word of a discharged Chinese cook and the Aboriginal servants.[69] In effect, it was not an absence of evidence that released Burrows from the probability of prosecution under the Aborigines Act, but the weight of prejudice against Chinese and Aboriginal testimony when unconfirmed by settler testimony. Officials had long tolerated such bias in the legal process, whereby convictions depended upon the corroborating evidence of Europeans.[70] However, the magistrate's decision to acquit Burrows, in spite of his personal conviction of Burrows' guilt, indicated more than a normalised distrust of non-white testimony. It also indicated the magistrate's concession, even if a reluctant one, to a more ubiquitous culture of settler authority that was supported by law and that sustained a cultural narrative of non-white men as inherently pernicious.

Although Gurdon allowed Burrows to avoid prosecution, he recommended that power over Aboriginal women should not be further 'placed in the hands of the squatters or their managers by making them protectors'.[71] Constable Barry, the district's other Aboriginal Protector, also wrote to his inspector asking whether the Aboriginal employment permits of men like Burrows and Bailey could be restricted to a condition 'that no native women be employed day or night at the house – [otherwise] the natives cannot be protected from them'.[72] A press report about Nellie's case voiced a similar caution. Tales 'waft themselves down from the Nor'-West' about wrongdoings relating to 'dusky maids of the bush', it stated, and '[h]istory has proved that the squatter is not the man to be trusted with the care of the blacks'. But while this report mirrored a wider discourse of moral disapproval towards white men's unspoken ownership of Aboriginal women, its disapproval was inextricable from distaste for the multiracial north itself. Burrows 'was the boss, and could do as he liked', the writer complained, and there was 'sufficient color in the evidence to show that the co-habitation of blacks and whites in the Never is an everyday occurrence'.[73]

If moral objection to Aboriginal women's sexual indenture in labour relationships was intermixed with distaste for porous racial boundaries, the deeper challenge to aspirational whiteness in the newly federated nation was interracial marriage. As historian Ann McGrath writes, intermarriage 'enacted the future nation in tangible and intangible ways', confounding 'both the color line and the colonizing line' and challenging a vision of settler sovereignty in ways that casual relations did not.[74] Anxiety about the north-west's blurred coloured line rose to a head the month before the police investigation into Nellie's case, when the local squattocracy gathered to protest the extent to which the Chief Protector allowed intermarriage to take place under the provisions of the Aborigines Act 1905. The act empowered the Chief Protector to give or withhold consent for a non-Aboriginal man to marry an Aboriginal woman, and local settlers complained that he was 'degrading white Australia' by granting his consent too freely.[75]

In fact, Prinsep supported the reinforcement of racial borderlines in ways that aligned his approach to that of Protectors in other jurisdictions during the early twentieth century.[76] He preferred that an Aboriginal woman should marry within 'her own people' and that young men of settler families should be protected wherever possible from their 'youthful ardour' for Aboriginal women.[77] But, he argued, the interests of both humanity and economy demanded his consent to marriage when white men fathered children who, with their Aboriginal mothers, would be a financial burden on the state if not supported by fathers and husbands. Those who preferred 'the old order of things', he concluded, were 'perhaps afraid of being brought to book themselves'.[78] In this hierarchy of humane governance, marriage trumped preference for racial segregation only when it avoided 'the old order of things' in which Aboriginal women and children held no claims to protection beyond that of the state. On the same grounds, the Protector gave his assent to marriages between Aboriginal women and Asian or other non-European suitors.

In reality, as many historians have shown, no amount of policing or government intervention could prevent the existence of interracial relationships, consensual or otherwise.[79] Yet when it came to the idea of Aboriginal women's continuing sexual exploitation in the multiracial north, the weight of suspicion still remained firmly placed on 'yellow', 'black', or 'coloured' men.[80] This was especially visible in the policing of northern goldfields and pearling towns where different racial groups mixed freely. Reporting in 1903 on police efforts to 'cleanse' the town of Broome, for instance, Corporal Feely described a setting of 'all colours', where Aboriginal men prostituted their women in exchange for grog, and the 'Chow, Malay & Manillaman' kept Aboriginal women for immoral purposes. Blurring the language of humanitarian concern with that of racial exclusion, he justified stronger policing measures 'in the interest of humanity ... to alleviate the misery of these poor people, and to remove this danger from our midst'.[81] In his annual report the following year, the Chief Protector was pleased to note that an increase in police patrols around the northern pearling districts had been helpful in preventing 'Manillamen' and other 'Asiatics' from 'soliciting native women' and 'hunting for them on the shore'.[82]

And what of Nellie's fate? Beyond her deposition in which she described how Burrows 'catch me' and 'no let me go', it is impossible to trace the degree, if any, to which she may have consented to the terms of her sexual indenture. Historians have cautioned us neither to overstate nor understate the scope of Aboriginal women's agency in colonial relationships, so just as it is likely that Nellie was without choice in the matter, it is also possible that she found some strategic advantage in her bonded relationship to her employer. Likewise, historian Ann McGrath stresses that while humanitarian campaigners and government policy-makers were setting out to 'save' Aboriginal people, Aboriginal people were securing their own futures through various means, which included interracial relationships, participation in settler industries and trade in resources.[83]

Rather than revealing anything specific about Nellie's circumstances, then, the investigation file of her case speaks mostly about a struggle of settler moral authority, in which settler men who held positions of guardianship in a juridified system of humane governance competed with one another as the Aboriginal woman's most legitimate rescuer. After Burrows's acquittal, Constable Barry made a determined effort to have him dismissed as a Protector of Aborigines, to restrict his right to employ Aboriginal women and to remove Nellie permanently from his custody. In following through with this plan, the policeman removed Nellie from Minderoo station and placed her in his own household as a domestic servant to his wife. Undeterred, Burrows 'pestered' to have Nellie returned to Minderoo station, persisting to the point where Barry threatened to lock him up.[84] Through a hired lawyer, Burrows continued to argue his case on grounds of his record as a respectable JP and employer of Aboriginal workers, the immorality of the Chinese cook Coon Chi, and the bad character of Nellie's husband, Dicky Dad.[85]

Ultimately, Burrows was not successful. Although he escaped prosecution, his certificate as a Protector of Aborigines was withdrawn and he was deemed unfit to employ Aboriginal women in the future. A short time later, the Forrest brothers released him from his duties as manager of Minderoo station.[86] In these ways a public sentiment of disapprobation washed over him, leaving him untouched by the law but reputationally tarnished. Nellie remained for the time being as a servant in the household of Constable and Mrs Barry, rescued from her sexual servitude to a settler master only by means of her alternative indenture as a domestic servant in the household of a policeman protector.[87]

Conclusion

The investigation at Minderoo station was not a singular case, but its timing brings into relief a coalescence of social unease around the turn to Federation about Aboriginal enslavement, the interracial intimacies of labour indenture, and the perceived need for more robust governance in multiracial settings. The legally braced protective bureaucracy that applied to all Aboriginal people by the early twentieth century emerged in part as an administrative response to humanitarian complaints about labour slavery and colonial violence that had aired for decades. It also emerged as a response to the hardening priority of settler society to consolidate its own racial sovereignty.

In such settings, the diversification of anti-slavery discourse that occurred through the late nineteenth century did not necessarily undermine a philosophy of white settler privilege. Rather, it provided an available vocabulary through which settler privilege could be bolstered. This was seen, especially in relation to the multiracial north, in the ways that greater culpability for Aboriginal slavery shifted discursively from white employers to pernicious 'Asiatics'. It was also seen in the way that moral objections to the slave-like systems of Aboriginal and Pacific Islander indenture became conflated with economic objections to the risk of white wage slavery. The problem with 'Slavery in the Nor'-West', ran one such commentary, was not just that it forced Aboriginal people 'to enter into lifelong bondage with the squatter', but also that it 'encourages cheap labour' across a market in which 'white workers have to compete'.[88] Similar arguments drawing out the causal relationship between non-white labour slavery and white wage slavery targeted Queensland's Pacific Islander indenture system and the indenture system across the British Empire, ultimately contributing to their decline.[89]

Of course, the rhetorical value of an early nineteenth-century humanitarian politics – one tied to the anticipated extension of individual rights and freedoms – did not disappear altogether. Scholars have traced how the legacies of older anti-slavery arguments were carried forward into the twentieth century in campaigns that challenged the embedded inequalities of settler societies and linked to a new international discourse of human rights.[90] However, arguably more influential in the settler world by the late nineteenth century was a double-edged colonial humanitarianism that could be put to the service of settler interests, while still appearing to uphold the interests of humanity. The translation of this settler humanitarianism into an increasingly juridified regime of humane governance in twentieth-century Australia worked less to protect Aboriginal people from systematic exploitation than to protect the sovereignty of the white settler polity. Although it was not anchored to the evangelical humanitarianism of the past, this protective bureaucracy was not entirely separate from it. Rather it was part of a historical continuum of humanitarian interventions which had always had a 'troubled rapport' with the demands of sovereignty.[91]

Notes

1 'The Native Question', *Coolgardie Miner* (Western Australia), 19 October 1896, p. 7.
2 Aborigines Protection Act (50 Vict. No. 25) 1886 (WA); Aborigines Protection Act Amendment (50 Vict. No. 912) 1886 (Victoria); Aborigines Act (6 Vict. No. 5) 1897 (WA); Aboriginals Protection & Sale of Opium Act (61 Vict. No. 17) 1897 (Qld); Aborigines Act (5 Edw. VII No. 14) 1905 (WA); Aborigines Protection Act (Act No. 25) 1909 (NSW), the Northern Territory Aboriginals Act (1 GeorgII V, No. 1024) 1910 (NT); Aborigines Act (2 GeorgII V, No. 1048) 1911 (SA).
3 Pacific Island Labourers Act (No. 16 of 1901); Immigration Restriction Act (No. 17 of 1901).
4 For instance, Samuel Moyn, 'Empathy in History, Empathizing with Humanity', *History and Theory* (2006), 45 (3), pp. 397–415; Michael Barnett, *Empire of Humanity: A History of Humanitarianism* (Ithaca, NY: Cornell University Press, 2011); Fabian Klose, *The Emergence of Humanitarian Intervention* (Cambridge, UK: Cambridge University Press, 2016).
5 Rob Skinner and Alan Lester, 'Humanitarianism and Empire', Special Issue of *Journal of Imperial and Commonwealth History* (2012), 40 (5), pp. 729–47; Lisa Ford, *Settler Sovereignty, Jurisdiction and Indigenous People in America and Australia, 1788–1836* (Cambridge, MA: Harvard University Press, 2010).
6 Alan Lester and Fae Dussart, *Colonization and the Origins of Humanitarian Governance* (Cambridge, UK: Cambridge University Press, 2014); Zoe Laidlaw, '"Justice to India – Prosperity to England – Freedom to the Slave!" Humanitarian and Moral Reform Campaigns on India, Aborigines and American Slavery', *Journal of the Royal Asiatic Society of Great Britain and Ireland* (2012), 22, pp. 299–324.
7 Russell McGregor, 'Drawing the Local Colour Line', *Journal of Pacific History* (2012), 47 (3), p. 345.
8 For instance, Kevin Grant, *Civilised Savageries: Britain and the New Slaveries in Africa, 1884–1926* (London, UK: Routledge, 2004), pp. 11–37; Richard Huzzey, *Freedom Burning: Anti-Slavery and Empire in Victorian Britain* (Ithaca, NY: Cornell University Press, 2012), pp. 5–20.
9 Hugh Tinker, *A New System of Slavery: The Export of Indian Labour Overseas, 1830–1920* (Oxford, UK: Oxford University Press, 1974); Kay Saunders, *Indentured Labour in the British Empire, 1834–1920* (London, UK: Croom Helm, 1984).
10 Jane Lydon, 'The bloody Skirt of Settlement: Arthur Vogan and Anti-Slavery in 1890s Australia', *Australian Historical Studies* (2014), 45 (1), pp. 46–70.
11 Jonathan Hyslop, 'The Imperial Working Class Makes Itself "White": White Labourism in Britain, Australia and South Africa before the First World War', *Journal of Historical Sociology* (2002), 12 (4), pp. 398–421; Brian Donovan, *White Slave Crusades: Race, Gender and Anti-Vice Activism, 1887–1917* (Urbana, IL: University of Illinois Press, 2006).

12 Fiona Paisley and Jane Lydon, 'Australia and Anti-Slavery', *Australian Historical Studies* (2014), 45 (1), pp. 1–2.
13 Adele Perry, 'Vocabularies of Slavery and Anti-Slavery: The North American Fur-Trade and the Imperial World', *Australian Historical Studies* (2014), 45 (1), pp. 34–5; Fiona Paisley, 'An Echo of Black Slavery: Emancipation, Forced Labour and Australia in 1933', *Australian Historical Studies* (2014), 45 (1), pp. 106–10.
14 For contemporary arguments for and against the existence of slavery in Queensland, see, for instance, 'Queensland Slavery', *Queenslander* (Brisbane), 14 December 1867, p. 4, and 'Queensland Slavery', *Northern Argus* (Rockhampton, Queensland), 11 September 1869, p. 2.
15 Penelope Hetherington, *Settlers, Servants and Slaves: Aboriginal and European Children in 19th Century Western Australia* (Perth, Australia: UWA Publishing, 2004); Ann Curthoys and Jessie Mitchell, *Taking Liberty: Indigenous Rights and Settler Self-Government in Colonial Australia* (Cambridge, UK: Cambridge University Press, 2018), pp. 361–84.
16 Chris Owen, *'Every Mother's Son is Guilty': Policing the Kimberley Frontier of Western Australia* (Perth, Australia: UWA Publishing, 2016).
17 'West Australia: Natives and Slavery', *Evening News* (Sydney), 9 April 1897, p. 6; 'Horrors of Slavery in Western Australia', *Herald* (Melbourne), 27 December 1897, p. 2; 'West Australian Slavery', *West Australian Sunday Times* (Perth), 30 April 1899, p. 5.
18 George Palmer, *Kidnapping in the South Seas* (Edinburgh, UK: Edmondston & Douglas, 1871); The Queenslander, *The Way We Civilise; Black and White; The Native Police: A Series of Articles and Letters* (Brisbane, Australia: G. and J. Black, 1880); J. B. Gribble, *Dark Deeds in a Sunny Land, or Blacks and Whites in North-West Australia* (Perth, Australia: Stirling Bros, 1886).
19 *Report of the Coolie Commission Appointed to Inquire into the Condition of the Indian Immigrants in the Colony of Natal* (South Africa: Government Printer, 1872); *Report of the Royal Commissioners Appointed to Enquire into the Treatment of Immigrants in Mauritius* (London, UK: William Clowes and Sons, 1875); Indian Immigrants Protection Ordinance 1876.
20 Reid Mortensen, 'Slaving in Australian Courts: Blackbirding Cases 1869–1871', *Journal of South Pacific Law* (2009), 13 (1), pp. 7–37.
21 Kristin Bergtora Sandvick and Dennis Dijkzeul, 'New Directions in Humanitarian Governance: Technology, Juridification and Criminialisation', *Global Policy*, 5 November 2019, accessed 1 May 2020.
22 Henry Reynolds, *North of Capricorn: The Untold Story of Australia's North* (Crows Nest, Australia: Allen and Unwin), 2003; Regina Ganter, *Mixed Relations: Asian-Aboriginal Contact in North Australia* (Perth, Australia: University of Western Australia Press, 2006); Ruth Balint, 'Aboriginal Women and Asian Men: A Maritime History of Color in White Australia', *Signs* (2012), 37 (3), pp. 544–54.
23 Victoria Haskins and Claire Lowrie, *Colonization and Domestic Service: Historical and Contemporary Perspectives* (New York, NY: Routledge, 2015).

24 On the longevity of this issue, see Alison Holland, 'Feminism, Colonialism and Aboriginal Workers: An Anti-Slavery Crusade', *Labour History* (1995), 69, pp. 52–64.
25 Ann McGrath, '"Black Velvet": Aboriginal Women and Their Relations with White Men in the Northern Territory, 1910–40', in Kay Daniels (ed.), *So Much Hard Work: Women and Prostitution in Australian History* (Sydney, Australia: Fontana, 1984), pp. 237–9; Victoria Haskins, '"Down the Gully & Just Outside the Garden Walk": White Women and the Sexual Abuse of Aboriginal Women on a Colonial Australian Frontier', *History Australia* (2013), 10 (1), p. 14; Liz Conor, *Skin Deep: Settler Impressions of Aboriginal Women* (Perth, Australia: UWA Publishing, 2016), p. 131.
26 'The Pilbarra Paradise: Motley Mongrel Melange', *Truth* (Perth), 30 July 1904, p. 2.
27 Andrew Porter, 'Trusteeship, Anti-Slavery and Humanitarianism', in Andrew Porter (ed.), *The Oxford History of the British Empire: The Nineteenth Century* (Oxford, UK: Oxford University Press, 1999), pp. 198–221.
28 Warwick Anderson, *The Cultivation of Whiteness* (Durham, NC: Duke University Press, 2006).
29 'Australia and White Slavery', *Richmond River Herald and Northern Districts Advertiser* (New South Wales), 21 April 1914, p. 4.
30 'A White Slave', *Advertiser* (Adelaide), 12 May 1906, p. 8; Shurlee Swain and Margot Hillel, *Child, Nation, Race and Empire: Child Rescue Discourse, England, Canada and Australia, 1850–1915* (Manchester, UK: Manchester University Press, 2010).
31 For instance, Damon Salesa, *Racial Crossings: Race, Intermarriage and the Victorian British Empire* (Oxford, UK: Oxford University Press, 2012).
32 'Society's Slaves: Dusky Handmaids and their Half-Caste Children: A Problem for the Protector', *Truth* (Brisbane), 13 January 1907, p. 3.
33 Gribble, *Dark Deeds in a Sunny Land*, pp. 33–5.
34 Gribble correspondence with Aborigines' Protection Society, March–December 1886, MSS British Empire S18/C137 and S22/G97, Weston Library UK; British Parliamentary Papers (BPP), *Correspondence respecting the Aborigines of Western Australia* (Colonial Office, October 1887), CO 881/8/3, National Archives (NA) UK.
35 Governor Broome to the Secretary of State, 12 July 1886, BPP CO 881/8/3, NA, p. 85.
36 Governor Broome to the Secretary of State, 9 June 1886, BPP CO 881/8/3, NA, p. 52.
37 'Slavery in the West', *Truth* (Brisbane), 16 June 1901, p. 5.
38 Regina Ganter, 'Living an Immoral Life – "Coloured" Women and the Paternalistic State', *Hecate* (1998), 24 (1), pp. 13–14. See also Ganter, *Mixed Relations*.
39 Balint, 'Aboriginal Women and Asian Men', p. 544; see also Reynolds, *North of Capricorn*, pp. 61–70; Kate Bagnell, 'Across the Threshold: White Women and Chinese Hawkers in the White Colonial Imaginary', *Hecate* (2002), 28 (2), pp. 9–32.

40 'Northern Territory Horrors', *Labor Call* (Melbourne), 17 November 1910, p. 6; 'Australia for the Asiatic', *Sunday Times* (Perth), 3 April 1910, p. 1; 'The Chinese Horror', *Labor Call* (Melbourne), 27 July 1911, p. 6.
41 'Awful Astounding Atrocities: Aboriginal Children Sold to Chinese', *Truth* (Brisbane), 16 December 1906, p. 10.
42 Liz Conor, '"Black Velvet" and "Purple Indignation": Print Responses to Japanese "Poaching" of Aboriginal Women', *Aboriginal History* (2013), 37, pp. 51–76.
43 'A Correspondent', 'The Native Question: Pastoralists and Their Native Supply: Asiatics and Native Degradation', *Western Mail* (Perth), 17 August 1901, p. 71.
44 'The Australian Aboriginals', *Western Mail* (Perth), 3 September 1904, p. 12; 'The Native Question', *Day Dawn Chronicle* (Perth), 1 July 1905, p. 2.
45 Jessie Mitchell, 'Corrupt Desires and the Wages of Sin: Indigenous People, Missionaries and Male Sexuality, 1830–1850', in Ingereth Macfarlane and Mark Hannah (eds), *Transgressions: Critical Australian Indigenous Histories* (Canberra, Australia: ANU e-Press, 2007), p. 230.
46 Neta Crawford, *Argument and Change in World Politics: Ethics, Decolonization and Humanitarian Intervention* (Cambridge, UK: Cambridge University Press, 2002), p. 241.
47 McGregor, 'Drawing the Local Colour Line', p. 345.
48 Walter Roth, *Report of the Royal Commission … on the Condition of the Natives* (Perth, Australia: Government Printer, 1905). The Roth Inquiry followed similar commissions of inquiry into the condition and management of Aboriginal people in other Australian jurisdictions between the 1850s and 1890s.
49 Roth report, pp. 6–12, 25–6.
50 Aborigines Act 1905, WA, sections 16–32; sections 42–4.
51 Ganter, 'Living an Immoral Life', p. 14; Aboriginals Protection & Sale of Opium Act (61 Vict. No. 17), 1897 (Qld).
52 Chief Protector of Aborigines to the Law Department Secretary, 1 November 1900, Acc 255, 1900/830, State Records Office of Western Australia (SROWA).
53 Chief Protector to Frank Wittenoom, 29 August 1898, Acc 255, 1898/1175, and Chief Protector to H. G. Leroy, 14 May 1901, Acc 255, 1901/406, SROWA.
54 Letter of Joseph O'Connell J.P., 29 April 1901, Acc 255, 328/1901, SROWA; Chief Protector, *Aborigines Department: Report for Financial Year Ending 30th June 1904* (Perth, Australia: Government Printer, 1904), p. 3.
55 'Goldfields Legrees – Coolgardie Slave Holders', *Sun* (Kalgoorlie, Western Australia), 27 August 1905, p. 9.
56 'Australian Slave Trade: Some Tales from the Far-Off North', *Sunday Times* (Perth), 28 October 1906, p. 5.
57 Julian Stuart, 'Nor-West Horrors: A Brand of Shame', *Sunday Times* (Perth), 26 February 1905, p. 9.
58 Jane Lydon, *The Flash of Recognition: Photography and the Emergence of Indigenous Rights* (Sydney, Australia: UNSW Press, 2013), pp. 39–55; Adrian

Graves, *Cane and Labour: The Political Economy of the Queensland Sugar Industry, 1862–1906* (Edinburgh, UK: Edinburgh University Press, 1993), pp. 225–6.

59 Chief Protector of Aborigines, memo to Sub-Inspectors of Police, 1 November 1906, Acc 255, 1906/949, SROWA.
60 John Slade Durlacher, *Landlords of the Iron Shore* (Perth, Australia: Hesperian Press, 2013), p. 4.
61 Depositions of Chi Coon, Nauwura alias Nellie, Booagoo alias Tommy, and Niabiddy alias Annie, 26–27 November 1906, Acc 255, 1906/820, SROWA.
62 Report of Constable J. Fogarty, 7 August 1906, Constable Barry to Inspector Drewry, 3 December 1906 and Inspector Drewry to the Chief Protector, 10 December 1906, Acc 255, 1906/1099, SROWA.
63 Aborigines Act 1905 (WA), section 7.
64 Circular from Premier John Forrest, 1 May 1898, Acc 255, 1898/53, SROWA.
65 George Burrows to Chief Protector, 22 June 1906, Acc 255, 1906/820, SROWA.
66 Deposition of George Crisp Burrows, 27 November 1906, Acc 255, 1906/820, SROWA.
67 George Burrows to the Chief Protector, 4 December 1906, and Burrows's lawyer Horace Joseph to the Chief Protector, 14 January 1907, Acc 255, 1906/820, SROWA.
68 Deposition of Kimberley Forrest, 27 November 1906, Acc 255, 1906/820, SROWA.
69 Resident Magistrate Gurdon to the Chief Protector, 1 December 1906, Acc 255, 1906/820, SROWA.
70 Jeannine Purdy and Hannah McGlade, '"No Jury Will Convict": An Account of Racial Killings in Western Australia', *Studies in Western Australian History* (2001), 22, pp. 91–106.
71 Resident Magistrate Gurdon to the Chief Protector, 1 December 1906, Acc 255, 1906/820, SROWA.
72 Constable Barry to Inspector Drewry, 3 December 1906, Acc 255, 1906/1099, SROWA.
73 'The Wonderful Nor'-West', *Sunday Times* (Perth), 16 December 1906, p. 2.
74 Ann McGrath, *Illicit Love: Interracial Sex and Marriage in the United States and Australia* (Lincoln, NE: University of Nebraska Press, 2015), pp. 1–2, 28; Kat Ellinghaus, 'Absorbing the "Aboriginal Problem": Controlling Interracial Marriage in Australia in the Late 19th and Early 20th Centuries', *Aboriginal History* (2003), 27, pp. 183–207.
75 Lewin Cooke to the Premier, 17 and 19 October 1906, Acc 255, 1906/827, SROWA.
76 Ellinghaus, 'Absorbing the "Aboriginal Problem"', p. 197.
77 Chief Protector to Abdullah, 5 November 1901, Acc 255, 1901/965 and Chief Protector to the Colonial Treasurer, 16 November 1906, 1906/827, SROWA.
78 Chief Protector to the Colonial Treasurer, 16 November 1906, 1906/827, SROWA.

79 On layers of consent in interracial relationships, see Ann McGrath, 'Consent, Marriage and Colonialism: Indigenous Australian Women and Coloniser Marriages', *Journal of Colonialism & Colonial History* (2005), 6 (3).
80 For instance, Henry Hunter to the Chief Protector, 6 September 1911, Acc 652, 1911/1243; Ellinghaus, 'Absorbing the "Aboriginal Problem"', pp. 188–9.
81 Report of Corporal Feely, 15 March 1903, Acc 430, 1903/123, SROWA.
82 Chief Protector, *Aborigines Department: Report for Financial Year Ending 30th June 1904* (Perth, Australia: Government Printer, 1904).
83 McGrath, *Illicit Love*, p. 99.
84 Police Constable Barry to the Chief Protector, 31 December 1906, Acc 255, 1906/820, SROWA.
85 Horace Joseph to the Chief Protector, 14 January 1907, Acc 255, 1906/820, SROWA.
86 Chief Protector to the Under Treasurer, 14 December 1906, Acc 255, 1906/820, SROWA; 'A Station Manager's Claim: Action for Wrongful Dismissal', *West Australian* (Perth), 22 August 1907, p. 7.
87 Constable Barry to the Chief Protector, 1 February 1907, Acc 255, 1906/820, SROWA.
88 'Slavery in the Nor-West', *Truth* (Perth), 22 July 1911, p. 3.
89 'Queensland Slavery', *Queenslander* (Brisbane), 14 December 1867, p. 4; Premier Griffith to Governor Musgrove, 30 September 1884, IOR/L/PJ/6/141, File 2560, British Library; Sascha Auerbach, *Race, Law and 'The Chinese Puzzle' in Imperial Britain* (New York, NY: Palgrave, 2009), pp. 15–50.
90 Fiona Paisley and Jane Lydon, 'Anti-Slavery and Its Legacies', special issue of *Australian Historical Studies* (2014), 45 (1), pp. 1–12.
91 Michael Geyer, 'Humanitarianism and Human Rights: A Troubled Rapport', in Klose (ed.), *The Emergence of Humanitarian Intervention*, p. 55.

8

Humanitarian priorities and West African agency in the British Empire

Bronwen Everill

In 1851 the famous Nigerian missionary Samuel Ajayi Crowther called on the British government to intervene on behalf of humanity in coming to the defence of the Church Missionary Society's settlement at Abeokuta.[1] Citing nearby slave trading and the threat it posed to the 'civilising mission' of the Empire, Crowther and others succeeded in encouraging the annexation of Nigerian territory to the British Empire. But this was neither the first nor the last appeal that West Africans would make to Britain's sense of itself as a global moral authority.

Less successful attempts to elicit British colonial intervention in other humanitarian crises – disease epidemics, famines, droughts – reflected the limitations of imperial humanitarianism and the mismatch between local priorities and imperial philanthropy. As historians Tehila Sasson and James Vernon have argued with regard to British famine relief in the nineteenth century, it 'generated a form of governmentality designed to produce a new type of colonial subject'.[2] The management of famine and disease was directed by colonial financial constraints, while at the same time helping to shape and sustain an argument about colonised people that limited the British government's responsibility by framing these humanitarian emergencies as problems of control and containment. As in managing the nineteenth-century colonial Irish and Indian famines, responses to local humanitarian crises in West Africa were often framed around 'educating' people out of poverty: 'relief was designed to teach men the virtues of industry' through a series of constantly changing approaches.[3] In the case of West African disease outbreaks, mistaking poverty for 'tradition' or 'racial characteristics', colonial administrators focused their resources on the European community in the belief that certain problems of development were inherent to other races rather than simply a matter of sustained investment.

In place of government intervention and investment, mutual aid societies – many with antecedents that predated colonial rule – stepped in to provide (limited) access for their members to welfare services, health care and forms of insurance. Humanitarianism was never purely the prerogative of the colonial government. West Africans in the British Empire defined their own humanitarian priorities, even when they had little in the way of resources, by mobilising the language of anti-slave trading and relying on their own civil society groups. The bifurcation of colonial and local humanitarian spheres of policy, however, had a legacy that continued through late colonial development and post-colonial humanitarianism.

This chapter will explore how Britain's humanitarian priorities in West Africa could be shaped by the demands of people like Crowther, the limitations of those claims on Britain's philanthropy, and how the relationship between the humanitarian promise and its reality affected West African attempts to control diseases like malaria. Ultimately, while British imperial humanitarian policy often responded to British West African subjects' appeals to intervene in the slave trade, other humanitarian concerns, including famine and disease, were regularly not prioritised by the colonial government, despite lobbying from the same groups. This chapter will contrast British responses to West African calls for anti-slave trade intervention with measures to reduce malaria and yellow fever and promote colonial welfare. Despite the strength of anti-slave trade feeling in the halls of power, humanitarian imperialism was not matched by humanitarian governance.

West African elites and the 'model' of imperial humanitarianism

West Africa held a unique position in the British imagination because of Britain's role as the leader of anti-slave trade interventions in the region. Although the tensions between humanitarianism and colonial governance were present throughout the Empire, West Africa presents a particularly useful example because of this clear antislavery mission.

Britain's long political and commercial involvement in West Africa began in the sixteenth century, long before it was connected with any humanitarian impulse, and its interests in trade and territorial control remained important as drivers of humanitarian policy.[4] The English Royal Africa Company's slave trading forts at places like Cape Coast Castle (modern Ghana), taken from the Dutch in the seventeenth century, required British traders to develop political alliances as well as commercial partnerships with local elites. Rebecca Shumway, Randy Sparks, Margaret Priestley and other historians have detailed how political and personal influence grew out of the transactions conducted at slaving forts and factories in the Gold Coast.[5] By the mid-eighteenth century, the era of the monopoly Company's dominance was over – though they still managed the forts on the coast – and 'free traders' spread out along the coast in order to take advantage of the potentials of competition. However, as historian William Pettigrew has argued, the free trade era was one that former Royal Africa Company employees characterised as rife with abuse, with competing traders dangerously overfilling ships and transgressing trading norms.[6] In the 1750s, the slave trader and Royal Africa Company lobbyist Malachy Postlethwayt wrote to encourage the expansion of British royal authority and regulation in trade in West Africa in order to curb the abuses associated with competition amongst traders. Postlethwayt's arguments for more regulation of the trade overlapped with an emerging Quaker sentiment against the slave trade more generally, showing how arguments against the practices of the slave trade emerged from both humanitarian and practical concerns.[7]

By the 1780s, Granville Sharp and Olaudah Equiano supported a plan to establish a new form of permanent British settlement near an existing private slave trading factory at Bunce Island in the Sierra Leone River. Their idea was to form a model settlement of free Black Britons in the region to counteract the influence of the slave traders, demonstrate the 'civilisation' of British values, and help to alleviate the poor conditions that faced Black Britons in London by giving them land 'back' in Africa. Their settlement, the Province of Freedom, established in 1787, would undergo numerous changes over the following century, changing its name to Freetown, operating under the governance of a British philanthropic company – the Sierra Leone Company – then becoming a Crown Colony, slowly expanding its territory and adapting its governance structures in response to local and imperial changes. At various points, the inhabitants of the colony of Freetown in Sierra Leone were joined by so-called 'native strangers', Maroons from Jamaica, formerly enslaved Americans who joined the British during the American Revolution and the 'Liberated Africans' resettled in villages around the colony after the slave ships they were transported on were captured and adjudicated in Freetown.[8]

It was this last group that numerous Sierra Leone governors pinned their hopes on in their quest to spread the notions of British 'civilisation, commerce, and Christianity' and end the slave trade. As historians Padraic Scanlan and Richard Anderson have argued, the policies of the British government in Sierra Leone toward the Liberated Africans was one that combined the paternalistic philanthropy of the British abolitionist and evangelical Clapham Sect with the emerging ideas of liberal imperial governmentality: Liberated Africans were assigned to villages; they were given apprenticeships; and their education was overseen by missionaries closely tied to the colonial government.[9] By the 1840s, British governors increasingly devolved responsibility to the residents of Freetown as colonial policy-makers (briefly) embraced the 'euthanasia of the mission'.[10] People like Crowther benefited from this approach, as he climbed the ranks of the Anglican Church hierarchy, and became an important political voice for the Sierra Leoneans who migrated to Nigeria.

The periodic swings between extensive (and expensive) philanthropic plans along the lines of the model of the Liberated African villages and the more hands-off devolution of governance to the emergent Liberated African middle class ultimately gave way to a 'golden age' for this group between the 1840s and 1870s, when they achieved positions of prominence in governance not only in Freetown but also in Nigeria, Gambia and the Gold Coast. In addition, they gained wealth through their success as merchants along the coast and as landlords in the colony, and gained political influence through the proliferation of their newspapers.[11] It was this group of Liberated Africans who made the greatest calls on the language of humanitarian imperialism, as work by historian Sandra Greene has outlined, asking for intervention in the slave trade.[12] But they gradually declined in authority from the 1880s, as the Empire-wide 'betrayal of the Creole elite' saw imperial favouritism swing towards so-called 'native authorities' (chiefs, headmen).[13] It is the example of this group of Anglophone Victorian African elites, however, that adds nuance to the question of who was the beneficiary of colonial humanitarianism in the British Empire, and what limitations colonial governance placed on humanitarian imperial ambitions.[14]

British antislavery intervention in West Africa was used as a model for nineteenth-century humanitarian interventions elsewhere in Africa. East African interventions, in particular, drew on both the reputation Britain had built for itself as an anti-slave trade leader and its experience in prosecuting slave ships and resettling trafficked people.[15] The antislavery mission in Sierra Leone has shaped much of the colonial history of the region. This legacy continued in the twenty-first century, with Britain's limited, 'surgical' military intervention near the end of the Sierra Leone Civil War (1991–2002) being used to demonstrate the principles of 'humanitarian intervention' and the doctrine of 'Responsibility to Protect'.[16] Addressing an acute threat, like the slave trade or war, represented an easily delimited investment of resources while complex issues of governance surrounded the provision of safe drinking water, sanitation systems, disease control or poor relief.

The 'success' of the civilising mission in creating a group of missionary-trained West African merchants, lawyers and colonial civil servants helped Britain to articulate its doctrine of developmentalism, as attitudes towards colonialism shifted in the interwar period.[17] Even as priorities shifted away from the slave trade and enslaved labour – though these still remained important for the League of Nations[18] – towards questions of health, disease control and economic development, these issues were regularly framed in terms of educational and civilisational terms, neglecting the long history of imperial under-investment and segregation.[19] Humanitarian imperialism was split into two distinct areas of governance – intervention and development – and over the course of the nineteenth and twentieth centuries, responsibility for those areas fluctuated between international and local authorities.[20] These contradictions of sovereignty and governmental responsibility were at the heart of humanitarian imperialism around the British Empire, but are especially evident in the case of British West Africa because of the unique circumstances of the Liberated Africans, who were cast as the prime example of Britain's humanitarianism in action, while also becoming a vocal group of colonial settlers; they were the object of humanitarian concern and a racialised colonial subject simultaneously.

Appeals to British imperial humanitarianism

During the second half of the nineteenth century, British humanitarians created a narrative in which missionary-educated West Africans instrumentalised the values of 'civilisation, commerce, and Christianity' to achieve local goals, largely in relation to territorial expansion and commercial competition with slave traders. From the period of the Sierra Leone Company's control of Freetown (1791–1807), the Black settler population used appeals to the anti-slave trading mission of the colony to demand intervention. Liberated African traders, operating beyond the bounds of the colony's jurisdiction, pushed for recognition of their British status and protection against accidentally being enslaved. In the 1840s Sierra Leoneans were extremely vocal in pointing to the inability of Liberia to control the slave trade in areas claimed by Liberia, a weakness of rule determined to be a sufficient cause for demanding that Liberia explicitly lay out their claims to sovereignty in places like Bassa Cove, a disputed area between the two colonies.[21] As noted above, Samuel Ajayi Crowther was one of a handful of West African missionaries involved in petitioning the British to expand their influence in support of abolishing the slave trade. Thomas Will was another Sierra Leonean who petitioned the queen 'to sympathize with her humble petitioners to establish a colony to Badagry that the same may be under the Queen's Jurisdiction and beg of her Royal Majesty to send missionary with us and by so doing the slave trade can be abolished'.[22]

But this influence of Sierra Leoneans on British policy was limited to examples of antislavery humanitarianism, or to cases where West Africans could successfully link their cause to antislavery. For instance, in the annexation of Lagos in 1861, Crowther was able to appeal to British philanthropists and mobilise the narrative of humanitarian concern for the mission station at Abeokuta in Nigeria by highlighting the slave raiding taking place in the adjacent Kingdom of Dahomey. Another call for British annexation, made down the coast at a British missionary and Liberated African settlement in Cameroon, was less successful, in part because despite the petitioners' desire for British intervention on behalf of missionaries and traders there, the slave trade was not a problem in the region: without a clear antislavery motive, the British government saw little reason to intervene.[23] Related attempts to expand British control of territory around Freetown usually relied on the mobilisation of the question of the slave trade's continuation in the interior and the threat it posed to the British African subjects resident in Freetown and the Freetown peninsula. Tensions between the British and French (in Senegambia, or in the Northern Rivers of what would become Guinea on the Sierra Leone border) or British and Americans (at Liberia) were often framed in terms of the laxity of French and American efforts to suppress the slave trade and the need for British intervention. A petition from a group of European and African traders based in Gambia complained:

> That so long as the Native Merchant can safely carry on this nefarious but lucrative trade, it is in vain to point out to him any other source of profit, however flattering or easy of attainment – and your memorialists are fully convinced that the utmost vigilance and exertion will be insufficient to the effectual abolition of the said Trade in Slaves while French Vessels are allowed free entrance and a French Settlement permitted to exist in the River Gambia.[24]

In 1857 the British finally gained control of Albreda, on the River Gambia, responding to the numerous complaints that French control of the fort was undermining British abolition efforts.[25] Sierra Leonean merchants, meanwhile, were able to gain concessions from Liberia through repeated appeals to British anti-slave trading goals in the contested Gallinas River region between Sierra Leone and Liberia.[26]

In the 1880s, when tensions with the French Empire were high, the *Sierra Leone Weekly News* included regular appeals from its readers to look into the allegations 'that some of the European merchants in the [Rio Nunez] are trafficking in human beings'.[27] The contested region was ultimately to fall within the territory of French Guinea, but the pressure on the British authorities to 'do something' about continued European slave trading in the Northern Rivers was an important part of the negotiating position of the government in the give and take of French and British territorial division in the 1890s.[28] The success of these appeals in shaping West African expansion and creating the sense in the metropole that there was a need for slave trade intervention – particularly in moments of European crisis – has been noted by scholars of West African colonial history.[29] Imperial expansion, in other words, regularly relied on a justification of humanitarian expediency that expressly invoked the campaign against the slave trade.[30] In fact, as numerous historians have detailed, even the claim of continuing enslaved labour was not enough to compel British action.[31] Humanitarianism was strictly circumscribed, and, as the examples above show, was often used to forestall European rivals rather than institute genuine humanitarian reforms.

Local humanitarian concerns

Appeals to Britain's antislavery mission were generally successful. What was less successful in imperial appeals were requests that extended beyond the expected victim narrative customary in antislavery discourse. Questions of public health and sanitation, housing, hunger and other humanitarian concerns were often dismissed by colonial authorities as matters of local culture, custom or unchanging environment. The colonial government only sporadically sought to address these problems for the African population of the colony.

During the early-modern period, West Africa had a reputation as a 'White Man's Grave', with high mortality from both epidemics of yellow fever and endemic diseases, such as malaria.[32] As Philip Curtin and other scholars of the settlement efforts in Freetown, Liberia, and elsewhere have noted, however, this high mortality was not limited to the European colonial officials and merchants, but extended to the wider population. Urbanisation and infilling in the mangrove regions and coast – areas that made sense to settle from the colonial perspective because of the ease of export and commercial traffic – did nothing to hinder the spread of these mosquito-borne diseases. The European population of Sierra Leone in the first decades of the nineteenth century, for instance, experienced a mortality rate of around 46 per cent, while the Black population's ranged between 30 and 50 per cent.[33] Sierra Leone's Governor, Zachary Macaulay, reported in the rainy season of 1798: 'The present has been the most sickly season I have ever known among the settlers. About a Week ago, there was scarce an individual belonging to the Colony who was not laid up with a kind of Influenza which did not however extend to the Europeans'.[34]

Despite the high mortality rate both within the local African population and among the Black settler population, contemporary ideas about health and foreign bodies shaped the colonial government's perceptions of the problem and its potential solutions. British military and colonial experience had led to the popularisation of ideas of health and sanitation that saw European (English) bodies as particularly susceptible to disease in tropical climates, and 'native' bodies as either unaffected or beyond the capacity of modern medicine to adequately address.[35]

Reports from British visitors to places like the Liberated African village of Regent emphasised the impact the civilisational mission was having on the population, in producing 'industrious' people who lived in 'remarkably neat and clean' houses.³⁶ In spite of these early observations, the later reports of both colonial officials and Freetown's elites emphasised the squalor of the city and its surrounds, and the need for more investment in long-term projects to manage sanitation and reduce the high mortality rate that resulted.

With the expansion of the local press in the 1870s and 1880s, Freetown's residents were increasingly able to vocalise their critiques of government responsiveness to a lack of progress in controlling the spread of disease. As one paper put it, 'suggestions have now and again been made by the public, through the medium of the press, to remedy the evil' of poor sanitation causing disease, 'but the authorities have given no heed'.³⁷ Concerns with sanitation and proposals for drainage and new hygiene measures regularly featured on the pages of both the *Sierra Leone Times* and the *Sierra Leone Weekly News*. An article published in 1885 summarised the requests for immediate aid that the residents of the city sought:

> The wet and malignant fever season to natives and Europeans alike is striding on with rapid steps apace with the exit of the present month. But though deadly the season generally is to all classes yet we regret to observe that necessary sanitary efforts have not been put forth to meet its usual emergencies. We had thought, that our authorities benefited by the experience of last year, would adopt in this, such precautionary measures as would save them a few £.s.D to their already impoverished exchequer. But in this, we are disappointed. And though we have from time to time in previous issues pointed out the neglected sanitation, or rather no system of sanitation at all which obtains with them at present, yet no definite action has been taken in the matter. Possessed with a ruler who is a medical man, we had hoped a discontinuance of this state of things.³⁸

Despite the repeated pleas of the residents, the colonial government's interest in preventative approaches to outbreaks of malaria and yellow fever was sporadic at best, and typically the more long-term solutions were deemed to be too expensive. Ensuring proper drainage, for instance, was not a one-time solution, but something the government would need to manage regularly.

As trade tax revenues declined in the 1870s, as a result of a recession, Sierra Leone and other parts of British West Africa were under increasing pressure to raise revenue locally through a mixed tax system that included direct and indirect taxes.³⁹ The British government did not want to fund the development priorities of the colonies from the London exchequer. But the amounts that the colonial governments could raise from the local population and from trade fluctuated annually, and the high salaries and benefits for colonial officials, defence of the borders and infrastructure developments aimed at commercial growth were an unmoving priority that typically superseded everything else.⁴⁰

Finally, in 1899, the Liverpool School of Tropical Medicine sent an expedition led by Major Ronald Ross to address a malaria outbreak in Freetown. His team found that the malaria-carrying Anopheles mosquitoes bred only in ground puddles near built-up residential areas, which meant that the measures that needed to be taken to prevent malaria outbreaks were limited to draining and sweeping up street puddles, using mosquito nets and, consequentially, moving the European population to the cooler hills around Freetown.[41]

The results in the implementation of the Report of the Malaria Expedition to Nigeria of the Liverpool School of Tropical Medicine at the turn of the twentieth century revealed that the colonial priority with regard to the endemic but devastating prevalence of malaria was primarily to segregate the European and African populations in the colonial capitals in West Africa. Preventative measures were deemed too onerous and expensive to implement and sustain in the face of what they believed to be intractable 'traditional' ways of living for the African residents of the cities.[42] The recommendations of the Nigeria expedition argued that segregation 'would have been unnecessary, of course, had the possibility of the suggestion of the use of quinine wholesale among natives been feasible, but the enormous quantity of the drug that would have been required, and the more or less uncivilised condition of West African natives, have been shewn to render the plan impossible'.[43] Other colonial journals took from the report that malaria should be addressed by 'the segregation of Europeans at a distance of not less than half a mile from the huts of natives', while plans to offer quinine to the whole community were deemed 'absolutely impractical'.[44] In other words, they interpreted the extant conditions – often fuelled by poverty and rapid urbanisation – as 'characteristic' of African peoples, rather than conditional on the colonial situation.[45]

Ross returned to Freetown in 1901 to attempt to implement some of his drainage ideas. He succeeded in clearing 90 per cent of mosquito breeding places, but Colonial Office officials ignored his report and the Governor of Sierra Leone deemed the continuation of his sanitation work 'too expensive to continue'.[46] But the African elites of Freetown were not impressed with this government response. In 1900 they complained about the British plan to move all Europeans to Hill Station:

> We view with disfavour the proposal to remove the European officials from unhealthy Freetown to the breezy hillsides and leave the African officials to the filthy and ill-kept surroundings of Freetown. If the chief Europeans were removed from Freetown less likelihood there would be than ever of the sanitary condition of Freetown being improved. The African official requires healthy surroundings as much as his European brother.[47]

Not only did this go against the idea of a 'civilisational' imperialism, but the writers worried that the removal of the Europeans would mean that there was no incentive for the colonial government to do anything about the conditions that made Freetown malarial: there was just too little interest in aiding the African residents of the town. A report five years later confirmed these concerns, highlighting that, after the expense of setting up Hill Station, 'it seems rather early to ask it to plunge into debt by adopting extravagant schemes, in order to bring about doubtful benefit to the Negro population which remains in the town'.[48] As the *Sierra Leone Times* commented, the expense of building Hill Station showed 'what a splendid thing the Government could have made of our streets and public buildings' had the sanitation campaign been followed through.[49]

Typically, and demonstrating their clear understanding of Britain's humanitarian priorities, Freetonians worried aloud about the increasing presence of immigrants to the colony from the interior, pointing out that they not only brought disease but also might attempt to kidnap people for the slave trade. This fear-mongering seems strange – there are no reported cases of kidnapping for slavery – but makes sense in the context of an understanding of what British authorities might actually take note of.[50]

It was clear that, although the population of Freetown suffered equally from problems of disease and sanitation, only the European population was targeted for relief by the colonial government. This became the standard approach across British West Africa. In Accra, Ghana, as in Nigeria and Freetown, segregation became standard. As historian Jonathan Roberts notes, Gold Coast 'government medical reports linked filth and contamination to the local Ga population, in line with theories of racial ecology that located sources of illness within African bodies', an underlying sentiment that continued even after mosquitoes were discovered as the disease vector.[51] Even once DDT and pyrethrum were being used to control mosquito populations during World War II, whole Ghanaian villages deemed 'too proximate' to airfields and other sites of military personnel were 'relocated'.[52]

Mutual aid

Colonial governments in West Africa repeatedly approached the issues of health care and epidemic diseases through methods of controlling population movements, rather than investing in the infrastructure that would have responded to their subjects' humanitarian priorities. This left a gap where basic needs – for health care, local sanitation campaigns, and other forms of community relief and development – were unmet by government policy. To respond to these needs, West Africa's British subjects relied on mutual aid societies. Many West African groups had pre-existing traditions of societies that looked after the welfare needs of members. The Poro societies in Sierra Leone were amongst the more well known of these societies, but the Humui and Njayei societies (of the Mende people), Tuntu, Thoma and Yasi societies (in Sherbro, off the coast of Sierra Leone) were all societies that historians have dated to the pre-colonial period.[53] While the Poro was specifically associated with a variety of governance functions, societies took on slightly different forms and functions during the nineteenth century in urban colonial settings.

As soon as Liberated Africans began to be settled in the villages surrounding Freetown, groups began organising themselves into mutual aid 'companies'. Christian relief societies were also organised by missionaries to replace the traditional companies, which they disapproved of as pagan.[54] In Sierra Leone, there were 'companies' specific to the Muslim community, as well as women's companies, men's companies, and those designated for the descendants of the various settler communities. These societies had 'disciplinary rules', as well as helping dues-paying members with medical expenses and other welfare needs, and they constituted an active and engaged civic community.[55] But, effectively operating as 'burial societies', they could offer little in the way of true intervention in preventing epidemics, famines or other local humanitarian concerns.

Sierra Leoneans took these societies across the British West African colonies as they settled in places like Badagry and Abeokuta, where they built on a common phenomenon throughout the region and became increasingly important in the colonial era. In Accra, Ghana, the urbanisation of the interwar period saw a flourishing of mutual aid societies that were not tied to hometown or kin-based affiliations. These societies operated as welfare insurance, covering sickness and funeral costs, but also providing 'excursions and picnics; concerts, singing, dancing and drumming; religious talks and discussions, literacy classes, debates, and cinema shows; first-aid service; initiation ceremonies for new members; and the laying of wreaths on graves of former members'.[56]

The colonial government looked askance at these societies as competing forms of civic organisation to the Church and the state that challenged governance in the early nineteenth century, but by abrogating their responsibility for local welfare concerns and humanitarian need, they effectively outsourced these state functions to the societies as the century progressed. When the missionaries withdrew from the management of the Liberated African villages after 1826, the role of the local mutual aid companies grew as they streamlined the devolved powers of the colonial government in the villages.[57] According to historian Christopher Fyfe, 'after 1856 village managers were only stationed at Waterloo, and in the Western District to watch for slave canoes from the Sherbro' while the rest of the villages were effectively left to the jurisdiction of the 'companies' and locally managed church societies.[58]

These parallel civil society structures operated beyond the purview of the colonial government, sometimes in direct competition with it, and sometimes co-opted to some of its functions. As African government scholar Peter Albrecht argues, the Poro are 'co-constitutive of a networked order-making arrangement where clear hierarchical or vertical relationships do not exist and where authority runs in a multitude of directions rather than from a clearly defined (state) centre'.[59] The unresponsiveness of colonial authorities and imperial philanthropists to any appeals for long-term solutions to questions of food security, sanitation and the provision of health care revealed the limitations of humanitarian governance and the strict prioritising of anti-slave trading interventions. As historian and anthropologist Benedetta Rossi notes of French colonial Niger, 'had the local administration fulfilled the role of purveyor of social security and welfare, labour and property could have become progressively individualised and separated from patronage and personalised dependence'; instead, 'pre-colonial hierarchies compensated for the incapacity of the colonial state to reach hinterland regions and protect its subjects in times of crisis'.[60] The same held true in British West Africa, where colonial administrator and theorist Lord Frederick Lugard's 'dual mandate' system formally recognised this reality.

But this was a poor solution to the concerns that plagued the colony. Without the ability to levy tax revenues that provided sufficient sums for development (contributions from members could not compete with export tariffs), and with little in the way of colonial resources to distribute, local humanitarians were hamstrung in their ability to attack colony-wide problems. Mutual aid could offer temporary solutions to sudden impoverishment, or help a community build a piece of infrastructure like a water pump, but it could not eradicate malaria.

The forms of civil society that emerged to deal with the weak colonial government response to demands for welfare and development aid took on a context of anti-modernity in the independence era of the 1960s, the period of national government sovereignty's height. As the British left Sierra Leone in 1961, they congratulated themselves on their progress in combatting disease: 'The devastating mortality from yellow fever, malaria, and other epidemic diseases, which decimated the non-immune European residents and visiting seamen in the 19th century, giving Sierra Leone its deadly reputation is a thing of the past. This has been made possible by vaccination, effective malaria prophylaxis, mosquito control, and improved hygiene and sanitation'. But despite these words of self-praise, the report also noted that 'the general population still suffers from a burden of endemic diseases which lowers efficiency and takes a great toll of human life'.[61]

As the post-colonial struggle to tackle these problems at a national level showed, however, endemic and epidemic disease and other crises of 'development' have in fact generated the very same kinds of global interventions that empires neglected. Historian Gregory Mann argues that this period saw a growing weakness arising out of humanitarian crises, such as famines, that saw West African governments asking for international interventions from non-government organisations.[62] Colonial governments that had been often unwilling to intervene in long-term solutions for health were now involved in a permanent, shadow–civil society response, inverting the 'disordered state' of the colonial period and resuming the outsourcing of these functions.

Conclusion

While British colonial political and economic intervention touched all aspects of daily life in West Africa, the limits of imperial humanitarian engagement were strictly drawn by the appeals to the antislavery mission. Who was Anglo humanitarianism for? In part, it was for the victims of the slave trade. But it was also for the public at home in Britain, who were proud of their nation's morality, but who believed in inherent differences between races. These beliefs made the humanitarian questions of health, hunger and sanitation 'local concerns', even as poor living conditions were exacerbated by the colonial presence.

Instead, West African colonial subjects organised themselves into their own societies to take care of the welfare needs of their members. Although these groups might sometimes operate on denominational or ethnic lines, they were just as likely to be organised along different civic lines – gender, locality, occupation – in ways that mirrored domestic aid societies elsewhere in the world. 'Development' – public health, infrastructure, education – was consistently driven by local organisations rather than by the repeated appeals to colonial governance because even when 'civilisation' or 'development' was a priority, the colonial government often underfunded the initiatives and operated on the assumption that only minimal improvements were possible, mistaking poverty for 'tradition'. Rather than 'solving' poverty, solutions were attempted that aimed to provide humanitarian relief and development aid as cheaply as possible, largely on the assumption that teaching people how to be self-reliant was the responsible approach to managing sanitation projects or health.[63] This was an Empire-wide response, and the case of West Africa echoes what other historians have illustrated with regard to the ways that these clashes between the supposedly humanitarian civilising mission and the realities of colonial governance operated in India and in the white settler colonies.[64]

The imperial assumption that people in the colonies were ignorant and they simply required education was belied by the mutual aid societies and the pleas from West Africa's leaders (at all levels) who asked for, and were denied, funding for these projects. West Africa was part of a wider imperial story, but the framing of British involvement in the region as driven by the antislavery mission starkly illuminates the tensions between the ambitions of humanitarian imperialism, and the realities of underinvestment and racialised rule on the ground. Humanitarianism justified and encouraged British imperial actors to intervene on their own terms – typically invoking the slave trade – and ignore the priorities of their West African colonial subjects.

Notes

1 Lamin Sanneh, *Abolitionists Abroad* (Cambridge, MA: Harvard University Press, 2002), p. 127; Kristin Mann, *Slavery and the Birth of an African City: Lagos, 1760–1900* (Bloomington, IN: Indiana University Press, 2007), pp. 91–102; Robin Law, 'Abolition and Imperialism: International Law and British Suppression of the Atlantic Slave Trade', in Derek Peterson (ed.), *Abolitionism and Imperialism in Britain, Africa, and the Atlantic* (Athens, OH: Ohio University Press, 2010), p. 158; Bronwen Everill, 'Bridgeheads of Empire? Liberated African Missionaries in West Africa', *Journal of Imperial and Commonwealth History* (2012), 40 (5), pp. 789–805.

2 Tehila Sasson and James Vernon, 'Practising the British Way of Famine: Technologies of Relief, 1770–1985', *European Review of History/Revue Européenne d'histoire* (2015), 22 (6), pp. 860–72.

3 Ibid., p. 861.

4 Miranda Kaufman, *Black Tudors: The Untold Story* (London, UK: Oneworld, 2017); John Thornton, *Africa and Africans in the Making of the Atlantic World, 1400–1800* (Cambridge, UK: Cambridge University Press, 2nd edn, 1998); Joseph Inikori, *Africans and the Industrial Revolution* (Cambridge, UK: Cambridge University Press, 2002); Jason Young, 'Fear of a Black Planet: Toward a Diasporic History of the Early Republic', *Journal of the Early Republic* (2020), 40 (2), pp. 201–8.

5 Rebecca Shumway, *The Fante and the Transatlantic Slave Trade* (Rochester, NY: Rochester University Press, 2011); Randy Sparks, *Where the Negroes are Masters* (Cambridge, MA: Harvard University Press, 2014); Margaret Priestley, *West African Trade and Coast Society: A Family Study* (Oxford, UK: Oxford University Press, 1969).

6 William Pettigrew, *Freedom's Debt* (Chapel Hill, NC: University of North Carolina Press, 2016).
7 See Trevor Burnard, this volume.
8 Paul Lovejoy and Suzanne Schwarz, *Slavery, Abolition and the Transition to Colonialism in Sierra Leone* (Trenton, NJ: Africa World Press, 2015).
9 Padraic Scanlan, 'The Colonial Rebirth of British Anti-Slavery: The Liberated African Villages of Sierra Leone, 1815–1824', *American Historical Review* (2016), 121 (4), pp. 1085–113.
10 Norman Etherington, *Missions and Empire* (Oxford, UK: Oxford University Press, 2005).
11 Gibril Cole, *The Krio of West Africa: Islam, Culture, Creolization, and Colonialism in the Nineteenth Century* (Athens, OH: Ohio University Press, 2013); Gustav Kashope Deveneaux, 'Public Opinion and Colonial Policy in Nineteenth-Century Sierra Leone', *International Journal of African Historical Studies* (1976), 9 (1), pp. 45–67.
12 Sandra E. Greene, 'Minority Voices: Abolitionism in West Africa', *Slavery & Abolition* (2015), 36 (4), pp. 642–61.
13 Vivian Bickford-Smith, 'The Betrayal of Creole Elites, 1880–1920', in Philip D. Morgan and Sean Hawkins (eds), *Black Experience and the Empire* (Oxford, UK: Oxford University Press, 2004), pp. 194–227.
14 See, for instance, the literature on trust and indirect rule, Dozie Okoye, 'Things Fall Apart? Missions, Institutions, and Interpersonal Trust', available from https://economics.uwo.ca/newsletter/new2014/Okoye_jun20.pdf, accessed 13 July 2020.
15 Lindsay Doulton, 'The Royal Navy's Anti-Slavery Campaign in the Western Indian Ocean, c. 1860–1890: Race, Empire and Identity' (PhD dissertation, University of Hull, 2010); Richard Huzzey, *Freedom Burning* (Ithaca, NY: Cornell University Press, 2012); Matthew Hopper, *Slaves of One Master* (New Haven, CT: Yale University Press, 2015).
16 Josiah Kaplan, '"Reading" British Armed Humanitarianism in Sierra Leone, 2000–2002', in Bronwen Everill and Josiah Kaplan (eds), *The History and Practice of Humanitarian Intervention in Africa* (Basingstoke, UK: Palgrave Macmillan, 2013), pp. 93–119.
17 Frederick Cooper, *Africa Since 1940* (Cambridge, UK: Cambridge University Press, 2002).
18 See Suzanne Miers, 'Slavery and the Slave Trade as International Issues, 1890–1939', *Slavery and Abolition* (1998), 19 (2), pp. 16–37.
19 Davide Rodogno, 'Non-State Actors' Humanitarian Operations in the Aftermath of the First World War: The Case of Near East Relief', in Fabian Klose (ed.), *The Emergence of Humanitarian Intervention: Ideas and Practice from the Nineteenth Century to the Present* (Cambridge, UK: Cambridge University Press, 2015), p. 187.
20 Gregory Mann, *From Empires to NGOs in the West African Sahel* (Cambridge, UK: Cambridge University Press, 2015); Paul Richards, Khadija Bah and James Vincent, 'Social Capital and Survival: Prospects for Community-Driven

Development in Post-Conflict Sierra Leone', Social Development Papers, World Bank Group, no. 12, April 2004.
21 Eugene Van Sickle, 'Reluctant Imperialists: The U.S. Navy and Liberia, 1819–1845', *Journal of the Early Republic* (2011), 31 (1), pp. 107–34.
22 Sanneh, *Abolitionists Abroad*, p. 143. See also Greene, 'Minority Voices', pp. 647–50.
23 Everill, 'Bridgeheads of Empire?', p. 800.
24 Gambia National Archives, CSO 1/1, Petition from Merchants, 1822.
25 Proclamation, Cession of Albreda, Freetown, 21 April 1857. C. W. Newbury, *British Policy Towards West Africa, Select Documents, 1786–1874* (Oxford, UK: Oxford University Press, 1965), p. 425.
26 Liberian Collections Project, Indiana University, Gallinas Documents 1840–1859, Part I of II, State Papers, vol. 33, 1844–45, pp. 314–15, Macdonald to Aberdeen, 31 December 1843; Adam Jones, 'Theophile Conneau at Galinhas and New Sestos, 1836–1841: A Comparison of the Sources', *History in Africa* (1981), 8, pp. 89–106.
27 'Slave Trade at Rio Nunez', *Sierra Leone Weekly News*, 27 June 1885, p. 3.
28 Christopher Fyfe, *A History of Sierra Leone* (Oxford, UK: Oxford University Press, 1962), pp. 524–5.
29 C. W. Newbury and A. S. Kanya-Forstner, 'French Policy and the Origins of the Scramble for West Africa', *Journal of African History* (1969), 10 (2), pp. 253–76; K. Mann, *Slavery and the Birth of an African City*.
30 Amalia Ribi Forclaz, *Humanitarian Imperialism: The Politics of Anti-Slavery Activism, 1880–1940* (Oxford, UK: Oxford University Press, 2015); Rob Skinner and Alan Lester, 'Humanitarianism and Empire: New Research Agendas', *Journal of Imperial and Commonwealth History* (2012), 40 (5), pp. 729–47; Fabian Klose, 'Enforcing Abolition: The Entanglement of Civil Society Action, Humanitarian Norm-Setting, and Military Intervention', in Klose (ed.), *The Emergence of Humanitarian Intervention*, pp. 91–120.
31 Sarah Delius, 'The Same in All but Name? Marriage, Slavery, Patriarchy and Politics: Sierra Leone 1890–1990' (PhD Dissertation, University of Witswatersrand, South Africa, 2020); Trevor Getz and Liz Clarke, *Abina and the Important Men* (Oxford, UK: Oxford University Press, 2011); Greene, 'Minority Voices', pp. 650–7.
32 Philip Curtin, *The Image of Africa* (Ann Arbor, WI: University of Wisconsin Press, 1964).
33 Ibid.; Leo Spitzer, 'The Mosquito and Segregation in Sierra Leone', *Canadian Journal of African Studies/Revue canadienne des études africaines* (1968), 2 (1), pp. 49–61.
34 Huntington Library, MSS MY 418, Macaulay's Journal, Folder 27, 5 July 1798.
35 Erica Charters, 'Making Bodies Modern: Race, Medicine, and the Colonial Soldier in the Mid-Eighteenth Century', *Patterns of Prejudice* (2012), 46 (3–4), pp. 214–31; Trevor Burnard, '"The Countrie Continues Sicklie": White Mortality in Jamaica, 1655–1780', *Social History of Medicine* (1999), 12

(1), pp. 45–72; Deb Neill, *Networks in Tropical Medicine: Internationalism, Colonialism, and the Rise of a Medical Specialty, 1890–1930* (Stanford, CA: Stanford University Press, 2012).
36 London Yearly Meeting, *Report of the Committee Managing a Fund Raised by Some Friends, for the Purpose of Promoting African Instruction; with an Account of a Visit to the Gambia and Sierra Leone* (London, UK: Harvey, Darton, and Co., 1822), p. 58.
37 *Sierra Leone Weekly News*, 'Sanitation in Freetown', 27 February 1886, p. 4.
38 'Extract from *The (Sierra Leone) Times*', *Sierra Leone Weekly News*, 25 April 1885, p. 2.
39 Laura Channing, 'Taxing Chiefs: The Design and Introduction of Direct Taxation in the Sierra Leone Protectorate, 1896–1914', *Journal of Imperial and Commonwealth History* (2020), 48 (3), pp. 398–9.
40 N. A. Cox-George, *Finance and Development in West Africa: The Sierra Leone Experience* (London, UK: Dobson, 1961).
41 Fyfe, *A History of Sierra Leone*, pp. 601–4; Spitzer, 'The Mosquito and Segregation in Sierra Leone', pp. 52–3.
42 H. E. Annett, J. Everett-Dutton, and J. H. Elliott, *Report of the Liverpool Malaria Expedition to Nigeria* (Liverpool, UK: University Press of Liverpool, 1901).
43 Ibid., p. 54.
44 'Review of The Report of the Liverpool Malaria Expedition to Nigeria', *Indian Medical Gazette*, February 1902, p. 69.
45 Eki Olumese, 'The Persistent Emphasis on Curative Care in Malaria Control in 20th Century Sierra Leone' (MPhil Dissertation, University of Cambridge, 2019); James L. A. Webb, Jr, *The Long Struggle Against Malaria in Tropical Africa* (Cambridge, UK: Cambridge University Press, 2014); Kalala Ngalamulume, 'Keeping the City Totally Clean: Yellow Fever and the Politics of Prevention in Colonial Saint-Louis-Du-Sénégal, 1850–1914', *Journal of African History* (2004), 45, pp. 183–202.
46 Fyfe, *A History of Sierra Leone*, p. 610.
47 'The Governor and the Citizens of Freetown', *Sierra Leone Weekly News*, 22 December 1900; Odile Georg, 'From Hill Station (Freetown) to Downtown Conakry (First Ward): Comparing French and British Approaches to Segregation in Colonial Cities at the Beginning of the Twentieth Century', *Canadian Journal of African Studies/La Revue canadienne des études africaines* (1998), 32 (1), p. 8.
48 F. Smith, 'Review of the Report on the Sanitation and Antimalarial Measures in Practice at Bathurst, Conakry, and Freetown', *Sierra Leone Weekly News*, 24 June 1905, p. 376.
49 'One Thing and Another', *Sierra Leone Times*, 16 January 1904, p. 2.
50 Fyfe, *A History of Sierra Leone*, p. 455.
51 Jonathan Roberts, 'Korle and the Mosquito: Histories and Memories of the Anti-Malaria Campaign in Accra, 1942–5', *Journal of African History* (2010), 51, p. 348.

52 Ibid., pp. 355–6.
53 Kenneth Little, 'The Political Function of the Poro, Part I', *Africa* (1965), 35 (4), p. 349; Trina Hogg, '"Our Country Customs": Diplomacy, Legality, and Violence on the Sierra Leone Frontier, 1861–1896' (PhD Dissertation, New York University, 2013), pp. 287–346.
54 Richard Anderson, *Abolition in Sierra Leone* (Cambridge, UK: Cambridge University Press, 2020), p. 172.
55 Ibid., p. 199.
56 Kenneth Little, 'Some Traditionally Based Forms of Mutual Aid in West African Urbanization', *Ethnology* (1962), 1 (2), p. 198.
57 Ibid., p. 182.
58 Fyfe, *A History of Sierra Leone*, p. 293.
59 Peter Albrecht, 'Secrets, Strangers, and Order-Making in Rural Sierra Leone', *Journal of Contemporary African Studies* (2016), 34 (4), p. 520.
60 Benedetta Rossi, *From Slavery to Aid: Politics, Labour, and Ecology in the Nigerien Sahel, 1800–2000* (Cambridge, UK: Cambridge University Press, 2015), p. 204.
61 Government of Sierra Leone, *Development Plan of the Health Services of Sierra Leone* (Freetown, Sierra Leone: Government Printer, 1962). John Manton and Martin Gorsky, 'Health Planning in 1960s Africa: International Health Organisations and the Post-Colonial State', *Medical History* (2018), 26 (4), pp. 425–48.
62 G. Mann, *From Empires to NGOs*, p. 11.
63 Richard Harris, 'The Silence of the Experts: "Aided Self-Help Housing", 1939–1954', *Habitat International* (1998), 22 (2), pp. 165–89.
64 Alan Lester and Fae Dussart, *Colonization and the Origins of Humanitarian Governance* (Cambridge, UK: Cambridge University Press, 2014); Sasson and Vernon, 'Practising the British Way of Famine'; Anna Clark, 'Humanitarianism, Human Rights and Biopolitics in the British Empire, 1890–1902', *Britain and the World* (2016), 9 (1), pp. 96–115.

9

The origins of exemption: The individual exception in the discourse of humanitarianism

Katherine Ellinghaus

In 1961 a meeting of federal and state ministers responsible for Aboriginal welfare was held in Canberra and agreed on a nation-wide policy of assimilation, which they defined as Aboriginal and Torres Strait Islander people eventually 'enjoying the same rights and privileges, accepting the same responsibilities, observing the same customs and influenced by the same beliefs, hopes and loyalties as other Australians'.[1] The Liberal Minister for Territories, Paul Hasluck, opened proceedings by evoking the rhetoric of humanitarianism.[2] He described what the eight ministers present were about to do as 'work that touches our humanity, our faith and our national self-respect ... work that demands a clear head but ... also warms the emotions. It calls for idealism as well as common sense'.[3] Over two days the ministers reported on their own states, each of which had its own history of oppressing and controlling Aboriginal and Torres Strait Islander people. They talked about discrimination, the meaning of the policy of assimilation, and the problem of the 'loose use' of the term 'citizenship' in relation to a group of people who were still specifically excluded from some state statutes and targeted by others.[4] Given this was a conference on assimilation, there was of course discussion about the usual postwar trinity of health, housing and education.[5] More broadly, the ministers emphasised the need to move Aboriginal and Torres Strait Islander people away from their communities and families living on reserves, missions and stations. The ministers knew this was a good idea because many of them could call on examples of individual people who had done it. 'Already, living unnoticed among the Australian population', said Hasluck, 'are some tens of thousands of coloured people who have found acceptance and usefulness to the general community'.[6]

Henry Winston Noble, Liberal Minister for Health and Home Affairs, had a personal example to draw on. In common with many wealthy Queensland families in the twentieth century, the Nobles employed an Aboriginal domestic servant whom they claimed was raised 'as one of the family'.[7] 'For some years', he said,

> I have had a very lovable half caste girl who has wonderful attributes and I do not think one would find a nicer girl anywhere. After a couple of years with us she could not be distinguished from a white person, apart from the difference in colour. I had her presented to Princess Alexandra, as a representative of the native people, and she looked lovely. She speaks beautifully. She lives in our house like one of us and has developed like one of our own children. Recently her mother took ill and she went back on the settlement for a while. On her return to us we found that her speech had deteriorated; her eyebrows, which she had kept plucked, had grown again. This was due to going on to the settlement, where she felt an inferiority complex. I think we will never get away very far if we let these people stay on the settlements where they get a complex and lose ambition. This girl now has her exemption and will never return to the settlement if I have any say in it. We must get these people off the settlements and out into the community ... unless we do something to get them off these places we shall develop an inferior and mendicant race.[8]

I acknowledge but set aside the way that the quotation above evokes the terrible history of Aboriginal girls and women employed as domestic slaves in white households. In recent years, historians have brought to light the abuse that Aboriginal and Torres Strait Islander domestic servants suffered at the hands of their employers, particularly those who had such an interest in their 'wonderful attributes' and 'lovely looks' and plucked eyebrows.[9] I also recognise the patronising racism evident in Noble's descriptions of 'these people' and the biological determinist and eugenic undertones of the phrase 'inferior and mendicant race'.[10] Instead I ask readers to take note of this nameless woman's 'exemption', mentioned at the end of the quote. Exemption was a status that would have freed her from the controls of the 1939 Aboriginal Preservation and Protection Act (Queensland) at the price of cutting ties with her non-exempt family and community. Exemption was also, I argue in this chapter, a reflection of the fantasy of the civilised, Christianised, acculturated Indigenous person that had been formed deep in the beginnings of British humanitarianism.

By 1961 Australian attitudes towards Aboriginal and Torres Strait Islander people were in flux, changing in response to international movements that recognised the need to ensure a common set of individual rights based on humanity. Aboriginal policy, though, was still expressed through state government protection acts designed to control and scrutinise Indigenous peoples, many of them amendments to legislation first passed in the late nineteenth or early twentieth century. These first 'protection' acts themselves borrowed the idea of 'protection' from a very different era in Australian history, a time dominated by settler violence and dispossession so ubiquitous that it caused a humanitarian-led reaction in Britain.[11] Exemption was thus an offshoot of what historian Amanda Nettelbeck calls the 'institutional framework' of Aboriginal 'protection', born from efforts in the mid-nineteenth century to end slavery in the British Empire and drawn from other examples of protection around the world.[12] In the late nineteenth century protection morphed from physical segregation in state-run reserves or missions to legislation with 'protect' in the title, versions of which were passed in nearly every Australian colony, state and territory from the mid-nineteenth century onwards. The first was enacted in Victoria in 1869. By 1911 every state and territory, including Tasmania, would have its own version of this legislation, and through most of the twentieth century, most Indigenous people lived lives 'under the Act', forced to remain on reserves or missions. Protection legislation gave government administrators the power to disrupt Aboriginal and Torres Strait Islander families by forcibly moving people, and determining where they lived, who employed them, whom they married and who looked after their children.[13] It also sometimes gave them power to exempt individuals who they determined did not require these controls.

In the context of Empire, exemption was deeply humanitarian – paternalistic, ameliorative and based on the conscience-salving idea that some deserving individuals could escape the controls imposed on the rest of their community. It embodied humanitarianism's dual focus on emancipation and mechanisms of control.[14] Exemption itself lasted to the bitter end of the protection era in the late 1960s, and its effects continue to impact Aboriginal and Torres Strait Islander families in the present day. In 1961, exemption, or a form of it, was on offer in Queensland, New South Wales, Western Australia, the Northern Territory and South Australia. Thousands of people had applied, and they and their families were attempting to live out its requirements of separation from family and community, and an outward demonstration of acculturation and economic independence. The total number of people granted exemption is unknown. According to Judi Wickes's research, between 1908 until 1967/68, a total of 4,092 certificates of exemption were issued in Queensland alone. In 2020, the 'Burden of Freedom? Aboriginal Exemption Policies in Australia' project has found evidence of 3,204 exemption applications across the country.[15] In many versions of the policy governments retained the ability to revoke the status, meaning the 'freedom' offered was limited at best. The effects of the policy were transgenerational and ongoing, an important part of the history of Australian Aboriginal policy that is still only just being understood.

There is no neat story about the origins of exemption. Exemption policies were introduced and operated at different times and places across the Australian continent. Exemption was introduced in Queensland in 1897, Western Australia in 1905, the Northern Territory in 1936, South Australia in 1939 and New South Wales in 1943, and was in use until it faded away after the 1967 referendum shifted the power to administer 'Aboriginal Affairs' from the states and territories to the federal government. At some times and places, exemption clauses were ignored and applications were rare, and at others it was emphasised. There was no government or philanthropic champion who named and promoted it as a policy, no government reports that particularly focused on it or speeches in Parliament that did more than mention it in passing. The few historians who have researched exemption have not speculated on why, if protection legislation was to control the Aboriginal and Torres Strait Islander population, so many of these acts had a literal escape clause.[16] No scholar has attempted to summarise this policy or its origins as a whole.[17] Instead, we know the history of exemption through personal (and thus local) stories – in biographies or autobiographies, or through case studies by historians.[18]

This chapter also shows how exemption clauses included in the legislation that controlled Aboriginal and Torres Strait Islander people's lives in the name of 'protection' during the twentieth century had century-long roots in humanitarian ideas about the possibility of 'civilising' individuals.[19] Even in the era of post-Cold War humanitarian intervention and after the United Nations 1948 Universal Declaration of Human Rights, Australian exemption policies aimed at giving rights to Indigenous people had little to do with a universal set of equal rights, but instead still relied on the pathways of 'progress' imagined by humanitarians in the eighteenth century.[20] Exemption was an echo of the humanitarian tendency to fantasise that some individual colonised subjects would embrace Christian and European belief systems and would consequently be rewarded with acceptance, equality and freedom. Despite exemption's long trajectory, it does not tidily reflect the contested relationship between humanitarianism and human rights which has received much attention from scholars in recent years.[21]

This chapter also shows how, though exemption coexisted with more well-known moments when human rights intersected with Indigenous affairs in Australia – such as the use of human rights discourse by Aboriginal activists from the interwar period onwards and the adoption of new policies of assimilation by the Australian Government in the post-World War II era in response to international changes in understandings of individual rights – exemption policies did not shift in response to these events. Rather, exemption exposes the tenaciousness of nineteenth-century humanitarian ideas about acculturated individuals and their continuing impact on state government policy in Australia.[22] Exploring the history of exemption in this context thus contributes to historians Rob Skinner and Alan Lester's question about the extent to which humanitarianism was bound up in developing the institutions of the colonial and nation state. Exemption was not just long-lasting, it was also a go-to solution for policy-makers at different times and places in Australia for more than six decades. The enduring nature of exemption policies, therefore, supports Skinner and Lester's argument that the histories of the nation state and humanitarianism are mutually constitutive.[23]

In the first section of this chapter, I examine the idea of the 'individual exception' in nineteenth-century humanitarian thought. In the second section I show how that idea was expressed obscurely in exemption clauses in various pieces of protection legislation passed by different states, colonies and territories between 1897 and 1944. I show how exemption was briefly reimagined in the postwar period as a way to demonstrate that Australia was not denying equal rights to Aboriginal people in welfare laws, until exemption policies were made redundant after the 1967 referendum. Ultimately, I conclude that the history of exemption policies shows us how humanitarian ideas, despite their apparent focus on emancipation and amelioration, led to policies that were ultimately harmful and oppressive.

The individual exception

Exemption's origins can be found in humanitarianism's imaginings of the civilised individual. One century before Noble pontificated on the qualities of his domestic servant, in Victoria in 1860, the newly formed Victorian Board for the Protection of Aborigines similarly preached at its 30 July meeting about the 'case of Thomas Bungaleene – an Aboriginal boy'. Bungaleene was the son of Bunjil Laen-buke, a headman of the Waiung clan whose Country was located around Lake King and Bairnsdale in the state's east. Bunjil Laen-buke, his two wives, Moonbulk and Parley (Kitty), and Parley's children had been taken hostage by Native Police as part of the hysteria caused by the so-called 'Captive White Woman' of Gippsland, a European woman rumoured to have been held against her will by the Kurnai people in the Gippsland region in the 1840s. Bunjil Laen-buke and Moonbulk died at Narre Narre Warren Native Police Barracks soon after. Parley (Kitty) and her two sons, aged two years (Kungudbar, later renamed Harry) and six months (Marbunnun, later named Thomas), were placed at the Merri Creek school under the supervision of Protector William Thomas.[24] In 1860 Marbunnun/Thomas was fourteen years old. The board discussed his case and he was then brought into a meeting and found to be of 'good mental endowment but an imperfect Education'.[25] Members of the board proceeded to take some interest in the child, dedicating time to discussion of his future in meetings across 1860 and 1861 and spending a significant part of their first report discussing him:

> Here, in the case of this young Aboriginal, an opportunity seemed to be presented to the Board of proving to the world that the Aborigines of Australia are degraded rather by their habits, than in consequence of the want of mental

capacity, and though the boy showed only an average ability, it was thought that by careful education, and instruction, he would probably become a good citizen, and of the highest usefulness as an agent in dealing with the Aboriginal race.[26]

Individuals like Noble's unnamed 'girl' discussed at the beginning of this chapter and the Victorian Central Welfare Board's idea of Thomas Bungaleene were a ubiquitous aspect of European civilising fantasies that accompanied colonisation, in which humanitarians imagined that colonialism would bring the 'benefits' of Christianity and 'civilisation' to 'heathen' and 'savage' lands.[27] In colonies all over the world, individual Indigenous people were seen as examples of the possibilities of assimilation, and this trope was persistent in the genealogy of humanitarianism, protection and assimilation that can be seen across the nineteenth and twentieth centuries in Australia. In the twentieth century, even when 'assimilation' rather than 'civilisation' was the order of the day, and when the 'protection' of the nineteenth century had been enshrined in regional legislation, the idea that *some* Aboriginal and Torres Strait Islander people should have their acculturation recognised and be 'out in the community', as Noble put it, was strongly in evidence.

From the earliest years of invasion in the continent that would become known as Australia, some British people were absorbed by an idea that can be traced to European empire-building of the early modern period and possibly even earlier: that they might entice individual Aboriginal or Torres Strait Islander people to take on the colonisers' language, custom and culture. In this urge we see the seeds of what would become more widespread and forceful efforts to assimilate and acculturate Aboriginal people in the late nineteenth and twentieth centuries. Settlers, missionaries and government officials often discussed individual people who demonstrated what historian Tracey Banivanua Mar called 'imperial literacy' – the ability to navigate colonial powers through not just reading and writing but also through knowledge about imperialism.[28] In common with humanitarians around the world, Europeans told stories about these individuals to raise awareness and inspire action, misreading their imperial literacy for acculturation, and their efforts to resist colonialism and deflect efforts to assimilate them as capitulation to Western forms of knowledge.[29]

While it was certainly not a ubiquitous view, there are plenty of examples of Europeans who believed in the ability of Aboriginal people to be 'civilised'. An early target of these views was Woollarawarre Bennelong, whom editor George Howe in his *New South Wales Pocket Almanac* of 1818 described as an 'early experiment' in European attempts to civilise the 'natives'.[30] We see it in the establishment of the Parramatta Native Institution by Governor

Lachlan Macquarie in 1814, described in the contemporary press as demonstrating that the Eora, the coastal clans whose lands encompassed the Sydney region, 'are capable of receiving instruction in all the useful arts of life; and their being so teachable, and in all other respects (accent and colour excepted) like unto the offspring of Europeans, furnishes an indisputable proof that the infant Aborigines may be civilized'.[31] As the nineteenth century continued, missionaries arrived in Australia with a commitment to the equal value of human souls in the eyes of God. They publicised their efforts to educate and Christianise Aboriginal people as part of their work.[32] They imagined promising acculturated individuals having a place in settler society and being better off away from their families and communities.[33] After the 1837 British House of Commons Select Committee on Aborigines published a report expressing concerns about violence against Indigenous peoples in British colonies, education was promoted as a way for Indigenous children to enter into civilised society.[34] As historical geographer Alan Lester has noted, from the 1830s the agenda of humanitarians and missionaries was not completely separatist but was also assimilationist.[35]

The introduction of policies to 'protect' Aboriginal and Torres Strait Islander people from settler violence and exploitation (which would later become the controlling protection legislation of the twentieth century) was directly driven by humanitarian thinking. The use of the word 'protection' was a nod to the humanitarian antecedent of the legislation in the 1837 Select Committee report which drew from a longstanding idea of the 'protector' in the early nineteenth-century British Empire and suggested that Indigenous peoples deserved protection, not violence.[36] The protectorate system, set up in the colony of Victoria in the wake of this report, is a well-known colonial attempt to put individual men in the role of protecting Aboriginal and Torres Strait Islander people (protectors were also appointed in South Australia and Western Australia at around the same time).[37] Those 'protectors', and the missionaries who accompanied them, then played a role in advising colonial governments about the policies and laws that they would eventually pass to control Indigenous people. For example, William Thomas, who began work as an Assistant Protector in Victoria in 1838, and the Reverend Johann Spieseke, a Moravian missionary who began a mission at Lake Boga, also in Victoria, in 1949, were both expert witnesses to the Select Committee of the Legislative Council appointed to enquire into the condition of Aboriginal people in Victoria in 1858, which was the precursor to the appointment of a Central Board and the very first piece of Protection Legislation passed in Australia in 1869.[38] Presbyterian minister Friedrich Hagenauer was one of the missionaries whose advice fed into new legislation in the 1880s. Methodist missionary Daniel Matthews was often away from Maloga, the northern Victorian mission he ran with his wife Janet, fundraising and advising government officials in Sydney.³⁹ As historian Alison Holland has argued, there was 'a complex, if embedded, relationship between governance and humanitarian interjections'. 'Humanitarianism', she says, 'may have shaped Aboriginal affairs far more than has traditionally been understood'.⁴⁰ Exemption is a clear and long-term example of the way in which humanitarian thinking, specifically the fantasy of the civilised individual, remained in the minds of administrators, philanthropists and politicians well into the twentieth century.

Humanitarian discourse in exemption policies

The differences in the ways where exemption clauses operated in the five states in which they existed were vast – they were worded differently, came into play at very different times, were applied to different populations and were operated in various ways by very different government administrators. I acknowledge the particular importance of these regional differences to the history of settler colonialism in Australia and also note that I cannot hope to encompass the diversity of language groups, peoples and perspectives found across Aboriginal and Torres Strait Islander Australia.⁴¹ What they do have in common, however, is the humanitarian ideals that were espoused in their wording, or in the processes that supported them. It is striking that these clauses, which caused the twentieth-century oppression of family dislocation and the categorisation of people, were couched in terms of civilisation and drew on what were believed to be the qualities of a good Christian person – temperance, modesty, morality and hard work – though twentieth-century ideas about economic independence and the importance of bureaucracy were also increasingly privileged.⁴²

The first exemption clause was included in the Queensland 1897 Aboriginals Protection and Restriction of the Sale of Opium Act. It read: 'It shall be lawful for the Minister to issue to any half-caste, who, in his opinion, ought not to be subject to the provision of this Act, a certificate in writing under his hand, that such half-caste is exempt from the provision from this act'.⁴³ Archibald Meston, a journalist who would later become Protector of Aboriginals in southern Queensland did not mention the idea of exemption in his 1896 government-commissioned report on how the then colony should treat Aboriginal and Torres Strait Islander people, which subsequently shaped the act itself. Nor was exemption mentioned in the debates introducing the act, although legislators clearly envisioned that some Aboriginal and Torres Strait Islander people would be able to live and work among settlers.⁴⁴ The need for cheap labour undoubtedly underpinned exemption, and individuals lauded for 'uplift' and 'civilisation' were often also asked, or forced, to work for Europeans. For the first few years after the clause was enacted, it was used particularly by employers wanting to have more freedom to move their female servants around the State.[45] Then, from the 1920s, the clause began to be used as a way of recognising individuals of mixed descent who, as Chief Protector J. W. Bleakley described in the 1927 report, 'by reason of their intelligence, education, character, and mode of living, are considered to be living a civilised life and well fitted to manage their own affairs'.[46] Their claims were 'carefully' investigated 'as regards the character, education, intelligence and breed'.[47] After 1939 the Queensland application for exemption form (which could be filled in either by the applicant or by a police or welfare officer) asked: 'Does applicant (or his family) habitually associate with aboriginals? Does applicant live in a civilised manner and associate with Europeans usually? Is applicant of good character, steady in employment, and industrious? Does applicant drink? Is applicant educated; to what extent? Is he (or she) thrifty and does he (or she) understand the value of money?'[48] These questions both evoked the 'civilised' individual of the nineteenth century, separate from their people and their culture, and knowledgeable about European life and demonstrating the qualities of a good Christian person, together with twentieth-century concerns about employment, industriousness, thrift and the imagined impact of having mixed ancestry.

In the rubric used by protectors and their staff to judge exemption, we see the same emphasis on morality, hard work, acculturation and 'breed' or 'caste' as appeared in the humanitarian efforts of the nineteenth century, though combined with twentieth-century notions of the productive, industrious member of society.[49] In 1905 Western Australia included an equally brief 'exemption' clause in its Act to Make Provision for the Better Protection and Care of the Aboriginal Inhabitants of Western Australia, which allowed the granting of exemption from the act to people who were 'lawfully employed', women who were 'lawfully married' to non-Aboriginal men, and those 'for whom, in the opinion of the Minister, satisfactory provision is otherwise made'.[50] In practice, the clause meant that the Chief Protector would take advice from local police officers, who in most places doubled as protectors, form an opinion about a particular person, and then advise the minister accordingly. Applicants were judged on their morality, Christianity, hard work, acculturation, education and, more than anything else, temperance.[51] Applicants spoke the same message back to the government in their letters: 'I am Christian. I read and write and Belief [sic] in the British Law same as heney [sic] white person'.[52] Applicants showed that they knew the discourses by which they were to be judged. One man wrote: 'I am not a wild native I am Christian. I read and write and I belief [sic] in the British Law same as heney [sic] white person'.[53] Another proclaimed, 'I am a land owner, also a contractor. And am entitled to a vote. I have never been in trouble for any offence. I have also been educated'.[54]

Intelligence, character and way of life continued to be characteristics required to be demonstrated by exemptees in the middle of the twentieth century. In 1939 a South Australian bill established a board to give 'more sympathetic and human treatment of our aborigines', along with a system of exemptions from the jurisdiction of the act, 'where the board is of the opinion that any aborigine by reason of his character and standard of intelligence and development should be exempted'.[55] As the bill was debated in Parliament, Malcolm McIntosh, the Liberal member for Albert, explained the need for exemption to balance the way the act would bring 'all persons of aboriginal blood … within the scope of the Act'.[56] Clement Smith, Independent member for Victoria, agreed the clause was necessary so that potentially white-passing, 'quarter-caste aborigines' should not be 'returned to the cesspits from which, to their eternal credit, they have emerged'.[57] As the world slipped into World War II, exemption was imagined as a way to rescue a few deserving individuals from the draconian controls of the legislation controlling the rest of the Aboriginal population.

As well as the idea of the 'civilised native', ideas about mixed ancestry, expressed through the offensive terms 'caste' or 'breed', were woven tightly through exemption clauses and their administration. While some clauses in the various acts particularly targeted people of mixed descent (such as Queensland's in 1897), others, like Western Australia's in 1905, did not. Nonetheless, in the way the acts were administered longstanding ideas about people of mixed descent being promising candidates for 'uplift' because of their white 'blood' or, as historian Tim Rowse has styled it, supposed to be 'not Aborigines or … only a "contaminated" version of a pristine and primitive race' are evident.[58] In 1936 the Northern Territory amended its Native Welfare Ordinance to include a new clause that declared that the 'Chief Protector may, by notice in the Gazette, declare that any person shall not be deemed to be a half-caste for the purposes of this Ordinance or of any provision thereof'.[59] The 1936 annual report of the Administrator spent little time discussing the clause, stating only: 'This new measure, in effect, offers the individual half-caste an opportunity of proving himself worthy of trust, thereby improving his outlook and stimulating his absorption into the white community'.[60] The view that only people of mixed descent should gain exemption was not, however, ubiquitous. In Queensland in 1939, a new act extended exemption to all people of Aboriginal descent, and in the Northern Territory in 1953 the definition of 'Aboriginal' was changed in the ordinance that extended exemption to all people of Aboriginal descent.[61] Racialisation often underpinned how exemption policies were administered, however, demonstrating how twentieth-century notions of biological racism played a part in the fantasy that people could gain equality by exhibiting certain behaviour.

World War II changed government policies, not just because of the global trend towards ending racial determinism or the growing influence of a discourse of human rights, but also because military activities in remote Australia put Aboriginal people in proximity to military and civil administrations.[62] There was a slow move away from understandings according to 'blood' and 'caste' towards policies that privileged the amount of time a person had spent in the company of white Australians. In New South Wales in 1943 exemption was first expressed as rewarding both individuals of mixed descent and those who were acculturated. Clause 18c of the Aborigines Protection (Amendment) Act (1943) allowed that the 'Board may upon application in writing issue to any aborigine or person apparently having an admixture of aboriginal blood, who, in the opinion of the board, ought no longer be subject to the provisions of this Act or the regulations or any of such provisions, a certificate in or to the effect of the prescribed form exempting such aborigine or person from the provisions of this act'.[63] The 1945 annual report of the Aborigines Welfare Board described exemptees as people who were 'equal in living standards and general intelligence to members of the general community'.[64] *Dawn Magazine*, published by the New South Wales Aborigines Welfare Board from 1952 to 1975, advertised what the board was looking for in exemptees: 'The issue of a Certificate of Exemption is determined after careful enquiry into the applicant's background, mode of living and general character'.[65]

In 1944 Western Australia introduced a policy of exemption in the form of the Native Citizenship Act. This Act was passed for familiar reasons: 'because it was desirable in respect to those natives who by reason of character, standards of intelligence, and development, were deserving of consideration in connection with the acquisition of citizenship rights'. The Chief Protector called the Act a 'most modern piece of legislation' that was inspired 'because it was realised that an enlightened policy was desirable in respect to those natives who by reason of character, standards of intelligence, and development, were deserving of consideration in connection with the acquisition of citizenship rights'.[66] It may have been a 'modern' piece of legislation, but the standards by which applicants were to be judged were the familiar ones of character, hard work, and good behaviour:

> When applicants lodge their applications with Clerks of Courts they must attach two references from reputable citizens certifying to the good character and industrious habits of the applicant. The application is then listed for consideration by a magistrate whose decision is final, but he must satisfy himself that (a) for the two years immediately prior the applicant has adopted the manner and habits of civilised life; (b) the full rights of citizenships are

desirable for and likely to be conductive to the welfare of the applicant; (c) the applicant is able to speak and understand the English language; (d) the applicant is not suffering from active leprosy, syphilis, granuloma or yaws; (e) the applicant is of industrious habits and is of good behaviour and reputation; (f) the applicant is reasonably capable of managing his own affairs.[67]

Ideas of 'civilisation', 'character' and 'intelligence' and qualities of 'industry', 'thrift' and 'temperance', now judged by magistrates and policemen, would have been familiar to the humanitarians of the nineteenth century. Though these concepts were now layered together with twentieth-century preoccupations with hygiene and economic productivity, the Native Citizenship Act created a familiar system that allowed non-Indigenous Western Australians to imagine that there was an escape clause for deserving individuals from the government's oppressive controls.

A final step in the story of exemption took place in the 1940s when the federal government slowly began to make Aboriginal and Torres Strait Islander people eligible for welfare. Exemption was again seen as a way of rewarding a select few, perhaps of appeasing the consciences of those who realised that excluding a segment of the population from the welfare system was racist. In 1941 an amendment to the Commonwealth Child Endowment Act gave Aboriginal people who could demonstrate that they were 'not nomadic', nor 'wholly or mainly dependent upon the Commonwealth or a State for his support' access to that payment.[68] In 1942 amendments to the Invalid and Old-age Pension Act 1908 and the Maternity Allowance Act 1912 made these schemes available to Aboriginal and Torres Strait Islander people who could prove their 'character, intelligence and development' or who had obtained exemption from a State Act.[69] The Social Services Consolidation Bill of 1947 made exempted Aboriginal people eligible for federal government welfare programmes such as old age, invalid and widows' pensions, and maternity allowances.[70] In 1951 assimilationist and anthropologist A. P. Elkin wrote to the new Liberal Prime Minister, Robert Menzies, to lobby for legislation to put the federal government in charge of Aboriginal Affairs instead of the states. Elkin saw exemption certificates as an imperfect means by which states were giving people access to social welfare. 'The Exemption certificate', he wrote, 'was only regarded as experimental and initiatory by those of us who proposed its introduction. The fiction cannot go on indefinitely. I see no reason why the Aborigines should die out, nor do I see any reason why we should have to issue Exemption Certificates in perpetuity'.[71]

As it was, exemption policies were made obsolete by the 1967 referendum which shifted responsibility for Aboriginal policy from the states to the federal government. Protection legislation was no longer the defining means by which Aboriginal and Torres Strait Islander peoples' lives were controlled. Only in Western Australia, where the Native Citizenship Act 1944 had detached exemption from the protection legislation, did it last a few years longer, limping into the early 1970s when the drinking habits of holders of citizenship rights were still being policed in some areas.[72]

The legacy of exemption

Exemption policies never offered the escape or the uplift imagined by their creators. They caused a traumatic loss of identity, culture and land, and had a very real impact on people's lives and families through generations. The ability to revoke the status, built at different times into the policies of all participating states, meant that surveillance and government control continued in the lives of exemptees, despite the promises of 'freedom' inherent in the status. Queensland continued to hold onto the earnings of exemptees; certificates in South Australia and Queensland were given with 'conditions attached'; and, most damaging of all, exemptees in all states and territories were expected to no longer have contact with non-exempt family and community.[73] The policies' ability to give legal exemption from complicated and all-encompassing pieces of legislation that were unique to each state and colony meant there are countless variances in the ways people came into contact with the policies, from the gaoling of artist Albert Namatjira for supplying relatives with alcohol while he was exempt, to white men lobbying to get their common-law Aboriginal wives the status in order that they might be legally married.[74] In the workings of the policy of exemption, there are also stories of activism, extraordinary and subtle examples of Indigenous resistance, ingenious manipulations of government policy, and day-to-day efforts of ordinary Indigenous Australians to live the best lives they possibly could in the face of the unrelenting racism displayed by white Australians and settler governments in the twentieth century. Overall, though, exemption was just another way in which Aboriginal and Torres Strait Islander people were treated as non-citizens.

Who then was exemption really for? It seems likely that exemption was obfuscation, an appeasement to the consciences of legislators and government administrators who needed to believe that there was a pathway for individuals who seemed perhaps confrontingly human. Administrators used the language of philanthropy and uplift and the possibility of 'equality' to distract from the abuses that were occurring under their watch. Despite this, exemption, though couched in the language of uplift and inspired by humanitarian thinking, was yet another way to control and document Indigenous people.

Conclusion

Exemption was the twentieth-century version of the same thinking that saw individuals held up as examples by missionaries and humanitarians. It was in some ways a fantasy masking the fact that protection legislation was really about control and surveillance. The 1961 conference on assimilation was the first time that all the Australian states concurred about their Aboriginal policies. Despite their different histories and trajectories of policy-making and the diversity of populations they oversaw, at that moment they could coalesce around humanitarian ideals, even though they notably paid no attention to decades-long Indigenous activism calling for equality, and continued to oppress Aboriginal and Torres Strait Islander people in the name of 'assimilation'. Noble's personal anecdote about his 'lovely' servant, whom he held up as a 'representative of the native people', might at first glance seem strikingly personal and out of place in a meeting of government ministers discussing Aboriginal policy. In actuality, it was right on brand, another example of what legal scholar Irene Watson calls the 'masquerade' that equality for Aboriginal peoples is available in settler states when in fact it is never really a possibility.[75]

Notes

1. Native Welfare Conference, *Verbatim Record of Proceedings*, 26–27 January 1961, Parliament House, Canberra (typescript), p. 1.
2. In this chapter I focus on the humanitarianism that Professors of English Kerry Bystrom and Eleni Coundouriotis define as the 'strand of humanitarian work linked to the abolitionism of the late eighteenth century and the civilizing missions of nineteenth-century colonialism' rather than the 'one associated with responding to the violence of war in the nineteenth century': Kerry Bystrom and Eleni Coundouriotis, 'Humanitarianism's Way in the World: On Missionary and Emergency Imaginaries', in Crystal Parikh (ed.), *The Cambridge Companion to Human Rights and Literature* (New York, NY: Cambridge University Press, 2019), p. 28.
3. Native Welfare Conference, *Verbatim Record of Proceedings*, pp. 1–2.
4. For information about the complicated history of Aboriginal citizenship, see John Chesterman and Brian Galligan, *Citizens Without Rights: Aborigines and Australian Citizenship* (Melbourne, Australia: Cambridge University Press, 1997), especially chapters 1, 2 and 3.
5. Native Welfare Conference, *Verbatim Record of Proceedings*, p. 24.
6. Ibid., p. 3.
7. Katherine Ellinghaus and Judi Wickes, 'A Moving Female Frontier: Aboriginal Exemption and Domestic Service in Queensland, 1897–1914', *Australian Historical Studies* (2020), 51 (1), pp. 19–37.
8. Native Welfare Conference, *Verbatim Record of Proceedings*, pp. 27–8.

9 Victoria Haskins, 'From the Centre to the City: Modernity, Mobility and Mixed-Descent Aboriginal Domestic Workers from Central Australia', *Women's History Review* (2009), 18 (1), pp. 155–75; Jackie Huggins, 'White Aprons, Black Hands: Aboriginal Domestic Servants in Queensland', *Labour History* (November 1995), 69, pp. 188–95; Aileen Moreton-Robinson, *Talkin' Up to the White Woman: Aboriginal Women and Feminism* (St Lucia, Australia: University of Queensland Press, 2000); Shirleene Robinson, '"Always a Good Demand": Aboriginal Child Domestic Servants in Nineteenth- and Early Twentieth-Century Australia', in Victoria K. Haskins and Claire Lowrie (eds), *Colonization and Domestic Service: Historical and Contemporary Perspectives* (New York, NY: Routledge, 2015); Michael Aird, 'Tactics of Survival: Images of Aboriginal Women and Domestic Service', in Haskins and Lowrie (eds), *Colonization and Domestic Service*, pp. 182–90.

10 Kay Anderson and Colin Perrin, '"The Miserablest People in the World": Race, Humanism and the Australian Aborigine', *Australian Journal of Anthropology* (April 2007), 19 (1), pp. 18–40; Russell McGregor, *Imagined Destinies: Aboriginal Australians and the Doomed Race Theory, 1880–1939* (Carlton, Australia: University of Melbourne Press, 1997); Warwick Anderson, *The Cultivation of Whiteness: Science, Health and Racial Destiny in Australia* (Carlton, Australia: University of Melbourne Press, 2005).

11 On this period and the humanitarian response to it, see Alan Lester and Fae Dussart, *Colonization and the Origins of Humanitarian Governance: Protecting Aborigines Across the Nineteenth-Century British Empire* (Cambridge, UK: Cambridge University Press, 2014); Amanda Nettelbeck, *Indigenous Rights and Colonial Subjecthood: Protection and Reform in the Nineteenth-Century British Empire* (Cambridge, UK: Cambridge University Press, 2019); James Heartfield, *The Aborigines' Protection Society: Humanitarian Imperialism in Australia, New Zealand, Fiji, Canada, South Africa, and the Congo, 1837–1909* (London, UK: Hurst, 2011).

12 Nettelbeck, *Indigenous Rights and Colonial Subjecthood*, p. 2.

13 For an understanding of life under Protection legislation, see Willie Thaiday, *Under the Act* (Townsville, Australia: N.Q. Black Publishing Company, 1981); Kevin Gilbert, *Living Black: Blacks Talk to Kevin Gilbert* (Ringwood, Australia: Penguin, 1978); Doris May Graham and Cecil Wallace Graham, *As We've Known It: 1911 to the Present* (Underdale, Australia: Aboriginal and Studies Teacher Education Centre, 1987); Lesley Williams and Tammy Williams, *Not Just Black and White: A Conversation between Mother and Daughter* (St Lucia, Australia: University of Queensland Press, 2015); Alick Jackomos and Derek Fowell, *Living Aboriginal History of Victoria: Stories in the Oral Tradition* (Cambridge, UK: Cambridge University Press, 1991). For a general historical overview, see Chesterman and Galligan, *Citizens Without Rights*. A comprehensive list of the legislation passed by each state that affected Aboriginal and Torres Strait Islander people can be found at https://aiatsis.gov.au/collections/collections-online/digitised-collections/remove-and-protect, accessed 25 January 2020.

14 Michael Barnett, *Empire of Humanity: A History of Humanitarianism* (Ithaca, NY: Cornell University Press, 2011), p. 55.
15 Judi Wickes, '"Never Really Heard of It": The Certificate of Exemption and Lost Identity', in Peter Read, Francis Peters-Little and Anna Haebich (eds), *Indigenous Biography and Autobiography* (Canberra, Australia: Aboriginal Studies Press, 2008), p. 77. See www.aboriginalexemption.com.au, accessed 16 October 2020, for more information on the 'Burden of Freedom? A History of Aboriginal Exemption project', funded by the Australian Research Council (DP150101847).
16 A number of historians have briefly discussed exemption in studies focused more broadly on the treatment of Aboriginal and Torres Strait Islander people in a particular time or place. For example, Heather Goodall discusses exemption in New South Wales in *Invasion to Embassy: Land in Aboriginal Politics in New South Wales, 1770–1972* (St Leonards, Australia: Allen & Unwin in association with Black Books, 1996), pp. 107, 267, 318; Russell McGregor addresses the subject in his studies of the meaning of assimilation in 'Avoiding "Aborigines": Paul Hasluck and the Northern Territory *Welfare Ordinance, 1953*', *Australian Journal of Politics and History* (2005), 51 (4), pp. 513–29, and in 'Nation and Assimilation: Continuity and Discontinuity in Aboriginal Affairs in the 1950s', in Julie T. Wells, Mickey Dewar and Suzanne Parry (eds), *Modern Frontier: Aspects of the 1950s in Australia's Northern Territory* (Darwin, Australia: Charles Darwin University Press, 2005), pp. 17–31. Richard Broome mentions it briefly in *Aboriginal Australians: A History Since 1788* (Sydney, Australia: Allen & Unwin, 4th edn, 2010), pp. 256. Darlene Johnson discusses exemption in 'Ab/originality: Playing and Passing versus Assimilation', *Olive Pink Society Bulletin* (1993), 5 (2), pp. 19–21. The pre-eminent historian of exemption is Judi Wickes, who focuses on the 'lived experience' of exemption: see Judith Anne Wickes, 'Study of the "Lived Experience" of Citizenship Amongst Exempted Aboriginal People in Regional Queensland, with a focus on the South Burnett region' (MA thesis, University of the Sunshine Coast, Queensland, 2010); Judi Wickes and Lucinda Aberdeen, 'The Diaries of Daisy Smith: The Experience of Citizenship for an Exempted Family in Mid-Twentieth Century Queensland', *Australian Journal of Politics and History* (2017), 63 (1), pp. 62–77; Judi Wickes and Marnee Shay, 'Aboriginal Identity in Education Settings: Privileging Our Stories as a Way of Deconstructing the Past and Re-Imagining the Future', *Australian Educational Researcher* (2017), 44, pp. 107–22; Wickes, '"Never Really Heard of It"', pp. 73–91; and Lucinda Aberdeen, Kella Robinson and Judi Wickes, 'Playing the Game: Aboriginal Exemption in Queensland and New South Wales', in Lucinda Aberdeen and Jennifer Jones (eds), *Black, White and Exempt: Aboriginal and Torres Strait Islander Lives Under Exemption* (Canberra, Australia: Aboriginal Studies Press, 2021), pp. 62–84.
17 Katherine Ellinghaus, 'The Poisoned Chalice: Exemption Policies in Twentieth Century Australia and the Writing of "History"', in Aberdeen and Jones (eds), *Black, White and Exempt*, pp. 24–41.

18 For example, exemption is mentioned in Sally Morgan, *Wanamurraganya: The Story of Jack McPhee* (Fremantle, Australia: Fremantle Arts Centre Press, 1989); Jackie Huggins, Rita Huggins and Lillian Holt, *Auntie Rita* (Canberra, Australia: Aboriginal Studies Press, 1994); Williams and Williams, *Not Just Black And White*; Gwen Baldini, 'A Whole World of Difference', in Jocelyn Scutt (ed.), *Country Women: Crossing the Boundaries* (Melbourne, Australia: Artemis, 1995), pp. 117–19; Jack Horner, *Vote Ferguson for Aboriginal Freedom* (Sydney, Australia: Australian and New Zealand Book Company, 1974); and Ruby Langford Ginibi, *Don't Take Your Love to Town* (Melbourne, Australia: Penguin, 1988).

19 Alison Holland has noted the lack of scholarly work that explores the nexus between humanitarianism and Australian Indigenous history in the twentieth century as compared with the nineteenth, and the importance of following humanitarian history into a twentieth century context: Alison Holland, 'Aboriginal Affairs: Humanitarian Intervention Then and Now: Dis/connections and Possibilities', *Australian Journal of Politics and History* (2017), 63 (4), p. 525.

20 This is, of course, not the only example of the long history humanitarian ideas: see Sarah Winter, 'Recounting history, locating precursors for human rights', in Parikh (ed.), *The Cambridge Companion to Human Rights and Literature*, pp. 13–17.

21 These debates largely centre on where idea of modern human rights can first be located, see Lynn Hunt, *Inventing Human Rights: A History* (New York, NY: W. W. Norton, 2007); Samuel Moyn, *The Last Utopia: Human Rights in History* (Cambridge, MA: Belknap/Harvard University Press, 2010); and the special issue of *Past and Present* (2016), 233, which features articles by Moyn, Hunt and others.

22 For discussion of the impact of human rights discourse on the political rights of Aboriginal and Torres Strait Islander people, see John Chesterman, *Civil Rights: How Indigenous Australians Won Formal Equality* (St Lucia, Australia: University of Queensland Press, 2005); Louise Chappell, John Chesterman and Lisa Hill, *The Politics of Human Rights in Australia* (Cambridge, UK: Cambridge University Press, 2009); Miranda Johnson, 'Connecting Indigenous Rights to Human Rights in the Anglo Settler States: Another 1970s Story', in Dirk Moses, Marco Duranti and Roland Burke (eds), *Decolonization, Self-Determination, and the Rise of Global Human Rights* (Cambridge, UK: Cambridge University Press, 2020), pp. 109–31. For histories of Aboriginal activism, see John Maynard, *Fight for Liberty and Freedom: The Origins of Australian Aboriginal Activism* (Canberra, Australia: Aboriginal Studies Press, 2007); Bain Attwood and Andrew Markus, *Struggle for Aboriginal Rights: A Documentary History* (Sydney, Australia: Allen & Unwin, 1998); and Gary Foley, Andrew Schaap and Edwina Howell, *The Aboriginal Tent Embassy: Sovereignty, Black Power, Land Rights and the State* (London, UK: Routledge, 2014).

23 Rob Skinner and Alan Lester, 'Humanitarianism and Empire: New Research Agendas', *Journal of Imperial and Commonwealth History* (2012), 40 (5), p. 731.

24 R. E. Barwick and Diane E. Barwick, 'A Memorial for Thomas Bungeleen, 1847–1865', *Aboriginal History* (1984), 8 (1), pp. 9–10; Ian D. Clark and Toby Heydon, *A Bend in the Yarra: A History of the Merri Creek Protectorate Station and Merri Creek Aboriginal School 1841–1851* (Canberra, Australia: Aboriginal Studies Press, 2004), pp. 58, 69.

25 Central Board Minutes, 30 July 1860, Item 1, B314, Central Board for the Protection of the Aborigines, Minutes of Meetings, Chronological Series, 1860–1967, National Archives of Australia–Victoria (hereafter NAAV).

26 Minutes of Meeting of Central BPA, 30 July 1860, 20 August 1860, 3 September 1860, 17 September 1860, 27 May 1861, 17 June 1861, and 29 July 1861, Item 1, B314, NAAV. See also Michael F. Christie, *Aborigines in Colonial Victoria 1835–86* (Parramatta, Australia: Sydney University Press, 1979), p. 173.

27 See Alison Twells, 'The Missionary Movement, the Local and the Global', in A. Twells (ed.), *The Civilising Mission and the English Middle Class, 1792–1850* (London, UK: Palgrave Macmillan, 2009), pp. 1–24.

28 Tracey Banivanua Mar, *Decolonisation and the Pacific: Indigenous Globalisation and the Ends of Empire* (Cambridge, UK: Cambridge University Press, 2016), pp. 51–62. See also Lester and Dussart, *Colonization and the Origins of Humanitarian Governance*, pp. 164–72.

29 Bystrom and Coundouriotis, 'Humanitarianism's Way in the World', p. 36.

30 Keith Vincent Smith, 'Bennelong among His People', *Aboriginal History* (2009), 33, pp. 19–20.

31 Australis Incoli, 'To the Printer of the Sydney Gazette', *Sydney Gazette and New South Wales Advertiser*, 26 July 1817, p. 3.

32 Patricia Grimshaw, 'Rethinking Approaches to Women in Missions: The Case of Colonial Australia', *History Australia* (2011), 8 (3), pp. 7–24.

33 For some examples, see Penelope Edmonds, 'Travelling "Under Concern": Quakers James Backhouse and George Washington Walker Tour the Antipodean Colonies, 1832–41', *Journal of Imperial and Commonwealth History* (December 2012), 40 (5), pp. 769–88; Patricia Grimshaw and Elizabeth Nelson, 'Empire, "the Civilising Mission" and Indigenous Christian Women in Colonial Victoria', *Australian Feminist Studies* (2001), 16 (36), pp. 296–7; Jane Lydon and Alan Burns, 'Memories of the Past, Visions of the Future: Changing Views of Ebenezer Mission, Victoria, Australia', *International Journal of Historical Archaeology* (March 2010), 14 (1), pp. 39–55; Felicity Jensz, 'Controlling Marriages: Friedrich Hagenauer and the Betrothal of Indigenous Western Australian Women in Colonial Victoria', *Aboriginal History* (2010), 34, pp. 35–54.

34 Rebecca Swartz, *Education and Empire: Children, Race and Humanitarianism in the British Settler Colonies, 1833–1880* (New York, UK: Palgrave Macmillan, 2019), p. 236.

35 Lester and Dussart, *Colonization and the Origins of Humanitarian Governance*.

36 See the *Report of the Parliamentary Select Committee on Aboriginal Tribes (British Settlements) Reprinted with Comments by the 'Aborigines Protection Society'* (London, UK: Aborigines Protection Society, 1837); Trevor Burnard,

'A Voice for Slaves: The Office of the Fiscal in Berbice and the Beginning of Protection in the British Empire, 1819–1834', *Pacific Historical Review* (2018), 87 (1), pp. 30–53; Lauren Benton, Adam Clulow and Bain Attwood, *Protection and Empire: A Global History* (Cambridge, UK: Cambridge University Press, 2017).

37 Amanda Nettelbeck, 'Colonial Protection and the Intimacies of Indigenous Governance', *History Australia* (2017), 14 (1), pp. 32–47.
38 *Report of the Select Committee of the Legislative Council on the Aborigines* (Melbourne, Australia: Government Printer, 1859), p. v.
39 Claire McLisky, 'From Missionary Wife to Superintendent: Janet Matthews on Three Independent Murray River Missions', *Journal of Australian Studies* (2015), 39 (1), p. 32; Grimshaw and Nelson, 'Empire', p. 301.
40 Holland, 'Aboriginal Affairs', pp. 534–5.
41 For an explication of the regional differences in twentieth century Aboriginal policies and experience, in particular the important differences between the 'north' and the 'south', see Tim Rowse, *Indigenous and Other Australians since 1901* (Sydney, Australia: UNSW Press, 2017).
42 Holland, 'Aboriginal Affairs', p. 531.
43 Aboriginal Protection and Restriction of the Sale of Opium Act 1897 (Queensland), section 33.
44 *Report on the Aboriginals of Queensland by Archibald Meston, Special Commissioner Under Instructions from the Queensland Government*, Presented to Both Houses of Parliament, Queensland 1896, p. 5.
45 See Ellinghaus and Wickes, 'A Moving Female Frontier'.
46 J. W. Bleakley, 'Aboriginal Department – Information Contained in Report for the Year Ended 31st December,1927' in *Reports upon the Operations of the Sub-Departments* (Brisbane, Australia: Anthony James Cumming, Government Printer, 1928), p. 6.
47 Ibid., p. 10.
48 'Report on Application by Aboriginal or Half Blood for Exemption from the Provision of the Act, No.85', blank form issued by Office of the Chief Protector Aboriginals, Queensland, undated (supplied by Kathy Frankland, Manager, Community and Personal Histories, Department of Aboriginal and Torres Strait Islander Partnerships, Level 6A, Neville Bonner Building, 75 William Street, Brisbane City, Queensland).
49 For a discussion of the ways in which the ideas and language of morality shifted across the twentieth century, see Melissa A. Wheeler, Melanie McGrath and Nick Haslam, 'Twentieth Century Morality: The Rise and Fall of Moral Concepts from 1900 to 2007', *PLOS ONE* (February 2019), 14 (2), pp. 1–12.
50 An Act to Make Provision for the Better Protection and Care of the Aboriginal Inhabitants of Western Australia, no. 14 of 1905 (Western Australia), Clause 13. This clause specifically referenced the 1897 Queensland Act, evidence that Western Australian legislators had drawn from Queensland's exemption clause.
51 Anna Haebich, *Spinning the Dream: Assimilation in Australia 1950–1970* (North Fremantle, WA: Fremantle Arts Centre Press, 2008), p. 76.

52 Applicant from Moora, 27 June 1918, Series 1644, Consignment 652, 1918–0827, Individual Personal Files, Department of Aborigines and Fisheries, State Records Office of Western Australia (hereafter DAF, SROWA).
53 Applicant to Chief Protector, 27 June 1918, Series 1644, Consignment 652, 1918–0827, Individual Personal Files, DAF, SROWA.
54 Applicant to Colonial Treasurer, 27 June 1919, Series 1644 Consignment 652, 1919–0856, Individual Personal Files, DAF, SROWA.
55 South Australia, *Official Reports of the Parliamentary Debates*, 19 September 1939 (Adelaide, Australia: Frank Trigg, Government Printer, 1940), p. 879; Aborigines Act Amendment Act 1939 (South Australia), section 11a.
56 South Australia, *Official Reports of the Parliamentary Debates*, 10 August 1939 (Adelaide, Australia: Frank Trigg, Government Printer, 1940), p. 467.
57 South Australia, *Official Reports of the Parliamentary Debates*, 7 September 1939 (Adelaide, Australia: Frank Trigg, Government Printer, 1940), p. 847.
58 Rowse, *Indigenous and Other Australians*, p. 2.
59 *Native Welfare Ordinance*, 1936 (Northern Territory), clause 3a (1). *Commonwealth of Australia Gazette*, no. 30, Thursday 19 March 1936, p. 474; *Northern Standard*, 3 April 1936, p. 12.
60 *Report on the Administration of the Northern Territory for the year ended 30th June*, 1936 (Canberra, Australia: L.F. Johnson, Commonwealth Government Printer, 1937), p. 12.
61 Aboriginals Preservation and Protection Act 1939 (Queensland), Section 3, available at https://aiatsis.gov.au/sites/default/files/docs/digitised_collections/remove/54685.pdf, accessed 16 October 2020; Northern Territory Aboriginals Ordinance (No. 2) 1953, Section 3 (c), at https://aiatsis.gov.au/sites/default/files/docs/digitised_collections/remove/52398.pdf, accessed 16 October 2020.
62 Rowse, *Indigenous and Other Australians*, p. 111.
63 Aborigines Protection (Amendment) Act 1943 (New South Wales), clause 18c.
64 Aborigines Welfare Board, *Annual Report of the Aborigines Welfare Board, 1945* (Sydney, Australia: Government Printer, 1946), p. 2.
65 'Exemption Certificates Granted – Many Seek Independence', *Dawn Magazine* (December 1954), 3 (12), p. 26.
66 Commissioner of Native Affairs, *Annual Report of the Commissioner of Native Affairs*, 1945 (Perth, Australia: Government Printer, 1947), p. 9.
67 Ibid., 9.
68 Child Endowment Act 1941 (Cth), s. 15. See Kartia Snoek, 'Marginalised Subjects, Meaningless Naturalisations: The Tiers of Australian Citizenship' (PhD thesis, University of Melbourne, 2019).
69 Maternity Allowance Act 1942 (Cth), s. 3 amending s. 6(2) of the Maternity Allowance Act 1912 (Cth).
70 Chesterman and Galligan, *Citizens Without Rights*, p. 162.
71 A. P. Elkin to Menzies, 2 July 1951, A462 743-1 Treatment of Aboriginals, National Archives of Australia – Canberra. Previously, Elkin had argued that citizenship 'should be accorded as soon as possible by a Certificate of Exemption ... to all persons with a preponderance of Aboriginal blood who

live under non-"nomadic" conditions and who have shown them capable of making a living ... The Incurable Nomadic Full-bloods ... must be "protected" in respect of food and health, and from possible ill-treatment by whites', in A. P. Elkin, *Citizenship for the Aborigines: A National Aboriginal Policy* (Sydney, Australia: Australasian Publishing Co. Pty. Ltd., 1944), pp. 43, 45.

72 Senior Constable Kevin Ronald Holmwood, 'The Problem of Citizenship Rights and Natives in the North Eastern Goldfields District', Western Australian Police Department Report, Cons 1910, Item 196–1910, Series S76, Status of Citizenship of Natives, State Records Office of Western Australia.

73 Wickes and Aberdeen, 'Diaries of Daisy Smith'.

74 Julie Wells and Michael Christie, 'Namatjira and the Burden of Citizenship', *Australian Historical Studies* (2000), 31 (114), pp. 110–30; 'Mrs. Reid. Exemption from Provisions of Aboriginal Ordinance, N.T.', A1, 1938/6142, National Archives of Australia.

75 Irene Watson, 'The Northern Territory Intervention: What Is Saved or Rescued and at What Cost?', *Cultural Studies Review* (September 2009), 15 (2), p. 45.

Part III

A new international order, 1918–95

10

Gender, personalities and the politics of humanitarianism: Nursing leaders of the League of Red Cross Societies between the wars

Melanie Oppenheimer

'I can't help recollecting ten years ago', enthused Cécile Mechelynck, a leading Belgian nurse and President of the National Federation of Belgian Nurses, as she addressed the graduating cohort of Bedford College in 1930: 'when my group, the first one, arrived in London ... 19 enthusiastic girls, rather lost ... How many struggles and difficulties we had, and how Miss Fitzgerald ... was trembling lest her idea, extravagant as it seemed, was perhaps having its first and the last experience together. How far we have gone! How the course changed later on under Miss Olmsted and Mrs Carter, and how, sometimes I regret having been a "pioneer"'.[1]

The international nursing course to which Cécile Mechelynck referred was established in London by the League of Red Cross Societies in 1920, barely one year after the formation of the League itself. The brainchild of Henry Pomeroy Davison, Wall Street banker and Chairman of the American Red Cross War Council, the League of Red Cross Societies was established by the Red Cross Societies of Great Britain, France, Italy, the United States and Japan on 5 May 1919. Responding to the calamity of World War I, especially its impact on the civilian populations of Europe, Davison wanted to establish a Red Cross organisation that focused not on war, as the Geneva-based International Committee of the Red Cross did, but on work in peacetime to prevent disease and promote health and welfare around the world.[2]

The one-year international postgraduate course for nursing training in public health has been described as a 'revolutionary dynamic'.[3] Offering both theoretical and practical training in sick nursing and public health work, it sought to assist in the development of public health nurses or health visitors (the two titles were used interchangeably) and standardise 'educational centres for training such nurses or visitors'.[4] The course was the first of its kind and attracted nurses from around the world. The first intake of nineteen nurses, of which Cécile Mechelynck was one, came from many countries, including Sweden, Italy, France, Greece, Poland, Czechoslovakia, Peru and

Venezuela, as well as Britain and the United States. By 1938, 296 nurses had completed the courses and were part of a who's who of nursing leaders who helped to transform public health nursing and education.[5] However, as suggested by Cécile Mechelynck, there were extraordinary challenges, and not only for the many foreign, non-English-speaking students.

This chapter takes as its focus the first three nursing directors of the League of Red Cross Societies, Americans Alice Fitzgerald (1919–21) and Katherine Olmsted (1921–27), and British nurse Maynard L. Carter (1927–38), all of whom experienced significant and at times overwhelming difficulties as they fought to consolidate the programme within the highly precarious environment of the League of Red Cross Societies in its foundational years. In particular, the chapter draws attention to the gendered nature of humanitarianism and how women struggled in the world of masculinist humanitarianism in the aftermath of World War I. The model of humanitarianism established by Henri Dunant and entrenched within the International Committee of the Red Cross promoted a gendered approach to medical matters with nursing the domain of women, and medical professionalism, organisational and infrastructure activities as best undertaken by men.[6] An analysis of the experiences of Fitzgerald, Olmsted and Carter within the context of one Western humanitarian organisation demonstrates both the gendered nature of humanitarianism and how it has been perceived and historicised in the first half of the twentieth century.

Nursing was feminised by the time of World War I, including within the Red Cross movement. Many national Red Cross societies, especially in non–English-speaking countries, established nursing schools in the nineteenth century, including in Sweden, Japan and Germany.[7] However, nursing practice was not a universal suite of craft knowledge; it was internationalised and slowly professionalised from the second half of the nineteenth century and beyond.[8] In some countries prejudice was rife, with religious orders the 'only nurses against whom there was no prejudice in the popular mind'. Considered a menial and degrading career, 'girls of good family and education were not allowed by their parents to become nurses'.[9] The war provided opportunities for women that most embraced with relish, especially those who had trained as nurses.[10] However, the war also changed the behaviour of nurses: younger women who were now enfranchised in Britain and the United States wanted different outcomes, and were not prepared to put up with the harsh conditions, long working hours and poor remuneration traditionally associated with nursing.[11]

During the war the nursing fraternity came into direct conflict with the Red Cross, specifically the 'snobbish, amateur and untrained Red Cross society lady nurses' as leading American nurse Lavinia Dock termed them.[12] In Britain, a deeply held prejudice against the Red Cross Voluntary Aid

Detachments (VADs) remained alive within the nursing fraternity, especially in the English-speaking world. It was feared that the quasi-trained and generally unpaid volunteers that worked in hospitals and convalescent homes would swamp the profession after the war. In some national contexts, however, such as in France, Japan and Germany, the Red Cross nurse was professionally trained to the standards of those countries. The result was a confusing situation where there were professionally trained nurses, volunteer trained nurses, and untrained and partially trained workers all working under the Red Cross banner as Red Cross nurses.[13]

Nursing historian Susan McGann has explored the powerful nursing cultures of Britain and North America, their competing agendas and philosophies in this period.[14] Foregrounding the debate between these two leading nations was the framework of the 'Nightingale model' of nursing and its local variants, a model of the second half of the nineteenth century that still held sway, both symbolically and practically, within the nursing fraternity. A feature of the League of Red Cross Societies' ambitious nursing training plan was to 'foster and promote transnational initiatives within the Red Cross network, to standardise, coordinate and promote health care'.[15] From 1863 and the beginning of the Geneva-based International Committee of the Red Cross, nursing within the Red Cross movement developed into a specific, gendered sphere of female humanitarianism. Ideas of female nurture were a powerful legitimisation for women's humanitarianism. However, the Red Cross was always hierarchical in nature, with nursing falling outside the standard norms of white, Christian, male leadership of large swathes of the Red Cross movement, the International Committee of the Red Cross, and humanitarian organisations more broadly.

In their edited book *Gendering Global Humanitarianism in the Twentieth Century*, historians Esther Möller, Johannes Paulmann and Katharina Stornig discuss the under-researched topic of the 'intersecting politics of gender and humanitarianism' and argue that women have been positioned as 'subordinate partners'.[16] The book took up the themes of the journal, *Gender & Development*, which, in 2019, published articles supporting 'humanitarian programming that promotes gender equality, women's rights, women's empowerment and leadership'.[17] This builds on the work of scholars who have sought to 'integrate women as the main agents within the history of humanitarian relief' and to open up the field, to explore the roles 'played by female agents who have been unrepresented' in the past.[18] Feminist and gender perspectives provide us with a better lens with which to see the unequal power dynamics and global hierarchies that women have had to negotiate within the histories of humanitarianism. Work by cultural historian Bertrand Taithe has exposed the patriarchal nature of humanitarianism and the specific ideas of masculinity as portrayed by Henri

Dunant and others around the origins and development of the Red Cross Movement.[19] Social and cultural historian Katherine Storr suggests a lack of focus on and studies of women and humanitarianism has occurred because they have been 'excluded from the record'.[20] This chapter takes up the challenge of exploring the dynamics and practices of gendered humanitarianism by using a biographical approach and focusing on the experiences of the League's first three nursing directors, Fitzgerald, Olmsted and Carter. In doing so, it reveals just how difficult it was for women to succeed in a world infused with gendered discourses, norms and practices of humanitarianism. Add to that the vested interests of the nursing profession and this becomes a highly gendered and political case study framed around care, compassion, humanitarianism and public health nursing between the wars.

Appointment of Alice Fitzgerald, first Director of Nursing

American nurse Alice Fitzgerald was appointed the inaugural Director of Nursing of the League of Red Cross Societies in October 1919 and commenced her role in Geneva the following month. Always interested in new ideas and opportunities, and an expert in multiple languages, including Italian, French, German, Spanish and English, Alice had attended the Cannes Medical Conference in April 1919, organised by Henry Davison and the five national Red Cross societies that later formed the League. Medical and health experts from around the world were invited to Cannes to 'shine the light of science upon every corner of the world'.[21] Alice appeared with the official nursing delegates as a translator. She saw the potential of the new League of Red Cross Societies and accepted the offer to lead its Nursing Bureau. 'Pioneering has always appealed to me, more than following in beaten tracks', she recalled.[22]

Born in Florence, Italy, in 1875 to wealthy American parents, Alice was educated as befitted a young woman of her generation and social standing. In 1902, and much to the horror of her mother, Alice enrolled at Johns Hopkins University School of Nursing.[23] After graduating, Alice returned to Italy and, in December 1908, immediately volunteered with the Florence branch of the Italian Red Cross dealing with the Messina earthquake disaster.[24]

Returning to America, Alice's restless curiosity in seeking out new experiences and her peripatetic work habits saw her employed at Johns Hopkins Hospital, then the Bellevue and Allied Hospitals in New York, before taking up a position at the Wilkes-Barre hospital in Pennsylvania. On the outbreak of World War I, Alice was superintendent of nurses at the Robert W. Long Hospital in Indianapolis. In 1916, she was selected as the Edith Cavell

Memorial Nurse, sponsored by the Massachusetts chapter of the American Red Cross to serve in the war. Alice left New York on 19 February 1916, sailing to England and enlisting in the Queen Alexandra's Imperial Medical Nursing Service Reserve. She served at the No. 13 General Hospital in Boulogne, a hospital in St Pol near Bethune, and the 2/2 London Casualty Clearing Station, 'buried in mud along the Somme Front, where the Germans surrounded us on three sides, and the guns belched, and the shells whined and Death held a festival day and night'.[25] After suffering what today we call post-traumatic stress disorder, and on the United States entry into the war on 6 April 1917, Fitzgerald resigned from the Nursing Service Reserve to join the American Red Cross, eventually becoming its Chief Nurse.[26]

Her work with the American Red Cross, both during and after the war, gave Alice valuable experience and insights into how the humanitarian organisation operated. Part of her role saw her travel with humanitarian relief worker, Lady Muriel Paget, to the new nation of Czechoslovakia, where Alice was instrumental in the American Red Cross organising a nursing school. Her last trip with the American Red Cross in the summer of 1919 was to the Balkans. On her return to Paris, she resigned to take up the position as Director of the Nursing Bureau of the League of Red Cross Societies, arriving in Geneva in November. The purpose and function of the Nursing Bureau evolved over time; however, at its base was to support national Red Cross societies that ran nursing programmes, co-ordinate training and share public health information across the global Red Cross network. Alice Fitzgerald was cautious and somewhat anxious about what was in store. 'I doubt if any one ever accepted a position with so slight a knowledge of what it entailed, with lesser opportunities for following any established precedents and with less data on which to build a program', she later wrote.[27] As the inaugural Director of Nursing, Alice commenced her position with 'bare walls, empty desks, a few pages of "Resolutions" for guides, and the knowledge that in [her] hands lay the immediate future of this service to humanity'.[28] Alice's philosophy towards the role of a public health nurse was directly linked to the problems in 'public welfare' that focused on *Tuberculosis, Infant Mortality, Lack of Supervision of School Children* and very general *Ignorance of Home Hygiene and Personal Hygiene*'.[29] At the time, the 'public health field had no boundaries, and there was no consensus about the best method of training nurses or others for the work'.[30] It became an emerging area of interest for Red Cross humanitarianism, one that was led by women. Even the term 'public health nurse' had various meanings in different countries, and covered 'a variety of workers in different countries, from health visitors and social workers to sanitary inspectors and charity visitors'.[31] These differences, both cultural and linguistic, created tensions and conflict among contemporary nursing leaders and caused innumerable problems for Alice Fitzgerald and her successors at the Nursing Bureau of the League.

Alice commenced her job by undertaking a survey of nursing across national Red Cross societies. Working through a cold Geneva Christmas, she drafted a questionnaire as well as an outline for possible schemes for the training of public health nurses. Alice was aware of the vast differences that existed between and within national Red Cross societies. 'Words were used by many nations with entirely different meaning in each case', she noted. The best way forward was to 'internationalise nursing according to the needs and resources of different countries', but she was unsure whether she could adequately capture that in the questionnaire.[32]

The questionnaire was divided into four sections. Section A, 'Red Cross nursing activities', included questions on whether there were voluntary or professional enrolled nursing personnel and their numbers; if the national society had established a Training School for Nurses, what the admission requirements and the length of training were and what were the numbers of graduates; whether the national society had established courses for instruction in home nursing and first aid; whether certificates were issued; and what efforts had been made by the national society to encourage public health nursing work generally. In Section B, 'Hospital and other nursing activities', questions sought information on other institutions that were providing nursing training; entry requirements; length of training; average salaries of graduated nurses; how untrained helpers were used; and whether the hospitals employed sisters of religious orders, Red Cross-trained nurses, trained nurses of other schools or voluntary nurses. Section C dealt specifically with army and navy nurses, and the fourth section, D, dealt with 'Public health nursing' and whether public health nursing was organised either by governments or privately.[33]

Fitzgerald received few responses from national societies and none have survived. She was left with the conclusion, however, that there was a need for public health nurses and that the League should facilitate their training.[34] She provided the Director-General of the League, David Henderson, and the General Medical Director, Dr Richard Strong, with two options for the training of public health nurses. The first was 'A League School for Training Public Health Nurses', situated in Geneva, where the League was based. Fitzgerald concluded this was not viable, largely due to the impossibility of finding relevant fieldwork sites for the students, as the clinical infrastructure did not exist, with none of the 'problems found in the poorer districts of the larger cities'.[35]

Fitzgerald's second idea (and her preferred model) proposed that the League make use of already existing schools of public health, and provide scholarships for students to complete the course. This would be less expensive for the League, Fitzgerald argued, as it would be 'an experiment to prove whether it is going to be profitable to bring together students from many countries and standardise'. It could be done for one year and then 'we might be ready to start the League training school', she suggested. The second idea was presented to the first General Assembly of the League of Red Cross Societies in March 1920. With twenty-seven national societies represented, it was resolved

> That the League of Red Cross Societies urge the establishment in Europe of one or more model training schools for public health nurses, but that until this can be realized there be founded under the supervision of the League nursing scholarships for the national Red Cross Societies of those countries where no such facilities exist, in a city chosen as being most appropriate.[36]

Once her proposal was approved, Alice Fitzgerald worked quickly to secure a course in theoretical and practical public health nursing run at the King's College for Women in London. Letters, information pamphlets and application forms were sent to national Red Cross societies. Applicants were to be selected by their national societies and be between twenty-three and forty years of age;[37] show evidence of continuous education up to the age of eighteen; possess a diploma or certificate as regulated by the highest nursing standards of the country which she represented; provide a medical certificate and reference for good character; and must be 'sufficiently familiar with English to follow lectures and take notes'.[38] In August 1920, just over twelve months after the League of Red Cross Societies was formed, and three months after its General Assembly agreed to the venture, the first international course in public health nursing opened in London. The classes included anatomy, physiology, hygiene, bacteriology, chemistry, elementary science, sociology and household work. Although all of the students spoke English, some students needed help with additional English classes.[39] The course provided the content that would support what the League hoped to do in its position as a federated agency representing the Red Cross national societies to assist in facilitating a public health agenda. Such an international postgraduate nursing course had never been attempted before and this inaugural year was highly experimental. Pioneers indeed.

At the beginning of 1921, it was decided to continue the course, but at Bedford College for Women within the University of London. Run from the Department of Social Sciences, lectures were shared with students of social work and health visiting. The normal strict entrance requirements were waived so that foreign students could enrol in a course tailored to each student's abilities, in recognition that 'each student is the product of a vastly different background of race, education and nursing standards, and as the work that each will undertake upon her return to her own country presents quite different problems'.[40] A 'somewhat elastic curriculum' was planned, providing as much individual instruction as possible according to the needs of the student. If language difficulties emerged, then special tutoring was arranged and 'lecturers handed out typed copies of their lectures as well'.[41]

For the period, this was a highly innovative approach, especially with the different views of national Red Cross societies towards nurses and public health training. However, this 'flexibility' was a source of great concern and disagreement among the nursing fraternity in Britain and the United States, who believed that public health visitors (as they were called in America) required a three-year nursing training first. This was to cause ongoing problems for the League and its nursing directors as nursing training varied from country to country with many countries requiring only two years' minimum training or even less. The financial costs of running the course, too, were substantial. The League guaranteed at least ten students per year and paid a tuition fee of £45 per student to Bedford College. The League paid for the salaries of the extra tutors and fees for special lectures and practical work. Each scholarship was worth £250 and the national Red Cross societies were asked to fund their own students. However, the League funded a scholarship if national societies could not find the money. Despite scholarships from voluntary organisations, such as the Commonwealth Fund and some students paying their own way, the financial commitment for the League remained substantial.

Other activities of the League's Nursing Bureau included the establishment of a school of nursing in Belgrade, Yugoslavia. In 1921 Alice Fitzgerald travelled to Romania as a League representative to assist in the establishment of a nursing school in association with the Serbian Red Cross and other local institutions. On the basis of her report, the League selected British nurse Enid Newton, who had a 'goodly supply of the pioneering spirit so necessary in such an undertaking', as Director of the new nursing school.[42] Alice made numerous visits to other countries as Director of the Nursing Bureau, including Czechoslovakia, where she visited child welfare clinics and public health centres in 1920 and 1921.[43]

Once it was evident that the international nursing programme was going to continue at Bedford College, and with another twelve nurses enrolled for the course from countries including Finland, Austria, Czechoslovakia, Japan, Canada and New Zealand, Alice Fitzgerald resigned her position. She left Geneva on 17 September 1921 and returned to the United States for a 'much needed rest'. Her life and career were framed around constant change; she rarely stayed in one position for more than a couple of years. Unhappy with the direction of 'League policies' that 'influenced' her resignation, it is likely that the less than helpful attitude of the American Red Cross and financial problems of the League were concerns that Alice was inclined to leave for others to sort out.[44] The latent hostility directed by the

International Committee of the Red Cross towards the League has been well documented by historians of the Red Cross movement.[45] Just as damaging was the lack of support from the American Red Cross. This national society came out of the war re-invigorated and triumphant. It did provide significant financial support to the League, but its lack of complete public support for the League, an international humanitarian organisation based outside of the United States, along with the ill-health and later death of the League's founder, Henry Davison, led to insurmountable difficulties for its staff in Geneva.[46]

Alice Fitzgerald continued to undertake work on behalf of the League of Red Cross Societies. Through the second half of 1921, she was the League's delegate to the American Red Cross Convention held at Columbus, Ohio on 4 October, the Conventions of the American Child Hygiene Association and the American Public Health Association, both held in New York in November.[47] After spending a short time in the United States, Alice went to Asia, working as Nursing Adviser to the Governor of the Philippines, and with the Rockefeller Foundation in Siam (Thailand) and China. In 1926 she attended the second Oriental Red Cross Conference in Tokyo as a delegate of the League. Her observations of nursing practices in these Asian countries were published in the League's *World Health*, as 'Eastern nursing through western eyes', in 1929.[48] Alice Fitzgerald returned to America, her pioneering days behind her. She continued to find employment at the Polyclinic Hospital in New York City as Director of Nurses and lastly at the Shepard Pratt Hospital in Baltimore where she was a housemother to nurses. In 1948, at age seventy-four and with ill-health, Alice retired, moving to a nursing home in New York City where she died on 10 November 1962, her career and legacy largely forgotten.[49]

Katherine Olmsted, second Director of Nursing

If, as the inaugural Director of Nursing for the League of Red Cross Societies, Alice Fitzgerald had problems in establishing the international nursing course in London, her successor, Katherine Olmsted, experienced enormous challenges to keep it going. Katherine was also a graduate of the Johns Hopkins nursing school and the Chicago School of Civics and Philanthropy, where she studied social work. With experience in public health nursing in America, Katherine had arrived in Europe in August 1917, as part of an American Red Cross commission to Romania to contain a typhus outbreak.[50]

Initially hired to work at the League as an Associate Director of the Nursing Bureau, Olmsted took up the position as Director of the renamed Public

Health Nursing Division at a precarious time for the League. Her work was directly affected by the politics of humanitarianism. The untimely death of the League's Director-General, Sir David Henderson, in August 1921 was followed by the passing of Henry Davison in May 1922. These were huge losses for the fledgling humanitarian organisation. Diminishing fiscal support from the American Red Cross and continuing disagreements with the International Committee of the Red Cross did not help. A growing pessimism infiltrated the corridors of the League. Budgets were cut, programmes were disbanded and, in 1922, the League relocated from Geneva to Paris.

Katherine Olmsted was described as an 'ardent and very well-meaning' young woman with an 'alarming independence'.[51] She had developed a keen opinion of what nurses required in the post-war world, believing that 'Those who wish to succeed as nurses must have brains and common sense. The more culture, refinement and education a young woman has, with "brains" to think for herself, the better nurse she will be'.[52] For Olmsted, nursing was 'not a profession for the ignorant, its call is to the intelligent, the educated young woman'.[53] She described the public health nurse as a 'teacher nurse' who 'makes her nursing profession serve the public as well as the individual ... by carrying her services into many homes, she has unlimited opportunities to act as an educator, to teach and demonstrate ways of disease prevention'.[54]

Katherine Olmsted's forthright personality, her energy and views ran foul of the nursing establishment as well as the powerful and well-remunerated Rockefeller Foundation whose foray into nursing education in Europe in the post-war period has been described as 'more by accident than design'.[55] Researchers who have explored the roles played by Edwin Embree, Director of the Division of Studies for the Rockefeller Foundation, and Elizabeth Crowell, the American nurse hired by the Foundation to survey public health nursing training in Europe and England in 1922–23 suggest that both were critical of the League of Red Cross Societies, its personnel, and the Bedford College programme.[56] Crowell held negative views of the international courses and believed that they were not 'the best means of giving European students the training they needed'.[57] This was in sharp contrast to the experiences and later careers of the nurses who completed the course.[58] These damaging views do not reflect the calibre of the League's directors of nursing, nor of Dr René Sand, the highly respected Belgian medical doctor described as one of the eminent leaders in public and social medicine in the first half of the twentieth century who was the League's Secretary-General and later Technical Counsellor from 1921 to 1927.[59]

Katherine Olmsted spent much of her time trying to find funds to enable the Bedford College nursing course to continue. In October 1921, her predecessor Alice Fitzgerald had approached the Commonwealth Fund to support a scheme to establish a League of Red Cross Societies Nursing Training School to the tune of US$300,000. Although initially expressing interest in the scheme, the Commonwealth Fund did not pursue the idea.[60] However, it did fund scholarships for Austrian nurses to attend the courses.[61]

In mid-1923, Edward Embree, representing the Rockefeller Foundation, held a number of meetings and informal lunches in both London and Paris with League officials, including Secretary-General Claude Hill, Dr René Sand and Katherine Olmsted. Embree visited Bedford College and met with nurses studying there on scholarships. He also dined with Olmsted, who discussed her work with the League, the difficulties she was having with American nurse leaders and her plans for a new administrator's course. Katherine Olmsted's forthright manner surprised Embree when she suggested that the Rockefeller Foundation cease 'work in nursing and finance [the] nursing division of League of Red Cross Societies'.[62] However, Katherine also advocated, without success, for the nursing fraternity more broadly, requesting Rockefeller support the International Council of Nurses with its regional conferences and publication of an international journal of nursing.[63]

Embree concluded that the League's public health nursing programme was not worth investing Rockefeller Foundation funds. It was not the product itself, as on his tour he met nurses who had successfully completed the international course and liked it. The problem was that he believed the future of the League was 'far from assured', and that it might not survive. Second, a lack of support from the American Red Cross as it continued its nurse training work in Europe independent of the League played a role in Embree's decision. If League leaders were not able to secure support for its nursing programme from national Red Cross societies, then why should the Rockefeller Foundation pitch in?[64]

Katherine Olmsted encountered considerable resistance from the International Council of Nurses, which was lukewarm in its support for the League's public health nursing programme. As Susan McGann has suggested, the Council, founded in 1899 by British nurse Ethel Bedford Fenwick as a federation of national nursing organisations, feared that the arrival of the League could supersede its role as the international body representing nurses.[65] Alice Fitzgerald was aware of this problem and had deftly navigated around it. However, once the Bedford College programme was underway, and successfully graduating nurses from across the world, the International Council of Nurses stepped up its pressure on a perceived threat to standards. Under pressure from the Council, the League established a Nursing Advisory Board. Led by Katherine Olmsted under the direction of the Council President, Baroness Mannerheim, the Advisory Board sought to exercise its influence over the League (and Olmsted). The International Council of Nurses was focused on getting the League to ensure that national

Red Cross societies that it represented and were in control of professional nursing training and standards in many countries adhered to the highest standards which were, they argued, 'a 3-year course, in connection with a hospital or hospitals providing medical, surgical and special services'.[66] The universality of the League made this edict difficult to achieve because only a few countries practised the so-called 'highest standard of nursing'.[67] The League continued to work to improve its Bedford College international nursing courses obtaining external advice through the commissioning of a report from Eunice Dyke of the city of Toronto's Department of Public Health in Canada. Dyke's report was sympathetic to the League and argued that the course and the League's position as a neutral arbitrator in the nursing education space were useful.

The relocation of the League of Red Cross Societies from Geneva to Paris in 1922 made it easier for Katherine Olmsted to oversee the Bedford College programme. She made flying visits to London, delivering lectures on public health nursing and meeting new students who were 'carefully selected, thoroughly prepared, well taught, sufficiently tutored, intelligently assisted upon their return'.[68] During her tenure, a second course for nurse administrators and teachers in schools of nursing was established at Bedford College in 1924. Most importantly, a home for the international nursing students was established at 15 Manchester Square, London. International House became 'more than a home for the students', it was a place where a welcome was extended to 'all foreign nurses visiting in London', providing students with a 'splendid spirit of internationalism'.[69] From 1923, a newsletter, edited and funded by the League kept the graduates connected, and in 1925 an 'Old Internationals' Association was formed (an idea of Maynard Carter, who had completed the course in 1922–23, worked for the League and succeeded Olmsted).[70]

Within five years, the success of the League's international courses was evident with sixty-eight 'Old Internationals' from thirty-four different countries contributing directly to global health practices. Forty-eight were directly involved in public health work, forty held positions as supervisors or directors, and eighteen were conducting courses in public health nursing. Thirteen were employed in hospitals with their work revealing 'vision, initiative, originality' in child welfare clinics, health demonstrations, new public health nursing services, newspapers and magazine articles, using the cinema for lectures: their work was described as 'unlimited' and often carried out 'in the face of unexpected disappointments and discouragements'.[71]

Other duties of the nursing director included overseeing the League's Public Nursing Division, its four female staff, and the dissemination of information to national Red Cross societies on nursing topics, the publication of pamphlets and articles, including a booklet entitled *Child Welfare Nursing*

(1925), and an illustrated booklet on Red Cross Public Health Nursing published in German and Spanish; collecting, compiling and distributing information on the development of nursing in different countries; and arranging nursing conferences, for example the Congress for Nurses held in Vienna in May 1925 under the auspices of the League, and attended by nurses from Austria, Germany, Czechoslovakia, Greece, Poland, Romania, Bulgaria, Hungary and Serbia.[72] Olmsted conducted missions to countries across Europe and regularly visited international graduates in their own countries.

Being in charge of the Nursing Bureau during a most precarious period of the League took its toll on Katherine Olmsted. In spite of the achievements, in particular the innovative international courses, the relentless pressures placed on League staff, and Olmsted in particular, in securing funding, the rejection of her approaches to the Rockefeller Foundation and the demands from the International Council of Nurses and nursing bureaucracies, were too much. 'Her irrepressible spirits, unfailing enthusiasm' and 'her courage' were not enough to overcome the 'great difficulties of which we can have no conception', wrote Nan Dorsey, President of the Old Internationals Association.[73] After the completion of a six-month study tour of the United States in 1926, where Olmsted delivered talks about the work of the League and Bedford College, and attended the Regional Pan American Red Cross Meeting in Washington on behalf of the League, she resigned.[74]

Once a three-year agreement with Bedford College was in place and the courses secured until 1930, Katherine Olmsted walked away from the League and her profession. In her final letter to 'My dear Internationals', written on board the SS *Providence* on 10 February 1927 as she sailed for the United States with her mother, Katherine described the 'inspiration of feeling the "Real Call" in this great international adventure ... into which some of us have given our all, our best, to win or lose it matters not'.[75] Turning her back on humanitarianism, the Red Cross and nursing, and after completing a Cordon Bleu cookery course, Katherine set up a French restaurant, called Normandy Inn, in Wallington, a small rural town surrounded by apple and cherry orchards in upstate New York. She ran the highly successful restaurant, styled with antique French provincial furniture and décor, serving French cuisine, including her famous French onion soup, until her death in 1964 aged seventy-seven. At least Katherine could maintain some control, creativity and independence in her second career.[76]

Maynard Carter, third Director of Nursing

Katherine Olmsted was succeeded by British nurse Maynard Linden Carter, who had successfully completed the international course in 1922–23, and worked for the League of Red Cross Societies' Nursing Bureau in London as Director of Studies. Olmsted believed that, in passing the baton onto Maynard Carter, she was doing so 'to a more capable person' than herself.[77] Born on 17 July 1886 in Brazil, where her father was an engineer, by the age of eleven Maynard Carthew was at boarding school in Shropshire. By 1911 she had completed her nursing training at St Bartholomew's Hospital, London, and during the war worked at the London General Territorial Hospital. Maynard married (Arthur) Cecil Carter in 1913, and when he died suddenly in 1921, she threw herself into humanitarian work, signing up with Lady Muriel Paget to provide medical assistance for a serious typhus and smallpox epidemic in Czechoslovakia (undertaking the same mission as her predecessor Alice Fitzgerald).[78] Moved by what she had witnessed, Maynard joined the staff of the League and worked under Katherine Olmsted and the Public Health Nursing Division while she was completing the course at Bedford College.

Maynard Carter held her position as Director of Nursing at the League for eleven years, providing stable leadership. She has been described as an outstanding leader, with a 'special tact and charm' and a 'wisdom and ability to delegate work clearly to others'.[79] She was awarded the prestigious Florence Nightingale Medal in 1937 for her contribution 'towards raising the professional standards of Red Cross nurses in all countries'.[80] During her time as Director of Nursing, she continued to refine the international courses, taking into consideration the competing agendas of the nursing fraternity and the continuing crisis with the budget. She oversaw an initiative of her predecessor, a highly successful refresher course and Summer School, held from 16 July to 4 August 1928. Seventy-nine of the 'Old Internationals' from twenty-seven different countries returned for the short course – further cementing the bonds among the alumni group, which by then extended across Europe to India, China, Mexico, the United States and Canada.[81]

For Maynard Carter, the aim of the international course was to provide students with foundational skills on which to base their teaching, and also to lead the nurse 'to think, to reason, to use her judgement, to give her a deeper understanding of human nature and human society' in order to assist them 'to overcome the difficulties with which she will have to contend in her own country'.[82] Other work of the League's Nursing Division included routine tasks of correspondence, attending to visitors at League headquarters in Paris, planning study visits, assembling information on nursing subjects, preparation of reports, including a comprehensive study of Red Cross Nursing Services, and dissemination of a Package Loan Library.[83] Maynard Carter was very supportive of the idea of air ambulances and supported national Red Cross societies' engagement in this innovative space. She gained her pilot's licence and flew regularly in France and England.

She travelled widely representing the League, undertaking numerous missions across Europe, the United States and Canada, as well as attending Red Cross and nursing conferences. On each trip, she was met and hosted by 'Old Internationals', who maintained a close and extensive alumni network. For example, in four weeks between January and February 1933, she visited seven countries, including Albania, Greece, Italy and Bulgaria, touring Red Cross hospitals, nursing schools and training facilities. Six months before, in July 1932, Maynard had travelled to South America and visited Red Cross and nursing facilities in Brazil, Uruguay (where she met up in Montevideo with Old International Leontine Adami-Roussel from the 1923–24 group) and Argentina.[84] In 1937, at the League's headquarters in Paris, and in co-operation with the League, she organised a Conference of Experts on Disaster Relief and the Role of the Nurse in War and Disaster.[85]

However, the precarious nature of League finances continued to cause anxiety. Before Katherine Olmsted had resigned, the League had negotiated a three-year deal (1927–29) with Bedford College, which became responsible for administering and conducting the nursing programme, with the League providing the funds.[86] This amounted to more than £7,300 a year, and included the maintenance and administration of the Manchester Square residence, housekeeper and clerk salaries, catering and cleaning, as well as £1,222 allocated to Bedford College for course improvements.[87] The League and national Red Cross societies continued to pay for scholarships, funded at £250 per student. Balancing the requirements of the 'very conservative' Bedford College in adapting to the international students and their language difficulties was one obstacle that Maynard Carter had to address. But finance remained the more pressing problem.[88]

The onset of the Great Depression deepened the crisis. Staff cuts saw the departure of Enid Smith, who had joined the Nursing Division in 1924, and Dutch nurse, Harriet Baud, who had completed the first Nurse Administrators Course in 1925.[89] The League looked for ways to extricate itself from the financial obligations of the courses. After extensive consultations with Bedford College and the International Council of Nurses, it was confirmed that the newly created Florence Nightingale Foundation would assume control. Since her death in 1910, the nursing fraternity had wanted to honour their 'founder' Florence Nightingale. Established in London, the Florence Nightingale Foundation was to be 'a living memorial – not a museum': it was to be an 'endowed foundation for postgraduate nursing education'.[90] It was led by representatives of the International Council of Nurses, the League of Red Cross Societies and Nightingale Memorial Committees to be formed around the world.[91] Foundation members included a who's who of the international nursing fraternity, with the League represented by its Secretary-General, Ernest Swift, and Maynard

Carter. She is credited with much of the behind-the-scenes negotiations, 'her tact and ability' as well as her 'happy relations' with members of the Council being key to the outcome.[92] The formal handover occurred in July 1934, with the League presenting to the Foundation the equipment and lease of 15 Manchester Square, the home for students taking the course and an office for the Foundation. The League continued to play a role, particularly through the Old Internationals Association.

In 1938, after eleven years in the job and suffering ill health, Maynard Carter resigned on medical grounds. She was succeeded by Swiss nurse and 'Old International' Yvonne Hentsch, who had attended the course in 1935–36. Her service to the League was recognised as 'extraordinary in its vitality and depth of understanding, and with that spirit of "it can be done"'.[93] During the war Carter worked as Lady Superintendent of the County of Buckingham Red Cross. She continued her position as Honorary President of the Old Internationals Association and remained in contact with many 'Old Internationals'. She also channelled her energies into the creative arts, as a skilled carpenter, woodcarver and potter. Maynard Carter died on 2 March 1962 aged seventy-six. She was remembered as a 'woman of many parts', 'ever in the front line of progress', a 'distinguished nurse and a devoted friend'.[94]

Conclusion

Applying a biographical approach, this chapter has explored the experiences and challenges of the first three women appointed as Directors of the League's Nursing Bureau from 1919 through to 1938. What it highlights is the gendered and political nature of humanitarianism, and the impact this had on individuals and their careers. Alice Fitzgerald, Katherine Olmsted and Maynard Carter were all highly professional nurses who lived independent and successful lives. They were energetic, experienced, committed, curious and fearless female leaders devoted to nursing and the development of their profession. All three encountered significant obstacles during their tenure as Director of the League of Red Cross Societies Nursing Bureau, much of it due to how Western humanitarian organisations viewed nursing, a distinctly feminised practice. The empire-building desires of international voluntary humanitarian organisations, such as the Rockefeller Foundation, as well as the infighting between the International Committee of the Red Cross, the American Red Cross and the League of Red Cross Societies, directly impacted the women charged with leading the new humanitarian organisation's innovative international nursing courses at Bedford College. Voluntary organisations led by men rode roughshod over one another to enhance their own status and position in the highly malleable post-war masculinist humanitarian world including the emerging area of public health.

Secondly, all three women appointed to the role of Director of the League's Nursing Bureau were caught up in the interwar politics of the nursing profession, which impeded their progress and created unforeseen obstacles. By stepping into the nursing world, the League ran into the struggle for international hegemony of British and North American nursing leaders. The result was that the League and its nursing directors came under sustained criticism from the nursing community. All three women were aware of the vast differences that existed across the Red Cross network in regard to nursing training and knew the difficulties this brought to the League of Red Cross Societies. Finding a way through that appeased all interested parties was the main challenge. It ultimately broke Fitzgerald, who walked away, as did her successor, Katherine Olmsted. Carter had better conciliatory skills than her predecessors, but it was under her leadership that the League relinquished the international courses to the International Council of Nurses through the Florence Nightingale Foundation. Despite this, the all-female student cohort, predominantly from Europe, as well as North America and Asia, helped to shape and influence the public health systems of multiple countries around the world. Through positions as heads of nursing schools, directors of public health programmes and instructors, the graduates were responsible for establishing public health programmes in their own countries on their return home and were instrumental in the development of public health policies and practices.[95] At the same time, the students developed a global network of friendships through the Old Internationals Association, one that worked to internationalise their perspectives and provide invaluable professional connections.

Finally, Alice Fitzgerald, Katherine Olmsted and Maynard Carter suffered from an ingrained conservative social and cultural approach to women's roles and capacities within the humanitarian space. Notwithstanding the complexity of the Red Cross Movement and the development of Western humanitarianism, the relationship of women, care and public health nursing, and its infusion into a post-war world, was framed around the discourses, norms and practices of a gendered humanitarianism. In addition, the three women were compromised by the nursing fraternity's vested interests and an inability to unite. The result was a highly gendered and highly political set of experiences. The establishment and running of the League of Red Cross Societies' international nursing programme provided the three nursing directors with a space where female activism, agency and humanitarian activities could flourish, a space where they were empowered to create new systems of nursing practices and achieve reforms that had a positive impact on global health policies and practices. How effective the women were in shifting the traditional gendered nature of women's engagement within the humanitarianism enterprise, however, is less well-identified and reveals the over-arching gendered nature of Western humanitarianism.

Notes

1 *International Newsletter, 1930–31* (Christmas 1930), p. 4, Old Internationals Association, League of Red Cross Societies, A0848/2 Box No R509626709, International Federation of Red Cross Red Crescent (hereafter IFRC) Archives, Geneva. A version of this paper was delivered at the Histories of the Red Cross Movement since 1919 conference in Geneva 12–14 June 2019. It is funded by the Australian Research Council's Discovery Project DP190101171 'Resilient Humanitarianism', 2019–23.
2 M. Oppenheimer and C. Collins, *Henry Pomeroy Davison* (Geneva, Switzerland: Société Henry Dunant, International Federation of Red Cross Red Crescent, 2019).
3 D. A. Reid and P. F. Gilbo, *Beyond Conflict: The International Federation of Red Cross and Red Crescent Societies, 1919–1994* (Geneva, Switzerland: International Federation of Red Cross Red Crescent, 1997), p. 96; see also A. M. Rafferty, 'Internationalising Nursing Education during the Interwar Period', in P. Weindling (ed.), *International Health Organisations and Movements, 1918–1939* (Cambridge, UK: Cambridge University Press, 1995), pp. 266–82; S. McGann, 'Collaboration and Conflict in International Nursing, 1920–39', *Nursing History Review* (2008), 16, pp. 29–57; J. Lapeyre, 'The Idea of Better Nursing: The American Battle for Control over Standards of Nursing Education in Europe, 1918–1925' (PhD Thesis, University of Toronto, 2013); J. Lapeyre, 'Public Health Nursing Education in the Interwar Period', in S. Grant (ed.), *Russian and Soviet Health Care from an International Perspective* (Basingstoke, UK: Palgrave Macmillan, 2017), pp. 217–42.
4 *Proceedings of the Medical Conference held at the invitation of the Committee of Red Cross Societies, Cannes, France, April 1 to 11, 1919* (Geneva, Switzerland: League of Red Cross Societies, 1919), p. 14. For details on the Cannes Conference and the emergence of the League of Red Cross Societies, see M. Oppenheimer, '"A Golden Moment?" The League of Red Cross Societies, the League of Nations and Contested Spaces of Internationalism and Humanitarianism, 1919–22', in J. Damousi and P. O'Brien (eds), *League of Nations: Histories, Legacies and Impact* (Melbourne, Australia: Melbourne University Press, 2018), pp. 8–27.
5 The numbers vary between 296 and 301, and seven special students who did not follow the Bedford College course. For an overview of the nursing programme, see M. Oppenheimer, 'Nurses of the League: the League of Red Cross Societies and the Development of Public Health Nursing Post-WWI', *History Australia* (2020), 17 (4), pp. 628–44. https://doi.org/10.1080/14490854.2020.1840290.

6 B. Taithe, 'Humanitarian Masculinity: Desire, Character and Heroics, 1876–2018', in E. Möller, J. Paulmann and K. Stornig (eds), *Gendering Global Humanitarianism in the Twentieth Century* (London, UK: Palgrave Macmillan, 2020), pp. 35–60. See also E. Möller, J. Paulmann and K. Stornig, 'Gender Histories of Humanitarianism: Concepts and Perspectives', in Möller, Paulmann and Stornig (eds), *Gendering Global Humanitarianism*, p. 287.
7 Oppenheimer, 'Nurses of the League'.
8 See C. Hallett, 'Nursing, 1840–1920: Forging a Profession', in A. Borsay and B. Hunter (eds), *Nursing and Midwifery in Britain since 1700* (London, UK: Palgrave Macmillan, 2021), pp. 46–73; B. Abel-Smith, *A History of the Nursing Profession* (London, UK: Heinemann, 1960); S. McGann, *The Battle of the Nurses: A Study of Eight Women Who Influenced the Development of Professional Nursing, 1880–1930* (London, UK: Scutari Press, 1992).
9 Alice Fitzgerald, Chapter X, War Diary (typed version), p. 211. Alice Fitzgerald Papers microform MS987, reel 1, Maryland Historical Society (MHS), Baltimore (hereafter Fitzgerald Papers, MHS, Baltimore). I thank Marian Moser Jones very much for providing me with copies during the Covid-19 pandemic in 2020.
10 See C. E. Hallett, *Veiled Warriors: Allied Nurses of the First World War* (Oxford, UK: Oxford University Press, 2014).
11 B. L. Brush, J. E. Lynaugh, A. M. Rafferty, M. Stuart and N. J. Tomes, *Nurses of All Nations: A History of the International Council of Nurses, 1899–1999* (Philadelphia, PA: Lippincott Williams and Wilkins, 1999).
12 Brush et al., *Nurses of All Nations*, p. 57.
13 'Report on the Section on Nursing', *Proceedings of Cannes Medical Conference*, p. 137.
14 McGann, 'Collaboration and Conflict', pp. 29–57.
15 N. Wylie, M. Oppenheimer and J. Crossland, 'The Red Cross Movement: Continuities, Changes and Challenges', in N. Wylie, M. Oppenheimer and J. Crossland (eds), *The Red Cross Movement* (Manchester, UK: Manchester University Press, 2020), p. 3.
16 Möller, Paulmann and Stornig, *Gendering Global Humanitarianism*, p. 2.
17 J. Lafrenière, C. Sweetman and T. Thylin, 'Introduction: Gender, Humanitarian Action and Crisis Response', *Gender & Development* (2019), 27 (2), DOI: 10.1080/13552074.2019.1634332.
18 D. Martín-Moruno, B. L. Edgar and M. Leyder, 'Feminist Perspectives on the History of Humanitarian Relief (1870–1945)', *Medicine, Conflict and Survival* (2020), 36 (1), pp. 2–18, DOI: 10.1080/13623699.2020.1717720.
19 B. Taithe and J. Borton, 'History, Memory and "Lessons Learnt" for Humanitarian Practitioners', *European Review of History* (2016), 23 (102), pp. 210–24.
20 K. Storr, *Excluded from the Record: Women, Refugees and Relief, 1914–1929* (New York, UK: Peter Lang, 2009).
21 Oppenheimer and Collins, *Henry Pomeroy Davison*, p. 57.
22 B. B. Scher, 'Alice and Her Wonderlands', *American Journal of Nursing* (June 1961), 61 (6), p. 74.

23 Ibid., p. 74. See also 'Memoirs of an American Nurse (Round the World and Back Again)', Fitzgerald Papers, MHS, Baltimore.
24 Diary of Alice Fitzgerald, p. 16, Fitzgerald Papers, MHS, Baltimore.
25 Alice Fitzgerald, Chapter II War Diary (typed version), p. 22, Fitzgerald Papers, MHS, Baltimore.
26 See Iris Noble, *Nurse Around the World, Alice Fitzgerald* (New York, NY: Julian Messner, Inc, 1964).
27 Quoted in Lavinia Dock, *History of American Red Cross Nursing* (New York, NY: The Macmillan Company, 1922), p. 1143.
28 E. H. Smith, GB RN, six-page typed article 'Bedford College for Women. An International Alma Mater', 1925, p. 2, Bedford College: League of Red Cross Society records 1925, BC/AL/333/1a/1/1. Bedford College, Royal Holloway Archives, University of London (hereafter, RHA), London.
29 Her italics. League of Red Cross Society General Council Minutes, 4th Session, Medical Section, 4 March 1920, p. 97, International Federation of Red Cross Archives (hereafter IFRC), Geneva.
30 McGann, 'Collaboration and Conflict', p. 29.
31 Ibid., p. 34.
32 Dock, *History of American Red Cross Nursing*, pp. 1143–4.
33 Memorandum from Alice Fitzgerald, 26 December 1919, League of Red Cross Societies Box 2, Folder 27, Alice Fitzgerald, Hoover Institute, Stanford, CA.
34 League of Red Cross Societies General Council Minutes, 4th Session, Medical Section, 4 March 1920, p. 98, IFRC, Geneva.
35 Memorandum from Alice Fitzgerald, 26 December 1919, League of Red Cross Societies, Box 2, Folder 27, Alice Fitzgerald, Hoover Institute, Stanford, CA.
36 Fitzgerald in Dock, *History of American Red Cross Nursing*, p. 1144.
37 Thirty are listed in the 1920 prospectus, but elsewhere it says it should be forty, which is more realistic, so perhaps it is a typographical error.
38 League of Red Cross Societies, 'Course of Training for Public Health Nurses. Program Prospectus, 1920', RHUL.AL.331.1, RHA; Fitzgerald in Dock, *History of American Red Cross Nursing*, pp. 1143–4.
39 *Canadian Nurse*, 1920 (republished from the *British Journal of Nursing*), 25.
40 Smith, 'Bedford College for Women', 1925, p. 4, Bedford College, League of Red Cross Societies records 1925, BC/AL/333/1a/1/1. RHA, London.
41 Ibid.
42 Alice Fitzgerald, Chapter XI, War Diary (typed version), p. 258, Fitzgerald Papers, MHS, Baltimore.
43 Ibid., p. 212.
44 Dock, *History of American Red Cross Nursing*, p. 1146.
45 C. Moorehead, *Dunant's Dream: War, Switzerland and the History of the Red Cross* (London, UK: HarperCollins, 1998), offers one of the first and most comprehensive accounts.
46 See, for example, J. Urwin, *Making the World Safe? The American Red Cross and a Nation's Humanitarian Awakening* (New York, NY: Oxford University Press, 2013); M. Moser Jones, *The American Red Cross from Clara Barton to the New Deal* (Baltimore, MD: The Johns Hopkins University Press, 2013).

47 Lillian Wald Papers, MssCol 3201, New York Library, New York.
48 *The World's Health* (January–March 1929), 10 (1), pp. 37–57.
49 Editor, 'This Way Forward: Alice Fitzgerald (1876–1962)', *Hopkins Nurse* (Summer 2014), https://magazine.nursing.jhu.edu/2014/07/this-way-forward-alice-fitzgerald-1876-1962/, accessed 19 October 2020.
50 See the Katherine Olmsted Collection, Alan Mason Chesney Medical Archives of the Johns Hopkins Medical Institutions, https://medicalarchives.jhmi.edu:8443/papers/olmsted.html, accessed 20 May 2020.
51 Quoted in M. Stuart and G. Boschma, 'Seeking Stability in the Midst of Change', in Brush et al. (eds), *Nurses of All Nations*, p. 80.
52 K. M. Olmsted, *Nursing as a Vocation for Women* (Madison, WI: University of Wisconsin Information and Welfare Bulletin, November 1916), pp. 8–9.
53 Ibid., p. 7.
54 Ibid., p. 18.
55 Rafferty, 'Internationalising Nursing Education', p. 267.
56 Lapeyre, 'The Idea of Better Nursing', p. 156.
57 Edwin R. Embree, diary, 13 June 1924, The Online Collection and Catalog of Rockefeller Archive Center, http://Dimes.Rockarch.Org, accessed 22 November 2021.
58 Oppenheimer, 'Nurses of the League'.
59 P. Zylberman, 'Fewer Parallels Than Antitheses: Rene Sand and Andrija Stampar on Social Medicine, 1919–1955', *Social History of Medicine* (2004), 17 (1), pp. 77–92.
60 The Commonwealth Fund was established in 1918 by Mrs Stephen V. Harkness for 'benevolent, religious, educational and like purposes'. Commonwealth Fund – Grants SGI, Series 18, Box 180, Folder 1489, RAC, New York.
61 See M. Oppenheimer, 'The Commonwealth Fund and Its Scholarship Programme for Austrian Nurses, 1924–1928', paper delivered at a two-day online symposium, Centre d'Histoire de Sciences Po, Paris, 14–15 June 2021.
62 Edwin R. Embree, diary, 26 July 1923, The Online Collection and Catalog of Rockefeller Archive Center, http://Dimes.Rockarch.Org, accessed 22 November 2021.
63 Exhibit A, 'Memorandum of Conference between Miss Olmsted and Dr Rene Sand of the League of Red Cross Societies and Miss Crowell and Mr Embree of the Rockefeller Foundation, Held at the Office of the League, Wednesday afternoon, 25 July 1923', Edwin R. Embree, Exhibits 1923, The Online Collection and Catalog of Rockefeller Archive Center, http://Dimes.Rockarch.Org, accessed 22 November 2021.
64 Exhibit C, 'A Program for Aid in Nursing Training in Europe', Edwin R. Embree, Exhibits 1923, The Online Collection and Catalog of Rockefeller Archive Center, http://Dimes.Rockarch.Org, accessed 22 November 2021.
65 McGann, 'Collaboration and Conflict'.
66 Recommendations of the Nursing Advisory Committee of the League of Red Cross Societies, 1924–1961, Box A0859/7. IFRC Archives, Geneva.

67 Minutes of the Nursing Advisory Committee, First Meeting, 1924 (23–30 April). Box A0829/1. Red Crescent and Red Cross Society Archive, quoted in Lapeyre, 'The Idea of Better Nursing', p. 170.
68 Report for the Nursing Advisory Board, 9–10 July 1926, p. 8, Nursing Advisory Committee Proceedings, 1924–1929, A0829/1, IFRC Archives, Geneva.
69 Smith, 'Bedford College for Women', 1925, p. 5. The house was destroyed by a bomb during World War II.
70 See the *Old International Newsletter*, published from 1923, IFRC Archives, Geneva. The Old Internationals Association was formed in 1925.
71 Smith, 'Bedford College for Women', p. 6.
72 *Old Internationals Newsletter* (Easter 1925), p. 13; League of Red Cross Societies, *Origins, Activities, Purpose* (Paris, France: League of Red Cross Societies, 1925), pp. 67–8, Lillian D. Wald Papers, New York Library.
73 *Old Internationals Newsletter* (Christmas 1926), pp. 3–4.
74 See League of Red Cross Societies, 1921–26, file 146, Rockefeller Foundation records, SG1, 1 Series 700: Europe, subseries 700C, Europe – Nursing Box 20, Rockefeller Archives.
75 *Old Internationals Newsletter* (Easter 1927), pp. 4–5.
76 See Katherine Olmstead/Normandy Inn (1886–1964), Town of Sodus Historical Society, at http://townofsodushistoricalsociety.org/hamlets/wallington/katherine-olmsted/, accessed 22 February 2019.
77 *Old Internationals Newsletter* (Easter 1927), p. 4.
78 I. H. Charley, 'Maynard Linden Carter ARRC, 1886–1962. A Memoir', *International Journal of Nursing Studies* (1966), 3, pp. 161–2.
79 Ibid., p. 163.
80 Reid and Gilbo, *Beyond Conflict*, p. 95.
81 See J. Browne, *The World's Health* (October 1928), ix (10), pp. 375–8; *Old Internationals Newsletter*, the Summer School edition (Summer 1928).
82 Report for the Nursing Advisory Board, 9–10 July 1926, p. 2, Nursing Advisory Committee Proceedings, 1924–29, A0829/1 IFRC Archives, Geneva.
83 Report of Nursing Division, 2–4 July 1928, p. 4, Nursing Advisory Committee Proceedings, 1924–29, A0829/1 IFRC Archives, Geneva.
84 *Old Internationals Newsletter* (Christmas, 1932), pp. 15–21.
85 Charley, 'Maynard Linden Carter', p. 164.
86 Exchanges of correspondence between Miss M. F. Tuke, Principal, Bedford College for Women, T. B. Kittredge (Assistant Director General) and K. Olmsted (Chief Nursing Division), in letters dated 8 October 1926, Bedford College files, RHA, London.
87 Memorandum, re Administration of Courses held at Bedford College, and Administration of 15 Manchester Square as a residence for students attending these Courses together with the office routine to be adopted, for the guidance of the Superintendent, revised 1 August 1928 BC/AL/332/2/40, RHA, London.
88 Report for the Nursing Advisory Board, 9–10 July 1926, p. 6.
89 *Old Internationals Newsletter* (Christmas 1930), between pp. 8 and 9.
90 'The Florence Nightingale International Foundation Inaugurated', *American Journal of Nursing* (August 1934), xxxiv (8), p. 786.

91 The Florence Nightingale International Foundation, four-page typed statement, undated c. July 1934, BC AL/333/1a/1/29, RHA, London.
92 Charley, 'Maynard Linden Carter', p. 165.
93 *Old Internationals Newsletter* (October 1938), pp. 32–3.
94 *Old Internationals Newsletter* (April 1962), pp. 19–20.
95 Oppenheimer, 'Nurses of the League'.

11

'Springs of love': Sentiment and affect in mid-twentieth-century development volunteering

Agnieszka Sobocinska

In late 1951, after six months in Indonesia, Australian volunteer Herb Feith wrote a letter to his former academic supervisor, political scientist William Macmahon Ball. The situation in Indonesia was 'undeniably one of suspicion of the foreigner', he wrote, and as a result, there is no trust and 'the foreign technical people here ... find themselves almost completely unable to use their skills'. Lack of emotional engagement, Feith believed, was limiting Indonesia's post-colonial development. Feith dedicated himself to improving this situation, both during his time as the first volunteer of the recently established Volunteer Graduate Scheme, and then later as part of its Executive Committee. Feith helped ensure that Australian volunteers received a salary that was equal to their Indonesian counterparts, and encouraged them to eat Indonesian food, learn the language and build genuine relationships with Indonesian co-workers. Volunteers' jobs, Feith later reflected, were important, but more important still was 'just to live normally and naturally in the Indonesian world, and to make friends among Indonesians'.[1] Feith's desire for emotional engagement was closely tied to wider political contexts: he sought to build trust with Indonesians in order to advance their postcolonial development and also improve bilateral relations with Australia. As Feith wrote to Macmahon Ball, the Volunteer Graduate Scheme's work was the manifestation of a new political philosophy, which brought sentiment and emotion into the coldly technical field of international development, and which he dubbed 'sentimental radicalism'.[2]

Tens of thousands of Western volunteers followed Herb Feith to Asia, Africa and Latin America in the 1950s and 1960s. Although Feith was uniquely capable of expressing his political philosophy, other volunteers were similarly emotionally engaged. This chapter explores sentiment and affect in three major development volunteering programmes: Australia's Volunteer Graduate Scheme, Britain's Voluntary Service Overseas (commonly known by its abbreviation, VSO) and the United States Peace Corps. It examines the sentimental rhetoric of development volunteering agencies to demonstrate how they brought emotion and affect into the technical sphere of international development. It then tracks the diffusion of sentimental rhetoric to intending volunteers. Based on the examination of hundreds of application forms, the chapter argues that most volunteers were motivated by an idealistic desire to help people worse off than themselves, as well as sentimental visions of global friendship. Fusing affect with theories of economic development, volunteering agencies helped collapse the distinction between international development and humanitarianism, and employed an emotional and moral lexicon in support of projects enmeshed in state, economic and cultural power.

Over the past three decades, historians have paid sustained attention to international development and humanitarianism. But the two historiographies have remained surprisingly separate. Recent scholarship has begun exploring how humanitarianism and international development met at the intersection of the Cold War and decolonisation. From the mid-twentieth century, humanitarianism changed from providing disaster relief to addressing the long-term economic, social and environmental causes of humanitarian disasters.[3] Recent work by historians Young-Sun Hong and Timothy Nunan suggest that by the mid-twentieth century, humanitarianism and international development were overlapping, if not mutually dependent.[4] Development actors used the altruistic rhetoric of humanitarianism to make their intervention palatable. Humanitarian organisations, in the meantime, actively assisted state- and bloc-based power through the provision of supplies and legitimacy to deeply politicised – and sometimes weaponised – power contests.

This chapter extends this scholarship by suggesting that the fusion between humanitarianism and international development depended on the translation of humanitarianism's sentimental rhetoric and affective register to the more technical field of international development. Historians and political scientists have taken an affective turn over the past decade.[5] Research into emotions and affect, and their relationship to political decisions, has flourished. These insights have been applied to international relations and international history.[6] They have also been probed in contemporary development studies.[7] Whereas the history of humanitarianism has long recognised the significance of affect in evoking concern for and action on behalf of distant others, historians of development have largely preferred to focus on state-based interventions and economic models, which are often assumed to be free of emotion.

This chapter argues that development volunteers brought the sentimental and affective traditions of humanitarianism to bear on international development. National and multilateral development agencies regarded international development as a rational and highly technical field, which historian Joseph Hodge has depicted as the 'Triumph of the Expert'.[8] Development volunteering was premised on the development paradigm, but it also cultivated a highly emotive register, claiming that volunteers participated in a sentimental project of humanitarian assistance and international friendship. Its appeal to Western empathy and fellow-feeling aligned it with humanitarianism, which has long relied on the strategic use of emotion.[9] Volunteers collapsed the distinction between international development and humanitarianism, and from the 1950s development volunteering agencies employed an emotional and moral vocabulary in support of the deeply political project of international development.[10]

The rise of development volunteering

Development volunteering was consciously tied to the emerging sphere of international development. The economic development of 'underdeveloped' nations was a key aim of the postwar period. The preamble to the United Nations charter had undertaken to 'employ international machinery for the promotion of economic and social advancement of all peoples' in 1945.[11] US President Harry Truman had announced the Point Four Program, to make 'the benefits of our scientific advances and industrial processes available for the improvement and growth of underdeveloped areas', in January 1949.[12] In 1950 the leaders of Commonwealth nations unveiled the Colombo Plan for technical assistance to Asia.[13] That same year, the United Nations initiated its Technical Assistance Administration (UNTAA).[14] The first development volunteering programme, Australia's Volunteer Graduate Scheme, was established in 1950. Its formation was sparked by an Indonesian request for Australian help to mitigate a skills shortage caused by the rapid departure of Dutch colonial bureaucrats following Indonesia's declaration of independence in 1945. The Volunteer Graduate Scheme's Executive Committee initially conceived of their programme as a contribution to Indonesia's development. Volunteers would work for two-year terms in technical roles – as scientists, doctors, university lecturers or English language specialists – to help fill vacant positions and train Indonesians to take their place. This proposal appealed to the Indonesian government, which was keenly focused on the nation's economic development in the early post-colonial years. As Indonesian Ambassador to Australia Dr R. H. Tirtawinata noted, 'every aspect of our life needs the stimulus of knowledge, of what the Americans call "know how". This is what you are giving us and what we most urgently need'.[15]

Originally conceived as a programme to assist Indonesia's development, the Volunteer Graduate Scheme soon shifted its rhetoric to attract the support of the Australian Department of External Affairs. When it first applied to the government for funding, the Executive Committee portrayed the Volunteer Graduate Scheme in the technical language of international development. Liberal Party Minister for External Affairs Percy Spender was not impressed: he thought technical experts were more desirable than well-meaning university graduates, and suggested that university students interested in assisting post-colonial nations would be better off getting some work experience, and in due course, registering as technical experts with the Colombo Plan for Cooperative Economic Development in South and Southeast Asia.[16] Spender's decision was confirmed by his successor, Richard Casey, who refused a funding request from the Volunteer Graduate Scheme soon after taking office in May 1951.

Recognising that it wouldn't convince Casey of the development value of non-experts, the Executive Committee began to define the Volunteer Graduate Scheme in a different way, using sentimental and affective language to suggest that volunteers could build friendships across the boundaries of race and nation, and in so doing help improve Australia's image in Asia. When the Volunteer Graduate Scheme re-approached the Department of External Affairs for a third time in 1952, its stated goal was 'to establish goodwill and understanding between our two countries' by sending personnel to 'assist in the technical and social reconstruction of Indonesia, and at the same time live with and get to know Indonesians'.[17] This sentimental re-framing of the scheme's aims was appealing amidst rising critiques of Australia's White Australia Policy. In this instance, the empathy demonstrated by Australian youth eager to devote themselves to Indonesia's post-colonial development aligned with the government's political agenda. From 1952 the Department of External Affairs paid for volunteers' travel to Indonesia, provided grants to cover additional costs and paid them a resettlement allowance upon their return to Australia.

The Volunteer Graduate Scheme also began to emphasise its sentimental and affective elements in appeals to potential applicants. An early pamphlet claimed: 'What [volunteers] do in their actual work is important ... But more important perhaps is the fact that these young people assert by the way they live, that racial equality is real. By having natural and friendly relations with Indonesians on a basis of mutual respect, they help to do away with the colonial legacy of mistrust and misunderstanding'.[18] Although the development aspect was always important, the scheme's Honorary Secretary wrote in 1955, 'the programme is essentially an idealistic one which aims to build international and inter-racial friendship'.[19]

Sentimental desires for friendships across the barriers of geography, nation and culture had been expressed in student exchange schemes, pen pal projects and other forms of cross-cultural interaction since the late nineteenth century.[20] Before World War II, most of these efforts were directed towards building relations across Europe, North America and Australasia. By the 1950s, however, this was starting to change. In Australia, the need to build contacts with Asian 'neighbours' became commonplace, as Australians came to recognise the region's strategic significance.[21] The Scheme's Honorary Secretary Jim Webb quipped: 'Friendship with Asia ... is a fashionable theme now in Australian university circles', and it was a theme that the Volunteer Graduate Scheme tapped into.[22] Although plans were hatched to expand the scheme across Asia and beyond, the Volunteer Graduate Scheme never extended beyond Indonesia. Originally started as a contribution to Indonesia's economic and social development, by the mid-1950s the programme's publicity material also emphasised the sentimental project of international friendship. The twin aims coexisted, with the Volunteer Graduate Scheme presented as 'a real contribution to technical progress and to the development of understanding and friendship'.[23]

The Australian Volunteer Graduate Scheme influenced Britain's Voluntary Service Overseas scheme, launched by former colonial official Alec Dickson in 1958. VSO proposed one-year terms for volunteers, most of whom were employed as teachers, civil servants or in community development in British territories and decolonising nations across Asia, Africa and the Caribbean. Like Australia's Volunteer Graduate Scheme, VSO was rooted in the concept of economic development, but relied on a sentimental narrative of cross-cultural friendship to gain supporters and appeal to potential applicants. Although it was nominally a non-government organisation, VSO was funded in large part by the Colonial Office under its Colonial Development and Welfare scheme, and the Commonwealth Relations Office, until responsibility for VSO shifted to the Department of Technical Cooperation in 1961. These connections bound it closely to Britain's effort for the economic development of its current and former dependencies at a time of decolonisation. But VSO also echoed, and even amplified, the Volunteer Graduate Scheme's rhetoric that affect and emotion were a key aspect of development volunteering. A 1960 VSO pamphlet claimed that, in West Africa, volunteers' 'warm and friendly sympathy with the people ... has made all the difference in the world and added greatly to the strength of Anglo-African friendship here'.[24] Again, empathy and sympathy were harnessed for political ends. The notion that young volunteers could turn around the bitterness accrued by decades, if not centuries, of colonialism was always a fantasy. But it was an appealing fantasy with wide purchase: depictions of volunteers in the British media routinely emphasised volunteers' capacities to build friendships across boundaries of race and nation.[25]

Where the Volunteer Graduate Scheme placed the stress on 'identification', Alec Dickson emphasised love as the emotional register of the VSO experience. Dickson believed that foreign aid could only be effective if it was accompanied by an emotional investment from both donor and recipient. Praising one of the earliest VSOs in Sarawak, Alec's wife Mora Dickson wrote: 'it was not ultimately his talents or his character or his usefulness to those who asked for him that made the best kind of volunteer, though all these things were important, it was the openness of his heart in loving his fellows and accepting their affection in return'. She believed that volunteers' youth was central to their capacity for emotional engagement, as they 'were at an age when the springs of love still ran freely outside set channels responding eagerly to the warmth in others and this was their priceless qualification'.[26] 'Love' in this context meant platonic, brotherly, love rather than the romantic variant, a fact considered so obvious that the Dicksons did not feel the need to define it explicitly. It was also strategically deployed for a political purpose. In the Dicksons' view, British hauteur towards 'natives' was a major problem in the context of decolonisation. In the future, post-colonial nations would be free to choose their relationships, and the Dicksons feared they would cut their ties if Britons continued to act with imperial disdain. The Dicksons recognised that most white Britons felt themselves to be racially and culturally superior, and they acknowledged that differences in education and temperament made cross-cultural friendship unrealistic. For this reason, they placed their faith in young people: both because they thought that young Britons had not yet absorbed the pervasive racism of their society, and because they held that the volunteers' relative lack of sophistication mirrored that of people in 'underdeveloped' nations.

This enhanced potential for 'love' was the primary reason VSO continued to send young volunteers straight from school, even as their lack of skills came under sustained criticism. The British government, focused on the development effectiveness of VSO, limited funding to qualified university graduates. But VSO insisted on retaining a separate programme for teenage 'cadets', funded from non-governmental sources, until the mid-1970s. This was because of the belief that, as Chairman of the VSO Council Lord Amory stated, 'the young person of 18–19 years is more uninhibited than the person of 21–22 years and, in certain situations, this can be of particular value in the making of friendships'.[27] The Dicksons were entirely convinced that VSO was effective on these terms. Alec Dickson decreed VSO a spectacular success even before the first contingent had returned from their year abroad, and the Manchester *Guardian* reported in 1959 that Dickson 'describes what has been achieved as "a breakthrough in human relations"'.[28]

Both the Australian and British schemes influenced the formation of the United States Peace Corps. The Peace Corps sent volunteers to dozens of countries across Asia, Africa and Latin America for two-year terms, predominantly in teaching or community development. Launched in 1961 by

President John F. Kennedy and headed by his brother-in-law, R. Sargent Shriver, the Peace Corps differed in key ways from its Australian and British predecessors. The Volunteer Graduate Scheme and VSO were nominally non-governmental agencies (despite being underwritten by substantial governmental funding), but the Peace Corps was a government agency from the start. This equipped it with considerable resources: the Peace Corps' founding budget of $40 million in the fiscal year 1961 eclipsed VSO's budget of £60,000 and was in a different category altogether from the Volunteer Graduate Scheme's modest £5,000 annual operating costs.[29] Yet, like both its predecessors, the Peace Corps accrued multiple aims. The objectives of the Peace Corps, as submitted to Congress, were threefold: 'to help the people of these countries meet their needs for trained manpower; to help promote a better understanding of the American people on the part of peoples served; and to promote a better understanding of other peoples on the part of the American people'.[30] These three aims spoke both to economic development and the sentimental project of cross-cultural friendship, and blurred the boundaries of development, humanitarianism and cosmopolitanism.

The Peace Corps had a high profile in the 1960s. In increasingly sophisticated public relations and media campaigns, the Peace Corps emphasised the humanitarian aspects of its programme. In 1963 *Time* magazine ran a cover story that claimed the Peace Corps as 'a US Ideal Abroad'. The article portrayed Peace Corps volunteers as well-meaning and altruistic Americans who were willing to make significant personal sacrifices to help distant others. In so doing, *Time* aligned Peace Corps volunteers to the popular image of humanitarianism, rather than international development. This was an important distinction. As a state agency, the Peace Corps was linked to geopolitics and profoundly implicated both in the Cold War and in the spread of northern economic hegemony.[31] Humanitarianism, on the other hand, was popularly thought to be removed from politics. Publicity that presented volunteers as humanitarians depoliticised the Peace Corps, decoupling it from political and economic power and symbolically realigning it with altruistic intentions. As the *New York Times* editorialised, 'Nobody's heart leaps at the thought of intercontinental missiles or of heroic efforts to save our own cities by destroying other peoples [sic] cities. The international crisis might come to this. But that isn't what we want'. Instead, 'What we want in our hearts is goodness and mercy, brotherhood and peace. And it is this yearning that a ... Peace Corps might help us to satisfy'.[32]

This rhetoric appealed to young Americans. It is difficult to overstate the popularity of the Peace Corps in the early 1960s. Even before it had been formally launched, a Gallup poll found that 89 per cent of Americans had heard of the Peace Corps, and 71 per cent were in favour of it.[33] The Peace Corps was inundated with applications from tens of thousands of hopefuls from its very first year. John F. Kennedy claimed that the volume of applications was 'most heartening of all … a convincing demonstration that we have in this country an immense reservoir of dedicated men and women willing to devote their energies and time and toil to the cause of world peace and human progress'.[34] Using a distinctly sentimental and affective register, the Peace Corps portrayed volunteers as altruistic humanitarians, and as citizen diplomats building bridges across boundaries of race and culture. This served to distance the Peace Corps from the United States government, even as it continued to finance every volunteer. It also served to appeal to ordinary citizens who hoped to make a contribution towards poverty alleviation and cross-cultural friendship at a time of heightened geopolitical tension and global economic disparity.

Empathy and optimism

The sentimental images portrayed by development volunteering agencies appealed to applicants in Australia, Britain and America alike. The National Library of Australia holds virtually every application the Volunteer Graduate Scheme received from its establishment in 1950 to its final disbanding in 1969. The total number of applications is relatively small – in the hundreds rather than the tens of thousands of applications received by the Peace Corps, for example – but questionnaires were descriptive and provided space for volunteers to describe their motivations at some length. The Peace Corps coped with a deluge of applications by turning to multiple-choice questionnaires, read by computers, as the first stage of the application process. The Volunteer Graduate Scheme never had to turn to labour-saving extremes. On the contrary, the Executive Committee had the leisure to enter into lengthy correspondence with intending applicants to clarify their desires and intentions. As a result, the diverse motivations of Australian applicants to the Volunteer Graduate Scheme are among the most accessible of any development volunteering cohort.

Development volunteering had taken off by the early 1960s, but in its early years the Volunteer Graduate Scheme struggled to attract applicants. This slow start points to the novelty of development volunteering, and also to its very real disincentives. Most obvious, perhaps, were the perceived financial sacrifices. In practice, most volunteers enjoyed a relatively comfortable lifestyle, but many assumed they would have been financially better off staying at home. At a time of low unemployment across Australia, Britain and the United States, most young people were assured of good jobs. Potential applicants feared that volunteering would delay or otherwise harm their career prospects and financial wellbeing. By going away for one or two years, volunteers delayed career advancement opportunities. Many worried about falling behind relative to colleagues who had remained at home, worked their way up the career ladder and saved money towards a home.

Volunteers also had to make social sacrifices. Leaving friends and family behind was bad enough in itself, but young applicants were particularly worried about deferring romantic relationships and, potentially, marriage. The possibility of 'missing out' on the marriage market felt very real in the late 1950s and early 1960s, reflecting that period's unusually high rate of marriage, and early age at marriage.[35] The pressure to find a spouse was particularly strong for young women, who often expected to retreat from paid work after marriage. For them, selecting a husband was a significant financial as well as emotional consideration. Some young women felt that two years out of the marriage market could materially hurt their prospects; even some of those who did end up volunteering felt anxious about whether any eligible men would be left by the time they returned home.[36] This remained true well into the 1960s. One 1965 study exploring the barriers to applying for the Peace Corps found the two most significant issues preventing application were 'desire to pursue career' and 'desire to get married'.[37]

The Volunteer Graduate Scheme's Executive Committee believed that a willingness to sustain personal sacrifice for the greater good was rare among Australian youth, and so 'do not consider that a huge flow of volunteers will ever come forward'. Indeed, they believed they would 'never attract more than a tiny percentage of students or graduates, the tiny percentage of "cranks", albeit the practical ones!'[38] And yet, numbers did grow, albeit slowly at first, and not only in Australia. In Britain, Alec Dickson personally invited twelve individuals to volunteer with VSO in its first year; the following year sixty were recruited and by 1963, 502 volunteers were selected from more than 1,500 applicants. The numbers climbed steadily before plateauing at 1,500 volunteers per year, drawn from an applicant pool of around 4,500, from 1966.[39] VSO's 10,000th volunteer departed from Britain in 1971.[40] The multitude of applicants for the Peace Corps is legendary. Over 11,000 applicants fronted for placement examinations during the organisation's first year.[41] In 1965 this had risen to 42,639 applications.[42] By the end of the 1960s, more than 300,000 Americans had applied for a term with the Peace Corps.

Why did they apply? Application forms sent to the Volunteer Graduate Scheme during the 1950s and 1960s point to a range of motives, but nearly all of them reveal a strongly personal engagement with international affairs that was both emotional and sentimental. These emotions were deeply felt and were strong enough to overcome the disincentives outlined above. But they were also closely tied to political outcomes. Emotions are not constant, but have been felt differently within different cultures and times.[43] Following two catastrophic world wars, the rise of the Cold War and the existential threat represented by nuclear weapons, by the mid-twentieth century international relations were front of mind for many otherwise ordinary citizens. In this context, emotions, including empathy, intersected with geopolitics. Many aspiring volunteers felt compelled to become personally involved in international affairs. Like Herb Feith, they thought that their emotions could be politically deployed amid decolonisation and the Cold War. Primed by the rhetoric and publicity surrounding development volunteering, they recognised that their feelings of empathy and goodwill could be politically useful and contribute to economic development and the building of a liberal international order.

A desire for cross-cultural friendship was also frequently expressed in applications to the Volunteer Graduate Scheme. Pharmacist Judith Gregory wished to work in Indonesia because of a desire 'to make a personal contribution towards better international relations.'[44] Teacher David Marchesi wrote of stating a 'general will to promote international understanding at an inter-personal level'.[45] Lois Griffiths, who was also a teacher, wrote that 'nothing could be of greater value than cooperation and understanding between Australia and neighbouring countries'.[46] The desire of these applicants to contribute to international friendship was premised both on a deeply personal and emotional register of internationalism and on an optimistic assessment of the power of individuals to shape international affairs.

Many Volunteer Graduate Scheme applicants linked the sentimental project of international friendship with the realpolitik goal of improving Australia's image in Asia. Some applicants believed that building personal friendships with Asians would demonstrate their nation's egalitarianism and lack of racism, which could contribute to more harmonious bilateral relations. One October 1955 application listed a desire to befriend Indonesians in order to 'help in bettering Australian relations with our Asian neighbours'.[47] An applicant the following year wrote of his intention 'to do my share of strengthening Asian–Australian relationships and understanding'.[48] Accountant Thomas Errey wrote, 'I conceive myself to be both a proud and patriotic Australian and still appreciative of the remarkable traditions, present qualities and potential renewed greatness of the Indonesian people & therefore a suitable person to promote goodwill between the two peoples'.[49]

Although such statements were common in Volunteer Graduate Scheme applications, they were exceptional in the broader context of 1950s Australia. Australia had a long history of anxiety about the 'rise' of Asia.[50] Although Indonesia had attracted only limited attention during the colonial era, a widespread belief that Sukarno sought to expand Indonesia's territory stoked anxiety about the potential threat to Australia in the 1950s and 1960s.[51] Volunteer applicants were unusual in expressing a desire for closer personal and national relations with Indonesia, and in believing that this would benefit the Australian nation. Significantly, they did so years before the government, or indeed a majority of the population, articulated similar views.

Where many applicants wrote of a sentimental desire to 'help' others, only a small number used the technical language of international development. Lois Griffiths noted: 'I have long followed with interest the achievements of the Indonesian people in developing their country ... I feel that I could make no better use of the professional knowledge which I have than in such a country'.[52] Among the most conceptually sophisticated applicants was twenty-six-year-old Hugh Francis Owen, who applied in 1959 to work in a teaching or economics advisory capacity. He listed a number of reasons for applying, among them 'Because I understand that a trained person can help Indonesia in its economic "take off"'.[53] Coming a year before Walt Rostow's *The Stages of Economic Growth* popularised the concept of economic 'take-off', this reflected a cutting-edge understanding of contemporary development economics that reinforced a personal desire to contribute to Indonesia's growth.

The history of humanitarianism has been premised on the mass mobilisation of empathy and compassion.[54] Typically, public empathy has been evoked in an atmosphere of despair, caused by vivid, and often shocking, representations of the pain and suffering of distant others.[55] Development volunteering was unusual in combining empathy with optimism. As we have seen, this optimism was private, in the sense that it reflected a belief that an individual could contribute to poverty alleviation and international relations. But it was also structural, related to the mutually affirming ideologies of decolonisation and development. Independence movements across Asia and Africa were marked by a striking optimism that freedom from colonial rule would bring both social justice and economic growth. This feeling was further encouraged by the optimism surrounding international development and modernisation theory during the 1950s and into the 1960s. As historian David Engerman notes, both north and south were caught up in the 'romance of development', and were equally optimistic about the success of development schemes.[56] Economic development theorists, and the multilateral and national agencies seeking to guide decolonising nations towards economic development, were optimistic about their prospects – perhaps unduly so, considering the vast handicaps of capital and expertise in many formerly colonised nations, and the extraction basis of their economies.

In addition to the secular sentiments described above, a significant proportion of Volunteer Graduate Scheme applicants cited religious beliefs among their motivations. Humanitarianism and religion have long been intertwined, and this relationship continued into the twentieth century. There was considerable overlap in both attitudes and personnel between the Volunteer Graduate Scheme and the Australian Student Christian Movement. The first significant influx of applications came after Volunteer Graduate Scheme Chairman Don Anderson presented at the Movement's 1951 National Conference, after which 100 delegates submitted preliminary expressions of interest to the Volunteer Graduate Scheme. Among them were several individuals who went on to volunteer posts, including Gwenda Rodda, Ollie McMichael and Ian Doig.[57] Subsequent Student Christian Movement conferences elicited further lists of 'interesteds', many of whom went on to volunteer in Indonesia.[58] The Movement also led direct recruitment campaigns including 'Operation 20+', co-ordinated by the General Secretary of the Australian Student Christian Movement, the Reverend Frank Engel, which aimed to send twenty volunteers to Indonesia with the Volunteer Graduate Scheme by 1955.

It is perhaps unsurprising, then, to find religious beliefs alongside secular motives in applications to the Volunteer Graduate Scheme. Many applicants referred to strong Christian beliefs, and expressed a desire to work in Indonesia 'in the name of Jesus Christ' or 'in some capacity of service for Christ's sake'.[59] Medical graduate Peter Graham applied because he wished 'to assist people towards the wholeness of life – physically, mentally & spiritually – by the practice of medicine and of the principles of Christ'.[60] Some were unsure of anything apart from their Christian calling: as one applicant wrote in 1954, 'I have been thinking rather seriously of answering a call which I have had to go to Indonesia in the service of Christ, and am a little worried, as I know nothing whatsoever about the conditions there, or those under which I would be working. I do not even know in what capacity I could go'.[61]

As an organisation, the Volunteer Graduate Scheme retained a secular posture that would make it acceptable to Indonesia's majority Muslim government and population. The personal motivations of its volunteers, however, often blurred secular and religious motives, reflecting the important role played by organised Christianity in mid-century Australia.[62] B. J. Richards was training for the Church of Christ Ministry when he declared he was 'interested in further information concerning Christian Missionary activity amongst those who have never had the opportunity to learn of Christ'.[63] Far from rejecting his application, Herb Feith (now a member of the Executive Committee) personally replied, noting that, although the Volunteer Graduate Scheme could not support overt proselytising, 'Almost certainly if you decided to go … you'd perhaps be able to do all sorts of work in the Church community, particularly among young people'.[64] Similarly, Peter Shedding of Castle Hill, on the outskirts of Sydney, wrote in 1959: 'I have felt for some time that God would have me carry out my employ as a Chemical Engineer in the South East Asian area where we could have the opportunity to tell others about the Lord Jesus Christ and to aid them in physical and material ways'.[65] Volunteer Graduate Scheme Chairman Don Anderson quickly replied, providing encouragement and further information, and suggesting Shedding contact the local volunteer representative to take his application to the next stage.[66]

There was little friction between secular and religious attitudes within the Volunteer Graduate Scheme. In the postwar period, the Australian Student Christian Movement espoused Christian intellectualism that related theology to current political, social and cultural questions. Its brand of progressive Christianity was notable for its early opposition to the White Australia Policy and support for closer ties with Asia.[67] Movement leaders thought that overt missionary activity should be replaced with secular service that was nonetheless conducted in the spirit of Christ. The kind of 'lay missionary' work they proposed included technical work, as long as it contributed to economic and social development. As a result, the sentimental desire for humanitarian assistance and international friendship of movement applicants was nearly identical to that of applicants from the broader community.

Sentimental and affective reasons were often joined by more down-to-earth motivations. Many intending volunteers also looked forward to travel and adventure. In 1953 Ian Spalding wrote to inquire about volunteering, explaining, 'My thoughts have occasionally drifted to the possibility of wandering off to the East for a while to see what life is like there'.[68] Michael Bradley, applying to work as a teacher in 1956, stated: 'I want a chance of seeing the country & people of Indonesia at first hand'.[69] Jillian Vial applied in 1960 because 'I want to travel and experience life, conditions and customs of Asia'.[70] Many more applicants mentioned a desire to see the world near the end of a long list of more 'worthy' or serious reasons. We can assume that other applicants felt a desire for adventure, but preferred not to mention it in their applications. But, as Herb Feith admitted, even for the most committed volunteer 'idealism would not be their only motive for coming here. Others would be the desire to go abroad and the desire to get experience'.[71]

The core motivations cited by Australian applicants were mirrored, with some minor regional variations, by British applicants to VSO and American applicants to the Peace Corps. Analysing 2,612 application forms for the Peace Corps in 1962, researchers Suzanne N. Gordon and Nancy K. Sizer found that 'what most of them want to do is to "help people" ... To them, serving as a volunteer is a way to work for peace, serve the United States, help to improve international relations, or participate in the progress of

'Springs of love'   277

developing nations'. In addition, they noted: 'More than half of the applicants mention potential advantages to themselves – experience, knowledge, a chance to develop as individuals and to further their careers or vocations', but that 'The advantage mentioned most often, however, is the opportunity the Peace Corps provides for learning about other cultures ... and becoming familiar with different customs, philosophies and ways of life'.[72] Although systematic research was never conducted in Britain, VSO volunteers were also thought to bear similar motivations. In 1963, the Lockwood Committee, tasked by the British government to oversee overseas volunteering programmes including VSO, reported that 'there was no single motive underlying overseas service by volunteers', but a basic factor was 'the undoubted need in developing countries for the temporary assistance of trained young men and women'.[73] VSO's sentimental tone, by which volunteering was thought to flow from springs of love, also appealed. Eighteen-year-old Briton Veronica Whitty applied in 1965 because 'I'm interested in what's going on in the world and I have a feeling I'd like to do something that would help the under-developed nations'. By 1965 applications such as Whitty's, which merged a humanitarian and sentimental desire to 'help' with the language of development, was entirely unremarkable. But it spoke to a decade and a half of rhetoric and publicity by development volunteering agencies, which had introduced sentiment and affect to the technical sphere of international development, and in so doing helped collapse the distinction between humanitarianism and international development.

Conclusion

From the early 1950s, volunteer agencies helped collapse the distance between humanitarianism and international development. Development volunteering programmes, including Australia's Volunteer Graduate Scheme, Britain's VSO and the United States Peace Corps, were all underwritten by national governments, and aimed to contribute to the economic and social development of 'underdeveloped' nations. But they also spoke to a sentimental desire to assist distant others and build friendship across boundaries of race and nation. Development volunteering both encouraged and harnessed feelings of empathy for the 'underdeveloped' nations among the youth of Australia, Britain and the United States. This affective register was strategically deployed by governments seeking to improve bilateral relations. Aspiring volunteers in the 1950s and 1960s responded with a heady affective cocktail in which the dominant emotion was empathy, and the prevailing disposition was optimism: an unusual and appealing combination.

Young volunteers signing up to work with the Australian Volunteer Graduate Scheme, British VSO and the United States Peace Corps were emotionally invested in international affairs, and sought to become personally involved in global issues of economic development and world peace. This sentimental and emotional investment was closely tied to geopolitics. The affective landscape of development volunteering is a crucial factor in the broader process by which humanitarianism transformed from disaster relief to long-term economic development from the mid-twentieth century. The emotions of development volunteering were deeply felt, but they were also highly political, binding tens of thousands of citizens to the politicised sphere of international development at the intersection of decolonisation and the Cold War.

Notes

1 'The Scheme for Graduate Employment in Indonesia: An Account of the Way the Scheme Works, and a Letter from Indonesia to Interested Volunteers', 1954 roneo letter, National Archives of Australia (hereafter NAA): A1893, 2032/5/4 Part 1.
2 Herb Feith to William Macmahon Ball, 10 December 1952, National Library of Australia (henceforth NLA): MS 2601, Box 4, Folder 43. See also Jemma Purdey, *From Vienna to Yogyakarta: The Life of Herb Feith* (Sydney, Australia: UNSW Press, 2011).
3 Michael Barnett, *Empire of Humanity: A History of Humanitarianism* (Ithaca, NY: Cornell University Press, 2011); Matthew Hilton, 'Oxfam and the Problem of NGO Aid Appraisal in the 1960s', *Humanity: An International Journal of Human Rights, Humanitarianism, and Development* (2018), 9 (1), pp. 1–18.
4 Young-Sun Hong, *Cold War Germany, the Third World, and the Global Humanitarian Regime* (Cambridge, UK, and New York, NY: Cambridge University Press, 2015); Timothy Nunan, *Humanitarian Invasion: Global Development in Cold War Afghanistan* (New York, NY, and London, UK: Cambridge University Press, 2016).
5 Sara Ahmed, *The Cultural Politics of Emotion* (Edinburgh, UK: Edinburgh University Press, 2004); Lila Abu-Lughod and Catherine A. Lutz, 'Introduction: Emotion, Discourse, and the Politics of Everyday Life', in Lila Abu-Lughod and Catherine A. Lutz (eds), *Language and the Politics of Emotion* (Cambridge, UK: Cambridge University Press, 1990), pp. 1–23; Ruth Leys, 'The Turn to Affect: A Critique', *Critical Inquiry* (2011), 37 (3), pp. 434–72.
6 Emma Hutchison and Roland Bleiker, 'Theorizing Emotions in World Politics', *International Theory* (2014), 6 (3), pp. 491–514; Janice Bially Mattern, 'On Being Convinced: An Emotional Epistemology of International Relations', *International Theory* (2014), 6 (3), pp. 589–94; Barbara Keys and Claire Yorke, 'Personal and Political Emotions in the Mind of the Diplomat', *Political Psychology* (2019), 40 (6), pp. 1235–49; Barbara Keys, 'The Diplomat's Two

Minds: Deconstructing a Foreign Policy Myth', *Diplomatic History* (2020), 44 (1), pp. 1–21.
7   Sarah Wright, 'Emotional Geographies of Development', *Third World Quarterly* (2012), 33 (6), pp. 1113–27.
8   See Joseph Hodge, *Triumph of the Expert: Agrarian Doctrines of Development and the Legacies of British Colonialism* (Athens, OH: Ohio University Press, 2007).
9   Jane Lydon, *Imperial Emotions: The Politics of Empathy across the British Empire* (Cambridge, UK: Cambridge University Press, 2019).
10 Michael E. Latham, *Modernization as Ideology: American Social Science and 'Nation Building' in the Kennedy Era* (Chapel Hill, NC: University of North Carolina Press, 2000); Michael Latham, *The Right Kind of Revolution: Modernization, Development and US Foreign Policy from the Cold War to the Present* (Ithaca, NY: Cornell University Press, 2010); Gilbert Rist, *The History of Development: From Western Origins to Global Faith* (London, UK: Zed Books, 2002); Corinna Unger, *International Development: A Postwar History* (London, UK: Bloomsbury, 2018); Sara Lorenzini, *Global Development: A Cold War History* (Princeton, NJ: Princeton University Press, 2019).
11 United Nations, Preamble to the UN Charter, signed 26 June 1945, at www.un.org/en/sections/un-charter/preamble/index.html, accessed 1 April 2020.
12 For a discussion of Point Four, see David Ekbladh, *The Great American Mission: Modernization and the Construction of an American World Order* (Princeton, NJ: Princeton University Press, 2011), pp. 77–113.
13 Daniel Oakman, *Facing Asia: A History of the Colombo Plan* (Canberra, Australia: Pandanus Books, 2004).
14 David Webster, 'Development Advisors in a Time of Cold War and Decolonization: The United Nations Technical Assistance Administration, 1950–1959', *Journal of Global History* (2011), 6, pp. 249–72.
15 Speech delivered by Dr R. H. Tirtawinata to the Volunteer Graduate Scheme Conference, Melbourne University, 23 August 1956, NLA: MS 2601, Box 2, Folder 21.
16 W. T. Doig to John Bayly, 29 December 1950, NLA: MS 2601, Box 2, Folder 9.
17 Don Anderson to A. Watt, 2 August 1952, NLA: MS 2601, Box 2, Folder 9.
18 'The Scheme for Graduate Employment in Indonesia'.
19 Jim Webb to F. G. East, 15 September 1955, NLA: MS 2601, Box 1, Folder 8.
20 Tamson Pietsch, 'Many Rhodes: Travelling Scholarships and Imperial Citizenship in the British Academic World, 1880–1940', *History of Education* (2011), 40 (6), pp. 723–39; Sam Lebovic, 'From War Junk to Educational Exchange: The World War II Origins of the Fulbright Program and the Foundations of American Cultural Globalism, 1945–1950', *Diplomatic History* (2013), 37 (2), pp. 280–312; Alice Garner and Diane Kirkby, *Academic Ambassadors, Pacific Allies: Australia, America and the Fulbright Program* (Manchester, UK: Manchester University Press, 2019).
21 David Walker and Agnieszka Sobocinska, 'Introduction', in David Walker and Agnieszka Sobocinska (eds), *Australia's Asia: From Yellow Peril to Asian Century* (Crawley, Australia: UWA Publishing, 2012), pp. 1–23.

22 Jim Webb, 'Why Not Work in Indonesia?', undated article draft, NLA: MS 2601, Box 13, Folder 133.
23 Jim Webb to John Thompson, Administering Secretary, Coordinating Secretariat of National Unions of Students, Leiden, Netherlands, 28 September 1954, NLA MS 2601, Box 2, Folder 19.
24 Pamphlet, 'Voluntary Service Overseas', current May 1960, TNA: CO 859/1445.
25 For example, see 'A Year in the Commonwealth for Young Volunteers', *The Times* (London), 1 December 1959, p. 4; 'Schoolboy Recruits for Central Africa: Improving Race Relations', *Guardian* (Manchester), 4 April 1959, p. 3; 'Wanted: 1600 Youngsters to Help Overseas', *Daily Mail* (London), 27 May 1965, p. 15; 'How the Young Ones Can Help Abroad', *Daily Mail* (London), 10 December 1964, p. 11.
26 Mora Dickson, *A Season in Sarawak* (London, UK: Dennis Dobson, 1962), p. 192.
27 'Confidential: Copy of a Letter from Lord Amory Dated 16 June, 1964 Addressed to Sir Andrew Cohen about the Future of the Cadet Programme', VSO Archives, Box 31.
28 'Schoolboy Recruits'.
29 Budget figures from Peace Corps, *1st Annual Peace Corps Report* (Washington, DC: Peace Corps, 1962), p. 64; 'Voluntary Service Overseas: Actual Income and Expenditure 1961/62', TNA: OD 10/4; Herb Feith to Ken Thomas, 6 February 1954, NLA: MS 2601, Box 2, Folder 13.
30 Peace Corps, *1st Annual Peace Corps Report*, p. 5.
31 David Engerman, *The Price of Aid: The Economic Cold War in India* (Cambridge, MA: Harvard University Press, 2018); Latham, *The Right Kind of Revolution*.
32 'Editorial: The Moral Equivalent', *New York Times*, 5 March 1961, p. E10.
33 George Gallup, 'American "Peace Corps" Proposal Wins Broad Approval from Public', *Washington Post*, 1 February 1961, p. A2.
34 'President's Message to Congress on the Peace Corps', *New York Times*, 2 March 1961, p. 13.
35 Willard L. Rodgers and Arland Thornton, 'Changing Patterns of First Marriage in the United States', *Demography* (1985), 22 (2), pp. 265–79; Betsey Stevenson and Justin Wolfers, 'Marriage and Divorce: Changes and Their Driving Forces', *Journal of Economic Perspectives* (2007), 21 (2), p. 31.
36 Diary 1961–2, Papers of Elinor V. Capehart, John F. Kennedy Presidential Library (hereafter JFK): RPCV, Box 102.
37 'The Peace Corps and the College Senior', Report to the Peace Corps presented by Young and Rubicam, New York, 1965, cited in Charles C. Jones, 'The Peace Corps: An Analysis of the Development, Problems, Preliminary Evaluation, and Future' (PhD dissertation, West Virginia University, 1967), p. 86.
38 Jim Webb to John Thompson, 28 September 1954, NLA: MS 2601, Box 2, Folder 19.
39 Dick Bird, *Never the Same Again: A History of VSO* (Cambridge, UK: Lutterworth Press, 1998), p. 201.

40 Minutes of VSO Executive Committee meeting, 5 October 1971, VSO Records, Box 31.
41 Peace Corps, *1st Annual Peace Corps Report*, p. 10.
42 George Nash and Patricia Nash, 'From Which Colleges Come the Peace Corps Volunteers?', Columbia University Bureau of Applied Social Research, JFK: RG 490, Series 1, Box 2.
43 See Lydon, *Imperial Emotions*.
44 Application questionnaire – Judith Anne Gregory, NLA: MS 2601, Box 1, Folder 8.
45 Application questionnaire – David Terence Marchesi, NLA: MS 2601, Box 1, Folder 8.
46 Lois Griffiths to Committee for Graduate Employment, NUAUS, 23 July 1954, NLA: MS 2601, Box 1, Folder 5.
47 Application questionnaire – Janice Mary McPhee, NLA: MS 2601, Box 1, Folder 5.
48 Application questionnaire – Kenneth John Tucker, NLA: MS 2601, Box 1, Folder 5.
49 Application questionnaire – Thomas George Errey, NLA: MS 2601, Box 6, Folder 62.
50 David Walker, *Anxious Nation: Australia and the Rise of Asia, 1850–1939* (St Lucia, Australia: University of Queensland Press, 1999)
51 Agnieszka Sobocinska, 'Measuring or Creating Attitudes? Seventy Years of Australian Public Opinion Polling about Indonesia', *Asian Studies Review* (2017), 41 (2), pp. 371–88. See also Prue Torney-Parlicki, *Somewhere in Asia: War, Journalism and Australia's Neighbours, 1941–75* (Sydney, Australia: University of New South Wales Press, 2000); Ross Tapsell, *By-Lines, Balibo, Bali Bombings: Australian Journalists in Indonesia* (Melbourne, Australia: Australian Scholarly Publishing, 2014); Simon Philpott, 'Fear of the Dark: Indonesia and the Australian National Imagination', *Australian Journal of International Affairs* (2001), 55 (3), pp. 371–88.
52 Lois Griffiths application letter, 1 August 1954, NLA: MS 2601, Box 3, Folder 26.
53 Application questionnaire – Hugh Francis Owen, NLA: MS 2601, Box 3, Folder 26.
54 Barnett, *Empire of Humanity*; Ian Tyrrell, *Reforming the World: The Creation of America's Moral Empire* (Princeton, NJ: Princeton University Press, 2010).
55 Susan Sontag, *Regarding the Pain of Others* (London, UK: Penguin, 2004); Lillie Chouliaraki, *The Spectatorship of Suffering* (London, UK: SAGE, 2006).
56 David Engerman, 'The Romance of Economic Development and New Histories of the Cold War', *Diplomatic History* (2004), 28 (1), p. 29.
57 'ASCM Volunteers for Graduate Employment in Indonesia, Jan '52', NLA: MS 2601, Box 1, Folder 5.
58 'Interesteds, 1954 SCM Conference', NLA: MS 2601, Box 6, Folder 62.
59 Application questionnaire – John Graham Francis, NLA: MS 2601, Box 1, Folder 5; Fay Bannister to Jim Webb, 8 March 1959, NLA: MS 2601, Box 1, Folder 4.

60 Application questionnaire – Peter John Graham, NLA: MS 2601, Box 1, Folder 8.
61 Eleanor Johnson to Jim Webb, 26 August 1954, NLA: MS 2601, Box 2, Folder 13.
62 David Hilliard, 'God in the Suburbs: The Religious Culture of Australian Cities in the 1950s', *Australian Historical Studies* (1991), 24 (97), pp. 399–419; David Hilliard, 'Church, Family and Sexuality in Australia in the 1950s', *Australian Historical Studies* (1997), 27 (109), pp. 133–46.
63 B. J. Richards to Miss Evans, 5 November 1953, NLA: MS 2601, Box 2, Folder 15.
64 Herb Feith to B. J. Richards, 18 November 1953, NLA: MS 2601, Box 2, Folder 15.
65 Peter Shedding to Jim Webb, 19 October 1959, NLA: MS 2601, Box 3, Folder 26.
66 Don Anderson to Peter Shedding, 29 October 1959, NLA: MS 2601, Box 3, Folder 26.
67 Renate Howe, *A Century of Influence: The Australian Student Christian Movement 1896–1996* (Sydney, Australia: University of New South Wales Press, 2009); Renate Howe, 'The Australian Student Christian Movement and Women's Activism in the Asia–Pacific Region, 1890s–1920s', *Australian Feminist Studies* (2001), 16 (36), pp. 311–23; Meredith Lake, 'Faith in Crisis: Christian University Students in Peace and War', *Australian Journal of Politics and History* (2010), 56 (3), pp. 441–54.
68 Ian Spalding to Betty Evans, 1 October 1953, NLA: MS 2601, Box 2, Folder 15.
69 Application questionnaire – Michael Charles Bradley, NLA: MS 2601, Box 2, Folder 13.
70 Application questionnaire – Jillian Claire Vial, NLA: MS 2601, Box 3, Folder 26.
71 Herb Feith to Dr Darmasetiawan, 16 November 1951, NLA: MS 2601, Box 6, Folder 55.
72 Suzanne N. Gordon and Nancy K. Sizer, *Why People Join the Peace Corps* (Washington, DC: Institute for International Services, 1963).
73 'Service Overseas by Volunteers – Weekend Conference at Farnham Castle, 22–24 February 1963', Lockwood Committee Minutes, 1962–1969, London School of Economics Women's Library: Returned Volunteers Abroad Records, Box 40.

12

Humanitarian activism during the Vietnam War: The case of Rosemary Taylor, Elaine Moir and Margaret Moses

Joy Damousi

In May 1972 five Vietnamese orphans were smuggled out of the war raging in Vietnam by the Australian humanitarian worker Elaine Moir. Moir, who worked in Vietnamese orphanages, took the children without the necessary landing permits or visas to enter Australia, said she 'got tired of begging the Australian authorities to let the children in so I went over and brought them myself'. The children had been given South Vietnam exit permits and Australians had arranged to adopt them, but there were bureaucratic delays in allowing the children to land in Australia. Moir said she was 'disgusted' with the attitude of federal and state governments in trying to stop children coming into Australia.[1] Moir's companion in Vietnam, the irrepressible Rosemary Taylor, a staunch advocate of inter-country adoption, justified these unlawful acts as a legitimate response to what she believed to be the Australian Government's inertia at the fate of children dying in the war. In a letter to the Labor Minister for Defence and Deputy Prime Minister, Lance Barnard (who had himself adopted two Vietnamese children), Taylor declared that the 'apathy of Australians and the Australian gov[ernmen]t to this issue of these orphan children is deplorable'. She continued, 'Never have I been so totally ashamed of my own country. I am not hysterical over this ... I am too ashamed'.[2] In an interview published in the *Australian Women's Weekly*, Moir said in defence of her illegal actions: 'I didn't want to embarrass the Australian government. I didn't consider I was breaking the law. I am a law-abiding person but I had no alternative. I wanted to get the children to Australia, to be able to say, "Here they are, do something!"'[3]

While supporters of inter-country adoption hailed Moir's act as heroic and visionary, her detractors deplored it. The *Australian* was quick to condemn smuggling children into Australia. 'Orphans of war', it editorialised, 'are tragedies which break everyone's hearts', but adoption was not the solution. Not only would this create a 'lottery', where only a few children 'would be saved', but also there is something 'unhappily reminiscent of nineteenth century paternalism about the suggestion that we should intervene, like lofty white gods practicing a patronising philanthropy, to snatch away a lucky few to be shown the good life in Western affluence'.[4] In Australia, this practice was formal policy, creating the long and devastating history of Indigenous children stolen from their families.[5] The rightful place to care for Vietnamese orphans, insisted the *Australian*, was in Vietnam: 'If all the money, effort, care and attention which it is suggested be spent on maintaining Vietnamese orphans in Australia were devoted to work in Vietnam, hope could be brought to hundreds instead of fortune to a few'.[6] Others believed Moir's act set a disturbing precedent. One H. T. McCrea, not persuaded by the sentimentality promoted by the press, wrote to the Department of Immigration: 'As a thinking person, I am disgusted and shocked at the irresponsible action of Mrs Moir, her defiance of Government authority and the Laws, in smuggling the five orphans, as she has done'. It would set a precedent: 'If this women [sic] gets away with this, the situation immediately arises where there is a law for those who adhere to law and order, and another law for those who defy. In other words she has made a mockery of the immigration laws of this country'.[7]

Rosemary Taylor (1938–2019), Elaine Moir (1937–2012) and their companion Margaret Moses (1940–75) became synonymous with the humanitarian operations involved in aiding war orphans during the Vietnam War. Much of the literature on Taylor, Moir and Moses has been framed through the history of inter-country adoption policy in Australia, charting the central importance of the Vietnam War in the evolution of that policy at both a Commonwealth and state level.[8] My focus here is a departure from this approach and instead explores the particular style of their humanitarian work and how this connected to the emergence of their advocacy and activism as humanitarians.

By examining the everyday activities of Taylor, Moir and Moses, I develop a threefold argument. First, their practice on the ground suggests that they operated in a way in which they worked largely as free agents, taking decisions and actions outside of any governing organisation. At different times they operated on their own, driving various activities, some illegal and others semi-legal, in wartime conditions. As a result, their day-to-day humanitarian work was consistently dangerous, chaotic, exhausting and ad hoc. By exploring this aspect of the activities of these three key actors, this chapter seeks to offer a distinctive contribution to histories of humanitarianism in the postwar period. Throughout the twentieth century, humanitarian activists have invariably been a part of a group or institution that has framed their actions and defined their objectives and practices, especially when dealing with refugee children in war. Before 1945, humanitarians worked within organisations such as the Save the Children Fund, the Foster Parents Plan (PLAN), the League of Nations, Near East Relief, and the International Social Service (ISS). Many of these organisations continued after 1945, but new ones also emerged, including the United Nations International Children's Emergency Fund (UNICEF), World Vision and the Oxford Committee for Famine Relief (Oxfam), which were especially active during the era of decolonisation and development. After World War II others, such as Holt International and various other agencies, also focused on the adoption of war orphans. Not all humanitarians, however, conducted their work under the directives of organisational structures. Others did so loosely, but also took matters into their own hands. Such humanitarians have drawn less attention from scholars but are worthy of study, as they can shed on the diversity of humanitarian work and cast a light on lesser-known activists, who are invariably women written out of the historical record or, in the case of the three activists I discuss in this chapter, not included in studies on humanitarianism.[9]

Second, I argue that this humanitarian practice allowed Taylor, Moir and Moses to take on a distinctive advocacy role for inter-country adoption of refugee children. Humanitarians such as these three women were outspoken, direct, interventionist, strident and blunt in their promotion of child adoption, which gained them extraordinary publicity and attention as they actively lobbied governments to influence public policy.[10] In doing so, they turned the humanitarian role into one of activism – a luxury not always afforded to other humanitarians who were compelled to abide by organisational rules and protocols, typically worked with governments to administer aid and relief and were invariably part of a wider web of bureaucracy, transparency and accountability. It is important to note that the international organisations that were active at this time in Australia in providing support for Vietnamese children – UNICEF, PLAN and ISS – did not support or promote inter-country adoption, and ISS actively opposed it. UNICEF undertook to provide supplies and provisions in aid, while PLAN promoted a child sponsorship programme. Moir and her two associates fiercely disagreed with ISS, which had a longstanding opposition to the adoption of children, beginning with the Korean War (1950–53).[11] While other groups began to emerge within Australia to lobby governments – largely comprising parents who wished to adopt – Taylor alone was pushing this line as a humanitarian within Vietnam.

Finally, this chapter intentionally moves outside of the debate between the relationship between humanitarianism and the reinvention of human rights which tends to dominate and define much of the scholarship of this period.[12] Studies of humanitarian activists in practice point to a more fluid, evolving and dynamic form of what could be termed a form of humanitarian activism, which was shaped on the ground, *in situ* and in action, and was less shaped by human rights declarations and other decrees. These humanitarian activists were proud to say that their actions spoke louder than words.

Rosemary Taylor, Elaine Moir and Margaret Moses

The Vietnam War (1955–75) provided a pivotal moment in the history of inter-country adoption. Australia's involvement in the Vietnam War began in 1962, when Australia sent military advisers as a part of the US effort to support the anti-communist regime in South Vietnam. The Liberal government led by Prime Minister Robert Menzies expanded its commitment by introducing military conscription in 1964 through the National Service Act and in 1965 deployed the first Australian troops. As a staunch ally of the United States and its foreign policy, Australia remained involved in the conflict until April 1975, when the war ended. By then, 3,000 Australians had been wounded; 521 had died; and more than 60,000 personnel had been sent to the war.[13]

The war created a large number of displaced and homeless children. The ISS estimated that there were 10,000 homeless children in sixty-three orphanages in South Vietnam in 1965. By 1973 the number of orphanages and orphans had almost doubled. Decades of war had made it increasingly difficult for orphaned children to be taken into families within villages, and the establishment of orphanages, funded by churches, US military and relief organisations, was seen to be the solution.[14] Australia's military entry into the war coincided in 1965 with the first legislation passed in Australia through which the state became the provider of adoption services and private operators required licences. Previously, adoptions had been undertaken through private agreements and negotiations.[15] Further, local adoption agencies in Australia in the 1960s and 1970s were ambivalent about inter-country adoption, even antagonistic towards it.[16]

Rosemary Taylor was one of the most high-profile Australian humanitarians at this time. Born in Adelaide in 1938, Taylor completed a Bachelor of Arts degree at the University of Adelaide, taught in Sydney and then travelled to the United Kingdom. Taylor had been a Catholic nun and a Sister of Mercy for five years, leaving the order in pursuit of a closed and more 'contemplative' order. She was accepted by a Carmelite order in Wales but by then had decided she 'could still live in a human way out in the world'. One such activity was to engage in missionary activities in 1962 among Indigenous peoples in Alaska. Working without a visa, she was soon expelled, but then returned once she successfully obtained one. When the visa ran out, she then returned to Adelaide. While she was waiting for a permanent visa, she answered an advertisement for volunteers to travel to Vietnam. She left in February 1967 to work in a refugee camp as an educational social worker for the Australian Council of Churches. She set herself up as 'a sort of one-woman task force', which, it could be said, precisely described her modus operandi. Soon she was acting as an informal liaison officer for arranging inter-country adoption with children in orphanages across Vietnam.[17] Her name became synonymous with the children she rescued. The Melbourne *Herald* called them 'Rosemary's babies'.[18] Taylor's efforts in Vietnam with child refugees and orphanages became a media sensation.

After two months Taylor decided to become an independent volunteer, because of what she believed were incompetent bureaucracies. She went to Phu My, an orphanage and a hospital near Saigon, and worked there until the end of 1967, when a Swiss nurse asked that she take over and organise overseas adoptions of war orphans for the Swiss organisation Terre des Hommes. Terre Des Hommes had been founded in Switzerland in 1960 by the journalist Edmund Kaiser to assist children in the wars of Vietnam and Algeria.[19] It was the only international organisation at the time that was involved in inter-country adoption in any substantial way. Taylor began collecting and caring for babies who were to be adopted abroad and she began to work on her own. Eventually, her work had to be formalised. In 1973 she became the director of the United States-based Friends of Children of Vietnam, but this association was short-lived. When Taylor and others raised concerns about adoptive practices within the group, an arm of it was formed called Friends for All Children, which Taylor controlled.[20] Between 1968 and 1972, she had arranged more than 1,132 adoptions across the world.[21] Taylor was airlifted out of Saigon two days after the tragic plane crash of the Operation Babylift US Galaxy flight in April 1975, in which, of more than 300 Vietnamese children and a number of volunteers on board, 153 were killed, including 76 children.[22] Subsequently, she travelled for two years overseeing the dispersal of children throughout the world. After that she took time away, studying philosophy and theology.[23]

Like Taylor, Elaine Moir became a champion of the movement for inter-country adoptions. Born in 1937, Moir was raised in Mount Barker in Western Australia. Her parents both died when she was young. Her father was killed on the Burma Railway and her mother when she was aged six. Raised by her grandparents, she married at nineteen and had two children. During the 1960s, she worked in Saigon as a photo-journalist and came into contact with children in orphanages, many of whom were fathered by US and Australian soldiers. She became relentless in the pursuit of saving Vietnamese child refugees.[24]

Perhaps the least known of three is Margaret Moses, whose name is most commonly associated with her tragic death. Moses joined Taylor in March 1971 when Taylor was running Friends for All Children (FFAC). Born in Launceston in 1940, she moved to Adelaide when her parents separated. She entered the Convent of Mercy in 1957 and professed in January 1960. She graduated from the University of Adelaide in 1963 and became a schoolteacher, but left the order in 1968. Thereafter she worked in the South

Australian Department of Education, but soon resigned. In April 1975, as communist forces were descending into Saigon, Taylor and her co-workers were evacuating children. Taylor and Moses switched places at the last minute on the fateful Galaxy flight in April 1975 and Moses perished when it crashed.[25]

Not only were these three women not aligned organisationally, but they were also not politically motivated: they were driven and absorbed by the emotional agenda of rescuing imperilled children in war. When the Labor Government of Prime Minister Gough Whitlam – a government committed to ending Australia's involvement in the Vietnam War – was elected in December 1972, Taylor seemed oblivious to the political implications of the election of this government. Three days after Whitlam was elected, she wrote to Moir with striking indifference: 'I suppose you are delighted with our change of government. I don't know enough about it to express any opinion at all'.[26] By adopting a humanitarian calling, the three women had no alignments and were prepared to lobby politicians on both sides of politics to promote their cause. In what follows I examine their humanitarianism in practice and then consider how this shaped an activist platform.

'Thief in the night': humanitarian work in war

In March 1975, in an extensive article in *Catholic Worker*, Taylor outlined the work she had undertaken in Vietnam. She described how she singlehandedly and independently rescued babies from war-torn areas and the dangers she faced as she laboured to do so. Under these conditions, the most humane solution, she believed, was evacuating children, placing them in orphanages and adopting them into Western families. She described how she would collect children in the orphanages from the provinces after bombing raids. Military and US officials assisted her in travel and provisions by allowing her to hitch rides with army trucks or whoever she could travel with in the regions.[27] In August 1968 Taylor described how she travelled across the country when she made extensive trips to the provinces. 'I hop from plane to plane depending on what's available: Caribou [small aircraft], helicopters, Beachcraft [sic] [light single-engine aircraft]'.[28]

Driven by her passionate conviction of the need to remove children from orphanages, Taylor's humanitarian work was frenetic, ad hoc and arbitrary. She worked independently and, in her steadfast commitment to save children, she believed that she was answerable to no one. Moses noted that this work demanded an approach where 'the moral responsibility of this or that or … the bureaucratic hassles of the local environment'[29] had to be at times suspended in the case of the former and bypassed in the latter.

The pragmatism required meant that 'The whole operation has an element of the thief in the night'.[30] This was a very apt description of their work. Taylor described how, following the Tet Offensive in 1968, movement in Saigon had become very limited. Courting danger was a part of their work – barbed wire and heavily armed guards lined the streets, and police headquarters where Taylor needed to go to secure passports for the children were guarded. 'Getting past the guards and barbed wire was a daily test of patience and ingenuity'.[31] The work also entailed a roller coaster of emotions. In December 1973 Taylor wrote that 'Our life is a kaleidoscope of emergency situations, new personnel, new nurseries, more children, sickness, epidemics, death and rising cost of living; new perspectives to old struggles; deluges and moments of sunshine. Today's statement will be an understatement tomorrow'.[32]

The sense of urgency and immediacy meant that Taylor worked at an accelerated pace. She was always snatching time: 'I am scribbling this while waiting for a passport in the U.S. Embassy', she wrote to Moir in October 1972.[33] Notes were written in haste and decisions were made on the run. 'Excuse this rambling', she noted in January 1973, 'in between I am feeding babies – resting a book on my knees to write – I am sort of trying to work out the situation as I go'.[34] She apologised that her letters were a 'mess', but they were written surrounded by children: 'I have 1 kgm babies I am watching here with me – one on a bed and one in a rocking chair'.[35]

Administrative logistics were challenging for most of the organisations Taylor interacted with in Vietnam, and, like Taylor, they were frustrated by local obstacles to their work. In February 1972 Taylor indicated she wanted to take a step away from one orphanage, Go Vap, because of the pressure and intensity of arranging adoptions, and the level of frustrations: 'I have been to the limits of frustration with this orphanage, and have decided some years ago that the time wasted at Go Vap can be more profitably spent elsewhere'. She was working under 'great pressure' and didn't have time for 'extraordinary deviations'. But Taylor expressed her deepest frustrations and irritations with the Australian government authorities. When Moir declared she was determined to take on the authorities Taylor replied with indignation and stated that she simply could not work with them:

> I certainly wish you luck in your fight against the ignorance and narrow-mindedness of the Australian authorities. From your point of view it may be worth the effort, but from mine it certainly is not worth the effort. I would prefer to send children to countries with a trace of understanding, and there are more than enough requests from these countries ... Sorry if that sounds unpatriotic but I prefer to speak my mind clearly on this point, so there will be no misunderstanding.[36]

Taking this responsibility on herself meant adopting a frenetic pace. Passports, entry visas and translation of adoption papers had to be arranged.[37] Applications for passports had to be made through the local authorities, which created problems for her: 'I dare not "walk it through" myself as they hate-my-guts to use a vulgar but appropriate expression. Moreover, Australian cases will be a very sore point with them now', following Moir's smuggling of the children in 1972.[38]

There was also tension with government embassies. In February 1973 Taylor was told she could stay in Vietnam only if she registered as a charity. The support from the Australian Embassy was minimal ('Really not an iota of interest from them'), but the United States was a greater support to her.[39] The Australian Government did not authorise her work. The strain of the relationship between Taylor and the Australian authorities rendered their relationship non-existent. She wrote in March 1973 that 'I myself have little to do with the [Australian] Embassy now. The U.S. have almost persuaded me to [change] my citizenship ... I even have been granted officially the status of SOCIAL WORKER ... I'm not sure if I get a university diploma out of it but at least I have a letter from the State Welfare dept. saying that my university credits and my experience would qualify me for the title of "social worker". (First time I've ever been anything!)'[40]

The negotiations with various embassies to arrange passports, visas and related paperwork could all become frustrating: 'During all this we are enduring a lot of "Bullshit" to use the vulgar american [sic] expression. We still don't quite know where we stand, but we are all pretty exhausted by the strain of it all'.[41] She thought the assistance given by Australia was never enough, and she said she felt 'very very disgusted' with the aid not given by the Australian Embassy, 'despite all the promises in Australia'. 'We are thoroughly disillusioned, and were it for the Australians, we would not be here at all. Their support amounted to NIL'.[42] There was also a personal, emotional dimension to her response. Describing the challenges of bureaucracy, she wrote to Moir:

> to save this poor child from a life of hell, just upsets me so much that I become unable to operate at all. I just have to recognise my own limitations. I think you know my feelings on the subject well enough by now. We are extremely grateful for your enormous efforts to aid the orphans, and for the material help we have been receiving from Australia, but here we just don't have the interest of the embassy which would be necessary to undertake adoptions on any scale, and we just can't afford the time to argue or fight with them.[43]

She continued to despair at the indifference of the Australian Embassy and the Australian authorities. The problem, Taylor believed, was that there was no international aid agency in Australia – other than the ISS, which did not support adoptions. While Taylor was involved in a number of organisations outside of Australia, Australia itself seemed to be disengaged.[44]

Taylor's strained relations with Australia also affected relations with wider aid organisations. The worldwide UNICEF fundraising campaign of 1973 brought out her frustrations about aid. She described how she had a visit from a reporter from the Melbourne newspaper, the *Herald* or *Sun* ('I forget which'), that was sponsoring the UNICEF appeal. Although she had 'nothing against UNICEF specifically', Taylor was in no mood to meet with them, as in her view the type of aid they provided was being wasted and didn't go where it should. Initially she was ready to immediately send the visiting reporter out, and 'then relented and offered him a cup of coffee as a friendly gesture between country men, and as a proof we had nothing against him personally'.[45] This friendly gesture was not, however, extended to the UNICEF appeal itself:

> But we would answer no questions. We said that we had nothing to do with UNICEF, and if he wanted honest stories he ought to go to the orphanages which might benefit from the UNICEF appeal. Moreover, I didn't feel like sponsoring any sort of official appeal at this moment, because we are just too aware of the VAST amount of foreign aid that is going into the pockets of the administrators up here.[46]

For Taylor, it was a matter of the dreadful waste of aid: 'It is a hideous state of affairs' as 'the money isn't getting anywhere near where it is needed'.[47]

The lack of food supplies and technical assistance became a central preoccupation for people working in the orphanages. Taylor relied on providing these supplies themselves. Moses asked Moir to supply milk and Lactogen (dried infant powder), as well as towelling shirts, hand towels and bath towels.[48] Taylor thanked Moir for her willingness to provide such supplies. Medical supplies, such as ventilators, were vital. Taylor wrote: 'we are tremendously relieved and excited by the prospect of a respiration monitor'. It came as a 'great relief' that she was purchasing one. 'This is precisely what we need ... as we have to hover over the babies watching respiration ... and everytime the baby stops breathing we have to give emergency treatment. This happens often'.[49] On material donations, Taylor requested shirts made of towelling as it is 'beautifully absorbent, and doesn't need ironing'. There were further requests as the weather became cooler: 'We like bunny-suits for the babies at night, but we would also like some flannelette nightdresses, where are sewn up at the bottom to form bags, and which zip up at the front. Since our older babies aren't wrapped up in blankets at night, we have to have them in something warm and these bags would be excellent'.[50]

Taylor thanked Moir for the materials she had sent: Farex (baby food), woollens and blankets, a respiration monitor, shirts, bulk milk and Lactogen.

The intensity of the work continued, as she reported she was 'keeping watch with 3 babies just now – are very ill – having oxygen – and 2 other tiny babies – well enough but needing constant supervision. I haven't got my wits enough to speak about anything else at the moment – just wanted to let you know that these packages have arrived'.[51]

Medical emergencies were constant and relentless. In November 1971 Moses described the medical routine in assisting war orphans: 'Not much news – and not much time to tell it. October has been a dreary month – TB, meningitis, pneumonia and the usual concomitants'.[52] At Go Vap, Taylor wrote that babies were just replaced with others when they died. 'We have to forget about the dead, and concentrate on the living'. She was aware how misguided that was in terms of understanding particular experiences: 'It is illogical I know NOT to be able to investigate further the reason for a death, and so prevent other deaths, but it is practically impossible'.[53]

Beyond the medical challenges, the adoptions themselves were complicated to organise, demanding immediate responses and urgent judgements, and causing a high level of frustration. In the case of one boy for whom Taylor was seeking support for adoption, time was of the essence: 'I tried to telephone you, but only have your house number, and couldn't get through. We cannot make calls to Australia at night, only during the day', and stressed 'so please send me a number where I can reach you, during the day. I feel as frustrated as hell over this case'.[54] Trying to fulfil requirements also created endless frustrations – in this case, the age of the boy was an issue and the need for a Catholic family to adopt him:

> I feel lousy about the whole thing. The seven year old boy at Phu My could certainly pass for 5 anywhere else, but as he already had a birth judgement made a short time ago, Sr Rose at Phu My is not keen on changing his name and age ... The frustrating bit is that I probably made up the age in the first place. Would seven be too old? You know from experience here that seven would be equivalent to about 5 in Australia.[55]

The power play of various agencies and organisations in any adoption was omnipresent: 'As for my position', Taylor noted, 'it gets more complex'. Negotiating the various government agencies was a delicate process:

> We are just in the middle of a sort of power struggle between the US Embassy and USAID. We have the Embassy right behind us. We have the Ambassador and the consul making decisions and telling us that it is O.K. and we have NOTHING to worry about ... that everything has been fixed up at the 'highest level' but we cannot seem to get the simple bit of paper that we need to present to the littlest man at the lowest level, who is actually in charge of putting his little paper clip in the dossier. It is just too extraordinary for words. We shall win through though.[56]

While this determination and resilience contributed to their success, it came at a serious personal cost. The repercussion of undertaking humanitarian work in this way resulted in severe emotional and psychological stress. The exhaustion that Taylor, Moses and Moir all expressed was a feature of the type of humanitarian work they undertook. It was almost sacrificial in nature and resonated with religious overtones, which was not surprising given the religious careers of Taylor and Moses.

Moses observed that, if they were to ever become an organisation, the motto would be '*Illegitimis nil carborundum*', which translates as 'Don't let the bastards get you down'.[57] This may have been a casual remark, but clearly the pace, pressure and strain of their work created exhaustion and stress. In April 1972 Moses noted that the 'only way you can get any work done is to refrain from luxuries like eating and sleeping'.[58] In August 1972, four months after this letter from Moses, Taylor wrote to Moir warning her not to contact Moses, who had arrived in Melbourne from Saigon:

> Margaret is home in Australia now ... but I want to warn you not to contact her. She needs a complete rest from Saigon affairs. I think it would be wisest not to phone her for any reason, or to discuss Saigon business with her. She was close to a breakdown on leaving Saigon, and I want her to have a good rest before she comes back. She is not home on business, but just to see her family and have a rest. It will defeat the purpose of her visit home if she has Saigon affairs on her mind.[59]

This continued in the following year. Writing in January 1973, Taylor described Moses's emotional and psychological condition: 'Marg is not too good – but she is going to France tomorrow – we have some business there so this will be an excuse – and I think the idea of the trip has boosted her morale a bit. She was in a bad state of depression for some time. She can't possibly pull out of it by staying around here. She will profit by escorting the group of children to Paris tomorrow'.[60]

Taylor was to later describe Moses's work and the breadth of her activities in detail. It was no wonder she needed time away, as hers had become an oppressive burden:

> Margaret knew the plumbers and the politicians, the military police and the milk distributors. She could lay her hands on surplus food and office equipment or command a plane, helicopter or a fleet of jeeps, and knew whom to phone for a fork-lift or a ten ton truck. Margaret was interpreter for the English speaking nurses and the French doctors, and knew the mortality rates of the Saigon hospitals.[61]

Her knowledge of individuals, processes and practices was equally breathtaking and all-encompassing:

Marg would be on a first name basis with possible allies before the rest of us were aware of their existence, and could sort out the hypocrites with a discriminating glance. She could be diplomatic, charming, and devastatingly articulate. She had the patience to suffer fools gladly but was never deceived by them. She scrounged vaccines and knew her way around all the courts and ministries. Margaret could calculate the electricity capacity of each nursery, then adjust it for new equipment. She devised new methods of clothes drying, rat control, sewage disposal, and the maintaining of hygiene. She could write lucid proposals or trenchant indictments. She kept vigil with dying babies and suffered in burying them.[62]

Taylor described Margaret Moses as offering 'personally the greatest support. Her friendship and loyalty sustained me through many morale shattering events'.[63] The fragility and tenuousness of humanitarian work was a feature of this practice on the ground. All of these challenges led her to exhaustion. 'All for now', she ended one letter, then, 'I am dead excuse this awful typing. I'm too tired ... to change the typewriter ribbon, and I keep typing errors in a freudian [sic] way'.[64] Moses captured this strain in her reflections on the uncertainties of what the end of the war would bring, after the various ceasefires during 1973: 'With peace looming nighmariashly [sic] on the horizon we don't know what to expect. Anyway, we'll soon know. Maybe. This is getting a bit like the boy who cried wolf'.[65] Tragically, Moses never did see the end of the war and what the world would look like after 1975.

This mode of operating which involved largely an individualised form of humanitarian work allowed for Taylor and Moir to play an advocacy role in promoting adoption as a humanitarian solution.

Contesting humanitarianism: advocacy and activism and their limits

Inter-country adoption was a hotly contested humanitarian issue in Australia during the 1970s. The debate was sharply divided between those who believed it was a humanitarian act to provide abandoned children in war with what was perceived as an opportunity to find a new home and family. Those who were opposed to the idea, largely social workers, argued that inter-country adoption was akin to theft and child abduction, as it was unclear how many children were genuine orphans, and that this act imposed a Western imperialist view, as it was underpinned by a belief in the superiority of Western family and culture, and children would lose connection with their heritage and language. The novelist, journalist and historian, Marina Warner encapsulated this view in an article in the *Spectator* in which she noted that, while adoption provided 'flight to ... affluent and tranquil worlds', it was a 'complete break' with 'country, language, race and heritage'. Warner concluded that sponsorship and other programmes should be supported so that children would not become institutionalised.[66]

As mentioned, many of the humanitarian aid agencies were also opposed to this adoption programme. The ISS in particular clashed with Moir and Taylor. The ISS was of the view that international adoptions and foster-parent schemes had limited the possibilities of local solutions and programmes and had, in fact, led to further abandonment of children. In the context of the Vietnam War, ISS believed it was often unclear if children were orphaned or abandoned at all, and claimed it was more productive to support efforts locally rather than pursue adoption.[67] The ISS became involved in Vietnam in 1966. The ISS also argued that inter-country adoption by proxy, through which children could be adopted in absentia, was contrary to the principle that the welfare of the child was paramount, and such programmes were to be fiercely resisted. In 1965 the director of Australia ISS, Margaret Kelso, wrote that she understood that people 'would feel emotionally roused to help children who have been the victims of political upheaval and war; that they should want to do so quickly, and that they should think the answer is to offer the children the good conditions of life enjoyed by themselves and their own children',[68] but this ignored the fact that the children would sever links with their culture and heritage, apart from the possibility of children being claimed by their birth parents later on. By 1972 these convictions had become even more resolute. Phoebe Leatherland, ISS Director at this time, stressed that it was better to try to encourage the strengthening of Vietnamese family ties; prevent abandonment; and make it possible for relatives to care for children.[69]

The limits of such a short-sighted programme were also an issue, for while these activities might have assisted the few, it was no solution for supporting the majority of children, who needed assistance over the long term.[70] The form of humanitarian activism promoted by Taylor and Moir saw the answer in the immediate and urgent circumstance of war, acting without the constraints of organisational structures, and they offered public and strident critiques of other aid agencies, Australian government authorities, and social workers, who particularly came in for scathing attack.

Moir and Taylor actively wrote in the media defending their decisions and actions, pleading from a humanitarian perspective that the most humane act was the remove children from a war zone. Inter-country adoption, they believed, was the most compassionate next step. Moir believed that these acts were not adequately recognised: 'I am heartily sick and tired', she wrote in 1977, two years after the end of the war, 'of the shrill accusations if those who sat in splendid isolation, 5,000 miles from the crumbling chaos of terror that was South Vietnam'. Due recognition needed to be given to 'the integrity of the people whose unheralded dedication salvaged a little joy for the fragile human flotsam of the Indo-Chinese conflict'.[71] Her detractors believed their acts were reminiscent of the most pronounced form of a compromised humanitarianism replete with cultural imperialism, denying children their cultural heritage and serving the needs of privileged white adoptees. In these discussions, their opponents believed there were explicit assimilationist overtones and an uncritical celebration of Australian values and lifestyle.

In a lengthy rebuttal to adoption retractors, Moir addressed the criticisms levelled at her and Taylor. She confronted the argument that it was 'not right' to remove Vietnamese children from their homes and transfer them to a foreign culture and environment, which would mean they would suffer an 'identity' crisis. Moir responded that the children in question were orphaned and abandoned, and had spent their lives in orphanages. Many of the children were 'mixed race', whom the Vietnamese communities discriminated against. The issue about 'culture' she argued was 'laughable', considering the wartime conditions and deprivations that children endured in orphanages. She drew graphic and dramatic images of children in these orphanages, whose situation, she argued, was a matter of life and death. Notions of identity crisis were not the priority, given the physical and emotional deprivations experienced by child refugees of the war. Indeed, she believed that the debate about identity crisis was 'immoral'. 'Does anyone really think his identity is protected in the environs of a typical Vietnamese orphanage?', she asked. Further, she believed that assimilating into an Australian environment, by adopting Australian values, would be the ideal: 'Last but not least is the fact that a child adopted into a loving family is not a stranger, nor does he grow up among strangers. Rather, he is a member of a family and as such is accepted for his own self by parents, siblings and friends. He is thoroughly inured in our culture, speaking our language and educated among Australian children. This is his culture by right of adoption'.[72]

A second theme was the argument that it was better to assist children in their own country than to send them overseas for adoption. Moir agreed with this argument, but believed that this policy was only viable in theory. In the context of war, severe deprivation, profound disruption and extreme poverty, orphans were unable to receive care in their own countries. In the future, she thought, such a policy might be possible, but at that time, it was impossible to provide for these needs. Even if material support could be provided, this would be a stop-gap measure: 'any technological aid will simply be a stop gap of material goods but can never hope to fill the vast emotional gap. Children do not live by food alone – they need the love and encouragement of parents who care about them as individuals'.[73]

The third argument related to channelling money to orphanages rather than funding costly adoptions. Her reply was that this assumed that an orphanage was a better place to raise a child than an adopted family. She believed no institution 'no matter how good, can cater to a child's needs as an individual human being'. Adoption, she believed, represents 'total salvation for one child which is infinitely preferable to sharing material support in an orphanage'.[74]

The fourth argument was to challenge a rebuke against adoptive parents who sought to adopt Vietnamese children as a 'status symbol', or that there was guilt relating to Australia's involvement in the Vietnam War. 'Are we really incapable of understanding that there are families, both here in Australia and all over the world, who do sincerely love their adopted children regardless of the race, colour or origin of that child?' She believed that if Australians could only accept and identify 'with a child who is a carbon copy in colour and race of ourselves' then we must be 'the poorer in spirit and Christian charity because of it'.[75] On the question of support for the Vietnamese people and their country, Moir commended the adoptive parents who acted in this way and saw it as a positive, not a negative. 'I can only applaud those Australians', she noted, 'who do feel guilt about what has been done to the people of Vietnam and to their country'. She agreed with those who abhorred Australia's involvement in wartime: 'Surely we are not intended to applaud and feel joy at our involvement in the horror of napalm, incendiary bombs, defoliation, vast refugee camps of homeless people and the slaughter at Mỹ Lai'.[76]

The main focus of their activities, Moir argued, was the *child* and how best to support the child. Moir believed that the evidence was indisputable that the welfare of the child could not be best served in a Vietnamese orphanage in a war-torn country. Above all, most of the children who were adopted would not have survived the ordeal had they been left in a 'typical Vietnamese orphanage'. Further, the argument that adoption would drain 'the next generation' of Vietnamese was an exaggeration, as only 1,000 children had left Vietnam for adoption overseas: out of a population of sixteen million, 'this hardly constituted the depletion of the next generation'. In her estimation, of this number 750 would have died and the remaining 250 would have been social outcasts if they had remained in Vietnam: 'emotionally crippled, physically deprived, uneducated, discriminated against because of their mixed blood and homeless in a culture which worships the family unit'.[77]

Moir and Taylor joined other activists and lobbyists in this debate: most notably, couples who had adopted children or were seeking to do so. In joining in local debates with prospective parents, Moir and Taylor continued their activism. Moir was central in the efforts of Thomas and Irene Williams, whose case to adopt a fourteen-month-old orphan child grabbed local headlines.[78] The Williamses joined the chorus of complaints against governments when the adoption of their child was approved by the South Vietnamese Government but not by the State Government of Victoria, which meant the Australian Government could not issue a visa to allow the child to arrive in Australia.[79] The tensions between professional social workers and those without any professional training in any aspect of child welfare, let alone diplomacy and political sensibilities, were amplified in these debates.

The opinions of Wendy and Allan Scarfe, both Quakers, and the adoptive parents of three children, reflect the position of fierce advocates of inter-country adoption. In 1976, they outlined their position in considerable detail. The Scarfes were critical of the attitude of social workers, accusing them of dismissing the views of adoptive parents, and of holding racist views. The Scarfes argued that the labels and terminology used by social workers were misleading, even promoting ignorance and prejudice. They challenged many assumptions they believed were promoted by social workers: that biological children should be a priority and that adoptive parents did not have the same link with children as biological parents; and unfounded claims that adoptive parents manipulated children.[80] The Scarfes fiercely challenged the arguments by social workers who opposed inter-country adoption and characterised them as out of touch with and removed from the direct experience of adoption.

The Scarfes believed that they were 'through training, working and long personal experience ... qualified to make intelligent observations and humane moral judgements upon the subject of inter-country adoptions'. The Scarfes also attacked the ISS, which for a long time had also challenged efforts to promote inter-country adoption. The Scarfes challenged the authority and expertise of ISS and accused the organisation of not working impartially, but actively blocking and preventing inter-country adoption. Questioning the extent of the ISS's role and power, the Scarfes accused the organisation of attempting to interfere in government agencies. Further, they believed ISS was ill-informed, ignorant and defamatory in the information they provided to the Australian Immigration Department. They ridiculed the arguments about removing children from their 'culture': 'No baby of 18 months is usually reading Shakespeare in Vietnamese'. They accused ISS of ignoring the emotional bonds children sought, and that helping the children was not simply a matter of 'providing developmental aid'.[81] It was 'particularly monstrous', the Scarfes said, that ISS would tell prospective parents to donate money to aid organisations rather than adopt.

The Scarfes claimed the ISS showed racist overtones, because it stated that couples should adopt an Australian 'white child', not a non-European child, and showed a distrust of adoptive parents, whom, they argued, ISS characterised as deviant, with ulterior, unbalanced motives. It was 'utterly contemptible' that they had adopted for the sake of a status symbol.[82] The Scarfes appealed to compassion, especially in relation to Vietnamese children in orphanages where there was a high mortality rate: 'Does I.S.S. live without pity?' They also asked why ISS allowed babies to die rather than allow 'human feelings to speed up impeccable procedures?'[83] They accused ISS of being a 'White Australian consultative service'. In effect, they were accusing ISS of racism in not promoting inter-country adoption.[84] Further, they said, the ISS was made up of social workers, the key target of attack for the Scarfes and Moir.

For Moir and Taylor, the debate over inter-country adoption was never a theoretical abstraction based on disconnected concepts, as they characterised the response by social workers. Their humanitarian activism extended to actively lobbying politicians to allow Vietnamese children to enter Australia for adoption. They received a sympathetic hearing from concerned politicians. In 1971 Moir wrote to Don Chipp, the Liberal Minister for Customs and Excise regarding the obstacles to Australians adopting Vietnamese orphans. These included issues of empowering the Immigration Department to allow Vietnamese children to enter into the country without the approval of individual state child welfare departments. Moreover, she wanted the Minister to 'pressure' ISS to review its anti-adoption measures, as its view was based on 'idealism in the parent-child relationship'.[85] Chipp passed on her letter to Jim Forbes, the Minister for Immigration, noting to Forbes that Moir was a 'passionate humanitarian' who was 'certainly not a nut' and 'judged by any standards of morality must be listened to'. He believed the points she raised 'are worthy of examination'.[86] Moir also wrote to Forbes and Andrew Peacock, Liberal Minister for the Army, requesting the easing of immigration laws to allow orphans from Vietnam to enter Australia for adoption.[87] Taylor contacted Lance Barnard, Labor politician and then the Deputy Leader of the Opposition with a plea in May 1972. She said that the attitude of the Australian government was 'deplorable' and Australia had 'no social conscience at all in the matter'. But she reserved her harshest criticism for social welfare bodies, which were 'archaic' and operated on 'theoretical principles' that the rest of the world recognised were inadequate. Taylor believed that through her extensive experience she was far more aware of the circumstances of children orphaned by war than social workers. Australians and their government had shown a lack of conscience and she hoped he would consider it his duty 'to work towards this enlightenment'.[88] Barnard was sympathetic to her cause. In writing to Forbes, on her behalf, Barnard said he was 'deeply concerned' with the matters Taylor raised and had every reason to believe that Taylor was 'not exaggerating', and passed on Taylor's letter with the following request: 'I would be very pleased ... if you could personally sympathetically consider what she had to say with a view to inducing your Government to adopt a more humane attitude to these helpless children'.[89] By the mid-1970s, through the humanitarian work of Taylor and Moir, politicians were increasingly offering their support to taking action on the issue of Vietnamese child refugees.

Conclusion

In February 1972 Taylor wrote to Moir that the winds of change were sweeping the world, with support for the flourishing inter-country adoption programmes. She expressed her deep frustration that her own country had not embraced these changes. 'Agencies all over the world are asking me to work with them in the placement of these orphans', she wrote, 'why bother with Australia?'[90] Taylor and her fellow humanitarians – Moir and Moses – became staunch advocates of this movement not only because of their experience in witnessing the plight of children in Vietnam, but also because their activism was made possible in the unique way in which they conducted their humanitarian work.

Taylor's independence from administrative and organisational constraints not only defined her humanitarian practice, but also allowed her to push this cause and challenge Australian laws in ways that other relief agencies did not. Inter-country adoption was such a contentious and highly problematic and dangerous venture that many of the more established and longstanding relief organisations in the region resisted it. Ultimately, Taylor, Moir and Moses and her fellow humanitarians became lobbyists for this cause. The selective nature of their humanitarianism, inherent in the deeply problematic practices underpinning inter-country adoption, was also reflected in the severe limits of their unregulated and unconventional humanitarian practice. This practice inspired them to look in the direction of inter-country adoption as the solution for orphaned children. But in doing so they missed that the mood for change was rather to look to alternatives, such as development programmes within Vietnam, rather than to outside of the country and to the affluent West as the saviour of children whose lives had been devastated by war.

Notes

1 'War Babies Smuggled in by Air', newspaper clipping, 'Saigon – Adoption of Vietnamese Children', National Archives of Australia (hereafter NAA), A4531, 62/6 Part 2.
2 Rosemary J. Taylor to Mr and Mrs Barnard, 19 May 1972, 'Vietnamese Children – Entry for Adoption Part 3', NAA, A446, 1972/76642.

3 *Australian Women's Weekly*, 21 June 1972, p. 5.
4 Newspaper clipping, 'Saigon – Adoption of Vietnamese Children', *Australian*, 30 May 1972, NAA, A4531, 62/6 Part 2.
5 See Katherine Ellinghaus's essay, Chapter 9, in this volume.
6 'Saigon – Adoption of Vietnamese Children'.
7 H. T. McCrea to Dear Sirs, 29 May 1972, 'Vietnamese Children – Entry for Adoption Policy', NAA, A446, 1972/76642, Part 3.
8 Patricia Fronek, 'Operation Babylift: Advancing Intercountry Adoption into Australia', *Journal of Australian Studies* (2012), 36 (4), pp. 445–58; Joshua Forkert, 'Refugees, Orphans and a Basket of Cats: The Politics of Operation Babylift', *Journal of Australian Studies* (2012), 36 (4), pp. 427–44; Joshua Forkert, 'Orphans of Vietnam: A History of Intercountry Adoption Policy and Practice in Australia, 1968–1975', PhD thesis, University of Adelaide, 2012.
9 One such study is Tarah Brookfield, 'Maverick Mothers and Mercy Flights: Canada's Controversial Introduction to International Adoption', *Journal of the Canadian Historical Association/Revue de la Société historique du Canada* (2008), 19 (1), pp. 307–30.
10 Rosemary Taylor and Margaret V. Moses, 'Copy of Letter Sent to the "Australian", 14 December 1971, "Adoption of Vietnamese War Orphans – General Representations, 1971"', NAA, A463, 1971/673; newspaper clipping, *Age*, 10 August 1971, 'Vietnamese Children – Entry for Adoption, Policy Part 2', NAA, A446 1968/70597; newspaper clipping, *Sunday Times*, 14 October 1973, 'Saigon – Adoption of Vietnamese Children', NAA A4531, 62/6 Part 2.
11 Joy Damousi, 'From Charity to Justice: The Australian Foster Parents Plan and Humanitarian Aid in Asia in the 1970s', *Australian Journal of Politics and History* (2019), 65 (4), pp. 549–65; Joy Damousi, 'Child Sponsorship, Development and Aid: PLAN and UNICEF in Australia, 1945–1975', *History Australia* (2020), 17 (4), pp. 711–27.
12 Andrew Thompson, 'Unravelling the Relationship between Humanitarianism, Human Rights and Decolonisation: Time for a Radical Rethink?', in Martin Thomas and Andrew S. Thompson (eds), *The Oxford Handbook of the Ends of Empire* (Oxford, UK: Oxford University Press, 2018), pp. 453–76.
13 See Peter Edwards, *Australia and the Vietnam War* (Sydney, Australia: New South Publishing, 2014).
14 Brookfield, 'Maverick Mothers'.
15 K. Dreyfus, M. Quartly and D. Cuthbert, '"Why Can't I Have My Baby Tomorrow?": A Legislative Periodisation of Intercountry Adoption in Victoria and Australia from the Early 1970s to the Present', *Victorian Historical Journal* (2015), 86 (2), p. 340.
16 Ibid., p. 341.
17 Newspaper clipping, *Herald* (Melbourne), 17 August 1974, in Biographical Cuttings, Rosemary Taylor, Social Worker, National Library of Australia (Hereafter NLA); Rosemary Taylor, in collaboration with Wende Grant, *Orphans of War: Work with the Abandoned Children of Vietnam 1967–1975* (London, UK: Collins, 1988), p. 1; *Australian Women's Weekly*, 15 February 1967, p. 13.

18 Newspaper clipping, *Herald* (Melbourne), 17 August 1974.
19 www.terredeshommes.nl/en/50, accessed 8 October 2020.
20 Friends of Children of Vietnam, 'Activity Report, Quarter Ending December 31, 1973', Papers of Elaine Moir, Folder 8, Box 2, MS Acc12.027 [hereafter all letters in the Moir collection to this reference unless otherwise stated], NLA; Taylor, *Orphans of War*, p. 87.
21 Taylor, *Orphans of War*, p. 71.
22 Newspaper clipping, *Bulletin*, 1 March 1986, p. 48, in Biographical Cuttings, Rosemary Taylor, Social Worker, NLA.
23 Ibid.
24 *Sydney Morning Herald*, 20 August 2012; *Sydney Morning Herald*, 28 August 2012.
25 Suzanne Edgar and Carmel Floreani, 'Moses, Margaret Veronica (1940–1975)', in *Australian Dictionary of Biography*, http://adb.anu.au/biography/moses-margaret-veronica-11184/text19931, accessed 27 May 2020.
26 Rosemary Taylor to Elaine Moir, 5 December 1972, Box 2, Folder 8, Papers of Elaine Moir.
27 Taylor, *Orphans of War*, p. 6.
28 Ibid., p. 23.
29 Margaret Moses to Elaine Moir, 8 August 1971, Box 2, Folder 8, Papers of Elaine Moir.
30 Ibid.
31 Taylor, *Orphans of War*, p. 19.
32 Rosemary Taylor, 'Dear Friends', 16 December 1973, Box 2, Folder 8, Papers of Elaine Moir.
33 Rosemary Taylor to Elaine Moir, 17 October 1972, Box 2, Folder 8, Papers of Elaine Moir.
34 Rosemary Taylor to Elaine Moir, 2 January 1973, Box 2, Folder 8, Papers of Elaine Moir.
35 Ibid.
36 Rosemary Taylor to Elaine Moir, 18 February 1972, Box 2, Folder 8, Papers of Elaine Moir.
37 Rosemary Taylor to Elaine Moir, 20 March 1972, Box 2, Folder 8, Papers of Elaine Moir.
38 Rosemary Taylor to Elaine Moir, 18 November 1972, Box 2, Folder 8, Papers of Elaine Moir.
39 Rosemary Taylor to Elaine Moir, 16 February 1972, Box 2, Folder 8, Papers of Elaine Moir.
40 Rosemary Taylor to Elaine Moir, 22 March 1973, Box 2, Folder 8, Papers of Elaine Moir, underline original.
41 Ibid.
42 Rosemary Taylor to Elaine Moir, 15 April 1973, Box 2, Folder 8, Papers of Elaine Moir.
43 Ibid.
44 Ibid.

45 Rosemary Taylor to Elaine Moir, 16 February 1973, Box 2, Folder 8, Papers of Elaine Moir.
46 Ibid.
47 Ibid.
48 Margaret Moses to Elaine Moir, 7 November 1971, Box 2, Folder 8, Papers of Elaine Moir.
49 Rosemary Taylor to Elaine Moir, 18 November 1971, Box 2, Folder 8, Papers of Elaine Moir.
50 Ibid.
51 Rosemary Taylor to Elaine Moir, 6 December 1971, Box 2, Folder 8, Papers of Elaine Moir.
52 Margaret Moses to Elaine Moir, 7 November 1971, Box 2, Folder 8, Papers of Elaine Moir.
53 Rosemary Taylor to Elaine Moir, 11 May 1973, Box 2, Folder 8, Papers of Elaine Moir.
54 Rosemary Taylor to Elaine Moir, 6 February 1974, Box 2, Folder 8, Papers of Elaine Moir.
55 Ibid.
56 Rosemary Taylor to Elaine Moir, 5 March 1973, Box 2, Folder 8, Papers of Elaine Moir.
57 Margaret Moses to Elaine Moir, 19 April 1972, Box 2, Folder 8, Papers of Elaine Moir.
58 Ibid.
59 Rosemary Taylor to Elaine Moir, 6 August 1972, Box 2, Folder 8, Papers of Elaine Moir.
60 Rosemary Taylor to Elaine Moir, 2 January 1973, Box 2, Folder 8, Papers of Elaine Moir.
61 Robert Strobridge, *Turn My Eyes Away: Our Children in Vietnam, 1967–1975*, with an Introduction and comments by Rosemary Taylor (Boulder, CO: Friends for All Children, 1976), not paginated.
62 Ibid.
63 Ibid.
64 Rosemary Taylor to Elaine Moir, 22 March 1973, Box 2, Folder 8, Papers of Elaine Moir.
65 Margaret Moses to Elaine Moir, 26 January c. 1973, Box 2, Folder 8, Papers of Elaine Moir.
66 Newspaper cutting, Marina Warner, 'Poor Little Bastards of Vietnam', *Spectator*, 12 August 1972, in 'Tom and Irene Williams – Adoption of Vietnamese Child', NAA, A1209, 1975/671.
67 Brookfield, 'Maverick Mothers', p. 316.
68 International Social Service, 'Note on Attitudes in Australia to the Welfare of Vietnamese Children', Australian Branch, 20 July, 1965', Adoption of Asia orphaned children by Australian families, NAA, A463, 1965/1778.
69 'Note on Intercountry Adoption', 5 April 1972, Australian Council of Churches, Box 107, 'Child Sponsorship and Adoption, 1965–1970', MS 7645, NLA.

70 Forkert, 'Orphans of Vietnam', p. 93.
71 Elaine J. Moir, 'No Conspiracy', *Bulletin*, 24 September 1977, p. 13.
72 Elaine Moir, 'The Primary Arguments Against the Adoption of Vietnamese Orphans by Australians are Set Out Below to the Best of my Knowledge and Understanding of the Subject', Item 3, Philosophies on Adoption, Box 1, Folder 3, Papers of Elaine Moir.
73 Ibid.
74 Ibid.
75 Ibid.
76 Ibid.
77 Ibid.
78 Newspaper cutting, *Age* (Melbourne), 24 May 1972; Tom and Irene Williams – Adoption of Vietnamese Child, NAA, A1209, 1975/671.
79 Ibid.
80 Wendy and Allan Scarfe, 'Terms and Attitudes in Inter-Country Adoption', pp. 1–17, in Item 3, Philosophies on Adoption, Box 1, Folder 3, Papers of Elaine Moir.
81 Ibid., p. 4.
82 Ibid.
83 Ibid., p. 6.
84 Forkert, 'Orphans of Vietnam', p. 93.
85 Elaine Moir to Don Chipp, 31 August 1971, Vietnamese Children – Entry for Adoption, NAA, Policy Part 2, A446 1968/70597.
86 Don Chipp to Jim Forbes, 13 September 1971, Vietnamese Children – Entry for Adoption, NAA, Policy Part 2, A446 1968/70597.
87 Andrew Peacock to Elaine Moir, 19 October 1971; Elaine Moir to Andrew Peacock, 12 October 1971; Elaine Moir to Jim Forbes, 27 August 1971; Folder 10: Correspondence – Governments and Semi-Governments, Papers of Elaine Moir, Folder 8, Box 2, MS Acc12.027, NLA.
88 Rosemary Taylor to Lance and Mrs. Barnard, 19 May 1972, Vietnamese Children – Entry for Adoption Part 3, NAA, A446, 1972/76642.
89 Lance Barnard to Jim Forbes, 25 May, 1972, Vietnamese Children – Entry for Adoption Part 3, NAA, A446, 1972/76642.
90 Rosemary Taylor to Elaine Moir, 18 February 1972, Box 2, Folder 8, Papers of Elaine Moir.

13

Humanitarianism in the age of human rights: Amnesty International in Australia

Jon Piccini

On the night of 2 March 1962, twenty-two people attended a meeting at the Owen Dixon Chambers on Melbourne's William Street that established Australia's first 'section' of what is now the world's best-known human rights organisation: Amnesty International.[1] The smattering of 'lawyers, social workers, women at home, businessmen, industrial workers, minister of religion and students' who attended that night had been inspired by Peter Benenson, a British lawyer, former Labour Party activist and Catholic convert, whose article 'The Forgotten Prisoners' had appeared in London's *Observer* newspaper ten months earlier.[2] The organisation's remit was novel: declaring itself above Cold War politics, members 'adopted' one political prisoner from each of a first-, second- and third-world nation – known as 'groups of threes' – and sought to use the power of the pen to have them released.

Those first twenty-two Australians had a mix of motivations, but Wendy Nott's seems particularly instructive. Hearing news of the organisation's founding over the radio 'while standing at the sink one evening' hit Nott, a homemaker from the working-class suburb of Essendon, Melbourne, like 'a bolt from the blue'. She had been involved in the Student Christian Movement and Aboriginal rights causes at university, and saw Amnesty as representing 'the idea of the brotherhood of man', an ambition not so distant from Benenson's own hope for 'a sort of secularised religious community which would "rekindle a fire in the minds of men"'.[3]

Nott's history and perceptions immediately reveal some of the contradictions that underlay Amnesty's emergence. Its novel deployment of human rights ideas and, like many organisations of the 1960s, its eschewing of binary Cold War hostilities, sat alongside a much older – indeed ancient – imperative to aid those in need. In this chapter, I use Amnesty as a window into the way humanitarian action was transformed and complicated by its ever-closer relationship with human rights in the second half of the twentieth century. Historian Samuel Moyn argues that 'the slow amalgamation of humanitarian concern for suffering with human rights', sped up from the 1970s onwards, culminating in the two becoming 'fused enterprises, with the former incorporating the latter and the latter justified in terms of the former'.[4] For Moyn, this process promoted humanitarianism's ever-closer relationship with the power of the state, and showed how human rights transformed from an expansive programme of delivering 'the good life' into basic guarantees to bodily autonomy, a process that organisations like Amnesty facilitated. Sean McBride, Amnesty Executive Chairman (1961–75) described the organisation as 'a humanitarian organisation that would do for political prisoners what the Red Cross did for prisoners of war'.[5] Historians Bruno Cabanes and Joy Damousi venture that this melding of charitable concern for immediate suffering with ideas of inherent rights and enforceable standards marks the emergence of 'humanitarian rights', whereby victims are owed not merely aid and amelioration of their conditions, but the right to lives of dignity.[6]

I argue that Amnesty's career in Australia shows how this amalgamation played out, highlighting that, while such overlap was productive, it could create significant conflict between two quite distinct optics. Such attentiveness to the local dimensions of international non-government organisations and humanitarian campaigns has concerned a growing body of scholarship.[7] Amnesty itself has been studied in its British, American, Dutch, Russian, Polish and, now, Australian iterations.[8] Such studies reveal not the appearance of a uniform global organisation committed to principles of impartiality and prisoner adoption, but instead how difficult it was to translate Amnesty's universal ideas into local contexts. 'It was by no means an instant success', but rather 'a depressingly slow task', as historian Jan Eckel puts it.[9]

In what follows I first locate Amnesty's Australian rise within what historian Tom Buchanan dubs its 'activist environment' – the causes, personalities and organisations that constituted Australia's humanitarian/human rights community in the late 1950s and early 1960s, which Amnesty responded to and borrowed from.[10] It was this background that determined the two key areas of tensions that overcame the Australian sections in the 1960s: Indigenous rights and conscientious objection to service in the Vietnam War. Such conflicts reveal a divergence between humanitarian and human rights-focused worldviews. After considering each in turn, I look to Amnesty's development in the 1970s. Its growing successes in this decade, including the establishment of the world's first parliamentary section of the organisation, demonstrate increasing complicity in state-based politics, which I argue replicate centuries-old ideas of 'humanitarian governance' that the organisation had initially rejected.

Humanitarianism and human rights in postwar Australia

Born as it was at the height of Europe's enlightenment, and the 'torrents of emotion' it elicited for suffering parties across the world, Australia has a long relationship with the practices and ideologies of humanitarianism.[11] This was animated first by opposition to convict transportation, and then the plight of Indigenous peoples in the early nineteenth century, the latter continuing into the twentieth century alongside more global concerns, particularly the plight of children and soldiers.[12] Contributors to this volume have revealed how such well-meaning gestures functioned to buttress colonial, and later national, rule, offering modes of humanitarian governance that served to simultaneously acknowledge and erase victims of empires and states.[13]

Such imperial benevolence was repackaged after World War II, in a world where formal empire was ending, and the idea of human rights was emerging as a corollary and sometimes competitor to the humanitarian impulse. Appearing almost accidentally in the 1940s, human rights made their way into the United Nations Charter at the behest of South African diplomat Jan Smuts.[14] These principles were viewed as 'ornamental remainders of original wartime visions' summed up in 1941's Atlantic Charter – a shiny gloss on the bigger ambitions of ensuring world peace and prosperity.[15] However, human rights took on somewhat of a life of their own, as the General Assembly created an eight-nation drafting committee to work on a declaration that enumerated them. While heralded at the time, scholars highlight how the Universal Declaration of Human Rights was overcome by Cold War tensions, which are apparent in the document's inclusion of both traditional civil liberties alongside more expansive guarantees of social and economic rights.[16]

One measure of the Declaration's 'death from birth' is the remarkably small number of grassroots organisations that emerged in the 1940s and 1950s that adopted its precepts. In Australia, one of the few such organisations was the Council for Aboriginal Rights, founded in 1951, with venerable communist, biochemist and nationally recognised folk dancer, Shirley Andrews, at the helm.[17] The council's founding constitution put its aims simply: 'to help the aborigines to win for themselves the liberties envisaged for all people in the Universal Declaration of Human Rights'. This reference responded to a brief wartime rights Zeitgeist, with the constitution's convoluted wording capturing something of the difference human rights made. The importance of Indigenous people 'winning for themselves' these rights, rather than merely being offered aid by distant strangers, spoke to the agency inherent in ideas of human rights as opposed to the benevolence of humanitarianism.[18] However, the Universal Declaration of Human Rights featured only rarely in the Council for Aboriginal Rights' activism into the 1950s, the success of which, including a central role in founding the Federal Council for the Advancement of Aborigines and Torres Strait Islanders in 1958, was attributable to Andrews's perseverance and energy.

The late 1950s also saw the emergence of new forms of humanitarian organisations, which exchanged ideas of the 'white man's burden' for discourses of development and social uplift.[19] Young-Sun Hong calls such transformations part of a 'global humanitarian regime' – the 'bridge by which ... asymmetries between the Global North and South, which had been constructed in the age of imperialism and colonial mandates, were re-articulated and reproduced across the 1945 divide'.[20] Some groups, like Save the Children, were reinvented for this new post-colonial climate, which 'made it impossible to separate emergency humanitarian relief ... from the overtly politicised development and medical aid, whose goal was to shape long-term postcolonial state-building projects'.[21]

This 'global regime' was also reflected in the foundation in Australia of the Volunteer Graduate Scheme (1951), activism around World Refugee Year (1959) and the founding of Freedom from Hunger (1960). The Volunteer Graduate Scheme, chronicled in this volume by Agnieszka Sobocinska, sent newly qualified Australian university students to needy Asian nations – in the first instance Indonesia – where they would undertake development work at a local's wages and conditions.[22] The latter two organisations emerged out of United Nations directives, with Freedom from Hunger becoming a permanent presence in the 1960s and 1970s. Each used novel campaign strategies – 'radio, television, print media, a more strategic approach' – to '*arouse* compassion'.[23] Yet they shared two key commonalities from the colonial era: a continuation of racialised ideologies, whereby 'volunteers were bound by colonial assumptions, even as they sought to overturn them', and heavily religious motivations.[24]

Amnesty International was born into an increasingly crowded field jockeying for the attentions of charitable Australians. As well as sharing many similarities with these new humanitarian groups, including a fondness for new forms of public relations and the religious affiliation of many members, there was also significant personnel overlap. Keith Dowding, Perth clergyman and internationalist, was at one point Secretary of Western Australia's Amnesty International section, as well as founding President of its Freedom from Hunger chapter, Chairman of Western Australians for Racial Equality, convenor of the Campaign for Nuclear Disarmament branch and Vice President of the United Nations Association of Australia.[25] Though such wide-ranging interests may not have been the case for all members, it is clear that Amnesty was deeply embedded in a broader world of campaigns and causes, while attempting to market its own approach to potential members and supporters.

Rather than forming a section covering all of Australia, Amnesty's haphazard formation saw separate, often conflictive, state sections emerge, perhaps speaking to 'the tyranny of distance' that so often afflicts antipodean history.[26] A national organisation, albeit without the Queensland section, would not be established until 1976, under significant pressure from the London leadership.[27] By mid-1965, the Victorian section – by far the nation's largest – claimed eighty-one financial members, an increase of fifteen on 1964, who were spread across ten suburb-based chapters.[28] Membership grew to 160 in 1967 and reached 385 by 1973. New South Wales proved even more sluggish, claiming some 120 members by 1973.[29] A sternly worded letter to the Victorian section in that year from Martin Ennals, a London Amnesty leader, reprimanded Australia for 'lagging behind much of the rest of the movement'.[30] There were some successes, however: the 1964–65 Victorian section annual report recording the release of prisoners in Greece, Portugal and East Germany.[31] These prisoners were provided to the sections, and subsequently local chapters, by the London headquarters. Amnesty was heavily hierarchical and all information flowed through the leadership and paid researchers, which contributed to tensions between London-based professionals and local volunteers.[32]

Amnesty's reception in Australia was overwhelmingly successful. Indeed, one Canberra commentator asked in 1965 why it had taken so long to found a local section, given its thoroughly agreeable nature.[33] In an interview with the *Canberra Times*, Liberal Party staffer and Canberra section President Michael McKerras claimed that Amnesty's model of adopting 'a prisoner of conscience in a Communist country, in a western country and in a non-aligned country ... ensures that the work is truly humanitarian and without political bias'.[34] Even the reform-minded Communist Party saw no reason to criticise the organisation, welcoming the foundation of a Western Australian section, and its adoption of a Rhodesian and a Polish dissident.[35] Another measure of the organisation's popular appeal is a letter from an unnamed university student to the *Australian Women's Weekly* in 1966, written to protest characterisations of young people like herself as loafers and a 'lunatic fringe'. This couldn't be further from the truth, the writer insisted, as 'during my first year at university in the Science faculty I learned to play a guitar, had poetry accepted for publication, wrote letters for Amnesty International ... and passed all my exams with credit'.[36] Amnesty activism was part of a thoroughly mainstream life, it would seem.

It was internally, however, where questions of Amnesty's role emerged. The organisation's adherence to political impartiality – seen as its path to acceptance by McKerras – entailed not campaigning on issues that related to one's home country. This exposed Amnesty to a longstanding criticism levelled at humanitarian groups: of ignoring what was happening on their own doorstep. Much as criticism was made of the World Refugee Year's focus on recipients abroad rather than 'refugees from poverty in Australia', in the words of Indigenous rights campaigner Mary Gilmore, at least some of Amnesty's membership grated against its inability to act against human rights abuses under its very nose.[37] I argue that this tension culminated in a clash of ideas and practices, between those with a prescriptive approach to human rights as a set of norms to be carefully read and acted upon at the national level, and humanitarians who enacted a more universal, benevolent script. This tension itself was nothing new: it had plagued the white supporters of Indigenous Australians for generations, a cause which demonstrated to some of Amnesty's early adherents that benevolence and rights were not necessarily bedfellows.

Amnesty and the challenge of Indigenous injustice

Aside from supporting prisoners abroad, Amnesty sections also took it upon themselves to recommend for adoption prisoners in their own countries. Kenneth Cmeil explains how groups like Amnesty invented 'ways to move this information to wherever activists had some chance to shame and pressure the perpetrators', crafting 'a politics of the global flow of key bits of fact'.[38] The Victorian section convened a study group in early 1965 to prepare a report on whether Indigenous Australians could become adoptees. The study group sought information from relevant organisations, principally the Federal Council for the Advancement of Aborigines and Torres Strait Islanders, and after seven months presented a final report, published as *The Situation of Australian Aborigines*.

Indigenous Australians, subject to punitive measures of displacement and genocide since colonisation, were organising and demanding their inclusion in the Australian nation with a new energy in the postwar period.[39] Everywhere, they remained second-class citizens: restricted from the vote at Commonwealth level and in most states, subject to restrictive 'protection acts' which controlled the daily lives of those under their mandates and often at the receiving end of punitive policing, particularly if living in remote areas.[40] Yet, the foundation of the Federal Council in 1958, and the decision to undertake a petition campaign demanding the removal of racially discriminatory clauses from the nation's constitution, made their cause increasingly visible, both to a sympathetic population and anti-colonial nations that aired Indigenous suffering in international forums.[41]

From the 1950s onwards, white Indigenous rights campaigners sought to utilise the Universal Declaration of Human Rights as a means of bringing Australia's policies into line with international standards. Yvonne Nicholls, a committee member of the Australian Council for Civil Liberties, wrote a pamphlet entitled *Not Slaves, Not Citizens* that explored the position of Aboriginal people in the Northern Territory in 1952.[42] Although the Northern Territory had been a focus of humanitarians and 'defenders' from the 1910s, the emergence of a 'world court of appeal' in the form of the United Nations' Human Rights Committee made such questions more pressing.[43] Nicholls found the Commonwealth denied all but one of the thirty articles in the Declaration to Indigenous Peoples in the Northern Territory, a situation requiring immediate attention to 'save our face and conscience' from being put 'before the councils of the world'.[44] Pastor, doctor and rights campaigner Charles Duguid delivered a similar message in that same year to over 1,000 people at the Melbourne Town Hall. He found that Indigenous Australians were not accorded the rights inherent in the majority of the Declaration's articles and concluded that 'common honesty demands no less' than the full realisation of the Declaration for Indigenous Australians, noting 'and Asia is looking on'.[45]

What differentiated Amnesty's approach from these earlier writers was its precise focus on 'to what extent is curtailment of Aborigines rights because of matters of policy which are outside the scope of Amnesty'.[46] This was a vital question: what constituted imprisonment? Amnesty was devoted to the release of non-violent political prisoners in line with Article 3 of the Declaration, a stance strengthened by the organisation's rejection of African National Congress leader Nelson Mandela from such status in the aftermath of his 1962 incarceration in apartheid South Africa.[47] But what of oppressed minorities within states who, as the Victorian section's first constitution read, were 'imprisoned because of race'?[48] This more metaphorical allusion to imprisonment, congruent with centuries of humanitarian appropriations of slavery and enchainment, did not sit well alongside Amnesty's restrictive remit.[49]

Much as Duguid and Nichols had found the status of Indigenous peoples and the articles of the Declaration to be incongruent in nearly all instances, Amnesty's final report laboriously mapped the inequalities of Indigenous Australians onto each relevant article, yet came to mixed conclusions on what role the organisation could play. While finding evidence of gross violations, particularly in terms of voting rights, lack of compensation for appropriated lands and freedom of movement, Amnesty members concluded that they could do little about these. While it 'would seem that work for the removal of legal disabilities of Aborigines comes within the spirit ... of Amnesty if not the letter', the report concluded, 'Amnesty's objects refer to "prisoners of conscience"' and '[i]n the absence of any militant pan-Aboriginalist movement, it is doubtful that there has ever been a true prisoner of conscience'.

Amnesty's disappointment was almost palpable, with the report concluding that 'Aboriginal people are certainly an enchained people', albeit one that Amnesty's human rights agenda could do little to help.[50] Amnesty

Victoria Secretary and amateur historian Clare Wositzky described the report as 'a milestone in the activities of the Victorian branch', albeit one which reinforced the organisation's commitment to a very limited terrain of activity.[51] Amnesty was not to offer an Indigenous Australian for adoption until a slackening of the definition of a 'prisoner of conscience' in 1988.[52] The other conclusion, that Amnesty could forward this information to the United Nations for action, however, drew critical attention to the report, both from the media and within Amnesty.

The *Canberra Times* carried a brief story on the report in April 1966, remarking that it compared 'the position of Aborigines in Australia ... to that of people living under a totalitarian state'.[53] While the report never explicitly said this, Kim Beazley Senior, Member of Parliament for the Australian Labor Party and self-described 'student of aboriginal affairs' penned a response 'expressing some fears' that Amnesty's work could have unintended consequences. Beazley attempted to undermine the report's credibility, describing Amnesty as an 'international "grievance" organisation' and condemning its authors for not inquiring with Indigenous people and their government-appointed Protectors, instead only engaging with previously published reports like those detailed above. Beazley described Amnesty's publication as a 'warning of the twists of interpretation and the damage to Australia of "investigations" of an abstract kind' – a less than subtle hint at the dangers of international eyes looking too closely in Australia's direction.[54]

The Canberra Amnesty section, in a remarkably public intra-organisational spat, expressed similar concerns. President Michael McKerras referred to the report as 'regrettable' and saw danger in the recommendation to 'refer the matter of Aboriginal rights to the United Nations, where it might be used to discredit Australia, before ... all means of promoting their rights within Australia' were exhausted. McKerras concluded by remarking, 'I personally do not feel that this comes within the scope of Amnesty', signalling a debate about the organisation's role and the relative merits of local campaigning that would continue to rage into the 1970s.[55] That one Amnesty section would take such a public step in shaming another points to its haphazard and shifting forms of politics. The Victorian section made a 'difficult decision' in 1968 to not publish an updated version of the report, owing to a 'new ... statute' from London 'which focused our work on ... political prisoners who are detained without trial'.[56]

This case makes it clear that Amnesty was far from a uniform organisation in these early years of its existence. Some members thought the organisation's global scope and media-savvy approach could serve as another front in an existing campaign of airing Australia's record on Indigenous rights at home and abroad. Others saw this as a threat to the very novelty that gave

Amnesty its significance: the 'apolitical', disinterested focus on prisoners of conscience. Such fault lines were not sealed by the public falling out of the Victorian and ACT sections, but instead were reinflamed only months later by the issue of conscription and the intensifying war in Vietnam.

Conscription and the limits of conscience

The issue of conscientious objection was to raise an even greater debate, this time between the organisation's Victorian and New South Wales sections. Australia entered the war in Vietnam in 1962, sending a thirty-man training contingent to aid the South Vietnamese government in containing communist rebels. In 1964 the Liberal government of Robert Menzies introduced a National Service scheme that allowed for potential overseas deployments, and in April 1965 joined the United States in committing ground troops – including twenty-year-olds conscripted via a lottery system – to the conflict for the first time.[57] Vietnam and the National Service scheme – soon labelled 'the Draft' following American nomenclature – became inseparable, inescapable issues during the late 1960s, and from early on encountered a small but growing number of protesters – often sparked by highly mediatised cases of 'draft resisters'.[58]

Bill White, a Sydney schoolteacher, announced his decision to defy a call-up notice to enter the National Service Scheme in July 1966, and was dragged from his home to a military prison in front of waiting media in November of that year. This case sparked a flurry of activity in Amnesty, with the cause of bringing those believed to be 'prisoners of conscience' to light initially uniting the organisation. The Victorian section released a statement in support of White's actions: 'we feel it impossible ... to doubt the sincerity of his convictions and are gravely concerned at the prospect of his continued detention under the provisions of military law'. Given 'the grounds for an appeal to the Government on White's behalf based on the sanctity of the individual conscience are substantial', the section recommended White's case to Amnesty's London office 'for appropriate action'.[59]

The New South Wales section expressed near-identical sentiments, reporting in August 1966 that 'Conscription had been the overriding issue in much of our new work'. The section was collecting material on Australian cases of draft resistance while campaigning for the release of conscientious objectors in the United States and East Germany. 'The fact that the predicament of Bill White is shared by young men all over the world' spoke, in the section President's view, to 'the immediate domestic value of Amnesty International to safeguard our own civil liberties and our international reputation'.[60]

The New South Wales section's commitment to the anti-conscription cause was not surprising, as section President Lincoln Oppenheimer was also a member of the recently founded Ex-Services Human Rights Association of Australia, a group of anti-war veterans whose leading members had been publicly forced out of the Returned Services League in 1967.[61] The two groups shared a morally focused form of politics, drawing on the Universal Declaration of Human Rights as one of their foundation documents, and consequently had significant organisational overlap. Association President Les Waddington was the speaker at Amnesty's 'Human Rights Day' event on 10 December 1967, and an Association member wrote to the group's journal, *Conscience*, imploring 'more of us' to join Amnesty 'and really delve into the plight of political prisoners all over the world'.[62]

White's public statement of conscientious objection, reproduced in the New South Wales section's newsletter, spoke of rights as 'unalterable' and inhering in a person rather than being a 'concession given by a government', and as such these were 'not something which the government has the right to take'.[63] White's statement reflected the development of a morally conscious form of politics percolating in both Amnesty and the Ex-Services Association at this time – that someone's humanity made them a rights-claiming subject, irrespective of their actions. 'I respect people, I respect their feelings, I respect their property [and] I respect their equality ... on the basic conscientious assumption that they, as I have, the unquestionable right to live', White concluded.[64]

White's release in December 1966 came before Amnesty could adopt his cause internationally, but more objectors soon followed. What became problematic, however, was when the politics of conscientious objection moved to one of downright refusal – non-compliance with the laws of the land. This was part of a broader trend within the anti-conscription movement towards more militant opposition to the National Service Act 1964.[65] Unlike White, who was released after being found a conscientious objector after a month in prison and a public backlash, part-time postman John Zarb applied, not on the basis of his opposition to all war, only that in Vietnam. He was gaoled for two years in October 1968. 'Free Zarb' became a rallying cry for the anti-war movement, with his imprisonment seen as representing the futility and double standards synonymous with the Vietnam War. As one activist leaflet put it: 'In Australia – it is a crime not to kill'.[66]

Convenor of the Lane Cove Amnesty Chapter in Sydney's affluent North Shore, Robert V. Horn described in a long memorandum to Amnesty's London headquarters how 'Conscription and Vietnam have become intermixed in public debate, and in contemporary style outbursts of demonstrations, protest marches, draft card burnings [and] sit-ins'.[67] Zarb's case was, however, nowhere near as clear cut for Amnesty members as White's had been. Horn described how Amnesty members held a 'wide spectrum of political, religious and moral views', and while 'one might guess that many members are opposed to Australia's participation in the Vietnam war' these individuals held 'many shades of views'. Such differences were particularly prominent around the acceptability of law-breaking.[68] Horn circulated a draft report on the situation in Australia that he had prepared for Amnesty's London headquarters to other Amnesty members within the New South Wales section and Victoria. The reactions to this report demonstrate just how divisive the issue of conscientious objectors and non-compliers was for an organisation deeply wedded to due legal process.

David McKenna, in charge of the Victorian section's conscientious objection work, put this distinction clearly in a reply to Horn, arguing that those who 'register for national service and apply for exemption', but whose 'applications fail either through some apparent miscarriage of justice or because the law does not presently encompass their objections … are prima facie eligible for adoption' as prisoners of conscience.[69] However, those who 'basically refuse to co-operate with the National Service Act' merely 'maintain a right to disobey a law which they believe to be immoral' – and were as such not a concern for Amnesty. McKenna here casts refusal as a purely political stand as opposed to those who hold a moral objection to conscription. By 1968 one of the Victorian section's primary objections to White's case – that the prisoner was held in a military gaol – was amended by Parliament in favour of civilian incarceration in state prisons.[70]

The Victorian section's 1967 annual report also questioned a resolution of Amnesty's most recent International Assembly, declaring that any person who refused to participate in a specific war was considered a prisoner of conscience, to which the section responded that 'there is a need for clarification of Amnesty's modus operandi in democratic countries'.[71] McKenna read the Universal Declaration of Human Rights as contradicting such a policy, noting that the limitations set forth in Article 29 meant 'freedom of conscience is not an absolute, nor is freedom to disobey in a democratic society'.[72] Concerns were raised about 'to what extent we uphold disobedience to the law by adopting such persons', noting that Amnesty had chosen not to adopt prisoners 'who refuse obedience to laws [such as] in South Africa or Portugal'. Adopting prisoners who refused to obey laws not only opened the road to what McKenna feared was a tidal wave of similar 'freedom to disobey' claims – 'are we to adopt people who refuse to have a T.B. X Ray on grounds of conscience?' – but also to what he saw as the possibility that in taking 'such a radical step … our high repute would be seriously damaged'.[73]

Horn and others in the New South Wales section 'decr[ied] such legalistic interpretation' – insisting 'the Non-Complier in gaol for conscientiously held and non-violently expressed views suffers no less than the [Conscientious Objector] who has tried in vain to act "according to the law"'.[74] While at first divisions on this issue were across and between sections, by late 1969 the Victorian section had solidly decided 'that non-compliers should not be adopted', and sent a memorandum to London to this effect in preparation for the Amnesty Executive Meeting to be held in Stockholm in 1970.[75] The position of the New South Wales section was equally clear, expressed in a resolution adopted during 'prisoner of conscience week' in November 1969 that requested Amnesty and the UN General Assembly to adopt 'firm restrains upon legal and political repression of conscience'.[76] '[P]rovided that the individual ... has not used or advocated the use of violence', the resolution asserted, 'the expression of honest opinions regarding matters of economics, politics, morality, religion or race is not a good and sufficient reason' to justify imprisonment, and 'no person should be penalised for refusing to obey a law ... which infringes the[se] principles'.[77]

The Australians' arguments reflected a much wider debate in Amnesty globally. Internationally, the organisation was convulsed with internal conflict over the period from 1966 to 1967, with evidence of Benenson's long collaborations with British intelligence and increasing signs of mental fatigue forcing Amnesty's 'founding father' to resign. This incident, while barely reported in the Australian sections, raised deep questions of whether it was 'legitimate for Amnesty to draw when necessary on the resources of state' or to collaborate with the state in achieving domestic or foreign policy objectives.[78] Calls for a decentring of the London secretariat's authority also grew, with large sections in Sweden and Belgium now making up a significant percentage of the organisation's global membership, and demanding more of a say in the organisation's affairs. The 1970 Stockholm gathering's decision to back the New South Wales section's views was blamed by the Victorian section on the strength of their Swedish counterparts – 'who have the same problem as Australia and have come to the opposite view'.[79]

This internecine conflict further demonstrates how the practices of humanitarianism and human rights found particular expression in the late twentieth century. For some, the image of an individual unjustly imprisoned for whatever reason – at home or abroad – was cause enough to render them assistance as 'a man and a brother', to recall an earlier humanitarian plea, within whom a right to life inheres. Such humanitarian sentiment was not, however, in keeping with the state-focused Zeitgeist of human rights in the 1960s, which saw rights as a contract between governments and their people – necessitating obedience and compliance with national authority. These two conceptions of Amnesty's role would continue to coexist within the organisation, as the 'human rights revolution' got underway.

Into the 1970s

On 10 December 1973 – International Human Rights Day – the Labor Party's Gough Whitlam became the first Australian Prime Minister to publicly support Amnesty International. A short press statement welcomed Amnesty's conference on the abolition of torture, then underway in Paris, as a positive step towards 'the abolition of torture and the observance of International Humanitarian Law' – adding that his government 'regards acts of torture as breaches of basic human rights and infringements of personal dignity'.[80] Keen to present himself as a multilateralist and friend of the liberal world order, Whitlam wanted to move Australian foreign policy away from US domination.[81] Yet, he no doubt shared the perspective that historian Barbara Keys identifies among many liberal Americans, that the cause of human rights provided a new moral foundation for international affairs in the wake of Vietnam.[82]

Amnesty had initiated contact with Whitlam almost immediately after his December 1972 election win – forming the first non-conservative government since 1949 – when the International Secretariat sent a message welcoming his release of remaining objectors to national service from prison.[83] In a follow-up note in May 1973, Amnesty President Sean MacBride reported being 'lost in admiration at the rapidity at which you and your government had moved' since its election, and exhorted Australia into supporting the newly launched Campaign Against Torture, and particularly its push for a UN Convention on the subject.[84] Having been granted consultative status with the United Nations Economic and Social Council, Amnesty pivoted with this campaign from a focus purely on freeing individual prisoners to greater attention on global human rights machinery, which necessitated increased work with sympathetic governments.[85]

MacBride's overtures proved successful, and Australia went on to play a significant role in the push for 1975's Declaration on the Protection of All Persons from Being Subjected to Torture and Other Cruel, Inhuman or Degrading Treatment or Punishment, adopted by the UN's General Assembly a month after Whitlam's dismissal. The creation of a parliamentary Amnesty group in 1974, at the initiative of members of the Victorian section, marked a further strengthening of the organisation's political impact, and its imbrication with state power. Established at the initiative of Labor Member of Parliament Richard Klugman, the group would not 'meet in the ordinary way to plan action on behalf of ... prisoners of conscience allotted to their care', but function as 'a group of MPs who ... support Amnesty International in their capacity as parliamentarians'.[86] This would include 'promoting in Parliament debate on "Amnesty issues"' and, importantly, 'interceding through channels of directly with governments when requested by Amnesty'.[87]

The group's first meeting in March 1974 was addressed by Clare Wositzky as representative of the Victorian section, attended by several dozen members of both houses, and elected an executive comprising David Hamer (Liberal) President, Klugman (Australian Labour Party) Vice President, Antony Lamb (ALP) and Phillip Ruddock (Liberal). Such political bipartisanship became a cornerstone of the Parliamentary Group's work. This did not mean, however, that it was not politicised. Indonesia was an early focus of the group, and Whitlam made representations directly to the Suharto government around its human rights abuses during a visit in 1975, overtures that demonstrated his 'substance', according to one parliamentary ally. By 'raising the humanitarian questions of Amnesty International' with a despotic leader, Whitlam demonstrated his independence from the 'small target' foreign policy of his predecessors, who, it was claimed, lacked 'the guts to raise in that environment the issue'.[88]

Further evidence of the Parliamentary Group's realpolitik potential is evident in parliamentary debates in 1976 around a choice to petition Soviet leader Leonid Brezhnev on 'the fate of the members of the Amnesty International group in Moscow' after a leading member had been sentenced to internal exile.[89] Liberal MP Peter Baume, Senator in the Fraser Government that had replaced Whitlam's in December 1975, rose to present the petition on behalf of the Parliamentary Group only to be interrupted by an Opposition member, who asked why this petition focused on Australia's Cold War enemy and not a problem closer to home, such as Indonesia. Baume's response – 'Our concern with the situation in Russia has nothing to do with the political system in that country; it has only to do with the people who are under threat' – showed how Amnesty's agenda could easily be utilised to further political agendas, particularly after the Helsinki Accords of 1975 made the Soviet Union increasingly vulnerable to criticism on human rights grounds.[90]

The Parliamentary Group sat awkwardly within Amnesty's unwieldy Australian structure, and its status within a proposed national Amnesty body became controversial in 1975. In that year, Labor MP Adrian Bennett joined Ruddock in writing to the Victorian section to protest a new constitution for a national Amnesty organisation. Under its provisions, the chairman of the newly founded National Executive would serve as Amnesty spokesperson, and would only be required to 'liaise' with the Parliamentary Group. Bennett and Ruddock implored that 'We would hope ... it was not intended to remove the right of the Parliamentary Group to express its views'.[91] More than this, though, the missive expressed hopes that not only would the National Executive 'consult with the Parliamentary group', but also 'be guided to some degree by these views'.[92] Indeed, the 'power to veto in relation to any executive decision' would be required for the Parliamentary Group, so that it could remain 'a viable inter-party organisation'.[93] It seems such a push for parliamentary control over the national organisations was rejected, as in the next year the Parliamentary Group broke off relations with the Victorian section, and established 'direct representation with London'.[94]

Previously termed an 'international "grievance" organisation' by even sympathetic members of government, the period from the mid-1970s onwards saw significantly greater usage of Amnesty reports in parliamentary debate and journalism, while Amnesty International's receipt of the Nobel Peace Prize in 1978 saw 'its prestige and demands made upon it ... increase out of all proportion to its income'.[95] Amnesty boasted 10,000 Australian members by 1986 and 130 local chapters.[96] In that same year, Labor Prime Minister Bob Hawke declared the group 'has the support of all Australians to whom the ideals of political and personal freedom and the value of free speech and open participation in government are important'.[97] Amnesty and Australia were one.

Conclusion

How compromised did this relationship with political power make Amnesty? No doubt, the existence of a Parliamentary Group was a powerful tool for meeting Amnesty's goals, but it also raised questions: particularly around the relationship between both humanitarianism and human rights with the power and entrenched interests of nation states. Could an organisation boast a significant number of politician members – no matter how cross-party they might be – and remain apolitical? Amnesty had been founded to represent the 'forgotten prisoners', individuals gaoled by states for expressing their political opinions. This is what gave the group its novelty, and its ability to intercede in regimes no matter their ideological temperament, in a crowded charitable marketplace. Nevertheless, a lack of clarity around what constituted imprisonment meant the organisation's aims were read quite differently by those members who saw Amnesty as a continuation of existing modes of humanitarian interest rather than an abrupt intervention in the name of newly consecrated human rights. Further growing pains emerged around draft resistance, as members, shocked by the dehumanisation of individuals by callous authorities, clashed with those who viewed rights and citizenship as interconnected, and overt criticism of governments a risk. Where did the limits of conscience lie? And was the state a friend or an enemy?

The 1999 stripping of Phillip Ruddock, founding member of the Parliamentary Group and then Immigration Minister in John Howard's Liberal-National coalition Government, of his membership badge posed such questions anew. Times had changed, and while soon-to-be Labor Attorney-General Gareth Evans could claim in 1978 that 'Australia is not a country where Amnesty has much work to do', by the turn of the millennium the organisation became an ardent critic of harsh immigration policies maintained by both sides of politics.[98] Policies like the mandatory detention of immigrants arriving by boat were 'in breach of the UN [Refugee] convention and it's in breach ... of international law', Amnesty national president Kathy Kingston protested.[99] Political scientist Stephen Hopgood argues in his 2013 book, *The Endtime of Human Rights*, that humanitarian law and its hardworking practitioners have been 'colonised' by 'Human Rights', 'a global structure of laws, courts, norms, and organizations that ... run international campaigns, open local offices, lobby governments, and claim to speak with singular authority in the name of humanity as a whole'.[100] The history of Amnesty International in Australia shows the awkward accommodations and recriminations that flow from this forced marriage, which can be felt to this day.

Notes

1 Clare Wositzky, *Lighting the Candles: The First Thirty Years of Amnesty International in Australia* (Northcote, Australia: Self-published, 1995), pp. 18–19.
2 Peter Benenson, 'The Forgotten Prisoners', *Observer* (London), 28 May 1961, p. 21.
3 Wositzky, *Lighting the Candles*, p. 19. For Benenson quotation, see Bastian Bouwman, 'Outraged, Yet Moderate and Impartial: The Rise of Amnesty International in the Netherlands in the 1960s and 1970s', *BMGN: Low Countries Historical Review* (2017), 132 (4), p. 55.
4 Samuel Moyn, *The Last Utopia: Human Rights in History* (Cambridge, MA: Harvard University Press, 2010), pp. 220–1.
5 Quoted in Stephen Hopgood, *Keepers of the Flame: Understanding Amnesty International* (Ithaca, NY: Cornell University Press, 2006), pp. 68–9.
6 See Bruno Cabanes, *The Great War and the Origins of Humanitarianism, 1918–1924* (Cambridge, UK: Cambridge University Press, 2014), and Joy Damousi, 'World Refugee Year 1959–60: Humanitarian Rights in Postwar Australia', *Australian Historical Studies* (2020), 51 (2), pp. 212–27.
7 See for example Amanda B. Moniz, *From Empire to Humanity: The American Revolution and the Origins of Humanitarianism* (Oxford, UK: Oxford University Press, 2016); Melanie Oppenheimer, 'Re-Alignment in

the Aftermath of War: The League of Red Cross Societies, the Australian Red Cross and Its Junior Red Cross in the 1920s', in Neville Wylie, Melanie Oppenheimer and James Crossland (eds), *The Red Cross Movement: Myths, Practices and Turning Points* (Manchester, UK: Manchester University Press, 2020), pp. 130–47; Anna Bocking-Welch, 'Youth against Hunger: Service, Activism and the Mobilisation of Young Humanitarians in 1960s Britain', *European Review of History: Revue européenne d'histoire* (2016), 23 (1–2), pp. 154–70.

8 Studies of local national sections in Amnesty International include Bouwman, 'Outraged, Yet Moderate and Impartial'; Sarah B. Snyder, 'Exporting Amnesty International to the United States: Transatlantic Human Rights Activism in the 1960s', *Human Rights Quarterly* (2012), 34, pp. 779–99; Christie Miedema, 'Impartial in the Cold War? The Challenges of Détente, Dissidence, and Eastern European Membership to Amnesty International's Policy of Impartiality', *Humanity* (2019), 10 (2), pp. 179–205; Tom Buchanan, *Amnesty International and Human Rights Activism in Postwar Britain, 1945–1977* (Cambridge, UK: Cambridge University Press, 2020); Jon Piccini, *Human Rights in Twentieth Century Australia* (Cambridge, UK: Cambridge University Press, 2019), pp. 108–16.

9 Jan Eckel, 'The International League for the Rights of Man, Amnesty International, and the Changing Fate of Human Rights Activism from the 1940s through the 1970s', *Humanity* (Summer 2013), 4 (2), p. 193.

10 Buchanan, *Amnesty International*, p. 10.

11 Lynn Hunt, *Inventing Human Rights: A History* (New York, NY: W.W. Norton & Company, 2007), p. 35.

12 On the nineteenth century, see Penelope Edmonds and Hamish Maxwell-Stewart, '"The Whip Is a Very Contagious Kind of Thing": Flogging and Humanitarian Reform in Penal Australia', *Journal of Colonialism and Colonial History* (2016), 17 (1), online (https://muse.jhu.edu/article/613283), accessed 12 May 2020; Penelope Edmonds, 'Collecting Looerryminer's "Testimony": Aboriginal Women, Sealers, and Quaker Humanitarian Anti-Slavery Thought and Action in the Bass Strait Islands', *Australian Historical Studies* (2014), 45 (1), pp. 3–33; Zoe Laidlaw, 'Indigenous Interlocutors: Networks of Imperial Protest and Humanitarianism in the Mid-Nineteenth Century', in Jane Carey and Jane Lydon (eds), *Indigenous Networks: Mobility, Connections and Exchange* (London, UK: Routledge, 2014); Amanda Nettelbeck, *Indigenous Rights and Colonial Subjecthood: Protection and Reform in the 19th Century British Empire* (Cambridge, UK: Cambridge University Press, 2019). On early twentieth-century discourses, see Melanie Oppenheimer, *The Power of Humanity: 100 Years of Australian Red Cross* (Sydney, Australia: Harper Collins Australia, 2014), and Allison Holland, *Breaking the Silence: Aboriginal Defenders and the Settler State, 1905–1939* (Carlton, Australia: Melbourne University Press Academic, 2019).

13 See contributions by Jill Beard, Ann Curthoys, Katherine Ellinghaus and Amanda Nettelbeck in this volume.

14 Mark Mazower, *No Enchanted Palace: The End of Empire and the Ideological Origins of the United Nations* (Princeton, NJ: Princeton University Press, 2009), pp. 28–9.
15 Moyn, *The Last Utopia*, p. 107.
16 On the Soviet involvement, see Jessica Whyte, 'The Fortunes of Natural Man: Robinson Crusoe, Political Economy, and the Universal Declaration of Human Rights', *Humanity* (2014), 5 (3), pp. 301–21.
17 On CAR, see Jennifer Clark, 'The Far Left and the Fight for Aboriginal Rights: The Formation of the Council for Aboriginal Rights, 1951', in Jon Piccini, Evan Smith and Matthew Worley (eds), *The Far Left in Australia since 1945* (Abingdon, UK:, Routledge, 2018), pp. 99–117; Piccini, *Human Rights*, pp. 1–3; 80–4.
18 'Council for Aboriginal Rights – Constitution', Council for Aboriginal Rights Papers, Box 5, Folder 6, State Library of Victoria.
19 In the Australian context for grass roots and organised humanitarian organisations in the postwar period, see Joy Damousi, 'The Campaign for Japanese-Australian Children to Enter Australia, 1957–1968: A History of Post-War Humanitarianism', *Australian Journal of Politics and History* (2018), 64 (2), pp. 211–26; Joy Damousi, 'From Humanitarian "Charity" to "Justice": The Australian Foster Parents Plan and Fostering Refugees in Asia during the 1970s', *Australian Journal of Politics and History* (2019), 65 (4), pp. 549–65.
20 Young-Sun Hong, *Cold War Germany, the Third World, and the Global Humanitarian Regime* (Cambridge, UK: Cambridge University Press, 2015), pp. 3–4.
21 Ibid.
22 Agnieszka Sobocinska, *Visiting the Neighbours: Australians in Asia* (Sydney, Australia: NewSouth Publishing, 2014), ch. 5; Agnieszka Sobocinska, 'A New Kind of Mission: The Volunteer Graduate Scheme and the Cultural History of International Development', *Australian Journal of Politics & History* (2016), 62 (3), pp. 369–87.
23 Damousi, 'World Refugee Year', pp. 213–14.
24 Sobocinska, 'A New Kind of Mission', p. 371.
25 'Crusader for Politics of Good', *Sydney Morning Herald*, 7 October 2008, www.smh.com.au/national/crusader-for-politics-of-good-20081007-gdsxsm.html, accessed 17 May 2021.
26 A term most famously articulated in Geoffrey Blainey, *The Tyranny of Distance: How Distance Shaped Australia's History* (Sydney, Australia: Macmillan, 1966).
27 'Editorial: A New Stage', *Amnesty Bulletin* (April 1976), 58, p. 2.
28 'Third Annual Report of the Victorian Section – March 1964 – March 1965', *Amnesty Bulletin* (April 1965), 10, p. 1.
29 *Amnesty International Victoria Section – Annual Report, March 1966 – March 1967* (Melbourne, Australia: Self-published, 1967), p. 1; 'Amnesty International Victoria Section: Eleventh Annual Report', *Amnesty Bulletin* (April 1973), 40, p. 2; Robert V. Horn to The Editor, *Lateline*, 10 May 1973, Robert V. Horn Papers, MLMSS 8123, Box 33, State Library of New South Wales (hereafter SLNSW).

30 'Eleventh Annual Report', pp. 2–4.
31 'Third Annual Report of the Victorian Section', p. 1.
32 On the organisational culture of Amnesty, and how it has led to past conflict, see Hopgood, *Keepers of the Flame*, ch. 2.
33 'Capital Letter', *Canberra Times*, 23 December 1965, p. 3.
34 Ibid.; 'Amnesty Group for Canberra', *Canberra Times*, 11 December 1965, p. 25.
35 'Amnesty Branch', *Tribune* (Sydney), 30 October 1968, p. 12. On the Communist Party's 1960s reforms, see Jon Piccini, 'More Than an Abstract Principle: Reimagining Rights in the Communist Party of Australia, 1956–1971', *Journal of Australian Studies* (2015), 39 (2), pp. 200–15.
36 'It's a Changing World', *Australian Women's Weekly*, 9 February 1966, p. 60.
37 Damousi, 'World Refugee Year', p. 219.
38 Kenneth Cmiel, 'The Emergence of Human Rights Politics in the United States', *Journal of American History* (1999), 86 (3), p. 1232.
39 See, in particular, Russell McGregor, *Indifferent Inclusion: Aboriginal People and the Australian Nation* (Canberra, Australia: Aboriginal Studies Press, 2011).
40 John Chesterman, *Civil Rights: How Indigenous Australians Won Formal Equality* (St Lucia, Australia: University of Queensland Press, 2005); Jennifer Clark, *Aborigines and Activism: Race, Aborigines and the Coming of the Sixties to Australia* (Crawley, Australia: University of Western Australia Press, 2008).
41 For the impact of such international shaming on Australian policy, see Jennifer Clark, 'Something to Hide: Aborigines and the Department of External Affairs, January 1961/January 1962', *Journal of the Royal Australian Historical Society* (1997), 83 (1), pp. 71–84.
42 Yvette Nicholls, *Not Slaves, Not Citizens: Conditions of the Australian Aborigines in the Northern Territory* (Melbourne, Australia: Australian Council for Civil Liberties, 1952).
43 Ibid., p. 3. On 'defenders', see Holland, *Breaking the Silence*.
44 Ibid., pp. 12–13.
45 Charles Duguid, 'The Universal Declaration of Human Rights as It Relates to the Aborigines of Australia', Council for Aboriginal Rights (CAR) Papers, Box 8, Folder 4, State Library of Victoria.
46 'The Situation of Australian Aborigines', *Amnesty Bulletin* (August 1965), 11, p. 3.
47 This was a decision on which the New South Wales and Victorian sections both agreed, see Wositzky, *Lighting the Candles*, pp. 57–8, and letter from Robert V. Horn to Peter Benenson, 'Your Recent Circular to Members', 31 June 1964, Robert V. Horn Papers, MLMSS 8123, Box 33, SLNSW.
48 Wositzky, *Lighting the Candles*, p. 98.
49 The women's movement in particular has made significant use of the slavery analogy, see Ana Stevenson, *The Woman as Slave in Nineteenth Century American Social Movements* (Basingstoke, UK: Palgrave, 2020).
50 *The Situation of Australian Aborigines: A Factual Report Compiled by Amnesty International* (Sassafras, Australia: Self-published, 1966), p. 36.

51 Wositzky, *Lighting the Candles*, p. 100.
52 Ibid., p. 101.
53 'Squalid Life for Aborigines Stressed', *Canberra Times*, 2 April 1966, p. 3.
54 K. E. Beasley MP, 'Amnesty Report Has Obvious Weakness', *Canberra Times*, 27 April 1966, p. 20.
55 'Regret at Haste on Aborigines', *Canberra Times*, 6 April 1966, p. 3.
56 Wositzky, *Lighting the Candles*, pp. 99–100.
57 For more on Australia's Vietnam War, see John Murphy, *Harvest of Fear: A History of Australia's Vietnam War* (St Leonards, Australia: Allen & Unwin, 1993), and Peter Edwards, *Australia and the Vietnam War* (Sydney, Australia: NewSouth Publishing, 2014). On the National Service Act, see Christina Twomey, 'The National Service Scheme: Citizenship and the Tradition of Compulsory Military Service in 1960s Australia', *Australian Journal of Politics and History* (2012), 58 (1), pp. 67–81.
58 Chris Dixon and Jon Piccini, 'The Anti-Vietnam War Movement: International Activism and the Search for World Peace', in William Knoblauch, Michael Loedenthal and Christian Peterson (eds), *The Routledge History of World Peace since 1750* (New York, NY: Routledge, 2018), pp. 371–81.
59 'Statement from the Victorian Section of Amnesty International. Bill White Case', *Amnesty Bulletin* (November 1966), 16, p. 4.
60 Lincoln Oppenheimer, 'President's Report', *Amnesty News* (August 1966), 10, p. 3.
61 The Ex-Services Human Rights Association of Australia is discussed in more detail in Piccini, *Human Rights*, pp. 99–108.
62 Waddington's speech is reproduced in *Amnesty News* (February 1968), 16, pp. 5–6; 'Not So Sweet', *Conscience* (May 1971), 63, p. 9.
63 'Copy of Statement by Mr W. White, Sydney Schoolteacher and Conscientious Objector', *Amnesty News* (August 1966), 10, pp. 2–3.
64 Ibid.
65 See Nick Irving, 'Anti-Conscription Protest, Liberal Individualism and the Limits of National Myths in the Global 1960s', *History Australia* (2017), 14 (2), pp. 87–201.
66 'Australia's Political Prisoner', Undated leaflet, State Library of South Australia, available at: https://web.archive.org/web/20060501083814/http://www.slsa.sa.gov.au/saatwar/collection/srg124_8_9.htm, accessed 29 April 2020.
67 Robert V. Horn, Untitled report on conscientious objection and noncompliance in Australia, Robert V. Horn Papers, MLMSS 8123, Box 33, SLNSW.
68 Ibid.
69 David McKenna to Robert V. Horn, 2 March 1969, Robert V. Horn Papers, MLMSS 8123, Box 33, SLNSW.
70 For more on these legal changes, see Murphy, *Harvest of Fear*, pp. 214–16.
71 *Amnesty International Victoria Section – Annual Report, March 1966 – March 1967*, p. 4.
72 David McKenna to Robert V. Horn, 2 March 1969.
73 Ibid.

74 Horn, Untitled report.
75 David McKenna to Robert V. Horn, 19 February 1970, Robert V. Horn Papers, MLMSS 8123, Box 33, SLNSW.
76 On the evolution of this concept amongst activists and in the United Nations, see Jeremy Kessler, 'The Invention of a Human Right: Conscientious Objection at the United Nations, 1947–2011', *Columbia Human Rights Law Review* (Spring 2013), 44 (3), pp. 753–91.
77 'Resolution – Prisoner of Conscience Week, November 1969', *Amnesty News* (February 1970), 24, pp. 15–16.
78 Tom Buchanan, 'Amnesty International in Crisis, 1966–7', *Twentieth Century British History* (2004), 15 (3), p. 288.
79 'International Council', *Amnesty Bulletin* (October 1970), 28, pp. 4–5.
80 E. G. Whitlam, 'Press Statement: Amnesty International, Paris Conference on Abolition of Torture', 10 December 1973, https://pmtranscripts.pmc.gov.au/release/transcript-3097, accessed 30 April 2020.
81 Carl Ungerer, 'The "Middle Power" Concept in Australian Foreign Policy', *Australian Journal of Politics & History* (2007), 53 (4), pp. 538–51.
82 Barbara Keys, 'Anti-Torture Politics: Amnesty International, the Greek Junta, and the Origins of the Human Rights "Boom" in the United States', in Akira Iriye, Petra Goedde and William I. Hitchcock (eds), *The Human Rights Revolution: An International History* (New York, NY: Oxford University Press, 2012), pp. 201–21; Barbara J. Keys, *Reclaiming American Virtue: The Human Rights Revolution of the 1970s* (Cambridge, MA: Harvard University Press, 2014).
83 Mentioned in *Amnesty International Annual Report 1972–3* (London, UK: Amnesty International Publications, 1973), p. 86, at www.amnesty.org/en/documents/pol10/001/1973/en/, accessed 17 May 2020.
84 Sean MacBride to Gough Whitlam, 11 May 1973, in National Archives of Australia (hereafter NAA): A1838, 929/6/3 PART 3.
85 This was not universally supported, however, with a strong tendency against United Nations work evident in the US section, whose leader declared it a 'sideshow'. Keys, *Reclaiming American Virtue*, p. 190.
86 'History of the Parliamentary Group of Amnesty International', in NAA A1838 929/33/3/1 PART 3. My thanks are due to Professor Barbara Keys for providing me with this document.
87 Ibid.
88 *Commonwealth Parliamentary Debates* (CPD), House of Representatives, 11 February 1975, p. 78.
89 *CPD*, Senate, 7 April 1976, p. 1165.
90 Ibid. On the Helsinki Accords, see Sarah B. Snyder, *Human Rights Activism and the End of the Cold War: A Transnational History of the Helsinki Network* (Cambridge, UK: Cambridge University Press, 2011).
91 Adrian Bennett and Phillip Ruddock to Vivian Abraham, 22 May 1975, in NAA M5048, 18.
92 Ibid.
93 Ibid.

94 'History of the Parliamentary Group of Amnesty International'.
95 Margaret Masterman, 'Amnesty International and Its Work', *Canberra Times*, 20 May 1980, p. 2.
96 'History of the Parliamentary Group of Amnesty International'.
97 R. J. L. Hawke, 'Prime Minister's Speech, Amnesty International Candle Lighting Ceremony, Kings Hall', 28 May 1986, https://pmtranscripts.pmc.gov.au/release/transcript-6935, accessed 19 May 2020.
98 Gareth Evans, 'Human Rights in Australia', talk at the ACFOA Summer School, Hobart, 22 January 1978, in Records of the Australian Council for International Development, Box 138, National Library of Australia.
99 'Ruddock Stripped of Amnesty International Badge' [Transcript], *AM*, 18 March 2000, available at: www.abc.net.au/am/stories/s111533.htm, accessed 18 October 2018.
100 Stephen Hopgood, *The Endtimes of Human Rights* (Ithaca, NY: Cornell University Press, 2013), pp. x, xiv.

14

Palliation, poverty and child welfare: Human rights and humanitarianism in the 1980s

Roland Burke

On 22 September 1982, Michael Posner, director of the Lawyers Committee for International Human Rights, defined the ambitions of human rights advocacy in austere terms. Speaking on his guiding creed of action to a US Congressional Subcommittee, Posner was clear on what might be achieved: 'At least for some of the people some of the time', human rights policy could 'make an awful situation slightly less awful'.[1] He conceded this was far from utopian. Palliation where possible 'may not be an ideal solution'; it was, however, 'worth doing'. Months earlier in Geneva, the Ugandan representative on the Committee, Olara Otunnu, faced with appalling poverty and the legacy of destruction wrought by comfortably exiled dictator Idi Amin, found the opposite.[2] Human rights for Uganda required radical reshaping of global economic and political structures, a so-called New International Economic Order, and its mildly less revolutionary counterpart, the Right to Development. 'There was a need', Otunnu argued, 'first of all, to democratize international economic relations'.[3] The delta between these two meanings, each fused to, and expressed within, 'human rights', had emerged in the mid-1970s. This chapter investigates the ways in which the minimalistic posture of what eminent historian Samuel Moyn described as the 'human rights breakthrough' interacted with the vestigial endeavour for international redistributionism across the late 1970s and 1980s. By the end of the 1980s it was a reconfigured minimalism that proved ascendant, drawing the ambitious vision of the 1948 Universal Declaration of Human Rights closer to its older sibling, humanitarianism.

Although the transformation of human rights in the 1970s has been subject to an imposing array of scholarship, the longer-term effects of the 'breakthrough' have yet to be fully assessed. It was in the 1980s that the cumulative impact of the 1970s renaissance of the human rights non-government organisations movement had begun to reshape the United Nations (UN), and many domestic polities across the Western world. Amnesty International continued to advance in its sophistication and reach, and was joined by new nodes and an expanding network of non-government organisation (NGO) groups that had mobilised around the treatment of Soviet dissidents, disinvestment from apartheid South Africa and the dark triptych of disappearances, death squads and torture in Latin America. Human rights campaigning was structured around restraining malign states from the outside where possible, and, for the incoming Republican administration of President Ronald Reagan in the United States, encouraging democratisation as a distant aspiration. Despite deep political differences, both human rights NGOs and neo-conservative cold warriors operated with a highly triaged concept of human rights – a pared-down canon of normative principles that mapped to limited means and modest expectations.

Conversely, the apparent momentum of the Third World, exemplified by the adoption of the New International Economic Order by the UN General Assembly, had faltered. While the precepts of global redistribution had been nominally agreed by the UN across the mid-1970s, and remained durable landmarks in human rights debates, the prospects of any real success beyond grandiose pronouncements had dimmed. In December 1986 the General Assembly adopted the Declaration on the Right to Development, a text which conjoined the logic of the New International Economic Order with human rights more explicitly, and with greater care to define the relationship. The edifice was impressive, but the revolutionary repartitioning of global resources, and the delivery of human rights it would purportedly ensure, remained undone.

This chapter argues that 'human rights' in the 1980s was a contest between an avowedly 'anti-political' human rights NGO movement, which constructed its activism around severe abuses practised by states, and a candidly political group of Third World governments, which cast human rights in terms of a massive repartitioning of inter-state economic power. The former found human rights, predominantly, in individuated humans. The latter viewed human rights as the means for dissolving 'existing, unjust' structures and reformulating them as a needed precondition for welfare and freedom. Rhetorically deadlocked for much of the time, international action and NGO activism settled into a new equilibrium, animated by grotesque harms, desperate conditions and distinctively vulnerable humans. Each of the identifiable successes of the 1980s was in areas of unique emotional valence and a deep heritage in the preoccupations of classical humanitarian campaigning: mutilating weapons, torture, subsistence and children. Major revisions to the international fabric, be it in the 'minimalist' liberal democratic key of the Western-dominated human rights NGOs, or the 'maximalist' key of the developing world, both appeared infeasible. Human rights' utopianism retreated to humanitarian palliation, and when re-factored into the austerity of humanitarianism, both species of 'human rights' could win victories that were impossible in the optimistic frame of rights.

Captivated by cruelties: the grim success of the Convention Against Torture

In Geneva, the new decade opened with the ratification of the Convention on Certain Conventional Weapons in October 1980, a small renovation in international humanitarian law. The Convention mostly avoided the intractable battles that characterised the wider 1970s endeavour to rebuild the 1948 Geneva Conventions, which had set out the contours of legitimate conduct in war.[4] Built on a perversely technocratic International Committee of the Red Cross examination of new weapons systems that caused exotic suffering, the 1980 Convention addressed weapons of mostly marginal military utility.[5] It applied the bounded compassion of Solferino to the technological terrain of cruelties new and anticipated, from thermobaric munitions and lasers employed to cause blindness to shrapnel transparent to x-ray imaging.[6] Unlike the almost paralysing debates of the late 1970s, which involved deep reconsideration of anti-colonial insurgencies, the Convention channelled the spirit of Red Cross founder Henri Dunant and the imperial dignitaries that pondered what constituted civilised warfare.[7] Where reforming Geneva law grappled with the outer bounds of what was permissible in 'wars of national liberation', the Convention patrolled the morbid demarcation of the time, manner and place through which lethal energy could be applied to the human body.[8]

The Convention was emblematic of the migration away from the structural and self-consciously ideological, and towards the pre-political corporeal.[9] A tight focus on the sufferings of the human person was consolidated as central to the human rights agenda of the 1980s, with the ongoing mobilisation against torture, and its inscription into a formal international treaty. With the drafting of the UN Convention Against Torture, the corporeal consolidated its place as a central priority in the first half of the 1980s.[10] Exemplified by Amnesty International's World Campaign, anti-torture was perhaps the defining theme of the human rights NGO 'breakthrough'. An initial Declaration Against Torture, concluded in 1975, moved – in UN procedural terms – very promptly through to the preparation of a Convention Against Torture, adopted in 1984.[11] Early steps after the 1975 Declaration were pursued by consensus, leveraging the intrinsic capacity for torture to be cast with absolute moral clarity. In his March 1977 summation of the recent session of the Commission on Human Rights, UK representative Sir Keith Unwin singled out forays on torture and arbitrary detention as amongst the more promising UN initiatives; they were 'useful things started without much controversy'.[12] Given a UN environment where tempestuous debates on the study of individual complaints from abused citizens, the decades-long effort to establish a High Commissioner for Human Rights and the hyper-political New International Economic Order often consumed the available time and energy, torture was an area where some progress could be made on a violation of especial gravity.

Torture was the emotional chaperone for advancing the institutional place of human rights NGOs, carried forward on the cumulative momentum gathered by Amnesty International's World Wide Campaign Against Torture. In May 1977 an impressive collection of human rights NGO representatives assembled, appropriately, at the Henri Dunant Institute in Geneva – a short trip from their local accommodations. Their strategy session set torture apart as a distinctively powerful – and useful – abuse. It was a violation that preceded and exceeded the human rights category. Amnesty International's position paper, introduced by Dick Oosting, who directed the World Wide Campaign, set out the rationale for a grand strategy based around anti-torture. According to Amnesty, the moment was now 'ripe for capitalizing on' the myriad gains of its World Wide Campaign, in public awareness, disappointment at government inaction and the emergent salience afforded to human rights in government policy – a development underscored by the election of Georgia's Democratic Governor Jimmy Carter to the US presidency in 1976.[13]

Torture was, for the attendees, seemingly *sui generis* in its capacity to harvest the energy of these trends, and potentially canalise outrage to impel wider advocacy. Strategic successes would be opened by 'the easy acceptance of torture being the most direct, obvious and abhorrent of all human rights violations'. Amnesty set out an ambitious 'general strategy', with anti-torture, as discrete and invincible moralism, puncturing obstacles to human rights protection.[14] An NGO alliance with friendly states 'would "use" torture as a universally acceptable "tool"'. Around this moralistic nucleus would 'form a loosely-knit international front that would aim at breaking through the existing frustrations and barriers of the inter-governmental mechanisms, especially at the UN'. Abolition of torture was at once innately good and effective instrumentalism. 'Once a breakthrough can be made on torture', Amnesty's strategists envisioned, the enabling precedent 'could then pave the way for more effective tackling on the inter-governmental level of other, obviously offensive human rights problems'.[15]

In a long disquisition on how to advance, the participants appeared sceptical of the burst of attention to rights heralded by Carter's election. Prominence in the new President's platform posed 'the risk that human rights might become a tired concept', and the term 'human rights' would degenerate into merely 'a tool in a Cold War situation'. The solution to politics was 'torture'. 'If we limit ourselves to torture', a discussant counselled, 'opportunities may be greater than the risks'.[16] For the Symposium's rapporteur, an emphasis on torture was recommended by its pre-eminence as a source of governmental shame and public revulsion. 'Most Governments', the Symposium noted, were 'ashamed of torture but not ashamed about killing and preventive detention'.[17] A state's vote against protections, and thus implicitly 'for' torture, was more than voting against a human rights measure: it was a vote against something more primordially tied to conscience and humanity. States that cheerfully voted down more comprehensive human rights treaties would 'not dare vote against humanitarian rights'.[18]

Those who negotiated this NGO strategy were acutely aware of a moralistic and affective dimension engaged by torture, an element that was seemingly attenuated in the general corpus of human rights. 'Moral Imperative Propaganda' was set out as a pillar in the proposed attack on torture. Its essence was simple – a metronomic reiteration of 'the fact that "there are simply certain things you don't do"'. An imposing affective weight was attached to the crime – 'the fact that torture is the grossest of violations mankind imposes' – which might transcend numerous political impediments. There was, in the assessment of the authors, 'considerable room for improvement in the propaganda that certain activities just violate humanity at its deepest level'.[19] 'Concentrated efforts', targeting a self-evident evil, would ensure 'stimulation of the moral force necessary to carry forward the whole action against torture'. Casting back to the mode of emotionally powerful appeal pioneered by abolitionists Thomas Clarkson and Elizabeth Heyrick two centuries earlier, the NGO Strategy group explicitly positioned itself as self-conscious successor to 'the two generations of moral indignation needed to generally abolish slavery'.[20]

In the conference rooms of the Dunant Institute, Amnesty and its circle had methodically wandered into the same mode of reasoning that generations of humanitarians had discovered in more personal terms. Enumerated points, prepared on an early word processor, lacked the wrenching misery recorded by humanitarian crusader Emily Hobhouse as she wrote amidst living – barely breathing – human destruction at the camps across the Orange Free State and Cape Colony.[21] From Johannesburg, Hobhouse wrote that her 'heart wept within', and related unstructured appeals to compassion on behalf of sick and starving mothers and children imprisoned by the Empire.[22] Advocacy was immediate, a direct entreaty to officials, where she sought 'to rub as much salt into the sore places of their minds' as she could.[23] Edmund Morel and Roger Casement began their humanitarian work in an investigatory mode, and arrived at revulsion at precipitous speed when they encountered King Leopold's atrocities in the literally mutilated flesh of Congo's people. Pioneering British abolitionist Thomas Clarkson himself began by preparing an essay demonstrating mastery of Latin expression and reason – and promptly collapsed in tears as he realised the implications of his argument. Human rights NGOs had a more studied and proceduralist road to epiphany: the pitiable human could activate in ways that technical legalisms and liberal phraseology could not. NGO grand strategy was to rebuild human rights from the litany of harmed humans, climbing from the corporeal back to the conceptual.

NGO advocates of the proposed Convention Against Torture studiously deferred engagement with any of those abuses that were predisposed to abstract discussion. Instead, they kept their gaze on the compelling quality attendant to the deliberate and meticulous enactment of pain – from here, they meditated on the need to build outwards to contexts. Torture was the unmediated encounter between the abusive state and the helpless individual. Equally, the arrival at that terminal point reflected human rights deficits that were much more systemic. While the Symposium proceedings conceded that 'from conscientization point of view, the strength of any programme to combat torture will continue to be built on specific cases', Amnesty gestured to the need for some effort to use the individually abused person as a thematic vector. More facility with 'the individual case' was needed in this context 'to draw attention to those situations which give rise to torture, that is, to link individual cases with broader (e.g. economic, political) questions'.[24] Again, while set in the prose of the Committee and the vernacular of international law, Amnesty's logic traversed the same routes that abolitionists, child welfarists and wartime palliators had pioneered decades earlier.

An individual's plight would, ideally, offer a bridge to some kind of counter-vision, as opposed to a total cauterisation of torture as an isolated and maximal type of abuse without deeper provenance. As late 1970s NGO strategy was translated into 1980s inter-state legal treaty, the persuasive facility of anti-torture activism was well proven, but any vision of it being a spearhead to more thorough transformation foundered. Anti-torture activism won major tactical victories, yet it did so amidst an ongoing strategic retreat. It successfully began to refigure human rights in terms closer to the archetypal humanitarian dispensations of the past: in the revealing terminology adopted by Amnesty, protection against torture was a 'humanitarian right'.

Shepherded by an alliance of NGOs and sympathetic states, international treaty protections against torture made substantial gains. Irritable and tense consensus, led by a UN working group, which ground away at a Draft Convention Against Torture across the first years of the 1980s, was aided by precisely the factors Amnesty had identified at their 1977 meeting – foremost the clarity and simplicity of focus. Considerable thought was devoted to parsing what, precisely, constituted the parietals of the barest humanity in a legal sense, but the normative intricacy and precarity inherent in other human rights instruments were less debilitating.[25] Similarly, the minimalist content of the protections assisted agreement on mechanisms for implementation and enforcement: legalistic defences and canards were less readily manufactured given the sparing content of the draft Convention Against Torture. Anti-torture campaigning was an exemplar of the rising power of the corporeal as a subject. It was a showcase for the efficacy of the performatively anti-political as a register through which to set down protection. It was a demonstration that human rights could make progress in a politically riven international organisation, albeit only if defined with exceptional parsimony.[26] The rapid adoption of the Convention Against Torture in 1984 indicated the promise of the 'breakthrough', which had re-partitioned human rights to the humanitarian floor, as opposed to the utopian ceiling. Corporeal causes could rebuild a rights architecture of claustrophobic but adamantine norms, grounded in pity and outrage.

Growing the right to food: corporeal human rights in another key

While anti-torture was the most striking monument to the successes of minimalism in the early 1980s, another focus, on the right to food, demonstrated that emphasis on the elemental physiologic wellbeing could be deployed toward less individual, less paradigmatically liberal ends. Bare subsistence provided another emerging site of accommodation between the transformational, sovereign-centric human rights of the Global South and the reflexive minimalism of the Western human rights NGOs. Proponents of structural change, typically encapsulated in the New International Economic Order, adopted a similar transliteration of abstract proposition to abused person, and an equivalent diminution of ambition. Subsistence became a symbolic avatar of the New International Economic Order and its crusading enthusiasm for a new collection of solidarity-type rights. Unlike this expansively drawn roadmap for global structural justice, subsistence was also sufficiently modest to be acceptable – or at least unanswerable – to even the most anti-statist liberals in the Western group. By the late 1980s, the New International Economic Order and its attenuated satellite, the Declaration on the Right to Development, were barely more than rhetorical talismans. By contrast, its radically diminished cousin, the Right to Food, was a consensual, bedrock article, and an accepted international priority. In subsistence and food, proponents of global structural change had found a humanitarian touchstone.

Food accessed an older wellspring of normative currency. In the early postwar years, with severe food crises in postwar Europe, provision of basic food had been a pillar of the then-new moral structure – a prerequisite for peace and freedom. The Food and Agriculture Organization (FAO) and the UN Relief and Rehabilitation Administration (UNRRA) programmes rested on compassionate and presumptively transient disbursement in the 1940s. Across the 1950s and 1960s, the sprawling UN complex of technical assistance, centred in the FAO and the World Food Program, gently moved universal sustenance away from the language of humanitarianism. Recognition of a particularised right to food was a novel hybrid of various moral species, old and new. When this refurbished right to food coalesced in the 1970s, it was distinct from the three moral accents on food that had preceded it. The Right to Food was less technocratic than the subsistence promised by FAO-led scientific progress. It was more emphatically asserted than food's position in the concert of economic and social rights of the Universal Declaration of Human Rights and International Covenant on Economic, Social and Cultural Rights. The right to food avoided the overt paternalism of the most established ancestral subsistence frame, that of charitable relief.

In November 1974, months after the UN Special Session devoted to a mostly empty recapitulation of debate between developed and developing worlds the World Food Conference was convened under the auspices of the FAO in Rome. Among the first in the new generation of global summits that began to punctuate the UN calendar, it drew together technocratic experts, NGOs and government delegations from the world's very divided states.[27] In its bold promises, the World Food Conference Declaration was a rededication to universalism, and, unlike the 1948 Universal Declaration of Human Rights, contained a timetable for realisation. Over a quarter century, however, the Declaration's blueprint extending the Four Freedoms had been reduced to one of especial urgency, in the carriage of the FAO. At the World Food Conference, the delegates proclaimed 'that within a decade no child will go to bed hungry' and 'no family will fear for its next day's bread'.[28] Given the cresting neo-Malthusian anxieties of crop yields, population growth, environmental damage and resource depletion, which were crossing from the specialist realm into popular culture, there was momentum for mobilisation on this particular right.

With food assurance in its charter, it was logical for the FAO to accord pre-eminence to universal subsistence, but the wider rights agenda at the UN was also hospitable to its elevation. Focussed on a remedy for one the most evocative effects of Third World impoverishment, the right to food was a potent nexus between the redistributionist abstractions of the New International Economic Order and a particularly striking misery. The televised grotesque of child starvation, particularly in Biafra, had been an exquisite source of activation of Western audiences in the late 1960s, and would be so again in 1984, with the Ethiopian famine.[29] Although food's place on the agenda of the late 1970s and early 1980s stemmed from the revolutionary demand for global redistribution, food was elevated for priority pursuit.[30] The Right to Food was the New International Economic Order made modest, and its abstractions were made manifest in despairing and upsetting flesh.

Despite its provenance in structural critique of global inequality, the right to food coincided with new trends in the scholarship, which recognised structural injustices, but approached them without any revolutionary zeal. Distinguished philosopher Henry Shue counselled a new modesty in moral pursuits. His 1980 monograph, *Basic Rights*, mapped well to the instincts of Western human rights diplomacy.[31] Shue's conceptual scaffold also departed from the almost monomaniacal focus on torture embraced by Amnesty, and proposed a scheme of 'basic rights' with much greater symmetry between the social and economic, as well as the civil and political. All rights, however, were substantially pared back. Shue advocated the ethical refoundation of what constituted the elemental – the titular 'Basic' of his work.

A right to 'subsistence', defined in wide but modest terms, was a central plank of Shue's scheme. He described the right to subsistence as 'to have available for consumption what is needed for a decent chance at a reasonably healthy and active life'.[32] Across his text, Shue established these rights as an essential floor: the hallmark of 'basic rights' was a standard that met but did not exceed absolute adequacy.[33] This return to 'basic' intersected with the inchoate desire for a new moralism that had accompanied the Carter administration in the United States.[34] As with so much in the 1980s, some evasive modus vivendi between corporeal minimalist and grand structuralist was discovered by deflating hopes.

In the UN, Asbjørn Eide, a well-published scholar and diplomat with proven expertise in human rights, was tasked with resolving the contours of the 'the right to food' and its domains of application. His report, presented to Commission on Human Rights in 1987, was a grand synthesis, more descriptive than normative, and rich in citations. Eide's investigation began with a venerable and secure genealogy, of US President Franklin Roosevelt's Four Freedoms of 1941, the creation of the United Nations and the promulgation of the Universal Declaration of Human Rights.[35] Prominent among the references, and a clear influence on Eide's approach, was the work of Indian philosopher, economist and Nobel laureate, Amartya Sen, who revised the study of famine away from a debate conducted around purely technical and economic distribution questions. Sen's pioneering insight on the ways in which accountability, legal and social equality and the aggregated features typical of healthy democracy were the key prophylaxis in famine was a study in how an often-vague phraseology of human rights' 'indivisibility' functioned, or tragically, malfunctioned.[36]

The right to food – or in Sen's term, 'food entitlement' – was an indissoluble composite of food itself, and a sub-set of civil and political freedoms. Eide's Right to Food report suggested the plausibility of a consensus between liberal and material visions of human rights. The rhetorical adoption of the concept of the Right to Food in the second half of the 1980s, and subsequently a steady technocratic programme to advance it, was the most rudimentary and frugal derivation of the bold demands for global economic justice that had rung out across Third World capitals and the UN General Assembly in the second half of the 1970s. Western human rights NGOs had descended from ambitions of a world of democratic welfare states, and found minimum altitude at the prevention of torture. Advocates of radical wealth redistribution had descended from global revolution to the prevention of starvation.

The consensus of compassionate paternalism: reviving the rights of the child

The Convention on the Rights of the Child was the capstone of the 1980s human rights enterprise – and the last major endeavour before the full dawn of the post–Cold War era.[37] Adopted on 20 November 1989, ten days after jubilant citizens dismounted their celebratory perch on Berlin Wall, the Convention followed a moribund adventure into the rights of children briefly pursued in the late 1950s and subsequently set aside as the preserve of UNICEF.[38] The rights and protection of children were revived as a formal UN human rights pursuit by Polish jurist, Professor Adam Lopatka, a minister in General Wojciech Jaruzelski's government.[39] With the adoption – in 1976 – of 1979 as the International Year of the Child, which served as a rededication to the 1959 Declaration, the plight of children was elevated as a theme for global public attention.[40] Evocative imagery of the young from across the world, often sickly, sometimes healthy – and always vulnerable – accompanied promotion of the Year.[41] These images resurrected a visual repertoire that had been deployed in the UN humanitarian appeals of the late 1940s and early 1950s, when photo essays on the precarious state of the children of postwar Europe, and later, the poverty of South Asia, were printed and disseminated en masse.[42] As part of the celebrations of the Year of the Child, the UN and UNICEF embarked upon their first tentative steps to a dedicated Convention.[43] Executive Director of UNICEF, James Grant, recalled that they anticipated the initiative 'would not progress very far', such was the perceived difficulty.[44]

In his outstanding analysis of the Convention, historian Linde Lindkvist demonstrates the ways in which the Convention was a text that revealed the normative contests around human rights in the 1980s.[45] While Lindkvist is primarily focused on the connections between humanitarian law and the Convention, his insight on the Convention as an index for the conflict within the language has wider application. Children's rights emerged as another sanctuary theme, where superficial disavowals of the political could be drawn upon, while simultaneously engaged with a special kind of force. Much like anti-torture, children's rights were reintroduced at the height of UN political dysfunction. Proposals for the Draft Convention on the Rights of the Child, introduced in 1978, were a slender channel of potential comity.[46] More prosaically, a Soviet-backed pursuit of work on children's rights was a procedural concession that allowed the Western- and democratic Southern-sponsored anti-torture item to proceed. Poland's representative, Bogumil Sujka, when recommending the Convention item to the General Assembly, emphasised that 'mankind should offer the child the best it possessed', a best, which given the generalised deadlock of most UN actions of the period, seemed unpromising.[47] Despite misgivings that the Convention on the Rights of the Child was designed for diversionary purpose – and it was – the new agenda item did no material harm to the key Western and NGO priorities, which were primarily torture.[48]

Much of the evolution of the Convention on the Rights of the Child was marked by a lack of contention.[49] As Lopatka's colleague, Wlodzimierz Kalinowki enthused, in his March 1981 summation of the encouraging proceedings of the Convention's Working Group, 'rights of the child enjoyed universal support because of its humanitarian nature'.[50] In a pan-ideological sense, the Convention was also predisposed to platitude, a facility well shown by the Director of the UN Human Rights Division, Kurt Herndl. Herndl reminded the 1984 session of the General Assembly that 'it was through the children of today that a future of peace, justice and freedom must be constructed'.[51] Even when Poland, the key sponsor of the Convention, was singled out for gross human rights abuses by the Commission on Human Rights at its 1982 session, work on the Convention continued without disruption. While railing against this supposed injustice, Poland could also advance a positive programme, and rehearse empty verbiage on the regime's commitment to social progress – even while it remained under martial law.

Numerous Third World delegations, including a growing array that was reacquiring democratic features lost in the years following independence in 1960, could emphasise the depth to which child poverty impaired capacity to secure health, literacy and physical security as envisaged in the Convention. Senegal's 1985 assessment, supportive of the Convention, was nevertheless emphatic that there were other fundamentals involved, humanitarian in character. Moussa Bocar Ly (Senegal), who was also a strong proponent of the right to food, and would go on to hold a senior position in the FAO, argued that the draft text, 'should focus on the situation of children in developing countries', a group 'often the victims of hunger, drought and illiteracy'. Ly represented the well-established government of

Abdou Diouf, successor to first President Leopold Senghor. While Diouf's government was comparatively liberal – winning an admittedly flawed election contested with a vote dispersed across eight parties – the former French colony remained desperately poor.[52] Even a well-crafted text depended on deeper improvements. 'It was', Ly lamented, 'a moot point whether it served any purpose to recognize the rights of children who were dying of hunger'.[53]

When shorn of any more sweeping demand for international economic revolution, and embodied in the vulnerable, the urgency of aid found no demur. As with torture, and with subsistence, the rights of children often found a strange sanctuary site from otherwise deeply inscribed political constraints. The most pitched contests on the substance of the Convention on the Rights of the Child, and the only area where major rupture seemed likely across its ten-year evolution, were on questions of military service. The adoption of the draft Convention on the Rights of the Child at the November 1989 General Assembly was, like much of the drafting work, bereft of open controversy. When presented to the UN Plenary, it was approved without a vote. In his celebratory address to the General Assembly on 20 November 1989, Secretary-General Javier Pérez de Cuéllar praised the Convention as something of a beacon for future human rights programmes. 'The process of its drafting', he enthused, 'was a model of how our organization can and should strive to achieve common goals'. He expressed his satisfaction that 'unproductive political confrontations were set aside': it was a showcase of how the UN could operate, to protect 'the needs of those who are humanity's most vulnerable'.[54] UNICEF Director James Grant declared 'that for children', the Convention was 'the Magna Carta'.[55]

At the turn of the decade, the Convention on the Rights of the Child and the cause of children were the face of a conjoined rights and humanitarian programme at the UN. In late September 1990, UNICEF convened the World Summit for Children, the most comprehensive assembly of heads of state in the history of international organisation.[56] Drawing outwards from the concepts that were set down in the rights of the child process, the Summit, which had been the object of years of exhaustive planning, cultivated sinews between children and a pared-down corpus of development milestones on vaccination, literacy and nutrition.[57] In its ruthless pragmatism and correlated lowering of horizons, it prefigured the focal point of the 2000s, the Millennium Development Goals.[58] Across 1989 and 1990, the Convention's opening for signature and associated promotional ceremonies were rich in symbolism – of children from around the world assembled at UN headquarters. The efflorescence of attention around the Convention on the Rights of the Child provided some of the few occasions where engagement with the young and the famous elevated the profile, prestige and promise of the human rights programme. Audrey Hepburn, a celebrated figure in film, served as a special ambassador for children from 1987.[59]

While the UN and UNICEF had parlayed celebrity into their profile for some time, Hepburn's experience before her screen career was an obvious point of affinity to the Convention on the Rights of the Child. When she was a child in Belgium, her father had abandoned the family to work for Oswald Mosley's British Union of Fascists. Her uncle was executed by Nazi occupiers in the Netherlands. She had witnessed the Gestapo firing squads at close range in her family's adopted home town of Arnhem. She later spoke of Jewish citizens being assembled for transport to death camps. During World War II she suffered severe malnutrition, developing kwashiorkor and anaemia during the Hunger Winter of 1944–45, a famine induced by the Nazi regime, when her family was compelled to survive on a starvation diet of tulip bulbs. She spoke of the 'rage' televised images of child starvation and suffering had induced in her, and her antipathy for 'politics'.[60]

Public outreach on children's rights tended to reinforce the humanitarian and palliative inflexion of the Convention's drafting – particularly its emphasis on the impacts of war, political violence and displacement. With several region-scale catastrophes, there was an almost gravitational association between the Convention and relief efforts. Hepburn travelled relentlessly across the late 1980s and early 1990s, witnessing first-hand the appalling conditions in El Salvador, Honduras, Ethiopia, Bangladesh, Sudan and Somalia.[61] She endorsed the UNICEF and UN plan for Corridors of Tranquillity – rivulets of mercy that would flow through areas of famine and conflict. In her address to the UNICEF Executive Board on 21 April 1989, as the Convention approached its final form, she spoke of 'phantoms carrying their sick transparent babies' to aid. These almost spectral parents were pressed forward by 'the one human quality which is the last to die; hope'. There was no soaring utopian promise in her closing words. 'There is', Hepburn stated, 'so much we cannot do'. Infant and juvenile victims of war, poverty, state-backed repression and famine would persist. Their parents would often perish. The promise was of some minima: 'we can return to them their most basic human rights, their right to health, cleanliness and life'.[62] These were impeccably humane sentiments, which maximised what was realistic in the circumstances. Yet they exemplified the retreat to compassion: this was a moralism that had its ancestors in Edwardian and interwar humanitarians, Eglantyne Jebb and Emily Hobhouse, and their ceaseless attempts at merciful ministration to the defenceless and destitute.[63]

Despite finding little success when framed in the ambitious and the abstract, the more radical human rights priority of remediating global structural inequalities could build similar arguments outwards from provocative, poignant examples. The logic of the Convention on the Rights of the Child, in the desperate plight of children, placed aspects of the Southern argument in a form that collapsed mediating abstractions, and also cast useful veils of pity, charity and mercy over sovereign economic claims. This rationale for a more equitable global system was recited with endorsement by UNICEF Director James Grant in 1988, who quoted Tanzanian President Julius Nyerere's plea: 'Must we starve our children to pay our debt?'[64] Much like the effective human rights NGO framing of torture as a moral absolute outside the political and cultural frame, the condition of starving, sick, shelter-less children were not answered by finely iterated talking points on aid conditionality and structural adjustment.

Conclusions

Both major monuments of the 1980s, the Convention Against Torture and the Convention on the Rights of the Child, were expressions of a human rights approach that sought to salvage elements of redemptive hope after three decades of disappointment. Each, in its way, was crafted in a register of the least worst, an attempt to re-base the currency of universal moral claims on reflexive human compassion. In terms of disposition, by the close of the twentieth century, the human rights movement had begun to resemble the approach of nineteenth-century humanitarians, orbiting the grim triptych of corporeal abuses, starvation and the abuse and deprivation of children. Much like the documentary humanitarians of almost a century earlier, human rights activism in the 1980s needed a sympathetic body, harmed by either abusive states or the capricious pathologies of the world economy, its institutions and the sovereigns within it.

Building on almost a decade of advocacy, the Convention Against Torture addressed the most grotesque abuses, the evidence of which had been documented and disseminated with sickening detail across pamphlets and testimonial reports. The Convention on the Rights of the Child represented a similar impulse in a different key: it articulated an expansive range of rights, but narrowed its protection to a vulnerable population which commanded enhanced sympathy. By the 1980s human rights had failed to deliver on any species of universal transformation, be it 'a world made new' of liberal and social democratic nation states, or the more radical project of global economic redistribution. Its rise in discursive purchase coincided with the fall in ambitions.[65] By the early 2000s, this re-factoring of human rights towards the immediate and limited – the desperation of the individual human – was the subject of searing critique. Most famously, Samantha Power, later UN Ambassador in the Obama administration, prepared a scathing jeremiad on the perils of palliationism in the context of genocide, *A Problem from*

Hell.⁶⁶ Released in 2002, shortly after the two most successful armed interventions against genocide – in Kosovo and East Timor – it was sufficiently compelling to win a Pulitzer Prize.

Power properly critiqued the perversity of ensuring besieged civilians were adequately fed while under artillery fire, when airstrikes, armour and aid might well have been more suitable responses. Power's vision of more ambitious liberal interventionism held deep appeal: its logic was powerful, and, at least episodically, vindicated. Nevertheless, Power's subsequent experiences with Libya, Iraq and Syria in the 2010s demonstrated the perils of this more fundamental, and kinetic, crusade. The two-decade descent from glittering, legalistic utopia of the late 1940s to clothed, isocaloric and sheltered individuals of the late 1980s was surely provoked by disappointment, but to dismiss it as 'mere' humanitarianism overlooks the commonality between the two moralisms. The priorities of the 1980s lacked the elegant maximalism of the postwar abstractions of universalist rights, but it had regained the urgency and desperation that reflected the best of the Edwardian and interwar humanitarians. Triaged and targeted efforts supplanted grandiose visions. Human rights had lost the interlocking, organic coherence of 1948, but had regained an emphatic focus on the primordial needs of the person: physical integrity, food and child welfare delivered humans back to the human rights programme.

Notes

1 *Hearings Before the Subcommittees on Asian and Pacific Affairs and on Human Rights and International Organizations of the Committee on Foreign Affairs, House of Representatives, August–September, December 1982* (Washington, DC: US Congress, 1983), p. 238.
2 Charles Delafuente, 'Ousted Dictators Living Like Kings', *Chicago Sun-Times*, 15 June 1986, p. 46.
3 (Olara) Otunnu (Uganda), Summary Records of the Commission on Human Rights, 22 February 1982, Geneva, E/CN.4/1982/SR.30, para 50.
4 Helen Kinsella, 'Superfluous Injury and Unnecessary Suffering: National Liberation Movements and the Laws of War', *Political Power and Social Theory* (2017), 32, pp. 205–31; and on earlier challenges to international humanitarian law, see Fabian Klose, 'The Colonial Testing Ground: The ICRC and the Violent End of Empire', *Humanity* (2011), 2 (1), pp. 107–26.
5 Convention on Prohibitions or Restrictions on the Use of Certain Conventional Weapons Which May Be Deemed to Be Excessively Injurious or to Have Indiscriminate Effects, Geneva, 10 October 1980.
6 International Committee of the Red Cross, *Report of the Conference of Government Experts on the Use of Certain Conventional Weapons*, 24

September – 18 October 1974, *Lucerne* (Geneva, Switzerland: International Committee of the Red Cross, 1975); International Committee of the Red Cross, *Report of the International Experts on Weapons That May Cause Unnecessary Suffering or Have Indiscriminate Effects* (Geneva, Switzerland: International Committee of the Red Cross, 1973); and 'Summary Records of the Ad Hoc Committee on Conventional Weapons', CDDH/IV/SR.1–7, in *Official Records of the Diplomatic Conference on the Reaffirmation and Development of International Humanitarian Law Applicable in Armed Conflicts, Geneva, 1974–1977*, vol. 16.

7 John Hutchinson, *Champions of Charity* (Boulder, CO: Westview, 1996).

8 For illustration, the deeply physiological quality in the analysis of Eric Prokosch, 'Trends in Fragmentation Weapons', *International Review of the Red Cross* (December 1975), 77, pp. 607–10.

9 Henry Shue, 'Torture', *Philosophy & Public Affairs* (Winter 1978), 7 (2), pp. 124–143.

10 On the role of Amnesty International, on torture and associated integrity of the person rights, protections from extrajudicial killing and arbitrary imprisonment, see the detailed survey by Ann Marie Clark, *Diplomacy of Conscience: Amnesty International and Changing Human Rights Norms* (Princeton, NJ: Princeton University Press, 2001); see also the earlier work, Helena Cook, 'Amnesty International at the United Nations', in Peter Willetts (ed.), *The Conscience of the World* (London, UK: Hurst, 1996), pp. 181–213. For illustrative example of Amnesty International advocacy around torture, see Amnesty International, *Report on Torture* (New York, NY: Farrar, Straus and Giroux, 1975).

11 United Nations, Declaration on the Protection of All Persons from Being Subjected to Torture and Other Cruel, Inhuman or Degrading Treatment or Punishment, General Assembly, A/RES/3452 (XXX), 9 December 1975; Report of the Secretary-General, Torture and Other Cruel, Inhuman or Degrading Treatment or Punishment in Relation to Detention and Imprisonment, A/10260, 3 October 1975; on the initial advancement of a Convention, see Commission on Human Rights, Draft Convention on Torture and Other Cruel, Inhuman or Degrading Treatment or Punishment, Commission on Human Rights resolution 18 (XXXIV), 7 March 1978.

12 Keith Unwin to Michael Simpson-Orlebar, Human Rights Commission XXXIII, 21 March 1977, FO 58/1149, C527586.

13 Summary Report, Internal working papers and agenda, 'International Symposium on Torture', Institut Henri-Dunant, 5–6 May 1977, Geneva, p. 5. Department of Foreign Affairs, Torture, 929/34/2, National Archives of Australia (hereafter, NAA), Canberra.

14 Ibid., p. 5, and extended in annexe, 'Presentation of Amnesty International, April 1977', p. 28.

15 Ibid., extended and elaborated in annexe.

16 Ibid., p. 8.

17 Ibid., p. 10.

18 Ibid., p. 16.

19 Ibid., p. 42.

20 Ibid.
21 Emily Hobhouse, *To the Committee of the Distress Fund for South African Women and Children* (London, UK: Friars Printing, 1901), pp. 3–17.
22 Emily Hobhouse, diary entry 9 December 1900, in *The Brunt of War and Where It Fell* (London, UK: Methuen, 1902), p. 72.
23 Elsabe Brits, *Emily Hobhouse: Feminist, Pacifist, Traitor* (London, UK: Robinson, 2016). This more candidly stated 'emotionalism' was set within a very sophisticated navigation of imperial conduits of activism, see the discussion in Rebecca Gill and Cornelis Muller, 'The Limits of Agency: Emily Hobhouse's International Activism and the Politics of Suffering', *Journal of South African and American Studies* (2018), 19 (1), pp. 16–35.
24 Summary Report, p. 41.
25 Jan Hermann Burgers and Hans Danelius, *The United Nations Convention Against Torture Convention against and Other Cruel, Inhuman or Degrading Treatment or Punishment: A Handbook on the Convention* (Dordrecht, Netherlands: Nijhoff, 1988).
26 For state of the text and its provisions, see Jan Hermann Burgers, Report of the Working Group on a Draft Convention against Torture and Other Cruel, Inhuman or Degrading Treatment or Punishment, E/CN.4/1984/72, 9 March 1984.
27 Report of the World Food Conference, 5–16 November 1974, Rome, E/Conf. 65/20.
28 FAO World Food Conference, Universal Declaration on the Eradication of Hunger and Malnutrition, Rome, 16 November 1974.
29 Lasse Heerten, *The Biafran War and Postcolonial Humanitarianism: Spectacles of Suffering* (Cambridge, UK: Cambridge University Press, 2017).
30 Summary Record of the Commission on Human Rights, 1392nd meeting, 16 February 1977, E/CN.4/SR.1392.
31 On Shue and his milieu, see the superb and significant inquiry from Samuel Moyn, 'The Doctor's Plot: The Origins of the Philosophy of Human Rights', in Duncan Bell (ed.), *Empire, Race and Global Justice* (Cambridge, UK: Cambridge University Press, 2019), pp. 59–65.
32 Shue, 'Torture', p. 23.
33 The sequelae of a human rights creed founded on 'adequacy' is superbly shown in Samuel Moyn, *Not Enough* (Cambridge, MA: Harvard/Belknap, 2018).
34 Henry Shue, *Basic Rights: Subsistence, Affluence, and U.S. Foreign Policy* (Princeton, NJ: Princeton University Press, 1980).
35 Asbjørn Eide, The New International Economic Order and the Promotion of Human Rights: Report on the Right to Adequate Food as a Human Right, E/CN.4/Sub.2/1987/23, July 1987.
36 The arguments he set out were sufficiently persuasive and powerful to win a Nobel Prize, see Amartya Sen, *Poverty and Famines* (New York, NY: Clarendon, 1982).
37 Convention on the Rights of the Child, A/RES/ 44/25, 20 November 1989. For assessment of the Convention's core features, see Dominick McGoldrick, 'The United Nations Convention on the Rights of the Child', *International Journal of Law, Policy and the Family* (August 1991), 5 (2), pp. 132–69.

38 Declaration on the Rights of the Child, A/RES/1386 (XIV), 10 December 1959. The text built on the precursor 1924 Declaration adopted by the League of Nations, which in turn was a re-adoption of the 1923 Declaration promulgated by the Save the Children organisation; see *World Child Welfare Charter*, 26 November 1924, subsequently endorsed and augmented by the UN in the late 1940s.
39 Lopatka would serve Polish government after 1981 on religion, and the peril posed by the purported subversions of 'antisocialist-minded clerics'. See 'Anti-Government Priests On Rise, Warsaw Says', *New York Times*, 21 May 1985, p. 7.
40 International Year of the Child (1979), A/RES/31/169, 21 December 1976.
41 For representative sample of the campaign, both heartening and harrowing, see International Year of the Child (series), 1 January 1978: UN Photo 64511, Lapland, Norway; UN Photo 149473, Casablanca, Morocco; UN Photo 149499 & 85683, Manila, Philippines; UN Photo 149500, Bangkok, Thailand; UN Photo 31426, Oslo, Norway; UN Photo 314700, Athens, Greece; 1 January 1979: UN Photo 117086, Cartagena, Colombia; UN Photo 380294, Chiapas, Mexico.
42 See imagery across David Seymour and UNESCO, *Children of Europe* (Paris, France: UNESCO, 1949); and UNESCO's *Book of Needs I and II* (Paris, France: UNESCO, 1947, 1949).
43 On the development and drafting of the Convention on the Rights of the Child, see Lawrence LeBlanc, *The Convention on the Rights of the Child* (Lincoln, NE: University of Nebraska Press, 1995); Paula Fass, 'A Historical Context for the United Nations Convention on the Rights of the Child', *Annals of the American Academy of Political and Social Science* (2011), 633, pp. 17–29; Cynthia Price Cohen, 'The Role of Nongovernmental Organizations in the Drafting of the Convention on the Rights of the Child', *Human Rights Quarterly* (February 1990), 12 (1), pp. 137–47; Cynthia Price Cohen, 'The Role of the United States in the Drafting of the Convention on the Rights of the Child', *Emory International Law Journal* (2006), 20, pp. 185–98; Cynthia Price Cohen, 'The United Nations Convention of the Rights of the Child: A Feminist Landmark', *William and Mary Journal of Race, Gender, and Social Justice* (1997), 3 (1), pp. 29–78; Jaime Sergio Cerda, 'The Draft Convention on the Rights of the Child: New Rights', *Human Rights Quarterly* (February 1990), 12 (1), pp. 115–19.
44 Interview with James Grant, UNICEF, 4 November 1989. UNICEF Archives, Strategic Information Section, CF/HST/INT/CRC/GRA; see also his delighted surprise when the Convention on the Rights of the Child was adopted, 'UN Assembly Adopts Doctrine Outlining Children's Basic Rights', *New York Times*, 21 November 1989, p. A6.
45 Linde Lindkvist, 'When the War Came: The Child Rights Convention and the Conflation of Human Rights and the Laws of War', in Lora Wildenthal and Jean Quataert (eds), *Routledge History of Human Rights* (London, UK: Routledge, 2019), pp. 183–200.

46 Draft Convention on the Rights of the Child, E/CN.4/L.1366/Rev.1, 7 February 1978; and UN General Assembly, Question of a Convention on the Rights of the Child, A/RES/33/166, 20 December 1978.
47 Bogomil Sujka (Poland), Summary Records of Committee III, 10 November 1978, A/C.3/33/SR.42, para 70.
48 Lindkvist, 'When the War Came', p. 183. The resolutions that determined the pursuit of both the Convention on the Rights of the Child and the Convention Against Torture were both successfully passed at the 1978 sessions of Commission on Human Rights and General Assembly Plenary.
49 See, for instance, the consensus passage of the work at both Committee III and Plenary in 1985, General Assembly Official Record, Plenary Meetings, 13 December 1985, A/40/PV.116, 24.
50 Wlodzimierz Kalinowki (Poland), Summary Records of the Commission on Human Rights, 10 March 1981, E/CN.4/SR.1635, para 51.
51 Kurt Herndl (UN Secretariat), Summary Records of Committee III, 19 November 1984, A/C.3/39/SR.44, para 7; see also Henryk Sokalski (Poland), Summary Records of Committee III, 23 November 1984, A/C.3/39/SR.48, para 14.
52 'Many Parties Competing in Senegalese Vote Today', *New York Times*, 27 February 1983, p. 12; Alan Cowell, 'African Democracy Has a Life of Its Own', *New York Times*, 22 May 1983, p. E2. On the orientation of the Diouf government, see Justin Mende, 'Diouf's New Directions', *Africa Report* (December 1982), 27, pp. 45–53.
53 Moussa Bocar Ly (Senegal), Summary Records of Committee, 22 November 1985, A/C.3/40/SR.51, para 32.
54 Secretary General, Provisional Verbatim Record of the General Assembly Plenary, 20 November 1989, A/44/PV.61.
55 'UN Approves Pact on Rights of Children', *Chicago Tribune*, 21 November 1989, p. 6.
56 For full list, see UNICEF, World Summit for Children (1990), catalogue of heads of state, available at www.unicef.org/wsc/country.htm, accessed 2 November 2018; see also, *Personal Messages of Heads of State and Government*, WSC (New York, NY: United Nations/UNICEF, 1990).
57 See the voluminous preparatory work conducted by UNICEF, series, Management Committee Meetings; Meetings in Preparation for WS Work, CF/RAF/ZW/S0337-1990-000072638.
58 On World Summit, and its moderated optimism, see UN and Specialized Agencies, *World Summit for Children: Give Every Child a Future* (New York, NY: United Nations, 1990); and Geraldine Van Bueren, 'Combating Child Poverty – Human Rights Approaches', *Human Rights Quarterly* (1999), 21 (3), pp. 680–706.
59 Hepburn was indelibly associated with the public presentation of the Convention on the Rights of the Child, see her featured across 'Children visit UN as General Assembly adopts Convention on their rights', UN Photo 275930, 18 November 1989; 'General Assembly adopts Convention on Children', UN

Photo 275929, 20 November 1989; 'UNICEF holds a press conference', UN Photo 275920, 20 November 1989; and 'Scouts visit UN in conjunction with a General Assembly convention on children's rights', UN Photo 275928, 20 November 1989.

60 See Robert Matzen, *Dutch Girl: Audrey Hepburn and World War II* (Pittsburgh, PA: Good Knight, 2019); and Hepburn's remarks on how her childhood shaped those she encountered, Audrey Hepburn in Her Own Words – Transcripts of statements, c. 1993. UNICEF Archives, Executive Director's Office, CF/RAF/USAA/DB01/2001 – 04735.

61 Summary of Audrey Hepburn's Activities as UNICEF Goodwill Ambassador 1987–1991. UNICEF Archives, Executive Director's Office, CF/RAF/USAA/DB01/2001 – 04735.

62 Audrey Hepburn's Statement to the UNICEF Executive Board, 21 April 1989. UNICEF Archives, Executive Director's Office, CF/RAF/USAA/DB01/2001 – 04735.

63 On the milieu of interwar humanitarianism, see Bruno Cabanes, *The Great War and the Origins of Humanitarianism, 1918–1924* (Cambridge, UK: Cambridge University Press, 2018); see also Ann Harries, *No Place for a Lady* (London, UK: Bloomsbury, 2007); Clare Mulley, *The Woman Who Saved the Children* (Oxford, UK: Oneworld, 2009); and Jebb's own writings. The resonance with the Convention on the Rights of the Child was noted by an expert on the drafting, who cited Jebb explicitly, see Thomas Hammarberg, 'The UN Convention on the Rights of the Child – and How to Make It Work', *Human Rights Quarterly* (1990), 12 (1), p. 98.

64 James Grant, Address and Report, Opening Session of the UNICEF Executive Board, 18 April 1988, New York, E/ICEF/1988/CSP. 9 Rev. 1, 11.

65 This quality is gestured toward in Martti Koskenniemi's apt diagnosis of a 'modesty' in 'postmodern human rights'. See Koskenniemi, 'Human Rights Mainstreaming as a Strategy for Institutional Power', *Humanity* (2010), 1 (1), pp. 47–57.

66 Samantha Power, *A Problem from Hell* (New York, NY: Harper-Perennial, 2002).

Index

Abbreviations: Aus = Australia; ICRC = International Committee of the Red Cross; LRCS = League of Red Cross Societies; USA = United States; WA = Western Australia

abolition of slavery 1–2, 6, 10–11, 13–16, 19, 37, 119–38, 179, 180, 183, 203, 331
  activism 9–10, 43–4, 121–4
  beginnings 37–8, 41–4, 49–52
  coerced labour *vs.* 122
  internationalism 18–21
  limits on 119–20
  morality 37–9, 43, 45, 46, 125, 133
  public attitudes 44, 120–4
  see also apprenticeship system, post-slavery; Benezet, Anthony; Clarkson, Thomas; compensation payments to slave owners
Abolition of Slavery, Act for the (1833) 119–23, 125–6, 131, 137
  exceptions/limits 119–20, 123, 126–30
Aboriginal and Torres Strait Islander people, Australian
  acculturation 222–3, 224–5
  activism 220, 229, 230, 307, 310–12
  ameliorating conditions 93–4
  assimilation 83, 154–5, 217, 222–4, 228, 230
  attitudes to 185, 188, 191, 217–19, 221–2, 229
  children, treatment of 91–3, 183
  Christianisation 91–2, 93–6, 150, 154, 156, 159, 160, 165, 222–5, 230
  citizenship 217, 227, 229, 310–11
  'civilising' agendas 91–6, 185, 222–8

  civil rights 179, 187, 310–11
  compensation for, lack of 154, 165, 166, 170, 311
  conciliation 10–11, 82–3, 96
  control of 219, 220, 229, 311
  education 217, 223, 225
  emotions and humanity 84–5, 87–96
  exceptionalisation of 16, 90, 96, 217–30
  exemption system 16, 217–30
  exploitation 179–92
  genocide 13, 15, 16, 148, 168–70, 310
  government *vs.* penal policy 155–6
  government welfare granted 228–9
  humanity, instilling 92–6
  inquiries into treatment of 185–9, 223–4
  invasion of lands 120–1, 136, 137
  labour 125, 154, 160–3, 167, 169, 179–92, 224, 225, 229, 310
  mixed descent 183, 190, 224–7
  property, ideas of 82, 90–1, 95
  protectionism 3, 15–17, 154, 156, 165, 166, 169, 179, 185–92, 218–19, 221–6, 228–9
  racism and racialisation 217, 218, 226–7
  redressing exploitation 187–8
  referendum (1967) 221, 228–9
  removal of 217–19, 310
  settler relations 10–11, 15–17, 82–3, 86–94
  treatment of 87–8, 181, 185–7, 217, 221–3, 311–12
  see also Aboriginal women, Australian; Australia; exemption system; Queensland, Australian Aborigines in; Rottnest Island prison (WA); Western Australia, Aboriginal people in

Aboriginal slavery in Australia 179–92, 310
  abuse 183–4, 186
  children 183
  colonial governments and 181–2
  government and 185–91
  humanitarianism, settler 180–5, 187–8, 190, 192
  interracial contact 183–5, 188–91
  northern Australia 179–92, 310
  race politics 182–5, 188–90
Aboriginal Tribes in British Settlements, Report of the House of Commons Select Committee on (1837) 13, 154, 156, 223
Aboriginal women, Australian 82, 191
  domestic service 183, 191, 217–18, 222, 230
  exemption system 217–18, 225
  government intervention 185–91
  marriage 189–90
  Minderoo station case 186–91
  morality 189–91
  as property 184, 189
  sexual exploitation 179, 180, 182–91
  see also Aboriginal and Torres Strait Islander people, Australian
Aborigines Protection Society 153, 156, 158, 184, 185
activism and activists, individual humanitarian 24, 25, 283–300
  see also Vietnam War orphans and adoption
adoption, inter-country
  advocacy 285, 294–300
  difficulties of 288–93
  see also Vietnam War orphans and adoption
Africa 3
  colonisation, effects of 41–3
  scramble for 18–19
  slavery in 14, 19, 21
  see also Africa, southern; Africa, West; Africans, European attitudes to
Africa, southern 3, 12, 14, 15, 18, 50–1, 135
  see also Cape Colony
Africa, West
  agency in, West African 199–212
  civilising mission 199, 201
  governance 200, 201–7, 209–10
  humanitarianism, imperial 200, 203–5
  humanitarianism, local 25–8
  mutual aid 199–200, 208–11
  racism 199, 205
  slave trading 14, 200–1, 203–4
  see also Nigeria; Sierra Leone
Africans
  European attitudes to 45–53, 130–3, 199, 205, 207–8, 212
  Liberated 1–2, 128, 201–4, 209–10
ameliorative action 12, 13, 21, 22, 93–4, 119, 219, 221
Amnesty International 5, 25, 305–6, 309, 316, 327
  anti-torture campaign 329–31
Amnesty International in Australia 25, 305–20
  conscription 313–16, 317
  government and 317–19
  human rights 311–12, 314
  human rights and humanitarianism 306–10, 316, 320
  Indigenous rights 309–13
  international body and 309, 315, 316
  membership 305–6, 308, 310, 317–19
  origins 305, 308–9
  parliamentary group 317–20
  role and scope 309–12, 319
  sectional divisions 305, 308–10, 312–16, 318–19
Angas, George Fife 135–7
anti-slavery see abolition of slavery
apprenticeship system, post-slavery 1–2, 120, 123–5, 127, 129–31, 133, 135
  Caribbean 123–4, 125–6, 130, 132–3
Armstrong, Francis 149, 151, 155, 158–60, 165
assimilation 15, 83, 154–5, 163, 217, 222–4, 228, 230
Australia
  colonial government 181–2
  convict labour 86, 125, 179–92
  Federation 179–81, 185, 191
  humanitarianism 17, 306–7
  investment in 12, 136–7
  settler colonial society 4, 15–17, 120, 135–7, 179–80, 222, 307

Index

white ascendancy 180, 183
  see also Aboriginal and Torres Strait Islander people, Australian; Amnesty International in Australia; Chinese in Australia; New South Wales; Queensland, Australia Aborigines in; South Australia; Tasmania (Van Diemen's Land); Western Australia
Australian Capital Territory, Aborigines in 219
Australian Council for Civil Liberties 310–12

Baartman, Sara 73–4
Bedford College for Women see public health nursing programme, LRCS
Benezet, Anthony 3, 9–11, 37–54
  attitudes 39–41, 45, 48, 51–4
  human rights 40–1
  influence on abolitionism 41–4, 53
  Sharp, Granville and 44–8
  Somerset case 48–51
Bennelong Woollarawarre 86–8, 94, 222–3
Blessius, Lawrence 66–8
Bosman, Willem 45–6
Brant, Joseph 70–1
Britain
  slavery in 44–5, 48–9
  voting rights, expansion of 14–15, 120–2, 138, 242
  see also abolition of slavery; Australia, settler colonial society; British Empire; humanitarianism; Indigenous peoples visiting Britain
British and Foreign Anti-Slavery Society 185
British Empire 3–4, 8
  Aboriginal vs. penal policy 155–6
  certainty of 7, 14, 61–2, 73
  consolidation 62, 64
  end of 5, 307
  expansion 6–7, 12, 63–4, 204
  restructuring 14, 119, 120, 133–8
  Seven Years War 6, 7, 9, 37–8, 43, 52
  slave trade 200–1
  transportation policy 125, 152, 156, 161, 162, 307
  see also Australia, settler colonial society; decolonisation; post-colonialism

Broome, Frederick 165–8, 184
Bullock, William 73–5
Bungaleene (Marbunnun), case of Thomas 221–3

Caitlin, George 75–6
Cameroon 203–4
Cape Colony 154
  abolition in 119, 128, 129, 131
  compensation, slave-owner 123, 129, 138
  Indigenous peoples 73–4
  slavery 126, 129
  see also Africa, southern
Caribbean and West Indies
  abolition of slavery 17, 119, 120, 122–3, 125–6, 134
  apprentices 123–6, 130
  attitudes to slavery 121, 127–8
  compensation 122–3, 128, 136, 138
  hybridity 52–3
  settler/Indigenous conflict 15
  slavery in 12, 13, 37, 44–50, 125, 129, 136
  see also Somerset case
Carter, Maynard L. 241, 242, 244, 253–8
Ceylon, slavery and forced labour in 75, 122, 123, 125, 126, 129, 131, 138
Cherokee envoys to Britain 56, 58, 64–6
child welfare 334–41
Chinese in Australia
  anti-Chinese sentiment 182, 184–5, 189, 191
  Minderoo station case 186–91
Christianity, evangelical 4, 12, 14
  Christianising agendas 83, 91–6, 150, 154, 156, 159, 160, 165, 201, 209, 222–5, 275–6
  humanitarianism and 6–11
  missionaries 3, 17, 46, 73, 93–4, 101, 121, 127, 128, 149–51, 154, 165, 167, 183, 185, 199, 201–4, 209, 222, 223, 230, 275–6, 286
  'civilising' agendas 15, 16, 19, 83, 91–6, 150, 156, 163, 185, 199–203, 205–6, 208, 211–12, 222–8
Clark, William Nairne 149, 152, 158–9, 170
Clarke, Andrew 159, 160

Clarkson, Thomas 9, 38–9, 41, 42, 53–4, 331
Cold War politics 265, 270, 305, 307, 330
Colombo Plan for Cooperative Economic Development in South and Southeast Asia 266, 267
Colonial Office 122–3, 124, 125–6, 127, 128, 129–30, 131–3, 135, 137, 138, 184
colonies, British *see* settler colonies
Commission of Eastern Inquiry on Indigenous peoples 75
compensation payments to slave owners 12, 122–3, 128–31, 134–6, 138
Congo 18, 19
conscientious objection in Vietnam War 25, 313–17
consumption, growth in 7–8
Council for Aboriginal Rights 307
Cowan, Walkinshaw 160–1
Creek envoys to Britain 64–5, 72
Crowther, Samuel Ajayi 201, 203–4
Cyprus 22

decolonisation 22–6, 265, 268, 269, 285
Defoe, Daniel 46–7
Demerara, slavery in 123–4, 125
development, international
  focus on 23, 264–8, 270, 276–8, 285, 308, 328, 333
  volunteering 264, 268, 276–8
Dickey (Thomas Walker Coke) 94
Dunlop, Alexander 73–4
Dutch East India Company 129

East India Company 12, 153
  charter renewal 120, 127, 134
  indentured workers 124, 125
  investment in Australia 12, 136–7
  opium trade 134, 135, 137
  restructure 120, 134, 136, 137
  shareholders 134–6, 138
  slavery 122, 123, 125–9, 134–5, 137
emancipation in British Empire 119–38
  changing attitudes 121–4
  civil rights and 131–3
  colonisation and 133–7
  defined 124–31
  free labour, attitudes of 124–5
  investment decisions 134–6
  transition to 123–4
  see also abolition of slavery; apprenticeship system, post-slavery; Sierra Leone; slaves, freed
emotion(s) 23–4, 84–5, 264, 265, 331
  cross-cultural readings 84–5
  humanity and 84–5, 87–96
  volunteering and 264–9, 271–4, 276–8
  empathy and compassion 17, 18, 119, 266, 268–9, 271–7
Enlightenment 4–5, 11, 83, 92–3
exemption system for Australian Aboriginal people 16, 217–30
  applications 219, 225–8
  control 219, 220
  defined 218, 219
  effects 219, 229
  end of 219–21
  examples of 220–2
  exception, individual 221–4
  humanitarianism and 220–1, 224–9
  human rights and 219–21, 227
  legislation 221, 224–7
  morality 225, 227–8
  origins 219–20
  racism 226–7
  revocation 219
  separation requirement 219–20
Ex-Services Human Rights Association 314

famine and famine relief 14, 17, 199, 334, 339
Federal Council for the Advancement of Aborigines and Torres Strait Islanders 310, 317
Feith, Herb 264, 273, 275, 276
Fitzgerald, Alice 241, 242, 244–50, 254, 256–8
Fitzgerald, Charles 159–61
Florence Nightingale Foundation 255–6, 257
Foster Parents Plan (PLAN) 284–5
France
  antislavery movement 2–3, 9–10, 13, 19, 204
  colonies 21, 37, 43, 63, 122, 126, 129–30, 133, 204, 210, 338
  humanitarianism 2–3, 10–11, 82
  nursing 241, 243, 244
Freedom from Hunger 308
Friends for All Children (FFAC) 287

gender and politics of humanitarianism 241–58
    see also Carter, Maynard L.; Fitzgerald, Alice; Olmsted, Katherine; public health nursing programme, LRCS
genocide 19, 23, 340–1
    Aboriginal Australians 13, 15, 16, 147–70 passim, 310
    defined 148, 168
Ghana (Gold Coast) 208, 209
Gillanders, Arbuthnot and Co. 124, 130
Giustiniani, Louis 149, 151–2
Gladstone, John 127, 129
Glenelg, Lord 127, 130, 132, 133
Gold Coast (Ghana) 46, 208
governance, humanitarian 4–5, 15–17, 19, 137–8
government and humanitarianism 119
    abolition of slavery 119–38
    colonisation 133–9
    expansion of electorate and 14–15, 120–2, 138, 242
    see also East India Company
Greece 12–14
Grey, George 154, 160
Gribble, John 165, 167–8, 183–4
Guinea 39, 47, 204–5
    see also Benezet, Anthony

Haiti 10, 13
Hepburn, Audrey 339
hospitals
    philanthropy and 100–1
    quarantine 106–7
    see also material culture; New York Hospital; Philadelphia Almshouse
humanitarianism
    British 2–27, 201–5, 208, 211–12
    colonial settler 2, 4, 6, 15–17, 179–85, 187–8, 190, 192, 205–8, 211–12, 306–7
    critiques of 17
    defined 1, 17, 38, 147
    development and 265, 270, 285
    diffusion 17–21
    French 2–3, 10–11, 82
    gendered approach 243–4, 250, 256–8
    imperial, late 18–21
    imperialist 200, 202–5, 208, 211–12

individual 24, 25, 284–5
intervention 4, 6, 12–13, 19, 22–6, 199, 211–12
local 25–8
objectives 179–80
rise of 4–5, 7–8, 11
West African 205–8, 211–12
humanity
    defined 84–5
    emotions and 84–5, 87–96
    Indigenous people 84–7
    instilling 88, 92–6
    savagery and 84–5
human rights 25–6, 29, 306, 327, 328, 330
    humanitarianism and 4–6, 24–6, 218, 285, 305–10, 316, 320, 340
    internationalist discourse 5–6, 192
    palliation and 327, 339–41
    transformation of 316, 327–8
    see also rights of man
Hutt, John 148, 149, 159, 164
    assimilation agenda 154–5
    punishment, views of 155–7, 160
    vision for Rottnest 147, 153–7, 160, 161, 166–9
hybridity, concern over 51–3

imperialism
    competitive 18–19
    humanitarian 202–5, 208, 211–12
    late 18–21
    see also British Empire; France
indentured labour 122, 179–92
    Australia 136, 179–92
    British Empire 120, 124, 125, 129, 131, 136–8, 182, 192
    India 130, 131, 136, 138, 182
    Mauritius 124, 125, 130
India 212
    attitudes to slavery in 126–9
    coerced labour 120, 125, 129
    exceptions to abolition act 126–9
    famine 14, 17, 199
    indentured labour 130, 131, 136, 138, 182
    indigenous slavery 122, 125, 126, 128–9, 131
    slavery 123, 126–9, 131
    see also East India Company
Indigenous peoples 145–237
    dispossession 3, 16, 25, 180, 218

emotions 84–5
  'exhibiting' 7, 58–62, 66, 73–6
  humanity, ideas of 84–5
  objects of humanitarianism 11, 14, 20–1, 29, 75, 311
  rights 25, 61
  settler colonies 12, 14–17, 50, 137
  slavery and forced labour 14–15, 75, 120–2, 125, 126, 128–9, 131
  treatment of 15, 69, 75, 154
  views of 17, 75, 84–5
  see also Aboriginal and Torres Strait Islander people, Australian; Africans, European attitudes to; assimilation; Christianity, evangelical; 'civilising' agendas; North America; protectionism; Rottnest Island prison (WA); savagery, ideas of; Western Australia, Aboriginal people in
Indigenous peoples visiting Britain
  Aboriginal Australians 72
  attitudes to 60–6, 70–3, 75–6
  Cape Africans 73–4
  early 62–6
  eighteenth century, late 70–2
  envoys 56, 58, 60–2, 64–7, 69–71
  exhibiting 7, 58–62, 66, 73–6
  government policy 155–6
  Inuit 70
  nineteenth century 72–6
  North American 62–3, 64–7, 69–71, 75–6
  Pacific Islanders 71–2
  public interest 60, 63, 70, 72
  racism 63–4, 66, 76
  rights 25
  savagery 64–6, 69–72
  Sun Tavern incident 60–2, 66–9
Indonesia, volunteering in 264, 266–7, 273–6, 278, 308
International Committee of the Red Cross (ICRC) 5, 22, 241, 242, 329
  early years 241–2
  hierarchies 243–4
  see also League of Red Cross Societies (LRCS); Red Cross societies
International Council of Nurses 251–3, 255
International Human Rights Day 317

International Social Service (ISS) 284–5, 295, 298–9
International Year of the Child 336
intervention and relief work 4, 6, 12–13, 18, 19, 22–6, 199, 211–12, 244, 245, 249, 254
Iroquois delegation to Britain 63, 64
Irwin, Frederick 149, 150, 159, 160

Jackson, William Dockwrey 162, 164
Jamaica
  apprenticeship system 132–3
  civil rights ex-slaves, limiting 131–3
  ex-slave owners 132
  racism 130–3
  slavery in 47–50, 131–2, 136
  see also Caribbean and West Indies

Kenya 22
kidnapping labour 181–2
Korean war 23, 285

labour, forced 119–21, 123, 125, 137
  convict 82, 125, 138, 152, 156, 161, 162, 179–92
  freed people of colour 120
  indentured workers 124, 125, 129–31, 136–8, 180–2, 192
  Indigenous people 120–1, 136, 147, 154, 157, 158, 160–4, 167, 169, 170, 179–92
  kidnapping for 181–2
  settler colonies 136, 137
  vs. slavery 122
  see also Aboriginal slavery in Australia; slavery
League of Nations 20–1, 23, 202, 284–5
League of Red Cross Societies (LRCS) 21, 251, 255
  ICRC and 249, 250
  Nursing Advisory Board 251–2
  Nursing Bureau 245, 248, 249, 254, 256
  Public Health Nursing Division 252–3, 254
  public health nursing programme 241–58
  see also public health nursing programme, LRCS
Legacies of British Slave Ownership database 134

Lemkin, Raphäel 148, 168
Liberia 205
　slave trade in 203, 204
Long, Edward 52–3
Lyon, Robert 148–52, 158

Macaulay, Zachary 128–9
McNab, Duncan 165–6, 167, 169
material culture 7–8, 11–12, 99–111
　Atlantic community 99, 103–8
　philanthropy and 100–1
　value of study 99–100
　see also New York Hospital; Philadelphia Almshouse
Mauritius 75, 122, 125, 151
　abolition of slavery 119, 123, 126, 129–31, 133
　apprentices 130–1, 133
　compensation, slave-owner 123, 130, 131
　indentured workers 124, 125, 130
Meyers, Hyam 61–2, 66–8, 73
Minderoo station case 186–9
missionaries see Christianity, evangelical
mixed race 52–3, 183, 190, 224–7
Mohawks at Sun Tavern 7, 11, 66–9
　attitudes, changing 61–6, 68–9, 72–6
　attitudes to 60–2, 71–3
　exhibition 58–9, 60–2, 76
　inquiry, House of Lords 60–2, 68–9, 74, 76
　moral vs. political discourse 61–2, 66, 68, 72, 76
　see also Indigenous peoples visiting Britain
Moir, Elaine 24, 285, 287–9, 291, 293
　defence of her work 295–7
　lobbying 299–300
　motivation 296–7, 299, 300
　smuggled orphans 283–4, 290
　see also Vietnam War orphans and adoption
Moore, George Fletcher 149–52, 154–5, 158, 170
Moses, Margaret 24, 284, 285, 287–8, 291, 300
　exhaustion 293–4
　see also Vietnam War orphans and adoption

Native Police Force 181, 221
New International Economic Order 327, 328, 330, 333–5, 338
New Norcia, Aboriginal people at (WA) 162–4, 168–9
New South Wales 86, 152
　Aboriginal people 82–96, 154
　conciliation phase 10–11, 82–3
　exemption rules 219, 227
　humanity in 85–7, 88
　see also Aboriginal and Torres Strait Islander people, Australian
New York Hospital
　African–Americans 12, 106, 109–11
　beds and bedding 99, 100, 104–11
　British humanitarianism 10–11
　care in 104–5, 107–11
　conciliation 10–11
　funding 103–4
　nursing 11–12, 99
　patients 104, 106–11
　welfare focus 12–13
　see also material culture
New Zealand 15, 154
Nicolay, William 130–1, 133
Niger 210
Nigeria 199, 203
Noble, Henry Winston 217–18, 221, 222, 230
non-government organisations (NGOs) 3–6
　anti-torture strategy 329–32, 340, 341
　donor appeals 22–3
　human rights 328, 330–1, 333, 336
　see also organisations, humanitarian
North America 12, 13, 40, 50–1
　Indigenous people 50, 60–7, 69–71, 75–6
　settler colony 2, 3, 12, 50–1, 135
　slavery 37, 40, 47, 50, 51
　see also Indigenous visitors to Britain; Sun Tavern incident
Northern Territory (Aus), Aboriginal people in 219, 226–7, 310–12
　see also Aboriginal and Torres Strait Islander people, Australian
nursing 11–12, 99, 111, 243
　attitudes to 99, 109–10, 242–4, 248, 256
　attitudes to public health training 248–52

Britain 242, 243, 248
  care work 104–5, 107–10
  professionalisation 108, 242–3, 248, 252, 257
  Red Cross volunteers 242–3
  USA 242, 243, 248
  wages 108–10
  see also New York Hospital; public health nursing programme, LRCS

Ojibwe in Britain 75–6
Olmsted, Katherine 241, 242, 244, 249–54, 256–8
Onslow, Alexander 167, 168
Operation Babylift 287, 288
opium trade 134, 135, 137
organisations, humanitarian 20–1, 24, 25, 308
  Anglophone 20–6
  war orphans 284–5, 295, 299–300
  see also International Committee of the Red Cross (ICRC); League of Red Cross Societies (LRCS); non-government organisations (NGOs); Red Cross societies
Oxfam 23, 284–5

Pacific Islanders
  indentured labour 180–2, 192
  Indigenous visitors to Britain 71–2
palliation 327, 339–41
Parramatta Native Institution 93, 222–3
Peace Corps (USA) 23–4, 264, 269–71, 276–7
  government and 270–1
  see also volunteering
Philadelphia Almshouse 108, 109
philanthropy 11–15, 99–101, 111, 200–3
  welfare and 11–15, 21
  see also New York Hospital; nursing
Phillip, Arthur 10–11, 82–3, 87–8
post-colonialism 3, 200, 211, 264, 266–7, 269, 308
Prinsep, Charles Robert 135, 136
Prinsep, Henry 186–90
Prinsep, John 135–6
protectionism 3, 15–17, 123, 154, 156, 165, 166, 169, 179, 185–92, 218–19, 221–6, 228–9
Protectors of Aborigines *see* protectionism

public health nursing programme, LRCS 21, 241–58
  antagonism to 244, 248–52
  funding 250–1, 253, 255–6
  gendered humanitarianism 242–4, 256–8
  goals 243, 245–6, 250, 254
  housing, student 252, 255
  location 241–2, 247–8
  origins 241–2, 246–9
  see also Carter, Maynard L.; Fitzgerald, Alice; League of Red Cross Societies (LRCS); nursing; Olmsted, Katherine

Quakers 9, 37–8, 40, 43, 201, 298
Queensland, Australian Aborigines in 217
  exemption system 219, 225, 226, 229
  indentured labour 180–2, 192
  protectionism 185–6, 218, 224–6

race and racism 7–8, 47–8, 52–3, 63–4, 66, 76, 130–3, 182, 186–90, 199, 205, 207–8, 212, 217, 218, 226–7, 269, 298–9, 308
  interracial contact 183–5, 188–91
Red Cross societies 21, 22, 246, 254, 255, 257
  American 241, 245, 248–51, 256
  British 22, 241
  European 241, 244
  Japan 241
  nursing, attitudes to 242–3, 248, 257
  relief work 18, 22, 244, 245, 249, 254
  see also League of Red Cross Societies (LRCS)
Reform Act (1832) 120–2, 138
refugees, postwar 20–1
Returned Services League 314
rights of man 5, 9–10, 13
  see also human rights
Rockefeller Foundation 250–2, 256
Ross, Ronald 207–8
Roth, William 185–6
Rottnest Island prison (WA) 16, 147–70
  Commission of Inquiry (1883) 166, 170
  conditions 157–67, 169
  deaths 147, 158, 166

education 155, 159, 160, 163, 165, 166, 170
employment 153, 155, 156, 160
establishment 152–4
forced labour 147, 157, 158, 160, 164, 169, 170
genocide 15, 16, 148, 168–70
harsh treatment 157–64, 169
Hutt's vision 147–57, 159–62, 166–9
investigations and recommendations 158, 160, 163, 166–7, 170
moral reform 156–7, 167
number of prisoners 157, 164–6
offences 151, 152, 154–5, 157, 159, 161, 162, 164–8
Protectors of Aborigines 147, 157–9
punishment 147, 155–7, 162, 169–70
release from 168–70
see also Western Australia (WA), Aboriginal people in
Royal Africa Company 200, 201
Royal Commission ... on the Condition of the Natives, Report of the (Roth inquiry) 185–6
Ruddock, Phillip 318–20

St Helena 123, 125–7, 129, 131
Salvado, Rosendo 162–4, 168–9
Sami people in Britain 74–5
savagery, ideas of 39–40, 42–3, 51, 64–6, 70–2, 83–5, 89, 148
Save the Children Fund 21, 284–5, 308
Scarfe, Wendy and Allan 298–9
Schuppe, John 61, 68
settler colonies 15, 17, 136, 137
    Africa, southern 3, 12, 15, 50–1, 135
    Americas 2–4, 12, 121, 135
    Australasia 3, 12, 120–1
    Australia 4, 10–11, 15–17, 82–3, 86–94, 120, 135–7, 147–8, 150, 154, 158–9, 162, 169–70
    Caribbean/West Indies 50–1
    donors, as 3–4
    expansion of 14–15, 120, 133–8
    humanitarianism 2, 4, 6, 15–17, 179–85, 187–8, 190, 192, 205–8, 211–12, 306–7
    Indigenous people 12, 14–17, 50, 137, 148–52, 158–9
    investment in 12, 134–7

law-making 50–1
nationhood 26–7
protectionism 15–17
slavery and 50–1, 134–7
see also Aboriginal and Torres Strait Islander people, Australian; British Empire; New South Wales; Sierra Leone
Seven Years War 6, 7, 9, 37–8, 43, 52
Sharp, Granville 9, 38
    abolitionism 42, 44–5, 49–51
    Africans, attitudes to 44–6, 48–53
    Benezet and 38, 44–8, 53
    Somerset case 43, 48–51
    on West Indian planters 44–5, 49–50
    xenophobia 45, 48–53
Sierra Leone 199–212 *passim*
    anti-slave trade mission 200, 202–5
    Christianising 201, 209
    civilising mission 201–3, 205–6, 208, 211–12
    elites 200–3, 206, 207
    free black colony 44, 201–3
    Freetown 201–4, 207–9
    governance 201–7, 209–12
    health and welfare 199, 202, 205–12
    humanitarianism, British 201–5, 208, 211–12
    humanitarianism, Indigenous 205–8, 211–12
    liberated slaves 1–2, 125, 128, 201–3
    missionaries 201, 203, 209–10
    mutual aid 208–11
    philanthropy 201, 202
    racism 199, 205, 207–8, 212
    taxation 206, 210
Sierra Leone Company 201–3
Singapore, investment in 136
slave owners 122–3
    abolition of slavery and 122–4
    attitudes of 48–51
    see also compensation payments to slave owners
slavery 42–3, 122, 123
    attitudes to 48–51, 121–9, 136
    chattel 119, 123, 125–6, 129, 131, 180
    East India Company 122, 123, 125–9, 134–5, 137
    Indigenous 75, 122, 125, 126, 128–9, 131

legality of 43–4, 49
modern 180–2, 186, 192
transition to free labour 123–4, 130, 135
types of 128–9
see also abolition of slavery; Aboriginal slavery in Australia; Aboriginal women, Australian; apprenticeship system, post-slavery; compensation payments to slave owners
slaves
as property 44–5, 48, 49, 123
revolts by 10, 122
treatment of 46–51, 131–2
slaves, freed 1–2, 121, 125–8
resettlement 201–3, 209–10
see also Sierra Leone
slave trade
abolition 1, 6, 9–11, 14, 37–9, 41–4, 121–2, 125, 128
African 14, 19, 37, 201–5
'Arab' 19
Atlantic and transatlantic 8, 13, 37, 39, 41, 42, 106, 125, 128
Australian 186–7
British 8, 43–4, 200–1
corruption, European 41–3
European 41, 42
intervention, calls for 12, 200, 202–5, 208, 212
racism 42, 44, 53–4
Sligo, Marquess of 131–2
Smith, Adam 8–9
Smith, Lionel 132–3
Société des Amis des Noirs 2–3, 10
Somerset case 43, 48–51, 75
South Africa see Africa, southern
South Australia
Aboriginal people 137, 219, 223, 226, 229
settlement 136–7, 154
South Australian Colonization Commission 136, 137
South Australian Company 136–7
Southeast Asia, labour 123, 182, 188, 190
see also Ceylon, slavery and forced labour in; Chinese in Australia; India
Spanish America 25, 51–2
stadial theory of progress 83, 92–3

Stephen, James 122–3, 124, 125–6, 127, 128, 129–30, 131–3, 135, 137, 138
Stirling, James 149, 151–3
sugar trade 127, 128, 130, 136
Sun Tavern incident 60–2, 66–9
Swan River Colony see Western Australia
Swing Revolts 125
Sydney Gazette, cross-cultural contact in 85, 89–92, 94–6
Symmons, Charles 155, 157, 158, 162

Tahitian visitors to Britain 71, 72
Tasmania (Van Diemen's Land) 13, 136, 152, 154, 156, 219
Taylor, Rosemary 24, 283–300
defence of her work 295–6
difficulties of work 288–94
independent work 286–7, 300
lobbying 299–300
motivation 288–9, 297, 299, 300
see also Vietnam War orphans and adoption
Tench, Watkin 82–3, 85–9, 95–6
Timberlake, Henry 65–7
Torres Strait Islanders see Aboriginal and Torres Strait Islander people, Australian
torture
campaign against 26, 317–19, 329–32, 340, 341
Convention Against, UN 26, 317–19, 329–33
transportation system, British 86, 125, 152, 156, 161, 162, 307

Uganda 326
United Nations 23, 339
Commission on Human Rights 329, 335
Convention Against Torture 26, 317–19, 329–33
Convention on Certain Conventional Weapons 329
Convention on Prevention and Punishment of the Crime of Genocide 23
Convention on the Rights of the Child 336–41
Declaration on the Right to Development 328, 333

Declaration to Indigenous Peoples 311
Economic and Social Council 317
Food and Agriculture Organization (FAO) 333–5, 337
Human Rights Committee 311
New International Economic Order and 327, 328, 330, 333–5, 338
Relief and Rehabilitation Administration (UNRAA) 333–4
right to food 333–6, 338, 341
Technical Assistance Administration 266
UNICEF 285, 291, 336, 338–40
Universal Declaration of Human Rights 23, 307, 310–12, 315, 327, 334, 335
United States *see* North America

Van Diemen's Land *see* Tasmania
Victoria (Aus), Aborigines in
  exemption system 221–2, 224–6
  protectionism 219, 221–4
Vietnam War 22
  conscientious objection 25, 313–16
  conscription 313–16, 319
  humanitarians in, individual 284–5
Vietnam War orphans and adoption 283–300
  Australian governments 183, 291, 298–300
  bureaucracy 287, 289–93, 299–300
  examples 297–9
  logistical problems 289–92
  numbers 286
  see also Moir, Elaine; Moses, Margaret; Taylor, Rosemary
Vincent, Henry 153, 157–62
Voluntary Aid Detachments (VADs) 242–3
Voluntary Service Overseas (VSO, UK) 23–4, 264, 268–9, 277
Volunteer Graduate Scheme (Aus) 23–4, 264, 266–9, 277, 308
  analysis of applications 265, 271–7
  Christianising 275–6
  goals 266–8
  government and 266–7
  motivations, participant 264, 267, 271–6
volunteering 23–4, 264–78
  development, international 264, 268, 276–8

emotion and sentiment 264–9, 271–4, 276–8
empathy 266, 268–9, 271–7
friendship, international 264, 265, 267–9, 273–4
motivation 264–5, 271–6
rise of 266–71
see also Peace Corps (USA)

Wakefield, Edward Gibbon 135–7, 153–4
Welch, Laurence 153, 157
Western Australia (WA)
  indentured labour 136, 181
  settler colony 136, 147–8, 150, 158–9, 162, 169–70
Western Australia, Aboriginal people in
  British law, application of 148, 154–5, 157, 160
  British policy 155–6
  British *vs.* Indigenous law 154–5, 160–1, 164, 166
  Christianisation 150, 154, 156, 159, 160, 165
  civilising agenda 150, 156, 163
  conciliation 150–2
  conflict, frontier 147–9, 154, 164–6
  culture, understanding 150, 151, 154, 162
  education 154–6, 163, 168–9
  execution of 149–50, 161, 165–6
  exemption system 219, 227–8
  labour 136, 154, 160–3, 167, 169
  legislation 184, 186–90, 227–8
  missionaries to 162–8
  prisoners 152–3
  protectionism and Protectors 147, 155–7, 160–1, 165, 166, 169, 184, 186–91, 223, 227
  punishment 149–51, 154–5, 161, 165–6, 169–70
  rights 157, 158
  Roth inquiry 185–6
  settler relations 148–52, 158–9
  treatment of 147–51, 153, 155, 157–61, 169, 170
  understanding of 149–51, 154
  see also Rottnest Island prison (WA)
West Indies *see* Caribbean and West Indies; Jamaica
White, Bill 313, 314
White Australia Policy 267, 276

white entitlement 180, 182, 189, 191, 192
white slavery 180, 183
white wage earners 180, 192
Wilberforce, William 2, 9–12, 38, 128
Williams, Thomas and Irene 297–8

World Refugee Year 308–10
World Vision 23–4, 285

xenophobia 42, 45, 48–51, 53

Zarb, John 314–15

EU authorised representative for GPSR:
Easy Access System Europe, Mustamäe tee 50,
10621 Tallinn, Estonia
gpsr.requests@easproject.com